Advance Praise for *Avant Rock*

"An invig   ·rimental
fringes. .   **DATE DUE**

"Martin addresses excellent analysis to a smart se...   cluding
Cecil Taylor, Sonic Youth, Jim O'Rourke, John Zorn, ... e, the New
Klezmir Trio, and Game Theory (one of many artists whose chess obsession he discusses). Martin relates their music to parallel developments
in philosophy and literature, citing influences from Adorno and
Debord to Nabokov and Harry Crews, and manages the neat trick of
combining the sharp personal enthusiasms of underground rock's
fanzine culture, with the cooler head of academic explorations, so that
the reader perceives why rock enthusiasts have stuck with it all these
years. . . .

"A trenchant and witty exploration, several cuts above typical surveys
written in the wake of the 'alternative' era."

—*Kirkus Reviews*

"A warning to the reader: Watch your wallets, because Bill Martin is
very good at what he does. He makes the supposedly esoteric music he
covers in Avant Rock *sound like so much fun, so full of possibility,
wonder, invention, and mischief, that his readers will want to instantly
buy all the albums he writes about so persuasively."*

—Greg Kot, *Chicago Tribune* rock critic

"In the era of the Backstreet Boys and Limp Bizkit, Britney Spears and
Eminem, it's unfashionable to talk about the music of ideas—even (or
especially) among people who write about popular music for a living.
Bill Martin refuses to accept this, and he dives into the deep end of
what he calls 'avant rock' to write with the insight of a superb critic,
the perspective of a scholar, and the passion of a fan."

—Jim DeRogatis, *Chicago Sun-Times* rock critic
Author of *Let it Blurt: The Life and Times of Lester Bangs*

Avant rock

Feed▨bACK

THE SERIES IN CONTEMPORARY MUSIC
VOLUME 3
SERIES EDITORS: BILL MARTIN AND KERRI MOMMER

BY THE SAME AUTHOR:

Matrix and line: Derrida and the possibilities of postmodern social theory

Humanism and its aftermath: The shared fate of deconstruction and politics

Politics in the impasse: Explorations in postsecular social theory

Music of Yes: Structure and vision in progressive rock

Listening to the future: The time of progressive rock, 1968–1978

The radical project: Sartrean investigations

Avant rock

Experimental music from
the Beatles to Björk

WITH A FOREWORD BY ROBERT FRIPP

BILL MARTIN

OPEN COURT
Chicago and La Salle, Illinois

Cover photos:
Sonic Youth: ©Chapman Bachler/Getty Images
Björk: ©Sin/Andy Willsher/Corbis

To order books from Open Court, call 1-800-815-2280.

Open Court Publishing Company is a division of Carus Publishing Company.

© 2002 by Carus Publishing Company

First printing 2002

Library of Congress Cataloging-in-Publication Data

Martin, Bill, 1956–
    Avant rock : experimental music from the Beatles to Björk / Bill Martin : with a foreword by Robert Fripp.
        p. cm.
    Includes bibliographical references (p.) and index.
    ISBN 0-8126-9500-3 (pbk. : alk. paper)
    1. Rock music—History and criticism.   I. Title.

ML3534 .M411 2001
781.66—dc21   2001059315

To the memory of

Toupee

landscape architect, moral exemplar,
hard worker, originator of the philosophy
of Superbism

Contents

Part 3: Rock out 177

Foreword

The act of music *is* the music.

Words don't, and can't, convey the experience of standing in the presence of music when music goes on download. So, why spend time and effort attempting to describe an experience inherently beyond our capacity to articulate?

One answer might be: because we are an Academic Ologist. And how much more might this be so were we also a Lefty Academic Ologist, even one given to reading weighty tomes by Ologists from the Gallic realms?

A second answer might be: because we have been so moved by music, and in awe of the effects music has generated in our lives, that we seek to make sense of a radically life-changing experience. Part of this search for understanding is through interrogating all that we can learn of the *activities* within the act of music. Perhaps we think our thinking out loud; even engage in discussion with whoever will listen, in the hope that they might confirm for us what we already know—that music is a quality, as if an act of grace.

But if we were an Ologist, particularly a lefty academic ologist of the Gallic persuasion, we would know that the conditions which surround the act of music may be, can be, and nearly always are, prejudicial to music appearing in our fallen world. If I have learnt two things in the forty-four years since I took up a guitar, they are these:

Music is a benevolent presence, freely, readily and directly available to all.

Music enters our world despite the characters that play it, not because of them. And if I have learnt one thing in the thirty-four years of being a professional guitarist and aspirant musician, it is this:

The music industry is not concerned with music.

Fundamentally, Prof. Bill is trying to explain, to himself and his readers, why the music that has touched him holds the value for him that it does. In doing this, he is too generous to those he likes and too dismissive of those he doesn't. Bill Martin's heart is in the right place, and his head follows. The head is an interesting head, and takes me places I wouldn't otherwise go. But his heart is what I trust.

ROBERT FRIPP

Thursday, 1st November, 2001
Chateau Belewbeloid
Mount Juliet, Tennesee

Acknowledgments

Before all else I must thank my editor and friend at Open Court, Kerri Mommer, for her enormous patience and encouragement in this project. My thanks, as well, to the rest of the folks at Open Court, especially Jennifer Asmuth.

In the past few years, and thanks to the publication of *music of Yes* in 1996, I have had the good fortune to hear from dozens of serious rock music listeners and musicians from many corners of the globe. I am deeply appreciative for our communications.

Among my closest friends with whom I have discussed music for many years, I would especially like to thank Garry Rindfuss and Chelsea Snelgrove.

I have also benefited greatly from the thoughts of a number of "rock intellectuals," in particular Robert Fripp, Christoph Cox, Deena Weinstein, and Jim De Rogatis.

The debts that I have to the larger intellectual community are too many to enumerate. I am thankful for a departmental and university environment that has encouraged my explorations of rock music, without imposing narrow academic categories. I am also very thankful for the large group of encouraging interlocutors in the institutions of philosophy and other intellectual pursuits.

In September 2000 I attended the Rethinking Marxism conference at the University of Massachusetts in Amherst. On the last day of the conference I happened to wear my King Crimson *Red* tee-shirt—it seemed appropriate, given the subject matter of the conference and the intersection of my intellectual interests. I was quite surprised when a number of people at the conference, some my age and some from other generations, mentioned their admiration for King Crimson. I told them that I had written a couple of books dealing with King Crimson and with progressive rock more generally, and several times the reaction was, "oh, you're *that* Bill Martin? I thought you were just the guy who writes on Derrida." In that light I want to also give a shout out to all of my friends who are trying to forge the connections and to work changes in the world.

Most of all I thank my dear life companion, Kathleen League, for her thoughtfulness and sweetness, and for her sustaining vibrations.

Prologue

Welcome to an odd little experiment. This book was exceedingly difficult to write, and undoubtedly it bears the marks of an internal struggle. As with rock music itself, books about rock music also quite often represent a negotiation between record label/publisher and musician/author. My leaning is toward theory, and yet not theory in the absolute abstract, but theory based in practice. Still, this book may not represent to some readers what they might have hoped for. This is not a book that deals in biography or the gossip that tends to accumulate around rock musicians. Although there are some outstanding examples of rock music journalism, I am not a journalist, and even less so am I a record reviewer. (All praise to the folks who are good at this, of course.) What interests me, apart from actually listening to the music discussed here, are the ideas in music. This approach, fundamentally oriented toward aesthetics, cultural criticism, social theory, and philosophy, is also quite different from what is more purely termed "musicology," which, in the narrow sense, sets out the formal structures of music in a technical language. I'm all for that, too, but it is not what I do here, nor is it what I could even remotely claim the competence to do. However, a philosopher who is also a musician can be well at home with avant-garde music, since, from John Cage and Cecil Taylor to King Crimson, Sonic Youth, Jim O'Rourke, and Björk, this is very much a music of ideas. One of the main ideas that one finds in avant-garde music is a questioning of the very notion of "form," and a good deal of avant-garde music consists in various ways of carrying out that questioning. So it is with avant-garde rock music.

The reader who is interested in musical and cultural theory, and in more abstract questions of social theory and philosophy, will find, I hope, much to chew on here. But what of the reader who picks up this text because she or he is simply attracted to the music of the artists (or at least some of them) who are discussed here? My hope is that you will find that your sense of what these artists are up to is deepened. I also hope that, in a world where connections are ever more difficult to forge, the reader who comes to this book first of all out of their enjoyment of some of this music will start to see the possibility of a larger artistic and intellectual culture.

One of the struggles I had writing this book was in how to arrange the chapters. For the longest time, I had intended to open with a long theoretical section, including a theoretical introduction that would most likely have been far longer than any of the other chapters. As I wrote the book, I was mindful of the worry that Jean-Paul Sartre had in appending his shorter book, *Search for a Method*, to the massive *Critique of Dialectical Reason*—it would appear that the mountain had brought forth a mouse, he said. Sartre "flipped the script," as the hip-hoppers say, and put the shorter book first. I had been having yet another night of bad sleep, worrying over this question, when I also remembered something that Pete Townshend had said about the making of *The Who by Numbers*. The band was not at all happy with the album, and considered not releasing it. Then it came to them to try putting the songs in a different order, and everything sounded quite different and better from that perspective.

The script was similarly flipped in the writing of this book—I arrived at the solution of sorting the priorities differently, and putting the parts that bear more directly on particular artists first. I have titled the first part of the book, "Practices, modalities," because I first of all discuss not only the Beatles and Yoko Ono, but also five musicians who played very significant roles in changing the definition of music and of their respective genres in the period out of which experimental rock emerged. For instance, we will explore some of the ideas and music of figures such as Glenn Gould and Cecil Taylor, and the discography for this part runs from Jean Sibelius to Ornette Coleman. The aim is to begin to understand rock music, especially its more experimental side, in its historical situation. I say "begin," because, on the one hand, rock music is a tradition that has only been around for about fifty years, and, on the other hand, fifty years seems like a long time for rock music to have been around.

The second part takes us into about thirty-three and a third years of rock music (give or take a month or two), from the Velvet Underground to Björk and Jim O'Rourke. The choices made in these chapters, in terms of what music to discuss, represent the arc of a diver into a very large and deep pool.

The third part of the book, "Rock out," consists in two theoretical essays. The first of these is something of a manifesto of avant rock, attempting to shape a justification for the existence of the rock avant-garde. One of the claims I argue there is that, if a person young in age or young in spirit was setting out to do creative and visionary things in music, they might just as well do these things in rock music as in any other kind of music. The second essay, "Rock in postmodern times," consists in reflections on where rock music seems to be at the turn-of-the-millennium, and where it might be going.

In each section in the second part there are discographies for the musicians discussed in the section. Each of these is followed by an "interlude" of sorts, where I provide a discography for some albums that fit roughly into the same timeframe as the musicians who are covered more extensively. Following these secondary discographies there are a few scattered comments that are meant either as guideposts or provocations. Many of the artists in these *secondary* discographies are worthy of book-length treatments in their own right. (In some cases such books have been written.) So, there is a lot of music discussed in this book—too much, but also not nearly enough. Really the idea is to create some snapshots of the world of experimental music out there, and also to see what sorts of sparks fly when certain pieces of music are placed next to one another. One of the hardest things about writing this book was trying to find the core connections that experimental rock music since the middle 1970s has to a larger culture. Culture itself is fragmented, to the extent that it exists at all in our time of hyper-commodification. Since the time of punk, rock music has seemingly gone in a plethora of different directions. Despite this, I want to know if there is a story to be told, or if there is any sense of thinking in terms of an unfolding or a logic. Have we now truly entered the period where history, including music history, only amounts to "one damn thing after another"? Of course, there is a logic to the creation of music "product," it is the logic of the commodity, which has nothing to do with the deeper aspirations that human beings might have. As regards more experimental or at least creative cultural trends, commodity logic has increasingly led to a situation where the middle falls out—everything is done either on a gigantic or a miniscule scale. There is a bifurcation between "mainstream" packaged pabulum culture, already fully commodified as it appears on the shelf, and the marginal culture of experimentation. We see this in music, in book publishing, in bookstores (where the megastores and dot.coms will not only determine where you buy your books, but more and more what books will be published), and perhaps ultimately in everything. And yet, in rock music, there might continue to be some hopeful signs, where the split between, say, Leonard Bernstein and John Cage in classical music, is not replicated, because there is still a dynamic interaction in rock between margin and "center."

Here and there I make reference to chess. In some sense, chess—whatever it is, game, science, sport, *art* (as some of its greatest practitioners have it)—provides a connection among John Cage, Yoko Ono, Brian Eno, John Zorn, and Björk (and even the progressive rock group Yes, whose song "Your Move" is based in chess imagery). There are a number of contemporary musicians, many of them in techno and electronica territory, who are or claim to be influenced by the French philosophers Gilles Deleuze and Felix Guattari. They had some interesting things to say about chess. There are many indirect connections as well. When one sits before the Muse, or when one sits before the muse of chess, Caissa, one is aware of a field of force—and one would do well to hesitate. *Where to begin?* That is the most difficult question, as Hegel said. If one is to disturb the blank page, then on what basis, according to what principle, with what strategy? But the page is never truly blank, the chess pieces are never entirely still, and the world is never truly silent, not as long as there is a subjectivity that might enter into fields of force. Well, the music/chess connection is not developed in any great depth here, but the comparison remains in the background of my search, in the music of recent decades, for the line that leads through the matrix. (I will gather a few of the threads of this comparison together in the final essay, which also serves as a conclusion of sorts.) The chess world has been in disarray in recent years, and so is the world of avant-garde art. Perhaps this is what happens when the "hypermodern" meets the postmodern. "Hypermodern" is the name for a trend in chess, originating in the 1920s, in which a radically new approach was presented to the question of controlling the center. Disturbing the center, because it cannot hold, might be the very essence of avant-garde art in the twentieth century.

This book is dedicated to the memory of a wonderful little friend, who was with us for about two and a half years, and who, Christ-like, was perfect and only brought joy. Any mountain would have been exceedingly pleased to have brought forth this superb fellow.

PART 1

....

Practices, modalities

Synthesis and new vocabularies

There has always been experimentation in rock music, but this took off in earnest in the late 1960s. The best rock musicians have always had open ears. What was different in the late sixties was that the aesthetic intersected with the social in such a way as to create new openings. Forms of experimentation that were seen as the domain of iconoclasts were taken up broadly, and this gave impetus to even more creativity. In avant-garde art before rock music, a tension developed that was to be given full play in post-sixties rock, a tension between an emphasis on "technique" and a certain refusal of technique. Clearly, in many of the experiments of dada, surrealism, abstract expressionism, and music that used randomizing procedures, technical ability with paintbrushes or musical instruments was not very much in the foreground. The idea was what was important.

In the work of a composer such as John Cage, it could even be said that the idea was more important than the execution, and thus one might wonder (as I argued in the first chapter) whether this is music or philosophy that we are talking about. Cage often found that the kinds of musicians who had put all of their effort into developing technique were just not up to the ideas that he was asking them to grapple with. Therefore, in a sense, technique was something that had to be broken through so that certain possibilities of music could be realized. Technique can sometimes get in the way of "letting music be." But things are not this simple, of course, and part of what I find interesting about the discussion of ideas and technical skill is that it leads to the conclusion that *materialism* is not that simple. Part of Cage's materialism is to compose ways that the world around us, or parts of it, that are not ordinarily understood as "musical," can in fact be or become music, if we pursue an active sense of allowing this to happen. In Cage's music, this requires a certain refusal of intentionality and expressivity, even if this involves one in the paradox that one must intentionally choose this course.

The *materialism* of John Coltrane and Cecil Taylor seems, by contrast, to be almost purely expressive, and, as well, inseparable from their extraordinary technical skills on their respective instruments. It is very difficult to imagine the music of Coltrane apart from his playing on the tenor and soprano saxophones, or the music of Taylor, apart from what he does with the piano (or Jimi Hendrix with the guitar)—this music is deep into its materials, so to speak. So, not to overly complicate this discussion by bringing in worries about metaphysics, but the point is that both the "through technique" and the "beyond technique" (or even "anti-technique") approaches involve a deep engagement with materiality, and yet they seem to go in very different, perhaps even contrary directions. Contrary possibilities where neither can really *exclude* the other, perhaps that is materialism in the age of quantum mechanics.

Recourse to questions of language and literature may be helpful. James Joyce's *Finnegans Wake*, which inspired several of John Cage's works, is perhaps the supreme example of a text where, on the one hand, language simply seems to speak itself, and, on the other, where the author has put on a virtuoso performance. Coltrane is no different, really: music, as a spiritual-material force, seems to simply express itself through his playing, and yet this could not happen except in the case of someone so supremely prepared. The virtuosos and near-virtuosos of progressive rock (this is the name for a certain genre of music, not a reference to all rock music that is some way "progressive," as will be explained in the third section of Part 2) sometimes demonstrated, however, that having a very large musical vocabulary did not necessarily mean that one had something to say. Some rock musicians with relatively meager technical skills, on the other hand, have had interesting and important things to say, and it is not especially clear that more technique would have improved the music—perhaps on the contrary. The rare case is where the extended vocabulary comes together with the important idea, though, fortunately, the rock avant-garde has attracted its share of musicians who can bring technique together with having something worth saying. Still, the tension between technique and its refusal or transcendence underlies the rock avant-garde just as it does other avant-gardes in the twentieth century.

In the late 1960s and early 1970s, as Lou Reed put it, there were those who were trying to become much better musicians, or much better players of their instruments at any rate, and those who were trying to forget what little they already knew. The presumption in the latter case was that technical skill was getting in the way of, or replacing, significance. So, we saw the later Beatles on the one side, or, perhaps even more to the point, Cream, Hendrix, the progressive rock groups, and the Velvet Underground, and then Patti Smith and punk on the other. Although these trends look like contrary paths for making rock music, what is perhaps even more significant, if one takes the larger view, is the way the dichotomy itself structured the trends. An especially stark form of the dichotomy can be seen in the fates of two of the most important punk bands, the Sex Pistols and the Clash. Most readers will know the dichotomy that Neil Young offered as the only way it can be for punk rock—either burn out or fade away. The Pistols rather dramatically went down the first road, but what about musicians who, instead of going down in flames or drifting into irrelevance, try to sustain and develop their language? It may be that sustainability and development are at odds with what punk was all about, but what is a musician then to do? Hence the options given by Mr. Young. The Clash tried something else, and Hüsker Dü and Black Flag would be other interesting examples. Part of what they did was to develop what they were doing with form, and also they became better musicians, they got better on their instruments. We will return to these issues as they specifically apply to punk, but the larger point is that the dichotomy continues to structure the ways that rock musicians approach experimentation.

Another way to come at this is to ask which path has been more influential and more fruitful—and these may not be the same thing—in more recent rock experimentation: that of the Velvets or that of the later Beatles? Sonic Youth, who may turn out to be the real heroes of this whole investigation, perhaps manifest traces of the later Beatles—though clearly more the *White Album* than *Sgt. Pepper's*—and even some progressive rock, but surely their real lineage goes back through punk to the Velvet Underground. If we bring Björk, Jim O'Rourke, or *Thrak*-era King Crimson into the conversation, the picture is really much more complicated. The tension around technique then also intersects with another dichotomy, that between improvisation and composition. In either case, the dichotomies are not so clear cut, which is of course the reason that they are able to structure the whole avant-rock field. Still, we might raise the question regarding this second dichotomy, which path has been more influential and fruitful. If we look to Sonic Youth, we will see much more emphasis on the refusal of technique and on improvisation, though there is technique to what they do, and they do compose songs and sections of their instrumental music, and they compose the *situations* in which their music is made. The way that these two dichotomies unfold and interact with each other will be helpful for understanding both the dynamic of avant rock in the post-sixties period, which is essentially what this part of the book is about, and what might be called the "post-post-sixties period," which is the subject of the second part.

One final comment on the question of technique. The issue is bigger than the question of how well one can play an instrument or place marks on staff paper. One way that avant-garde *rock* music tends to transcend technique, even in the case of musicians such as Robert Fripp who have an abundance of the stuff, is in drawing on a basic characteristic of all rock music. Rock music, in synthesizing diverse elements from elsewhere in the musical world (first of all from African-American and therefore African traditions and from British Isles traditions, lines that intersected in the American South), tends to be imitative. It is not a jab at abstract expressionist painters that some young people saw the paintings of Jackson Pollock, Mark Rothko, Franz Kline, and others as an incentive to create avant-garde art of their own, often without going through a course of formal schooling. Nor is it a denigration of the work of John Cage, Karlheinz Stockhausen, and Luciano Berio to acknowledge the way that rock musicians in the middle and late 1960s, unschooled for the most part, said, "yeah, I'd like to incorporate some stuff that sounds like that." But in the case of imitative painters, what came out was almost always merely derivative, whereas in the case of rock music the result could be quite original, because assimilation, synthesis, and imitation are integral parts of the language of rock.

Jean Sibelius, *Symphony No.2 in D, Op.43*; Boston Symphony, conducted by Colin Davis (Philips LP, 1976; composed 1901–1902).

Igor Stravinsky, *Le Sacre du Printemps*; London Symphony Orchestra, conducted by Claudio Abbado (Deutsche Grammophon LP, 1976; composed 1910–13; recording is of 1947 revision).

Arnold Schoenberg, *Pierrot Lunaire*; Jan DeGaetani, voice; The Contemporary Chamber Ensemble, conducted by Arthur Weisberg (Nonesuch LP, 1971; composed 1912).

Charles Ives, *Concord Sonata/Three Places in New England/ Central Park in the Dark*; Roberto Szidon, piano; Boston Symphony, conducted by Seiji Ozawa; Boston Symphony, conducted by Michael Tilson Thomas (Deutsche Grammophon CD, 1994; composed 1910–1915).

Heitor Villa-Lobos, Carlos Chavez, Alberto Ginastera, *Latin American Ballets*; Simon Bolivar Orchestra of Venezuela, conducted by Eduardo Mata (Dorian CD, 1995; composed 1917–1941).

Edgard Varèse, *Offrandes/Integrales/Octandre/Ecuatorial*; The Contemp-orary Chamber Ensemble, conducted by Arthur Weisberg (Nonesuch LP, n.d., pieces from 1921–34).

Jean Sibelius, *Symphony No.7 in C, Op.105*; Boston Symphony conducted by Colin Davis (Philips LP, 1975; composed 1923–24).

George Gershwin, *Rhapsody in Blue/An American in Paris*; New York Philharmonic, conducted by Leonard Bernstein (Columbia LP, 1973; composed 1924, 1928).

Béla Bartók, *Music for Strings, Percussion and Celesta*; London Philharmonic, conducted by Georg Solti (Turnabout LP, n.d.; composed 1936).

Karlheinz Stockhausen, *Electronic Music: Song of the Youths/ Contact* (Deutsche Grammophon LP, n.d.; pieces from 1955–1956, 1959–1960).

————. *Kontakte, for Electronic Sounds, Piano, and Percussion*; James Tenney, piano; William Winant, percussion (Ecstatic Peace CD, 1997; recorded live, 1978; composed 1959–1960).

▼ Ornette Coleman, *The Shape of Jazz to Come* (Atlantic LP, 1959).

Many years ago I attended the tragi-comic wedding of a college friend. Among the many freakish elements of the wedding was a tape of Bach organ music that jumped up to double speed in the middle of the ceremony. (If memory serves, the tape was an 8-track, which makes the story even funnier in hindsight.) From the sublime to the ridiculous. That high-pitched organ whine was not unlike the voice of Adele Bertei's on Thomas Dolby's fantastic dance hit, "Hyperactive." "Like an itch in your headphones," she sang. Bach that day was not unlike that itch, having already gone through the click and clank and electronic crackle of Glenn Gould's *Goldberg Variations* and John Cage's and Lejaren Hiller's *HPSCHD*. Now put on the headphones, set the tape for quadruple speed (8-track if you have it), and climb aboard the roller coaster for a brief tour of a tiny slice of the twentieth century. If you place the starting point of this section next to the place where the chapter ends, it appears that we have a history of rock music from Finland to Iceland. Does this mean that avant rock is the cold stuff? Could be, could be.

"Rock music from Sibelius to Björk"—there's a provocation for you.

I am aiming for a bit of Foucauldian "archeology" here—Michel Foucault proposed a methodology for treating ideas and works of art as "found objects," so to speak, the meaning and logic of which is at first unclear. Rather than immediately insert the productions of earlier ages into a teleology of progress that ultimately arrives at and therefore verifies our own supposed enlightenment, let us first assume that these artifacts are alien to us. Well, as strange as the twentieth century will increasingly come to seem, I do not know if a true critical distance is entirely possible. But this is where the device of a certain kind of "mere list" comes in. Probably a true disciple of Foucault would say that there is nothing of archeology here. But the archeology is not found in the "artifacts" given by the list, whether those be piano sonatas of Charles Ives or James Brown *Live at the Apollo*, but instead in the overall shape of this queer list, the idea of starting with a kind of culmination of the Romantic and the initiation of the Modern in European classical music, and somehow ending with Rage Against the Machine. So, in fact, the list is almost to be thought of as merely something to just look at, something from which some ideas may spring, something to provoke the reader into saying, "hmm, that's interesting." (Please note: the appearance of only one or two albums for a given year is not meant to indicate that I think there was only one "good" album that year.)

"For what else is this collection but a disorder to which habit has accommodated itself to such an extent that it can appear as order?" This question, raised by Walter Benjamin at the outset of his charming essay, "Unpacking My Library," could be asked of any attempt to say, "this is what it means to create an overview of a field"—the field in this case being twentieth-century music. Obviously, there are many discussions of this field where it never would have occurred to the participants to include Chuck Berry or the Beatles, or even Duke Ellington and Charlie Parker, to say nothing of Björk or Jim O'Rourke. From that perspective, the discographies provided here would seem to have washed up on the beach of some quite alien world. And yet carriers of such lists walk among us.

Periodization is not a simple matter, especially when humanity has entered a time when: (1) many, many different cultures, each with their own sense of periodization are rubbing against one another—mainly thanks to imperialism and colonialism; (2) global communication capabilities begin to create some basis for Marshall McLuhan's "global village." The twentieth century, through wars and the new forms of communication, was a time of "many *other* present eras" and of the beginning of a single era of global society. The forging of this new "village" has occurred in a not altogether happy way, indeed, mostly on the contrary; Chinua Achebe's novel *Things Fall Apart* pretty well sums up a good bit of what has more recently been called "globalism."

What, then, constitutes the "change of the century" (to borrow the title of Ornette Coleman's 1959 masterpiece)? To open the discography with Sibelius, Stravinsky, and Schoenberg certainly shows a bias toward the Western timeline, if not necessarily a prejudice. Probably what is most evident in this choice is a Kantian, Hegelian, and Marxist (or is it Jewish and Christian?) orientation toward seeing history in terms of certain underlying dynamics. These dynamics then bring about "world history" insomuch as they "progressively" subsume parts of the world beyond Western Europe. It was in this sense that, in the *Communist Manifesto*, Marx and Engels called the bourgeoisie the most revolutionary class in history. This was not meant entirely as praise, but instead as an analysis of those forces that were creating a society "sprung into the air." There is a paradoxical movement to the twentieth century, one that replicates on a global scale the motion of monopoly capital—the world is both bound more tightly together, and at the same time violently ripped apart. In cultural terms, the interesting things tend to happen on the edge, in the margins.

When I proposed, a moment ago, a history of twentieth-century music from Sibelius to Björk, I also had in mind that Helsinki and Reykjavik have been what geographers in recent years have called "edge cities." (The term is used in a number of ways, but quite often to designate cities that are on the edge of empire or the edge of technological development.) Two of the liveliest scenes for punk in the 1980s were Helsinki and Salt Lake City, Utah. Helsinki in the time of Sibelius (1865–1957) was on the edge first of the Russian empire, then of the Soviet Union. As a composer, Sibelius can also be understood as having been on the edge of Wagner. Sibelius took all of the harmonic innovations of Wagner and pared them down into symphonic works that are models of economy. For this Sibelius has often been called the most original composer of symphonies after Beethoven. And yet the Seventh Symphony, completed in 1924, does not present a celebratory summation of Beethoven's heroic, humanist project, but is instead thoroughly dire throughout—and the final measures cannot be heard as anything other than a gasp. An eighth symphony never materialized, even though Sibelius was to live for more than another thirty years.

Ironically, his retirement from composition seems to have paralleled that of Charles Ives (1874–1954), whose William Jamesian brand of anti-imperialism led him to abandon composition in disgust at the First World War. Ives would also live a good while longer. The irony is that Ives singled out Sibelius for scorn, because the latter had been adopted as the national composer of Finland and received a government stipend. This offended Ives's highly American sense of independence, and also allowed him to place Sibelius into the "sissy music" category—where the Finn was in the good company of Mozart and Chopin, among others. For Ives, as well, the tragedy of the First World War was that it signaled the folding of the United States back into European ways, which he saw as world-weary and imperialistic. Ives sought a music that was not only its time, but also its place, congealed in sound—to paraphrase what Hegel said about philosophy.

In the first half of the twentieth century, a good deal of ink was spilled in comparisons of Arnold Schoenberg and Igor Stravinsky. Indeed, there is a dynamic to this comparison that describes well what happens when traditions seem on the verge of exhaustion. Schoenberg was extolled by Theodor Adorno for his systematic deconstruction of tonality, while Stravinsky was sometimes denigrated for his expressivism and exoticism. Part of the latter accusation, and the related charge of "Orientalism," seems based on the strange assumption that some of the sounds and ideas in *The Rite of Spring* have something to do with Africa. Superficially, this notion probably comes from two sources. The Paris of the latter years of the nineteenth century and the first decades of the twentieth was often called the cultural capital of the world, and there was a great deal of importation of "exotic" culture, everything from Balinese gamelan music to Sub-Saharan musicians and dancers. (An interesting account of the Paris exhibitions of that period and their influence on music from then until recent times is found in David Toop, *Oceans of Sound*, pp. 1–22.) The African-American expatriots such as Sidney Bechet and Josephine Baker were to come later (after the First World War), but the images all tend to congeal around the idea that Stravinsky was on to something African. The other superficial source, which came even later, was the Walt Disney film, *Fantasia* (1940), which uses the opening section of *Rite of Spring* in its score, and which again makes us think of jungles with tigers, giraffes, and big, lumbering, purple elephants. Who could remember, then, at least when we look back to the origins of the experimental trends in twentieth-century music, that *The Rite* was subtitled, "Scenes from pagan Russia"?

What is perhaps slightly less superficial is that, even considering the Russian countryside and not Africa as the source of Stravinsky's inspiration, surely the composer was reaching for a kind of *vitalism*, a *Lebensphilosophie* (life-philosophy) as the Germans called it. In some respects a reaction to the increasingly technocratic and bureaucratic nature of modern European urban existence, life-philosophy sought renewal in the rural and the so-called primitive. (After many years in which the subject has been ignored, a fascinating reevaluation and updating of this philosophical trend has been provided by David Farrell Krell, in his book, *Daimon Life: Heidegger and Life-Philosophy*.) In this respect, one might certainly pursue the exoticism/Orientalism charge, and wonder if neo-primitivism constitutes little more than a raiding party on the cultures of peoples who have been subjugated by European (and American) imperialism.

This charge is never completely avoidable, I think, and yet there might be a more positive way of looking at the question. Schoenberg's move to the dodecaphonic (twelve-note) system can be seen as the next step in the progression from the extreme

chromaticism of Mahler. At the same time, the "next logical step" does give us a transformation of quantity to quality, as it were, because Mahler's use of all the notes of the
scale was marshaled to the task of what might be called a supercharged expressivity,
whereas Schoenberg "regularized" the chromaticism, even to the point of clearly opening the door to what John Cage would do next—logically?—namely diminishing the
role of intentionality and "personality" in music. But, you see, I want my *Pierrot
Lunaire* and *Moses und Aron* (Schoenberg) *and* my *Firebird* and *Rite of Spring*
(Stravinsky), and other works besides (by these and other composers), and I reject the
idea that there is simply a way to know what the "next logical step" is in music. This
contrary to Adorno, even if I accept his arguments about what made Schoenberg great
(while rejecting, for the most part, his reasons for thinking Stravinsky not great). In
some sense Stravinsky, who also comes after Mahler (though also after Debussy, in a
way that probably does not apply to Schoenberg, and I am reminded of the general
antipathy of cultured Germans such as Adorno toward much of anything French),
instead of asking what the next step was for "the scale" and for harmony, asked what
this "scale" was all about, anyway. Along with Béla Bartók, and, in a somewhat different context, Charles Ives and even George Gershwin (and Henry Cowell, who numbered
among his pupils Gershwin, John Cage, and—briefly—Burt Bacharach!), there was a
desire to be liberated from Western tonality altogether. This meant both "breaking" the
Western scale, and recognizing that there were other cultures where music had been
created with other scales for many centuries.

I find it undecideable which is the more "valid" approach—"Schoenberg" and
"Stravinsky" standing here as emblems—to the question of what to do next in music. I
think such undecideabilities are in the nature of true creativity and the avant-garde current in art. On either side there is a stricture. On the "Schoenberg" side the question is
one of finding the "next step" that is not so "within the logic" of what has come before
that nothing truly new is achieved. On the "Stravinsky" side the concern is one of mere
cultural imperialism—the "dazzling" display of, say, polyrhythms or unusual timbres
that would actually be commonplaces in the music of the cultures they were stolen
from. There is a fine line between a certain "integration," something more akin to
learning from different cultures, and assimilation, theft, and so on. In either case, isn't
the real question one of whether we are hearing something new? Doesn't this remain
the question even if, sometimes, what we thought was new turns out to be quite old?

In this regard, I would argue that there is a good deal more to George Gershwin's
"classical" works than simply a superficial synthesis of "light" classical music and
bowdlerized jazz. For one thing, there were two additional elements to Gershwin's
music beyond what he was trying to pick up from Louis and Maurice (Armstrong and
Ravel, respectively). In collaboration with his brother, Ira (and, in *Porgy and Bess*,
Dubose Heyward), George Gershwin was one of the most brilliant practitioners of the

songwriting craft. And, as more recent commentators have argued, there was a Klezmer connection in Gershwin, the "Jewish jazz" that came from Eastern Europe and found something of a home in New York City. Most famously, the clarinet opening of *Rhapsody in Blue*, taken by some to be "bad" jazz, is pure Klezmer. Well, personally, I think the "classical" works of Gershwin, from the *Rhapsody*, to the *Piano Concerto in F*, *An American in Paris*, *Porgy and Bess*, and the three *Piano Preludes* are great stuff, and I wish that Gershwin had lived longer (he died at age 39) and written more. He opened some doors.

This "next step in the logic"/"another logic altogether" dynamic came to define, I would argue, the avant-gardes of classical music, jazz, and then rock—and I would daresay that this dynamic still defines the avant-garde in art and intellectual pursuits generally. What I find especially interesting are those points where the strategies meet, connect, overlap, and engage in creative contestation. Taking the "next step" sometimes lands one in "another logic altogether," but meanwhile (and perhaps with twenty-twenty hindsight) this supposed "other logic" may not be as unrelated to the "occidental" logic as one might at first think. If chess were truly exhausted, and there really were no new games to be played within its system of rules (as some suggested at the end of the nineteenth century, just before Aron Nimzovich and Richard Reti launched their hypermodern revolution—the parallels to what Einstein was told about the exhaustion of physics are remarkable, as well), then I suppose that one might turn to a new game, or "an other" game, for example, Go. This is a model that Gilles Deleuze and Felix Guattari set up in their *A Thousand Plateaus*, a work that has had some influence within the contemporary music scene. (Many readers will know that a techno compilation album was produced—on the *Mille Plateaux* label—with the title, *In Memorium Gilles Deleuze*.) I think chess still has something to give, so I have some questions about the D&G (as they say) argument; I will return to this question in the conclusion (and a little bit in the discussion of Yoko Ono). But perhaps here, in the context of what was just said about the avant-garde dynamic, I may be permitted the assertion that what would be truly interesting is if there was a way for chess and Go to speak together. Or perhaps it is Bach and Brazil, which is why I included a work by Heitor Villa-Lobos in the discography.

On another note altogether, part of what came out of the attack on "the scale," and the concomitant turn to other scales and sounds, was an elevation of percussion. One sees this not only in Stravinsky and Bartók, but even more in the music of Edgard Varèse, John Cage, and Karlheinz Stockhausen among many others. In some sense, even in "classical music" (whatever this means after the aforementioned), the "rhythm section" steps forward, which is something that connects this music to jazz and then to rock.

Many of the interesting developments in rock music, at least on a formal level, can be connected to transformations in the role of the "rhythm section"—the drums and bass guitar. I place the term in scare-quotes because these transformations dislodge the standard sensibility about what is the background and what is the foreground. I would go so far as to say that there are various developments in avant-garde rock music that fail to be nearly as interesting as they could be because, even despite the use of very extended harmonic or timbral ranges, the bass and drums are "back there," just sort of plodding along. Just to say something rather tendentious . . . I like Yes and I like Sonic Youth, and I appreciate the very different contributions that each has made. It is probably accurate to say that most aficionados of avant rock are more inclined toward Sonic Youth than toward Yes. But one problem I have with Sonic Youth is that there is rarely anything going on in the bass guitar and drums that serves as interesting counterpoint to the noise explorations of Thurston Moore and Lee Renaldo. In the music of Yes, on the other hand, what Chris Squire and Bill Bruford, and then Alan White, have done with the roles of the bass guitar and percussion is truly remarkable—there are other good examples, though mainly in progressive rock (although I would cite the Beatles and The Who as at least important precursors), but no one has equaled the way that they displaced the rhythmic "center" and distributed it throughout the group. What is to be made of the fact that very few rock critics—oriented toward avant rock or otherwise—have commented upon this? I would say they need to clean the wax out of their ears.

In jazz and rock, one way of "breaking the scale" is to leave the piano out of the mix, or to emphasize the especially percussive qualities of the piano. The latter is one of the strategies of Cecil Taylor, and more will be said about him in the next section. In the case of the former approach, what at one time was referred to as "pianoless" jazz, Ornette Coleman's *The Shape of Jazz to Come* is the place to start and perhaps the place to finish.

Amusingly, the Ben Folds Five has more recently been referred to as a "guitarless" group (but then, the Five is actually three), as though *not* having a piano or a guitar is what defines the music. But then, after Schoenberg died, and after resisting it all his life up until that point, Stravinsky turned in his last years to dodecaphony. Perhaps it is time to turn from this gloss on some developments in twentieth-century classical music toward rock music.

When John met Yoko: The Beatles come apart

One of Yoko Ono's most inspired pieces was her *White Chess Set* of 1966. Instead of two opposing sides, one black and one white, she painted everything—the board and the pieces—white. Since one cannot tell which pieces belong on which side, the game quickly falls apart. "The players lost track of their pieces as the game progresses; Ideally this leads to a shared understanding of their mutual concerns and a new relationship based on empathy rather than opposition. Peace is then attained on a small scale." But with Lennon, she and he could attempt to achieve peace on the largest scale—could use art to transform minds.

—Arthur Danto, "Life in Fluxus"

Readers will probably not be surprised to learn, if they do not know it already, that there have been a number of web sites devoted to attacking Yoko Ono. One site that I found particularly amusing in an obnoxious sort of way had the lovely title, "Yoko Ono crushed my balls." I wonder if the creator of this site realized how revelatory that title is. After all, this *webmaster* had devoted significant effort to express once again what has been one of the most persistent myths in the history of rock music, namely that it was Yoko Ono who broke up the Beatles, thereby destroying the greatest rock band of all time. Keeping in mind that, just because a story is a myth does not mean that it is not true, or at least that it does not have its truth, I think we could say that the claim is both false and true. The relationships in great bands are like marriages. If these intimate bonds come apart, this is rarely the result of some tampering by someone outside the relationship, but instead the result of internal tensions. Someone inside the band may flirt with or otherwise hook up with someone outside the band, and this may exacerbate tensions and it may even be for the purpose of exacerbating tensions, but the basic shape of this dynamic is defined internally, even if in the context of the world and society and larger forces that are whipping around.

Those of us old enough to remember the breakup of the Beatles certainly can attest to the shock it sent through the world. Obviously there were other very important things going on at the time, too, and the breakup of a rock band seems rather inconsequential if one develops the full context. But it was because the Beatles were so much a part of their cultural and historical context, indeed emblematic of it and inseparable from it, that Paul McCartney's announcement on April 10, 1970 left us speechless and gasping for air. The Beatles were more than a band, they were a *force*—and this quality to what they did makes us forget that they were indeed a band, they were guys who played instruments and wrote and sang songs, and put out recordings. It didn't help matters that, only shortly before the announcement, we had been listening to some of the band's most brilliant work, *Abbey Road*. There are those who think the Beatles are overrated, or who argue that this or that other band was really the first to do things that are popularly attributed to the Beatles (some of my friends from Texas propose the Red Crayola as a candidate). Well, was there anything with the Beatles that was truly new under the sun? Rock music is synthesis and transmutation, often with a beat that is danceable and a melody that can be sung, hummed, or whistled—or something like these qualities are down in there somewhere or being related to somehow. What was original about the

Beatles is that they synthesized and transmuted more or less *everything*, they did this in a way that reflected their time, they reflected their time in a way that spoke to a great part of humanity, and they did all of this really, really well. Having said this, I am sure it is obvious to the reader that, far from thinking the Beatles are overrated, I think instead the opposite, that we still do not entirely understand how they did what they did. We do not understand them as a force, and part of this failure to understand is that the Beatles actually remain underrated as musicians.

Suppose one wants to know what rock music is all about. Then first go to the source, what I call the "trinity" of rock's originators—Little Richard, Chuck Berry, and Jerry Lee Lewis (and certainly with appreciation for Ray Charles and Louis Jordan just before them, and Bo Diddley just after)—and then, to have a sense of what rock music is when it becomes "developmental," go to the Beatles. One might argue, and people have argued, that a group such as the Rolling Stones is more faithful to the spirit of rock, that the Beatles really depart from that spirit. In at least one sense, that is true. The Rolling Stones have stayed much closer to blues and rhythm and blues roots of rock-'n'roll, and their one significant departure from that was their attempt to make their own version of *Sgt. Pepper's*, *Their Satanic Majesties Request*. This is most likely my favorite Stones album, and this is probably something that would only be said by someone more oriented toward the Beatles and toward experimental rock, and very few Stones fans would say this. The Beatles set rock music on a course where the idea was that it would develop *as music*, in its formal aspects and in the range of its content. There were other innovative groups, of course, but the Beatles consolidated a trend and at the same time created a remarkable series of examples of experimentation.

Was there any real point to those endless "Beatles versus the Stones" debates and shouting matches some of us used to have back in the day? To some extent we were comparing apples and oranges. That is to say, however, that there was an implicit recognition, even if we are just coming to understand it, that different genres were opening up within rock music, and that rock'n'roll was going to keep with one direction and experimental rock was going to go somewhere else. The reality was that rock'n'roll was going to remain "faithful" to one set of impulses in early rock music, primarily centered on blues forms, while experimental rock was going with another set of impulses, mainly having to do with synthesis and expansion, that would lead in not one, but many different directions. There is more to it than just "you go your way and I'll go mine," however, and this is what made those between-classes or late-night dorm-room arguments so heated. On either side, there was a kind of moral imperative—this really seemed to go beyond aesthetics. Around the late 1960s is when we started to hear the "that ain't rock'n'roll" critique. John Lennon even contributed to it with his "just give me that rock and roll music" line, which included formulas for not straying too far from orthodox rockism (backbeats and the like); then, of course, he strayed quite far from this orthodoxy himself. (Lennon was like that, one minute saying that, if you carry pictures of Chairman Mao, no one is going to listen to you, and the next minute—or a couple of years later, anyway—wearing a Mao button and waving the Little Red Book.) The "Stones" side of the debate held strongly that "rock should stay rock," which meant being tied to blues progressions, while the "later Beatles" side argued that rock should develop and go in whatever direction it wanted.

Which side in the debate was more "political," in the sense of being in touch with the politics of youth in the late sixties? That question divides into two (as Mao liked to say) as well. After all, weren't the Stones and their sound more in line with what was going on in the streets? Didn't the rockers seem more down with the people—or, at least, would we not think that is the case, looking back on it now? There has been a longstanding debate, beginning at the end of the nineteenth century, concerning the relationship between radical politics and avant-garde art. The relationship between the two has been very uneasy, precisely because the perception—not by any means always inaccurate—has been that artists and intellectuals tend to be not very well connected to the masses. Indeed, the perception is that most artists and intellectuals have a condescending attitude toward "common people." This goes doubly for avant-garde artists, because, for one thing, a person has to be something of an intellectual to be this kind of artist.

From about 1910 to 1940, there were various attempts on the part of avant-garde artists to bridge this gap, or at least to bring radical politics and avant-garde art together. Dada, surrealism, constructivism, and cubism were four movements that had this ambition (or at least some of the practitioners did). In many ways these and other forms of experimentation were politically marginalized not by being so "far out" that "ordinary people" just did not like them, but instead by the aesthetic orthodoxy that took hold in the international communist movement, led by Joseph Stalin. Despite the conventional wisdom of more recent years, not everything produced under the heading of "socialist realism" was dreck. In particular, much of the music of Shostakovich and Prokofiev was very good, sometimes great even, though of course they struggled with some of the more restrictive cultural edicts of Stalin. Instrumental music seemed to fare the best, and prose (especially the novel and poetry) and painting the worst. However, stylistic orthodoxies tend to stifle creativity—big surprise, that—and socialist realism was probably more stifling than most. (Mao Tsetung was especially critical, in a lecture that he gave in Yenan in 1942, of what he called "the poster and slogan style in art.")

This was a time when many artists, not only those adhering to the contours of the socialist experiment in the Soviet Union (which became less and less of an experiment, and increasingly what Sartre calls a mere "institution"), were looking for *the* form of art that would serve revolutionary ideals and practices. For example, there was an argument that cubism and collage techniques (such as those used by Sergei Eisenstein in his films) were especially suited to the all-round, universal, and dialectical perspective of the working class. Bertolt Brecht was an advocate of defamiliarization in theater—making the familiar seem strange—as well as of moments when the theatrical suspension of the real is rudely disrupted. Theodor Adorno thought Schoenberg and his school (Webern and Berg) pointed the way forward in music, with their twelve-note technique (also called serialism). In the 1930s, the Communist Party of the United States determined that folk music was the true music of the proletariat, and this led, ultimately, to those tomatoes that were thrown at Bob Dylan when he first appeared onstage with an electric guitar. While these positions are certainly worthy of study and discussion, the post-World War 2 scene in art was one where demands for aesthetic consensus were mostly on the wane, except for two very broad trends—the one at least asking for "relevance," the other for experimentation. The happy situation at the end of the 1960s, however, was one where a great deal of experimentation seemed entirely relevant, and the Beatles played a major role in consolidating this position.

Then, one tale of male paranoia goes, Yoko Ono smashed the Beatles to pieces. Here was someone with no "rock credentials," someone not known to players or listeners in the rock world, who came from the circle of John Cage and the avant-garde scene of the plastic arts, whose very name came to mean "interloper." Now, thirty years later, some critics argue that Yoko Ono's album, *Plastic Ono Band* (1970), laid "the groundwork for the punk revolution of 1976" (as the liner notes for Rykodisc's reissue put it). Even so, doesn't an album that features so much noise and screaming and screeching ("caterwauling" is a term often heard to describe Ono's singing) seem a rather rude interruption of the project of the later Beatles? There was something of a precedent with "Revolution 9" from *The White Album*. The interesting thing, as Allan Kozinn points out, is to listen to all of the "Revolutions" as a sequence—the slow version, that Lennon later called "Revolution 1," from the album, then "Revolution 9," then the fast version that was put out as a single. The sequence encapsulates the trajectory of the late Beatles and the post-Beatles period of Lennon and Ono, in that three elements are present: the songcraft that the Beatles had developed to a very high level from their beginning but especially since *Rubber Soul* (1965), avant-garde collage techniques that owed a good deal to Ono's involvement with John Cage and with the Fluxus group of conceptual artists in New York, and a more raw, primitivist rock. While the emphasis up through *Abbey Road* (the final album the group made, although *Let It Be* was released a year later) was on the first of these elements, the other two would play a role as well—for example, in the "disoriented," bad-reception radio sounds found in the middle of "I am the Walrus." (See Kozinn's illuminating analysis of the entire *White Album* and the period in which Ono came onto the Beatles' scene, pp. 161–84.) "But they could have gone on making great albums the way they did with *Sgt. Pepper's*" is the refrain of the anti-Ono faction. Like millions of people I was also heartbroken when the Beatles split up, but, in retrospect, I have to respect them for taking that step. Rather than settle comfortably into being an institution, they somehow knew—even if they might not have understood—that the world was at a turning point. As always, they turned with it.

The Beatles gave us late sixties utopianism in musical form. In splitting up, they also gave us something that we needed, even if we did not want it at the time, a certain wistfulness and melancholy without which utopianism is just the sort of triumphalist attitude that Western imperialism excels in. This is not a matter, as some so cynically think today, of realizing that "peace and love" are just a load of bollocks or that visions of universal humanity—which John Lennon never gave up, even if he certainly had his cynical moments—are hopelessly naïve. Instead, the Beatles brought an emotional sophistication to music that broke through the orthodox orientations of adolescent rock. Paul McCartney, contrary to popular conceptions, made his own contribution to this sophistication. Consider, for instance, "She's Leaving Home," where growing up, "liberation" if you will, and sorrow are inextricably intertwined.

Still, Lennon's songs often had an edge that was lacking in McCartney's. (For simplicity's sake I am leaving aside George Harrison's songs, many of which are wonderful, simply because considering them does not contribute to the line of argument I want to pursue here.) This edge found its most pained expression in Lennon's first post-Beatles album, *Plastic Ono Band*. Both Lennon and Ono released albums under the same title in 1970, with almost identical cover art (with the exception that the positions of Ono and Lennon are reversed). Lennon's is an exceedingly lonely, "existential" album. Almost all of the songs deal with loss or refusal. Perhaps what comes through most strongly, on a personal level, is that, even after all of those years of being one of the most famous, and sometimes notorious, people on the planet, Lennon was basically a shy person and Ono was the flamboyant one. My view is that this speaks to differences in their class backgrounds most of all. Lennon came from a working-class background, from a gritty, rough, port city, and from a broken home. Ono came from a wealthy family that encouraged her avant-garde artistic pursuits. As many in the art world are saying in more recent years, though the notion has yet to get across to those who are worrying about having their testicles crushed, it is clear that Ono was becoming and would have been a figure in the avant-garde scene, perhaps a major figure, had not a certain open-minded rock star taken an interest in her. On Lennon's side, this was just as much an intervention into his Liverpool background and his marriage (concerning which the bitterness of Cynthia and Julian continues to this day), as it was into his band. The relationship with Ono resulted in a very strange combination, but one that we see in perhaps the larger part of avant rock from the late sixties until now: the meeting of the avant-garde artiste with the rock primitive.

Call this the "Ono effect." Yoko Ono barely knew who John Lennon was when she met him; after they married, she was often frustrated at having become "Mrs. John Lennon, destroyer of the Beatles." Indeed, in the middle 1970s, there were periods when she sent Lennon away, so that she could have some space for her own creativity, and also in the hope that John would grow up a bit. Certainly one could say that Ono became a rock musician, if that is what she became, quite by accident. But isn't that true of everyone? Rock music itself is an historical accident. I'm being a little facetious, but there is something to rock music being the result of the contingent (if also historically brutal) meeting of two cultures (many more than two, in reality, but the simple picture of the meeting of British Isles and African cultures in the American South is demonstrative enough), and there is something to the provincial, shy John Lennon, in some sense a Liverpudlian to the end, reaching out to the sophisticated cosmopolitan from Tokyo. Indeed, the primitivist and the experimenter were already conjoined in Lennon himself (and certainly in the Beatles), and Ono played the role of consolidating an avant-rock trend that went beyond the point of no return.

What of the actual music, however? Is it more than an interesting idea, the sort of thing that makes Yoko Ono and John Cage, among many others, more philosophers than composers or musicians? Perhaps one can be an artist in some other field besides music, and approach one's art with a rock sensibility—the painter Jean-Michel Basquiat springs to mind (as well as Andy Warhol). But Ono, at the time she met John Lennon, was primarily a conceptual artist. Her work in the early to middle 1960s ranged from "Laugh Piece"—"Keep laughing a week"—to "Bicycle Piece For Orchestra"—"Ride bicycles anywhere you can in the concert hall; do not make any noise." Often her pieces asked that one endeavor to not make "noise" or sound—at least *try* to do that, she implores. As philosopher Arthur Danto writes, "[t]he most robust of her works were subtle and quiet to the point of near-unnoticeability. One of her performances consisted, for example, of lighting a match and allowing it to burn away" ("Life in Fluxus," *The Nation*, Dec. 18, 2000). Her musical works were not different in kind from her visual ones—both primarily involved the opening of spaces in the imagination, first of all, and only secondarily the eyes or ears.

Having said all of this, however, it would be very hard to deny the prescience of Ono's catalogue as "rock musician." 1970's *Plastic Ono Band* was made with the same group that played on John Lennon's album of the same name—Lennon on guitar, Klaus Voorman on bass, and the inestimable Richard Starkey on drums. For sure the album anticipates punk, or at least a certain side of it—perhaps most of all the instrumental aspects of Richard Hell and the Voidoids and even Gang of Four. But I would also say that the album anticipates Sonic Youth and even some of the electric music of Ornette Coleman. Significantly, *Plastic Ono Band* contains a seven-minute track titled "AOS" ("area of specialization"?) that is a rehearsal tape with Ornette Coleman and his group.

Coleman said of Ono that her music "has the sounds of all the ethnic cultures of the present civilizations" (*Walking on Thin Ice* liner notes), preparing the way for one of the main aspects of avant rock—avant-rock musician as "transmuter" and "transmogrifier" of all available musical material. *Plastic Ono Band* is true avant rock, in the sense that Ono is absorbing the most contemporary sounds of Ornette Coleman and John Cage, and putting these sounds in a rock context—if, by such a context, one can mean that rock musicians are playing instruments such as bass guitar and drum set as part of the ensemble.

Then, there is the "instrument" that most stands out here and with most of Ono's albums, her voice. With twenty-twenty hindsight, I think that it is safe to say that if people had been a bit more broad-minded at the time, not so hung up on Yoko Ono as a woman and as "Mrs. John Lennon," this instrument would have been regarded as being in the same class as Jimi Hendrix's Stratocaster. John Cage was critical of music that is "expressive," music that attempts to reflect the emotional state of the composer or improviser (and, on this score, Cage was especially critical of the latter, and of jazz in general). It is interesting to think about what Ono does with her voice in the context of her having come from the circle of Cage. Certainly it would be hard to not think of Ono's singing as expressive, no less than with Hendrix's guitar playing. The comparison shows, I think, the way that avant rock has taken different paths to similar results. On one level, despite everything that hits the ear as quite similar in the "screams" and "moans" of Ono's voice and Hendrix's guitar, they are coming from different places. Hendrix is pushing the limits of the blues, while Ono borrows some sounds from blues and rock along with every other musical genre. But on another level, this is a matter of expanding the aural experience (and one contradiction—though perhaps in the dialectical sense—in Cage's approach is that he attempts to negate expressivity while valuing experience), and so Hendrix and Ono are in the same ballpark after all—and the ballpark where such a thing could happen is rock music.

For a good example of Ono's voice as Hendrix-like guitar fill, check out the version of "Cold Turkey" on John Lennon, *Live in New York City* (1972). In the rendition of "Come Together" at this Madison Square Garden concert, Lennon sings "come together, right now. . . stop the war!" This is thought to have been the straw that broke the camel's back, in terms of the campaign initiated by Richard Nixon to have Lennon and Ono thrown out of the United States.

There are albums by Ono where more space is given to something like conventional songs. This is especially the case with two albums released in 1973, *Feeling the Space* and *Approximately Infinite Universe*. (The latter consisted in two LPs and has been reissued on two CDs.) I find that Ono's songs succeed perhaps one-third of the time—she accomplishes much more when she "intervenes," so to speak, in the world of rock songcraft than when she tries to fully occupy this world. These albums, however, were also interventions into the emerging radical feminist movement of the early 1970s—what is sometimes called the "second wave." Indeed, with a reference to one of the mothers of that second wave, Simone de Beauvoir, *Approximately Infinite Universe* is dedicated to "my best friend John of the second sex," while *Feeling the Space* is dedicated "to the sisters who died in pain and sorrow and those who are now in prison and in mental hospitals for being unable to survive in the male society." With titles such as "Yellow Girl," "Angry Young Woman," "She Hits Back," and "Woman Power," many of the songs from *Feeling the Space* have an anthem-like quality, verging on and sometimes crossing the line into agit-prop. This is also true for many of the songs on *Approximately Infinite Universe*, but some of the anger and bitterness of *Feeling* is taken even further, as evidenced by titles such as "What a Bastard the World Is," "Is Winter Here to Stay?," and "I Felt Like Smashing My Face in a Clear Glass Window." The last of these is not only anticipatory of a thousand punk songs about smashing and glass, but also eerily and worrisomely prophetic as regards the "season of glass" that Ono would experience seven years later, when John Lennon was assassinated. My favorite song from either of these albums, and one of my favorites from all of Ono's songwriting, is "Death of Samantha," from *Approximately Infinite Universe*. The soi-disant refrain, "People say I'm cruel . . . yeah . . . I'm a cruel chick, baby," not only forms part of a powerful statement appropriate for the political moment in which it was made, it clearly had an influence in the new wave music of the late 1970s and early 1980s, and the punk and new wave feminist musicians who came out of that period, from Natalie Merchant to Kim Gordon to the Riot Girl groups.

The other album that might be said to form a trilogy with the two just discussed, 1971's *Fly* (also a double LP/CD), is more instrumental and experimental, especially on the second disk. Parts of the album make me wonder what Ornette Coleman sounded like when he played tenor saxophone with R&B bands in Texas (his switch to alto sax, and indeed to the famous white plastic alto that he is holding on the cover of *The Shape of Jazz to Come*, was precipitated by his being beat up and having his horn smashed in the middle of a roadhouse gig)—there is a deliberate clash of more mainstream and "out" elements. For sure, Ono is deliberately putting a sound into rock music that would seem to not belong, in a sense upping the ante from what the Beatles and others thought they were doing after they heard and were influenced by John Cage and other contemporary classical figures. Other parts of *Fly* consist in collage and jungle percussion, and are very much in the vein of other experiments in contemporary chamber music of that period.

It may be that Ono made her best collection of songs immediately preceding and in the aftermath of Lennon's murder, with her controversial album from 1981, *Season of Glass*. Ono-haters were quick to jump on the fact that the album cover features Lennon's blood-spattered eyeglasses, as though she were "cashing in" once again. As a matter of fact, the inspiration for the album was John Lennon's having heard some then-recent new wave records on the radio, and calling Ono to tell her that rock music seemed to be catching up with her a bit. The rush to find any pretense to put down Yoko Ono—or Linda McCartney, for that matter—as someone who would never have made it except for the patronage of a famous man, is a testament by negative example of how she got under the skin of rock music and its emerging establishment. One stellar irony here is that Ono confronted the establishments of at least three cultures—of rock music, of "art" music in the Western world, and, not least, of Japan, where to become a composer was considered "too hard for women." Going up against these barriers, in a form that integrated post-Cage experiments into rock, makes a good deal of Ono's work unpalatable to an androcentric mainstream that has a fairly clear idea of what nice girls are supposed to be doing, if anything, with rock. But for others it opened many doors.

To be crude about it, we might ask the question that has been raised many times: Why in the world would John Lennon trade his bandmates in the Beatles for Yoko Ono and the Plastic Ono Band? There are overwhelming standards that were set for rock music in the late 1960s, with the Beatles in the vanguard. One has to wonder if perhaps it is better if young people today simply ignore all of that for the most part, attributing it to something that had to do with their parents. You can't trade Creed for Cream, and it was already said in 1970 or earlier that you cannot trade Ono for Beatles. But the former comparison is not the latter. Of course, we wanted to hang on to the Beatles forever; they made us happy. The *White Album* opened the way to the fracturing of that narrative, however. For McCartney, there were more of the nice stories to be told—and not all of the stories that he told after that time were without merit, it should be recognized. But what happened in the moment when John met Yoko meant something for the future of those forms of rock music committed to experimentation.

At the beginning of this section I quoted Arthur Danto, a well-known philosopher who has written a column on art in *The Nation* for many years. The occasion of his article, "Life in Fluxus," is a major exhibition of Ono's work at the Japan Society, in New York City. The title for the exhibition is "Y E S," and an impressive book, with Ono's works both famous and virtually unknown, as well as essays on her work by scholars of the avant-garde, has also been published under this title. Danto's final paragraph bears quoting in full:

> Yoko Ono is really one of the most original artists of the last half-century. Her fame made her almost impossible to see. When she made the art for which her husband admired and loved her, it required a very developed avant-garde sensibility to see it as anything but ephemeral. The exhibition at the Japan Society makes it possible for those with patience

and imagination to constitute her achievement in their minds, where it really belongs. It is an art as rewarding as it is demanding.

In 1995 Ono came more fully into contact with the post-punk milieu of her son, with the album, *Rising*, a collaboration with Sean Ono Lennon's group, IMA. Many of the songs were occasioned by the fiftieth anniversary of the nuclear bombing of Hiroshima. The singing is often reminiscent of "Death of Samantha"—cool and spare. There are also hints of techno, at least in the use of mechanistic break-beats, while at the same time there is a good deal of grunge as well. While the temptation is to think, "Okay, she's trying to get into what the kids are doing now," what is more the case is that experiments that Ono conducted before, during, and after her time with John Lennon are continuing to work their way into basic rock music. (Further adventures in this realm can be heard from the other group that Sean Ono Lennon plays in, Cibo Matto, especially their 1999 album, *Stereo Type A*.) There is an excellent article on Ono's music, by Edward M. Gomez, from the *Y E S* book. Titled "Music of the Mind from the Voice of Raw Soul," Gomez's concluding paragraph is also worthy of citation in full:

> Ono, once a determined transcriber of bird song [which places her in the excellent company of Oliver Messiaen], became a confident performer, an accomplished composer in diverse genres, and a skilled record producer. "When I create, I'm obsessed with it, I'm driven by it," she has said. "The sheer joy and excitement surpasses all other considerations. A good composer knows what she wants to use—and eliminate—step by step, note by note, as she enters the sound world created by design and chance." It is in that realm of aural adventure and expressive possibilities that Ono has spent a lifetime charting her "music of the mind" in many forms and manners—and amplifying it for the world through an irrepressible voice of raw, unfettered soul. (p. 237)

Step by step, move by move. The *White Chess Set* of 1966 was transformed from 1987 to 1999 into a series of works called *Play It By Trust*. As Joan Rothfuss and Midori Yoshimoto write in the *Y E S* volume,

> Ono's interest in chess is contextually linked to that of Fluxus mentor Marcel Duchamp, who in the 1920s announced his withdrawal from art-making to pursue his passion for chess. Some Fluxus artists dealt with the game in their works; Ono herself conceived several variant objects, including a "game of go, all transparent," a game of chess with no queen—that must be imagined," and a chess set in which the pieces were hidden inside identical individual containers. None of these appear to have been realized. (p. 136)

But what is "realization," especially in an art of the imagination such as Ono's? What is it about the game of chess with no queen that must be imagined—the whole game, or the lack of a queen? Imagine that we are playing this game without its most powerful piece, the queen—certainly anyone who fears having their testicles crushed would enjoy this fantasy. Gilles Deleuze and Felix Guattari, in *Mille Plateaux* (*A Thousand Plateaus* is the English translation, though the French term also refers to a many-layered pastry), devote a couple of pages to an interesting comparison of the games of chess and Go. In the West, chess and music have an association going back several centuries, at least from Philidor to Ono. François André Danican Philidor, 1726–1795, was both the "most respected French composer," as well as "far and away the greatest chess player of his time" (Schonberg, *Grandmasters of Chess*, pp. 34, 36). Harold Schonberg, for many years the senior music critic at the *New York Times*, as well as a long-time observer of the chess world (he covered the 1972 Fischer-Spassky match in Reykjavik—hometown of Björk), quotes former chess world champion Max Euwe: Philidor "laid the first stone in the edifice of modern position play. He took chess out of the narrow confines of Euclidean observation into the boundless realm of Cartesian thought" (p. 37). It would not be hard to imagine Deleuze and Guattari arguing that Cartesianism is not so boundless after all, and, in the comparison of chess and Go, to the extent that I understand it, it seems that the former occupies something of the realm that encompasses Descartes and Marxism (which, in French philosophy might mean someone whom Ono read with enthusiasm as a young woman, Jean-Paul Sartre), while the latter bursts Western metaphysical boundaries in the manner of a Nietzschean anarchism ("nomadology" is the term Deleuze coined elsewhere). Certainly, what appears to be the formalism and division of labor of the chessboard seems as though it would be much more a part of the music of Mozart or even Prokofiev (by all accounts a fine chess player), than it would be the art of Marcel Duchamp, John Cage, or Yoko Ono. And, a work such as *White Chess Set* (1966), or "Revolution #9" from the *White Album* for that matter, disrupted settled, foundational subjectivity as much as the post-Sartrean philosophical trajectory—from Althusser to Derrida and Deleuze—did. However, as with Schoenberg, Cage, and Derrida, Yoko Ono searched for the creative interstices that arise from within a certain logic. The rootless, "rhyzomatic" music that is inspired by Deleuze, or perhaps by something in our time and culture that inspired him, for all that it might have sonic affinity with Cage or Ono, is really coming from somewhere else. This may be a way of saying that, even to the great extent that Yoko Ono's work of the 1960s and 1970s foreshadows much that comes after and is perhaps still to come, this work is still very much the reflection of a dynamic that remains rooted in that period. Techno and turntablism, for all that it also has roots in John Cage and other composers who were already using electronics and turntables by the 1950s, may also be the first truly "post-1968" music, the first music reflective of a sensibility that no longer takes its fundamental orientation from the social and cultural vibrations of the late 1960s.

Meanwhile, speaking of the waning of social hope, right-wing mayor Rudy Giuliani cancels funding for New York City's Chess-in-the-Schools (CIS) program. Yoko Ono steps in with the funding, and hosts the annual Imagine Chess Tournament. In his report for *Chess Life* magazine on the Third Annual Imagine Tournament (March 2000), Brian Killigrew observes the arrival of the host:

> Yoko Ono came in and was mobbed by the press. After a few photos were taken, Yoko went straight to a chessboard and played a CIS student. . . . At the awards ceremony, Yoko spoke to the children about believing in themselves and imagining a great future that they can create. Yoko then proudly posed behind each group of winners. When a member of the press called out for her to stand in front of the groups for photographs, she wouldn't budge. (*Chess Life*, June 2000, pp. 36–37)

Beatles, *Rubber Soul* (Capitol LP, 1965).
——, *Revolver* (Capitol LP, 1966).
——, *Sergeant Pepper's Lonely Hearts Club Band* (Capitol LP, 1967).
——, *Magical Mystery Tour* (Capitol LP, 1968???).
——, *The Beatles* ["The White Album"] (Apple LP, 1968).
——, *Abbey Road* (Apple LP, 1969).
——, *Let It Be* (Apple LP, 1970).
Yoko Ono and John Lennon, *Unfinished Music No.1: Two Virgins* (Apple LP, 1968).
John Lennon, *Plastic Ono Band* (Apple LP, 1970).
Yoko Ono, *Plastic Ono Band* (Rykodisc CD, 1997; orig.1970).
——, with the Plastic Ono Band, *Fly* (Rykodisc CD, 1997; orig.1971).
——, with the Plastic Ono Band, *Approximately Infinite Universe* (Rykodisc CD, 1997; orig.1973).
John & Yoko/Plastic Ono Band/Elephant's Memory, *Some Time in New York City* (Apple LP, 1972).
Yoko Ono, with the Plastic Ono Band, and with Something Different, *Feeling the Space* (Rykodisc CD, 1997; orig.1973).
Yoko Ono, *Season of Glass* (Rykodisc CD, originally 1981).
——, *Starpeace* (Rykodisc CD, 1985).
——, *Walking on Thin Ice* (compilation; Rykodisc CD, 1992).
Yoko Ono/IMA, *Rising* (Capitol CD, 1995).
Yoko Ono, *A Blueprint for the Sunrise* (companion CD for the book, *Y E S Yoko Ono*; Japan Society/Harry N. Abrams, 2000).

John Cage

In a Landscape; Stephen Drury, Keyboards (Catalyst CD, 1994; composed 1938–1983).
Singing Through: Vocal Compositions by John Cage; Joan La Barbara, voice; Leonard Stein, piano; William Winant, percussion (New Albion CD, 1990; composed 1942–1985).

Four Walls; John McAlpine, piano; Beth Griffin, voice (Largo CD, 1995; composed 1944).

Sonatas and Interludes for Prepared Piano; Joshua Pierce, piano (Tomato LP, 1977; composed 1946–1948).

String Quartet in Four Parts; The Concord String Quartet (Turnabout LP, 1973; composed 1950).

Concerto for Prepared Piano and Orchestra; Yuji Takahashi, piano; Buffalo Philharmonic Orchestra, conducted by Lukas Foss (Nonesuch LP, n.d.; composed 1951).

4'33", for any instrument or combination of instruments. (Edition Peters sheet music, 1960; composed 1952).

26'1.1499" for a String Player; Bertram Turetzky, contrabass; from *The Contemporary Contrabass* (Nonesuch LP, n.d.; composed 1955).

John Cage and David Tudor, *Indeterminacy* (Folkways LP, 1959).

John Cage and Lejaren Hiller, *HPSCHD,* for harpsichords and computer-generated sound tapes; Antoinette Vischer, Neely Bruce, David Tudor, harpsichords (Nonesuch LP, n.d.; composed 1967–1969).

Etudes Australes for Piano; Grete Sultan, piano (Tomato LP, 1979; composed 1974).

Thirteen; Ensemble 13, conducted by Manfred Reichert (Classic Produktion Osnabrück CD, 1993; composed 1992).

Glenn Gould

J. S. Bach, *The Goldberg Variations;* Glenn Gould, piano (Columbia LP, first released 1955; composed 1742).

Schoenberg/Berg/Webern; Glenn Gould, piano; CBC Symphony Orchestra, Jean-Marie Beaudet, conductor (Canadian Broad-casting Corporation CD, 1995; pieces recorded 1952–1954; works composed 1907–42).

Paul Hindemith, *The Piano Sonatas;* Glenn Gould, piano (Columbia LP, 1973).

Ludwig van Beethoven, *Bagatelles;* Glenn Gould, piano (Columbia LP, 1975; composed 1782–1802).

Jean Sibelius, *3 Sonatines, Op.67/"Kyllikki," Op.41;* Glenn Gould, piano (Columbia LP, 1977).

Glenn Gould, composer, *The Solitude Trilogy: Three Sound Documentaries (The Idea of North, The Latecomers, The Quiet in the Land)* (CDC Records CD, 1992).

Herewith, an abbreviated journey through the prehistory of avant rock—dealing with those whom might be called the more immediate precursors: John Cage, Glenn Gould, John Coltrane, Cecil Taylor, Miles Davis.

Deconstruction of the European classical tradition: John Cage and Glenn Gould

The truth of one of John Cage's well-known remarks comes homes to me on a regular basis. A trivial example will suffice. On a bike ride, I passed a house that was under construction. There were perhaps ten workers carrying out various operations, at least half of them hammering nails into wood. Intermittently there were the sounds of drills and of a high-pitched circular saw. The overall effect was not unpleasant (though living next door to the cacophony, or waking up to it, would most likely be something else again). Without especially reflecting on the matter, a thought asserted itself: this is music. Not simply that the sounds I was hearing *could* be music, or heard "as musical," but that they were already music.

Cage's famous remark was, "I do not hear noise, I hear music."

Incidentally, and this topic will come up repeatedly, it is interesting to think about the implications of the "logical next step" from dodecaphony being "cacophony." The latter is generally used as another name for "noise." John Cage studied with Arnold Schoenberg when the latter was based in Los Angeles (Cage grew up there). One of the famous stories about their interaction was that Schoenberg told Cage that, until he mastered certain techniques, he would always find himself coming up against a wall when it comes to harmony. Cage's response was that he would dedicate himself to banging his head against that wall. That is a rather "material" response, one might say, and it calls to mind that the root of the term "cacophony" is the Greek expression, *kakia*, which comes down to us today as a euphemism for excrement, *ka ka*. Neo-Platonist thinkers of a gnostic orientation, especially Plotinus, denigrated matter, and they used the Greek *kakia* to designate it. The alternative is to revel in the goodness of the world and all of its sounds and possible sounds. Hence, to go beyond the twelve-note system into cacophony, or what at first may seem to be "noise."

Now, why would a book about experimental rock music contain a discussion of figures such as Cage and Coltrane? Surely it cannot be argued that these figures played much of a role in the emergence of rock'n'roll from rhythm and blues. In the nexus from Ray Charles and Louis Jordan to Chuck Berry, Little Richard, and Jerry Lee Lewis, we can safely assume there was little awareness of (or interest in, at any rate) works for prepared piano based on procedures of randomization, strange interpretations of Bach's *Goldberg Variations,* or modal improvisations and percussive, intense harmonies that strain the jazz tradition to the breaking point. Rock music was busy making its own new sounds, new syntheses, out of popular materials. To say that the strange brew that gave rise to, say, Elvis Presley, was more "social" than "aesthetic" would be to ignore the fact that musical materials are rooted in the materiality of cultures and cultural interactions. (For the present example, see the impressive book by Michael T. Bertland, *Race, Rock, and Elvis.* The title might as well have included class and gender, which are clearly part of the author's story.) Their cultural backgrounds and traditions are no less important for John Cage or Cecil Taylor, than for people in the American South who were hearing intersections of country music, blues, gospel, and mountain ("hillbilly") music, and whose receptivity to the emerging mix was also bound up with class.

And yet, within a relatively few years, it was clear that rock musicians were paying attention to the larger trends of the European classical and jazz traditions and much else besides. The dynamic of rock is that it always seems to throw the doors wide open.

One could see why something like the "spirit," if not always the actual work or ideology, of John Cage would sooner or later come into contact with rock music and play a role in it. This has to do with something specific about the way that both Cage and rock music are "American," something deep in the American grain, namely, the centrality of experience. Cage's experiments with music from the 1940s onward, and the ethos of rock music especially in the midst of and after the social upheavals of the sixties, were both aimed at erasing any hard and fast distinction between "music" and "life." Both might even be taken as an assault on what Paul de Man called "aesthetic ideology," the idea that the aesthetic constitutes an autonomous domain, akin to the sphere of life occupied, at least in modern, secular times, by religion or the spiritual. The transcendence of the compartmentalization of life, which perhaps otherwise can be understood as the distinction between the public and the private or even between the life of action and the life of contemplation, is seen not only in Cage's work, but in all of the protagonists discussed in this section. In each case, this occurs through the enlargement of the syntax of music. The aim was never to "prepare" the way for rock music and its avant-garde possibilities, of course—except perhaps in the case of Miles Davis, who created a significant overlap between jazz and rock. However, rock since the middle and late sixties has opened its doors to this enlarged syntax; therefore, it behooves us to grapple with the innovations that rock later absorbed. This discussion is not meant on any level as an authoritative introduction to these figures, but instead as a set of thematic renderings of some important ideas in music that have made their way into avant-rock.

We might speak of John Cage and Glenn Gould in terms of the "deconstruction" of the European classical tradition. To discuss these two figures together may seem strange to some readers. The former is known primarily as a composer, the latter as a performer, a pianist to be specific. Significantly, in either case there are those who would challenge these designations, though not for the purpose of proposing other terms. Both figures have legions of detractors. What sort of "composer" allows randomness to dominate the process of setting down musical instructions, and what sort of pianist creates such eccentric interpretations as to seemingly do fundamental violence to the works of canonical composers? What sort of composer composes works for tree branches and pine cones and conch shells, and what sort of respectable classical pianist uses recording technology, including innumerable tape splices, to produce novel interpretations of Bach, Beethoven, and other figures major and minor? On many important questions, Cage and Gould seem completely at odds with one another, holding opposing positions (for example, on the matter of recorded music), and yet each assaulted the Western classical tradition in wave after wave. In some sense, each could be seen as responding to a simple question: After Schoenberg, what next? As composer and "interpreter," Cage and Gould, respectively, each attempted that next step. Each created work that, on the one hand, can be understood within the logic of what came before, but, on the other hand, also seems to explode that logic. Indeed, what one might find frightening about both Cage and Gould is that their steps beyond make almost anything else in music that is not equally far out, at least in the tradition from which they come (but to some extent in music more generally), seem as though it is a step backward. Certainly, one could speak with some legitimacy about "John Cage, Glenn Gould, and the end of music"—but I have invoked the term "deconstruction" instead. The point to speaking of deconstruction rather than ends is this. If Cage and Gould leave us with the question of what to do with music after their work, one central claim of the present book is that even exploded logics leave trails and generate consequences.

Jacques Derrida coined the term "deconstruction," and he has also written about the "ends of man." This is an appropriate reference in the present comparison because both Cage and Gould, in raising fundamental issues regarding what music is after certain logics have been taken to the breaking point, also raise questions about who is the "subject" of music—who is making music. In Cage, there is the sense that music does its own "speaking." In Gould, the dialogue between composer and interpreter is complicated both by Gould's "eccentric" readings and by the continuous interjection of hitherto supposedly "foreign" elements of sound production and recording.

As always under the premise that the point here is not to present an exhaustive account of any given figure, what follows are some fragmentary comments on some of the things that John Cage and Glenn Gould were up to, things that bear on the subsequent development of music and in particular avant rock.

Cage was something of an amateur mycologist (mushroom expert). He once won six thousand dollars on an Italian game show answering questions about mushrooms—he needed the money to pay for an operation for his mother. Cage was also interested in Buddhism, and an old legend tells us that the Buddha died from eating a poison mushroom. In one of his books, Cage supplies a recipe for mushroom catsup, which he called "dogsup." Cage was inspired by Yoko Ono to take up a macrobiotic diet, though I do not know if the mushroom dogsup discovery came in that context.

Cage argued that if you take silence seriously, then you must conclude that the most basic element of music is not counterpoint, harmony, timbre, rhythm, or dynamics (loudness), but instead duration. This is because, of the aforementioned attributes, only duration applies to silence as well as sound. A crucial element of Cage's music and philosophy, and perhaps the most important element, is to give silence its due—which leads, ultimately, to a piece such as *4'33"*.

"Isn't he the guy who wrote that thing that doesn't actually have any notes in it?" Well, there are notes in it, if the incidental sounds that happen to occur during the performance happen to have a particular pitch.

With duration as the basic building block, the musical "measure" becomes a little box of time, and "notation" can become a set of instructions that says, for example, "in the next thirty seconds, do the following . . . ."

Cage was a pioneer in the use of new forms of notation and, just as some of his musical ideas can be said to be more philosophy than music, some of his notations can be said to be more akin to graphic art.

Cage is often associated with the prepared piano, which he invented, having been inspired by Henry Cowell. Less well known, at least popularly, is Cage's invention of the "water gong," a gong played under water. The original inspiration for this instrument was a water ballet for which Cage was asked to compose the music.

Perhaps Cage's sensibility about duration was reflected in the extended improvisations of Coltrane, and in psychedelic rock jams, where time is a key element, even if the idea is also to transport the listener "beyond time." Of course, it can be argued that these genres have to do with expressivity, whereas Cage was attempting to remove this quality from music. But the expressivity is not entirely "personal" in these examples, there is the desire to let music itself—or perhaps, in the case of Cage, the stars, water, electronic oscillations, life, the universe, everything and nothing—speak.

Two of my favorite works by John Cage are written for piano, the one for prepared piano, the other for the piano left to itself. The *Sonatas and Interludes for Prepared Piano* were composed in the period from 1946 to 1948. Numerous recordings have been released over the years, and the work is performed often. The *Sonatas and Interludes* are considered to be Cage's masterwork for the prepared piano and the most important of his works in the mid-1940s. This work is not the product of random procedures but rather is a result of Cage's engagement with Indian aesthetics. (The influence of Indian philosophy and of art historian and critic Ananda Coomaraswamy is discussed in depth in James Pritchett's *The Music of John Cage*, pp. 29–39.) Indeed, and perhaps even more surprising, given what has been said about expressivity, the *Sonatas and Interludes* purportedly deal with the "attempt to express in music the [eight] 'permanent emotions' . . . and the common tendency toward tranquility" (Pritchett quoting Cage, p. 30). However, it can be argued that this progression in the work, from the earlier of the twenty pieces that make up the *Sonatas and Interludes* where there is some sense of emotional charge, to the later pieces where emotion seems increasingly absent, represents Cage's first systematic attempt to transcend intentionality. It is interesting to listen, in this regard, to the *Etudes Australes,* a work for piano where the notes are generated by placing transparencies over charts of the stars as seen from Australia. This work, from roughly thirty years later (1974), is reminiscent of the *Sonatas and Interludes* in its elegance and simplicity, its magical quality. Cage's "noise," as evidenced in works such as *Indeterminacy, Cartridge Music, HPSCHD,* and *Imaginary Landscape #4 for Twelve Transistor Radios,* is important and compelling, and obviously very important for understanding the trajectory that runs from the Velvet Underground to Sonic Youth and beyond. But there is something about these two piano (prepared or otherwise) works that distills Cage's project with great clarity.

Much is made of Cage's use of concepts such as indeterminacy, chance, and randomness (Cage makes a distinction between the latter pair that is perhaps too subtle for discussion here), but the terms "intention" and "intentionality" are rarely brought into the discussion. These are important terms, however, for many of Cage's experiments can be seen as attempts to depart from the intentionality of the composer, performer, or listener (sometimes by breaking down these categories as well). In this attempt, Cage's "next step" can be said to also break with the European model of Enlightenment and rationality. In this latter model, the aim is to bring anything that is obscure, even one's own processes of thought, into the light of reason. If there is anything to my earlier argument about a kind of Schoenberg/Stravinsky dialectic, Cage's "next step" might be seen as a crossing from the former to the latter, but not in terms first of all of what is done to the scale or to rhythm, or to any "musical" element per se, but instead in terms of Cage's search for ideas from non-European cultures, most often from India, China, and Japan. The next step after dodecaphony might be the use of chance operations in the choice of notes, in which case Cage is going further in the logic of Schoenberg, but Cage also found a philosophical basis (the point being that Cage went first to the idea rather than the sound itself, which is something different from the search for sounds outside the European classical canon that was conducted by Stravinsky, Bartók, and many others) for indeterminacy and chance in his explorations of Buddhism. As John Pritchett puts it, in the early to middle 1950s Cage went from an aesthetic of "making" to one of "accepting" (p. 76). Pritchett's formulation is very much worth pondering: in order to "explore freely the infinite space of musical possibilities, chance was essential" (p. 76). A longer passage from *The Music of John Cage* is helpful:

> Cage gives the reason for the necessity of chance in "Experimental Musical Doctrine": "In view, then, of a totality of possibilities, no knowing action is commensurate, since the

character of the knowledge acted upon prohibits all but some eventualities." The assertion here that musical knowledge limits the scope of compositional action has its parallels in passages from Cage's earlier writings: in "Lecture on Nothing," where he describes
how materials can be "worn out" by thought about them; in the part of the "Lecture on
Something" that deals with the way in which thought (as expressed in traditional musical
continuity) tends to exclude "non-profound" events; and in the "Juilliard Lecture," where
he adapts a Zen metaphor to point out that "sounds are sounds and men are men"
and that "the wisest thing to do is to open one's ears immediately and hear a sound suddenly before one's thinking has a chance to turn it into something logical, abstract, or
symbolical" . . . (p. 76)

The paradoxes involved in these formulations, starting with "the necessity of
chance," are most likely lost on no one, least of all Cage. And yet, these paradoxes are
emblematic of what is perhaps paradigmatic of all avant-garde music, the attempt to
hear with "other ears" and "new, fresh" ears.

Although Cage looked eastward for philosophical systems in which sense can be
made of the necessity of chance, his contemporary, Jean-Paul Sartre, was also setting
out a philosophy of radical contingency in the years following World War Two.

Comparisons have been made between Sartre and Buddhism, especially as regards
a concept that Cage also takes up, namely that of "no-mindedness." Personally, I do not
accept the comparisons, and on some level I am skeptical of Cage's connection to
Buddhism—I think there is a difference between a kind of unraveling or even deconstruction of Western Enlightenment ideas and a philosophy that starts from seemingly
different premises.

Instead, Cage's music can be understood as an experiment in freedom and responsibility, and perhaps as having as much to do with Ralph Waldo Emerson as with
Buddhism. But let's stay with the paradoxes for another moment. Recall that I titled this
section of the book, "Practices, modalities." I will say more on practices, as this notion
relates to Cage, in a moment. There is a sense in which the dialectics that motivate the
avant-garde—"next step"/"something else," "music"/"noise," advanced technique/
refusal of technique, and so on, are encapsulated in the play of modalities: possibility,
necessity, contingency, actuality, impossibility. Cage's "necessity of change" and refusal
of intention invoke another modality: impossibility. To knowingly "not know," to intentionally attempt to surmount intention (Cage, incidentally, was disdainful of the path that
some took toward this end, drugs), is to attempt the impossible. But this again gives us
a definition of the avant-garde since, to use the language of Jacques Derrida, to "invent"
is impossible and yet this is where our responsibility lies.

Cage's music invites performers and listeners into an experiment in the practice of
freedom. In a documentary film on his work (*John Cage,* part of the "4merican
Composers" series—yes, that is how they spelled it), Cage remarks that he was look-

ing for a way that people could be free without becoming foolish, and he goes on to discuss problems that he has had with classically trained performers. When some of these performers took Cage's scores as a license to do anything they pleased (other than actually playing the score), he said that he realized his basic problems were "social, not musical." Given that Cage's music is in some sense (as he suggested in the quotation cited above) more about listening than "making sounds," one can find a politics at the intersection of these social and musical problems. I would say that it is a politics of possibility and, to use Derrida's phrase, "letting the other speak."

In purely "musical" terms, the transition to listening, or "acceptance," as method, is connected with Cage's arguments about silence. In the "making" model, silence is simply what is left out, it is the place where the composer or performer chooses to not do any making. In the "acceptance" model, silence asserts itself, at least to the attentive listener.

However, there is no "real" silence. One of John Cage's most famous stories ("anyone who knows me knows this story") concerns his experience in an anechoic chamber at Harvard, sometime around 1950. (As Cage biographer David Revill remarks, despite the fame of the story, no one has been able to pin down exactly when it took place.) An anechoic chamber is one that allows no outside sounds to enter in. Cage wanted to spend time in the chamber so that he could experience complete silence. What he found instead is that he heard two sounds: his own heartbeat, and the sound of his blood rushing through his veins. David Revill's account of this experience is very perceptive—and one can see from his reading of the experience why he titled his biography *The Roaring Silence.*

> "I had honestly and naively thought that some actual silence existed," Cage recalled. "So . . . I had not really put silence to the test." Now he realized that silence, as he had construed it, did not exist. "Try as we may to make a silence, we cannot," Cage observed. "No silence exists that is not pregnant with sound."
>
> If "silence" was to remain a valid concept, Cage had to redefine it in light of his experience. Up to this point, his advocacy of the principle of non-dualism and interpenetration had not stopped him maintaining a division between sound and silence. Now experience had corrected him; he saw the split was in the head. The dichotomy had to be refined in such a way that its source was made apparent: intention versus non-intention.
> (p. 163)

Yes, that way of putting it really captures the paradox, and in a way shows how Cage's concern with chance might really come into communication with Sartre's radical contingency. It is often thought of Sartre that he was some sort of throwback Cartesian who has been superceded by folks who have shown the constructedness of the subject. Certainly Sartre had some Cartesianism in him—but I say this as someone who finds titles such as "Descartes' Error" a bit laughable. (The book of that exact title does argue convincingly that there is no absolute divide between "reason" and the emotions, but unfortunately this sort of expression has been taken as indicating that Descartes was some sort of misguided fool, with his notions of "reason" and subjectivity.) Part of the genius of Sartre's argument about subjectivity is that, in his philosophy, the subject can be both "constructed" in a social fabric and irreducible. The subject is irreducible *for us.* The paradox of subjectivity that this recognition involves us in seems to be the same as what Cage understood from his experience in the chamber.

There is a very funny moment in the Cage documentary film, speaking of contingency. The film includes excerpts from a concert that was held to celebrate Cage's seventieth birthday, with Cage as a participant. At least part of the concert was a marathon session during which a number (at least seven) of Cage's works were being performed simultaneously, in the same hall. One of these works involved the use of a radio, tuned to a station that was broadcasting live. There was a moment in the performance when, miraculously, relative silence prevailed—and a voice from the radio entered that "silence," saying: "Let's move on to music."

Amazing moment, really. Everyone in the audience laughed, including John Cage.

Cage was interested fairly early on in the possibilities of amplified "small" sounds, and he pioneered the use of contact microphones in music-making, though often with objects that would not conventionally be thought of as musical instruments. Among his later works that used this technique are "Branches" (1976) and "Inlets" (1977), the former using tree branches, pinecones, and a cactus (technically, "Branches" is termed a work for percussion, using "amplified plant materials"), and the latter using conch shells both blown and filled with water for unpredictable sloshing sounds, and "the sound of fire," preferably generated live. When I was in college, a review of performances of these pieces in the Village Voice (by critic and minimalist composer Tom Johnson) fascinated me, and played a role in bringing me even closer to Cage. My roommate in those days, a superb fellow who had (still has) tremendous talent as a folk musician, but who thought Cage was ridiculous, for awhile would ask me on a regular basis if I had heard any good concertos for pinecone lately.

Cage was always looking for sound sources. Someone played him the Beatles song "Back in the USSR" and he commented that he appreciated the use of the jet-plane engine at the beginning. "Cartridge Music" (1960), one of the "amplified small sounds" works that used the cartridges of turntables, is one of the sources of what turntablists would later render as scratching. *Imaginary Landscape #4 for Twelve Transistor Radios* (1951) is an early instance of sampling. It would be interesting to compare a performance of this piece from its time of composition to one from more recent years as an example of larger transformations in the social and cultural landscape. These and similar sound source discoveries, along with the prepared piano and pieces that require the performer to play inside the piano can also be related to the "language of effects" that one hears in John Coltrane and, more predominantly, Pharaoh Sanders. The conch gurgles from Inlets would also make excellent loops for techno mixes.

Cage was generally not very favorable to the idea of improvisation except in the case of what he called "non-intentional improvisation." Spontaneity, as Cage understood it, is too closely linked to intentions and personal likes and dislikes. Biographer David Revill, himself a percussionist, provides an insightful critique of Cage's views on this subject (as did Cecil Taylor, with a single, biting remark—to be quoted later). In a nutshell, as Revill writes, "[F]or many players the experience of improvisation is not at all personal; it is as if a certain sound has to be made at a particular moment, or, more accurately, one makes it, with no gap between decision and action" (p. 170). Revill calls Cage's attitude toward improvisation one of the latter's "rare prejudices." Though I agree with Revill's critique, there is also something to this idea of "non-intentional improvisation," which might be summed up by Cage's question (quoted by Revill), "How can I get a B-flat to come to me of itself, and not just out of my memory, tastes, [and] psychology?" (p. 171) The fruitfulness of this approach can be seen in the improvisations of Derek Bailey, AMM, and, more recently, Chris Cutler (the percussionist from Henry Cow who has performed solo, with drums and live electronics, in recent years) and Jim O'Rourke (in his performances using laptop computer).

Referring to a performance of his later works, the James Joyce-inspired Roaratorio (1979), Cage said, "I'm sure it'll be noise, but I doubt that it will be white."

For Cage, to compose a piece of music often means to come up with the methodology for its composition. The idea is the piece.

Cage did not like recordings, and claimed to not own any records. At home, he would often listen to two radios at once. He claimed that records destroyed the musical experience.

Cage was taught to play chess by Marcel Duchamp in the mid-1960s. "I was using chess as a pretext to be with him" (Revill, p. 214).

Since his game was much weaker than that of Duchamp, Cage generally played with Teeny [Duchamp's wife, Alexina Sattler]. Duchamp sat smoking at the other end of the room and would periodically glance at their game and make criticisms, "and in between take a nap. He would say how stupid we both were. "Don't you ever want to win?" he barked at Cage. "He didn't say it was likely, but he said it very accusingly," Cage recalled. "I was so hurt that I was wondering whether to leave altogether. The next day when we met he was all smiles and friendship. I think that Teeny had said something to him." "I was so delighted to be with him," explained Cage, "the notion of winning was beside the point." He was delighted, too, when he heard that Duchamp, on being asked what kind of relationship they had, replied, "We're buddies." (Revill, p. 214)

Cage wrote at least two works that involve chess. One is actually a chance-modified film of a game that he played with Teeny Duchamp. The other, Reunion, is Cage's only work for the year 1968: "for diverse performers, a plurality of electronic musics gated by a game of chess played on an electronically prepared board."

In almost every photograph of John Cage, he is smiling broadly, if not laughing.

John Cage disliked recordings. Glenn Gould gave up a lucrative concert career to devote himself to recording. John Cage favored the performance context where composer, musicians, and audience could be involved in a common experience. Glenn Gould was highly skeptical of the live performance situation, though not, perhaps, of the category of "experience" itself. The length to which Gould would go to avoid direct contact with other people has become the subject of legend, and certainly his departure from the concert stage cannot be understood apart from his hermit's temperament. But Gould felt, and provided cogent arguments for his inclination, that the concert situation has very little to do with listening, and therefore not much to do with the musical experience as he understood it. Therefore he kept his music-making to his apartment, the recording studio, and perhaps to the solitary excursions that he would make to Canada's desolate northern areas.

This is only one example that is illustrative of a paradox involving John Cage and Glenn Gould. The paradox is not that they held diametrically opposite positions on various fundamental issues, both musical and philosophical, but that they held these positions out of quite similar motivations. The question of the possibility of listening is fundamentally about the character of experience. Cage tended to be a very public person and yet his conception of experience is heavily indebted to Zen. The form of inwardness here is complex, and it might be argued that Zen is a form of radical empiricism without any need for a centered "self." Experience just is, and experience of self is just one among all the other experiences—and not necessarily a trustworthy guide to reality. Put this way, Zen sounds like the philosophy of David Hume—one of the originators of the form of radical empiricism in the West that, in the more recent one hundred years, has been associated with diverse figures such as William James, Gilles Deleuze, and Richard Rorty. However, at least in Cage's version, Zen is clearly not only about "pure, unmediated experience," but also an attitude of acceptance towards whatever reality presents. (A detailed discussion of Cage's interest in Zen is found in Revill, esp. pp. 110–18.) Here we find once again the paradox of intentionality in Cage.

Where do things stand on this score with Gould? First of all, especially for those readers who might not be familiar with Glenn Gould, we should mention that he was not primarily a composer. Gould did do some composing, most significantly of what he called his three "contrapuntal radio documentaries," also known as the *Solitude Trilogy.* (He also wrote a string quartet and a choral work with the title, "So You Want to Write a Fugue?") And certainly he played a role in breaking down the distinction between the "composer" and the "performer" or interpreter. Still, this deconstruction took place on the foundation of Gould's skills as a pianist. That was the store of "street cred," so to speak, on the basis of which he was able to get away with everything else. (If I may offer a disclaimer here, my intention is to deal with some of Gould's ideas, especially his sense of what "interpretation" of a tradition entails. My aim is not to compare the particulars of Gould's piano practice with those of other virtuoso interpreters of the Western classical tradition.) For sure, even Gould's first and probably still most famous recording, of J. S. Bach's *Goldberg Variations,* was immediately recognized as eccentric. The things that Gould would do to the classical repertoire, the "liberties" that he would take (in a moment they will be categorized), were tightly controlled, not the result of chance operations. Still, why not compare John Cage to a composer who, rather than having opened music to chance and non-intentional structures (or possible structures), went in the opposite direction, toward a kind of hyper-serialism where every element of the music is controlled with mathematical precision? That is a "next step" also, and the person with whom it is most associated is composer Milton Babbitt, who aimed to take the approach represented by Schoenberg's twelve-note system into the determination of not only pitch, but also timbre, rhythm, dynamics, and so on (see Paul Griffiths, *Modern Music and After,* pp. 59–69). That step is interesting in its own right, but there is something about what John Cage and Glenn Gould did that not only seems more like two equally valid forms of *deconstruction* of the tradition they inherited (though as an American and a Canadian, not as Europeans; Babbitt was American also, but arguably more European in his approach to Schoenberg), but there is a further deconstruction in the way that they stand as antinomies to one another.

Gould's post in the antinomy has been called "radical conservative," a conservatism so deep that it is radical. This is the assessment presented in the film, *Glenn Gould: A Portrait,* a documentary made by the Canadian Broadcasting Corportation (1985). The approach of the film, however, is what I would call "conservative conservative," a rendering of the nutty and eccentric Gould safe for the tea-and-biscuits-at-the-club set. (But then, the film is distributed by a company based in Long Beach, California, with the German name, "Kultur," the sort of thing that led to the Dead Kennedys "uber alles . . . .") The film is good, however, for the footage of Gould and interviews with his associates, as long as you can ignore the "august" tone of the narrator. Cage and Gould are both about "receiving" a certain tradition, but they both also appreciated the ocean that exists between themselves and the "centers" of that tradition. Cage was once asked by a European composer—and this became one of his famous, oft-repeated stories—how he was able to work, being so far from the centers of the European tradition. Cage asked in response how his interlocutor was able to work, being so close to the centers of European tradition. In the Portrait film, Gould remarks that, "in Toronto you can carve up your own musical space"—and, as I remarked already, Gould was fascinated by what he called "the idea of North," meaning not only Canada, and Canada in relation to the United States, but also the northern reaches of Canada.

There a person could clear his or her mind, free from the chatterings of other people. Gould did enjoy conversations with animals, incidentally—birds, horses, elephants, dogs. Any reference to "chatter" after the late 1920s is also a reference to Martin Heidegger, who might also be called a radical conservative (which led him to an involvement with fascism and Nazism, as many readers will know, though there are some other elements in his thought that speak better of him). In his philosophy, most remarkably *Being and Time* (*Sein und Zeit,* 1927), one finds the notion of "das Man"—often rendered as "the they," with the connotation of something like the "mindless crowd." The main product of this crowd, qua crowd, is chatter. (Lest anyone think there is nothing more to this idea than pure condescension, Heidegger thought that most people spend most of their time on the level of chatter, and this applies even to deep thinkers—such as himself, of course—and it applies increasingly as society comes more and more under the sway of technology and mass media. On the other hand, one can easily find more than one's share of condescension when in the company of what might be called Heideggerian camp-followers.) Certainly one can hear more than a little resonance of Heidegger in what Gould says about audiences. Here is an especially acerbic example quoted from the biography by psychologist and musician Peter F. Ostwald, *Glenn Gould: The Ecstasy and Tragedy of Genius:*

> There's a very curious and almost sadistic lust for blood that overcomes the concert listener. There's a waiting for it to happen, a waiting for the horn to fluff, a waiting for the strings to become ragged, a waiting for the conductor to forget to subdivide . . . it's dreadful. There's a kind of gladiatorial instinct that comes upon the case-hardened concertgoer, which is why I suppose I don't like him as a breed and don't trust him, and I wouldn't want one as a friend. (pp. 130–31)

Harsh stuff, and the word "breed" is troubling, too, in the context of Heidegger's nationalism. If we can set these nasty associations aside for a moment (even if they cannot be dismissed altogether), there is a point here, and every person who attends musical performances with an ear toward *listening* knows this.

It is hard to imagine rock music without rock concerts, even though there have been periods or subdivisions within rock music that might have been more about listening to a record by oneself or with a friend or two (progressive rock or Nick Drake, or some of the recent women singers who mainly appeal to adolescent girls). Besides the fact that it can be an interesting experience to see musicians perform their music in a live setting, and the live setting can propel the music in ways that it would not have encountered in the studio, there is also the whole idea of the rock concert as "happening." However, what does it mean when this experience comes to be about almost everything under the sun except listening—especially when, thanks to digital innovations, there may not be so much playing coming from the stage, either?

At some rock performances, too, there seems to be a strange new sound coming from the audience. What I am going to say here is a bit speculative, and I don't quite know how one would go about studying the question more objectively. You can hear this sound when artists or groups are introduced on *Saturday Night Live,* or on many live albums (a recent example that I heard is Ben Harper, *Live from Mars*). There is something about this shrill and rising sound coming from a mass of voices that seems to say, "He is here! And we are not worthy! It is too good for us!" Perhaps the first time I noticed this was when the host on *Saturday Night Live* announced that "Cher is with us!"—as though the messiah had arrived. I once heard similar sounds at an Itzak Perlman concert, so this reaction is not confined to rock music. People are going nuts over something—it would be hard to say that it is music; instead, it seems that we are into a further stage of the society of the spectacle, with a more recent addition of what might be called celebrity messianism (even when the celebrities are throwaway, here today/gone tomorrow-types). None of this necessarily speaks against the music, but it doesn't speak for the music, either.

Avant rock attempts to shift the focus back to the music, which is what Gould also tried to do by leaving the concert stage. The music most often recorded by Gould was that of Bach, Beethoven, Mozart, and Schoenberg. In the case of most classical musicians who emphasize such a repertoire (perhaps excluding the Schoenberg), we might find a mainly backward-looking sensibility. With Gould, the comparison that comes more to mind is when a philosopher such as Derrida reads Plato or Montaigne, or when Deleuze reads Hume, or when Antonio Negri reads Spinoza. The comparison is apt because Gould enters not only the sound-world of Bach, but also the idea-world, and he enters these worlds not only as an explorer, but also as an interlocutor, someone looking for a fruitful conversation. Gould's solitude, finally, is not entirely that of the hermit or spiritual recluse (though, to be sure, he was as much of a hermit as one can be living in a high-rise apartment in a large, cosmopolitan city), but more that of the writer. At the piano, or with a musical score, whether in his apartment or in the recording studio, he was alone, but not alone—he had conversations with Bach and Beethoven, and he did not leave the transcripts of those conversations in a desk drawer, but instead prepared them for public release.

For Gould, then, the piano was an instrument of thought, of thinking. Heidegger connected the thoughtlessness of common chatter with the increasing domination of society by *techné* (akin to what Marxists call "instrumental reason"), which then led to a critique of technology. Gould, in turning away from live audiences, and instead toward making connections with individuals one by one through the medium of the long-playing record, embraced technology seemingly without reservation. Many sources could be cited on this question, but two in particular are especially interesting. First, let us turn to Gould himself, in a review of the record, *Switched-On Bach,* by Walter Carlos. Released in 1968, *Switched-On* is an interpretation of Bach on the then-new Moog synthesizer. Gould called it the "record of the decade." (Many readers will know that, subsequently, Walter became Wendy Carlos.) Gould was a prolific writer of essays and reviews, and the following comes from *The Glenn Gould Reader.*

> The whole record, in fact, is one of the most startling achievements of the recording industry in this generation, certainly one of the great feats of "keyboard" performance, and . . . the surest evidence, if evidence be needed, that live music never was best. (p. 430)
>
> [T]he real revelation of this disc is its total acceptance of the recording ethic—the belief in an end so incontrovertibly convincing that any means, no matter how foreign to the adjudicative process of the concert hall, and even if the master is white with splicing tape, as this one surely must have been, is justified. (p. 432)

It would be fair to read the latter comments as saying that music-making that negates or stands against the concert hall is the way to go. For his views on technology, and the "recording ethic"—surely a notion that would appeal to avant-rock musicians—Gould was sometimes referred to as "Bach in the age of Marshall McLuhan." The latter, "patron saint" of Wired magazine and of cyberculture in general, was also a resident of Toronto; Gould and McLuhan exchanged views on a few occasions, including twice in radio debates. McLuhan's book, *Understanding Media: The Extensions of Man* stands with another book from 1964, Herbert Marcuse's *One-Dimensional Man,* as quite fresh and illuminating, even in our postmodern times. One of McLuhan's many terms that have entered popular discourse is "global village"—the new media makes such a thing possible, McLuhan thought. It is interesting to ponder what use Gould would have made of the Internet and World Wide Web. Clearly, Gould resonated with the idea of being in communication with many people even while living a physically solitary existence.

We can keep these themes in mind while turning to another source. *Glenn Gould: Music and Mind,* by the late University of Toronto philosopher Geoffrey Payzant is one of the really interesting books about music, I think, because it deals primarily in ideas. An entire chapter with the provocative title "Creative Cheating" is dedicated to the aforementioned "recording ethic." Here are a few important passages:

> In the 1960s Glenn Gould was frequently referred to, by journalists and publicity people, as "the philosopher of recording." He does not speak of himself as a

philosopher, but the expression "a new philosophy of recording" is his. It refers to what he saw as an emerging attitude toward recorded music and not to a philosophical system or discovery of his own. He has written numerous articles and scripts explaining how technological progress would make it possible for musical recording to advance from its early archival stage to a higher stage in which technology and technicians would participate in the creative process actively and in their own right.

In our European tradition, philosophical work is to a great extent done by the Socratic method of argument and counter-argument, by ongoing dialectical exchange. It is a contentiously cooperative activity. Since Gould is a solitary, and wants to be in complete control of all that he does, he is not in that tradition; he has no taste for dialectics. . . .

In his mid-twenties he told an interviewer that if he had not been a musician he would have been a writer. He said that part of the appeal of being a writer was that this vocation would allow him to set his own working hours. (p. 119)

A slightly different reading is possible here. Although, if one is fortunate enough to sustain oneself through writing, then there is a good deal of flexibility as regards working hours, there is also a sense in which writers write when something that needs to be written calls to them. That is where the dialectic (or at least the dialogue) is found, in a way similar to what I said earlier about Gould's conversations with Bach, Beethoven, and other of his muses. Gould tested the limits of Beethoven interpretation; that is not the same thing as saying that anything might count as an interpretation of Beethoven. Likewise, though Gould certainly pursued an antiseptic regime with unending passion (he was an extreme hypochondriac, among other things), and though part of his "eccentricity" as a musician was the way that he would take great liberties with musical scores, he was not a free jazz musician after all, he was mainly an interpreter of Bach, Beethoven, Mozart, and others in the European classical tradition. He had to come to terms with the musical scores of these composers—but what I would propose is that, in keeping with his views on live performance, he came to these conversations in a way that can be called anti-authoritarian and anti-logocentric. That is, Gould approached the interpretive process as someone who also had rights in the conversation, and who did not take the presence of the voice—whether it was the composer's or the audience member's—as authoritative, the last word.

As for the particulars, there are four main ways in which Gould's interpretations are "weird"—and I use that term because of its resonances with both the uncanny (or, better, *das Unheimlich* in German) and the "weirding ways" of those who practice witchcraft. These can be set out quite simply. First, Gould would almost always sing along with his piano playing, and his singing can be heard on most of his recordings. He refused to talk about why he sang, other than that it was part of how he played the piano—and, as such, he did not want the engineers to filter the singing out from the recording. (Once, in response to a question about why he sang, Gould mentioned the story of the centipede that was unable to walk when asked how she was able to coordinate her one hundred legs.)

Second, Gould would take liberties with musical scores, but not in the manner of past interpreters, who might play a baroque work in a somewhat Romantic style or something of that sort, but instead in a more systematic way. He would play passages upside-down, for instance. Or he would play passages marked "very soft" very loud, or vice-versa. Often there is an element of dialectical inversion, taking a passage in just the opposite way from what the composer instructs, to see if another and at least equal truth about the passage might be found.

The third and fourth weird things have to do with the recording situation more directly. As musicians who are reading this will know, with any instrument and even with the human voice there are pesky sounds that are supposedly incidental to the "true sound" of the instrument. For instance, if you play the guitar or bass guitar, you are well familiar with "string noise" that is caused by moving your hands up and down the neck. A piano, when you think about it, is a rather large, clumsy, and clunky instrument, and its hammer mechanisms are capable of making all kinds of little noises. As with his singing, Gould took these noises to be a part of the music—after all, the noises are part of the piano, and the piano is what is making the music, in collaboration with the pianist. Most classical recordings (or jazz and rock recordings, for that matter) have the "noises" filtered out. If anything, Gould went out of his way to have them present in the recording. There is a clear connection to John Cage's understanding of "noise" here, but, just as clearly, Gould is different on this point. For Cage, the "nonmusical" sounds of the piano apparatus are "incidental," but we cannot make a hard-and-fast distinction between what really belongs to music and what does not. For Gould, the sounds are not incidental, they are fully a part of playing the piano. Two different perspectives lead to a similar result.

Finally, and what was most controversial in the classical-music world, Gould never hesitated to employ tape splices to get the final sound that he wanted. A word of caution on this point: ever since such technology became available (now, of course, "splicing" is a whole other affair in the digital domain), classical musicians made use of it. What made Gould different was that he not only admitted to the use of splices, he championed the idea. As Payzant shows, Gould's philosophy of splicing was integral to his recording ethic generally—the irony being that, if anything, this ethic was set against any notion of the "integral" or integrity that depended on a nostalgic organicism. As Payzant puts it, a common objection to splicing is that it "breaks the integrity and sweep of a performance" (p. 123). This objection "presupposes the existence of, as one pianist put it, 'the sense of a long line stretching across the whole piece,' which 'can rarely be achieved unless the playing continues from beginning to end without stopping'" (p. 124). Gould's response to this line of reasoning would appear alarming to anyone for whom some notion of "authenticity" is important, whether that be in music, life, or social institutions. "[S]plicing doesn't damage lines; good splices build good lines, and it shouldn't much matter if one uses a splice every two seconds or none for an hour so long as the result appears to be a coherent whole" (quoted by Payzant, p. 124; italics in original). One is reminded of Kurt Vonnegut's famous statement that "we are what we pretend to be, so let us be careful what we pretend to be." But doesn't such an approach offend the idea of some core that individual human beings possess, a core that is then expressed by artists in their works? Here we again see Cage and Gould coming together from different directions. The position expressed by the pianist whom Payzant quotes is dependent on the idea that live performance is the ideal, and recording is parasitic upon this ideal, it is absolutely secondary. Gould flips this over even to the point of having little or no regard for live performance at all. I'm not sure we have to go to that extreme to see the deconstruction that takes place when the hierarchy is reversed—the situation here is completely reminiscent of Jacques Derrida's famous argument about speech and writing, where he also reversed the hierarchy and argued that the "mediated" form, writing, comes before that which presents itself as fully present, speech.

Payzant approaches the question by an analogy to filmmaking—which reinforces the "Bach in the age of McLuhan" idea.

> On the back lot of a motion picture studio we might find a street with, among other structures, a saloon, a bank, a saddlery and a funeral parlor, each with a hitching post in front. From certain vantage points we might not be able to see that these are façades, supported out of sight at the back by crude, sloping timbers. But we would not be tempted to hitch our horse and enter any of these buildings in the hope of doing our banking or buying refreshment, because we would know the rules and could not be deceived about actualities underlying "mere" appearances. The appearances are sustained not by actuality but by sloping timbers.
>
> A piece of music in performance is . . . like the movie set . . . . It exists as and for appearance; the music is its own appearance. There is no actuality underlying it. Its coherence comes from the ways in which musical appearances in general are related among themselves, each to every other, each to the whole of a piece, and the whole to each of its apparent parts. It is entirely phenomenal, entirely separate from any noumenal ground. (pp. 124–25)

Yet again there is a Cage connection, and it has to do with the relationship between performance and emotion. The "live performance ethic," as opposed to the recording ethic, is about emotion and expressivity. The artist, in this scenario, is expressing his or her inner core through music. The film analogy (which Gould was also fond of) is helpful here, because we do not really expect of the actor on the screen that she is really feeling, in the inner core of her "real" self, whatever emotional state is being portrayed on the screen. The performing musician is acting no less than the performing thespian. Of course, there is a big difference between Cage and Gould here. For the former, the aim is to create a music that is not expressive, and this means an active sense of letting the world speak through music, and getting out of the world's way. Gould, on the other hand, is not anti-expressivity per se, but instead argues that, as far as the performance goes, as embodied quintessentially in recorded form (whether that be film, long-playing vinyl record, or data stream), there is no difference between the "real" and the carefully constructed "façade." Indeed, the latter is often superior:

> Gould: . . . I love recording because if something lovely does happen, there is a sense of permanence, and if it doesn't happen, one has a second chance to achieve an ideal.
>
> Interviewer: Then you have no objection to splicing tapes from several performances into one?
>
> Gould: I can honestly say that I use splicing very little. I record many whole movements straight through. But I can also say that I have no scruples about splicing. I see nothing wrong in making a performance out of two hundred splices, as long as the desired result is there. I resent the feeling that it is fraudulent to put together an ideal performance mechanically. If the ideal performance can be achieved by the greatest amount of illusion and fakery, more power to those who do it. (Payzant, p. 125)

As always, Gould's words are sharp and provocative.

Gould even goes so far as to extrapolate from the recording ethic to a larger morality: "I believe in the intrusion of technology because, essentially, that intrusion imposes upon art a notion of morality which transcends the idea of art itself." The sensibility is not unlike that of Bach—the composer who could write the exquisite *Suites for Cello* as exercises for his students (Pablo Casals revived them, as "artworks," in the twentieth century), and for whom aesthetic value, no matter how great, is secondary to awe at the greatness of God. Gould was similarly motivated by the values of transcendence and ecstasy. If new means have appeared that would allow the "ideal performance" to come closer to these values, then we are in fact obligated to employ these means, even if we are engaged at the same time in "creative cheating" or "illusion and fakery."

What remains difficult is to square the critiques of subjectivity in Cage and Gould with the way that the commodity logic of postmodern capitalism whips people around into any old shape that suits its ends. Even without some overly Cartesian essentialism of the self, surely there is a difference between the person who has some sort of center and the one who has no backbone. Capitalism does a great job of taking what was radical at one moment and making the new things part of its own apparatus the next. One of the great examples is the way that educational reforms that were demanded by French radical students in the late 1960s later turned out to be useful, at least in part, to imperatives of industrialization and urbanization that the French economy needed anyway. This does not mean that the demands, when the students and workers made them, were not radical, but that the recuperative powers of capitalism, if it is not defeated, are immense and often overwhelming.

Finally, just a few stray thoughts about Glenn Gould.

Gould was blessed, but also cursed, with both a photographic memory and absolute pitch.

He was a high-school dropout.

His childhood was not happy; he felt that he had nothing in common with other children; he didn't "relate well." What happiness he did have as a child came from his pets, with whom he often had lengthy conversations.

Gould created three radio dramas, consisting primarily of overlapping conversations and soliloquies that he conducted with himself, through the device of multi-track recording. Among his writings are many self-interviews. Clearly this man contained multitudes, even as he isolated himself from most other people. There was something about the romance of radio that also linked Gould with Cage, and the *Solitude Trilogy* with works such as *Imaginary Landscape #4 for Twelve Transistor Radios.* Well, radio is not so magical these days, at least not in countries such as the United States, where all of the stations are owned by a handful of media conglomerates. It's hard to hear that intimate voice late at night, whispering in your ear, revealing secrets. Art Bell, perhaps.

Gould did not record too many "out of the way" composers, but he was a champion of Schoenberg, and he recorded music by composers not very much associated with the piano—Paul Hindemith (sometimes thought of as the very antithesis of Schoenberg, but whose music was also banned by the Nazis for being "degenerate"), Georges Bizet (composer of the opera, Carmen), Jean Sibelius.

In 1962, Gould published an article titled "Let's Ban Applause!"

On October 4, 1982, Glenn Gould died of a stroke. He was barely fifty years old, and was survived by both of his parents.

● John Coltrane

Giant Steps (Atlantic LP, 1959).
My Favorite Things (Atlantic LP, 1960).
John Coltrane and Don Cherry, *The Avant-Garde* (Atlantic LP, 1960).

Africa/Brass (MCA LP, 1961).
Impressions (MCA LP, 1961).
Duke Ellington and John Coltrane (Impulse LP, 1962).
Coltrane (Impulse LP, 1962).
Afro Blue Impressions (Pablo LP, 1977; live performances from 1962).
John Coltrane and Johnny Hartman (Impulse LP, 1963).
The Best of John Coltrane: his greatest years (Impulse LP, n.d.; live performances from 1961–1963).
A Love Supreme (Impulse LP, 1964).
Ascension (Impulse LP, 1965).
Kulu Se Mama (Impulse LP, 1966).
Interstellar Space (Impulse LP, 1974; recorded February 1967).

Cecil Taylor

In Transition (Blue Note LP, 1975; recordings from 1955, 1959).
Jazz Advance (Blue Note CD, orig. 1956).
Looking Ahead (Fantasy LP, 1959).
Nefertit, the Beautiful One has Come (Arista LP, 1975; live performances from 1962).
Silent Tongues: Live at Montreaux '74 (Arista LP, 1975).
Air Above Mountains (Buildings Within) (Inner City LP, 1978; live performance from 1976).
Cecil Taylor and Mary Lou Williams, *Embrace* (Pablo LP, 1978; live performance from 1977).
Cecil Taylor (New World LP, 1978).
One Too Many, Salty Swift, and Not Goodbye (Hat Hut LP, 1980; live performance from 1978).
Three Phasis (New World LP, 1979).
Max Roach and Cecil Taylor: Historic Concerts (Soul Note LP, 1984; live performances from 1979).
Calling it the 8th (Hat Hut LP, 1983; live performance from 1981).
Segments II (Orchestra of Two Continents)/Winged Serpent (Sliding Quadrants). (Soul Note LP, 1985).
For Olim (Soul Note LP, 1987; live performance from 1986).
Live in Bologna (Leo Records LP, 1988; live performance from 1987).
Tzotzil Mummers Tzotzil (Leo Records LP, 1988).
Cecil Taylor and Derek Bailey, *Pleistozaen mit Wasser* (FMP CD, 1989; live performance from 1988).
In Flourescence (A&M LP, 1990).
Cecil Taylor and Dewey Redman, Elvin Jones, *momentum space* (Verve CD, 1998).

Blues into fragments: John Coltrane and Cecil Taylor

The thought that forcefully asserts itself when I listen to an extended work by John Coltrane or Cecil Taylor is, What minds these are! Coltrane and Taylor ought to be especially appreciated by Marxists, for what they demonstrate is the materiality of mind, the co-implication of mind and matter in the material parameters of musical sound. Theirs is no reductive materialism, but instead a magical one, perhaps best represented by the recording of the children's song, "The Inchworm," from the 1962 album, *Coltrane*. Trane unfolds the simple melodic material of the song into near-infinite harmonic and rhythmic space, underscoring the profound message of this seemingly innocuous little tune:

> Inchworm, inchworm, measuring the marigolds,
> You and your arithmetic will surely go far.
> Inchworm, inchworm, measuring the marigolds,
> Seems to me you'd stop and see how beautiful they are.

Unfortunately, many Marxists are precluded from understanding this truth by their hang-ups with what they think of as a "scientific worldview." I think there is something better, and perhaps it is all encapsulated in something that Mao Tsetung said: "If you want to make revolution, it is good to know some poetry."

In the late 1950s and early 1960s, when Coltrane and Taylor were first being recognized for their innovations, their music was described with such terms as "sheets of sound" and "energy" and "fire music," more positively—and, negatively, as "anti-jazz," "noise," "ugly." Their music still has the power to shock and rattle (the nerves, the eardrum), perhaps in a way that Mozart's or Beethoven's does not anymore. It may even be that Cecil Taylor's music will never be "normalized," its harmonic and rhythmic complexities never assimilated to some more standard conception of "swing." When Beethoven's music becomes "easy" to listen to, we might say that in fact no one is hearing it anymore. Still, musical innovations tend to "trickle down" by and by, and we stretch our ears to accommodate and normalize what had earlier sounded strange to the point of being "unmusical." Even a few minutes of Cecil Taylor's music is difficult for many people to deal with, and the same could be said for Coltrane's epic improvisations, from the longer versions of "My Favorite Things" to the raucous duets recorded with drummer Rashied Ali not long before Trane's great soul passed into eternity.

Whereas Cage's music conjures "possible logics"—of the moon, the stars, and the sun, of branches and pinecones and sea creatures and tidal forces—what I hear in Coltrane and Taylor is an extraordinary line that leaves no doubt as to its logic. For sure, every possibility of the chord is pursued. Coltrane's sheets of sound, especially as he moved into improvisations that lasted ten to twenty minutes long and longer, really are a way of saying that there is an entire universe in a musical grain of sand. Coltrane's music is *science*, really, a material demonstration that what appears at first to be "chaos" is instead a complexity that defies comprehension. What are the "proper" notes that may be harmonically associated with the root notes of the chord? Can one get *there* from *here*? The longer improvisations seem to demonstrate that one can in fact get anywhere and everywhere from "here," if one builds the right kinds of roads and bridges.

The best demonstration of this aspect of Coltrane's playing—and I have mentioned the harmonic and rhythmic dimensions of his extrapolations (and not forgetting the contributions of the other musicians in his groups), but there is also his use of tone color (timbre), and even the almost "athletic" way that he could do seemingly *impossible* things with the tenor and soprano saxophones, not unlike Michael Jordan's unbelievable feats on the basketball court—is arguably to be found by following the trajectory of his recordings of "My Favorite Things." For those who are not familiar with Coltrane's music, this is indeed the song by Richard Rogers and Oscar Hammerstein, made famous by Julie Andrews's performance in *The Sound of Music* (1959). Coltrane's 1960 album, named for the song, began to show what he was capable of with the soprano. Before Coltrane, the soprano saxophone was most famously used by the great Sidney Bechet—a New Orleans musician of the generation before Louis Armstrong, and a friend and promoter of Josephine Baker—and Steve Lacy, Coltrane's contemporary and fellow avant-jazz artist. In fact, it was after hearing a performance by Lacy—whose vita also contains a stint with Cecil Taylor—that Coltrane was inspired to take up the soprano. Lacy is still with us, and long may he remain so, and he has made a goodly share of important recordings over the past forty and more years. On *My Favorite Things*, Coltrane's recording of the song is adventurous for its time, and yet it sounds tame against the background of the extrapolations and fragmentations that Trane would generate in the seven years that were left to him.

When a jazz musician or group states the main theme of a piece at the beginning of a performance, that is called playing the "head." In most jazz before 1960 or so, the general rule was that the musicians would come back around to the head on a regular basis, and most improvisations never get too far from the head. Put in a disarmingly simple way, the story of blues into fragments is one where this "rule" is progressively tampered with or broken. In the last recordings of Coltrane and his group, live performances in Japan and at the Village Vanguard in New York City, only a fragment of the head is stated in the versions of "My Favorite Things." Only fragments of the well-known melody appear thereafter. And yet, as with Glenn Gould's deconstructions of Bach, or Jacques Derrida's of Descartes for that matter, the weight of accumulated historical practice hovers over the performances. Gould, Coltrane, and

Derrida hear those voices and translate them into a different space—but what about other listeners and readers?

This last question is raised because, especially in the last three or four years of his life, Coltrane was increasingly charged with obscurantism. This went beyond what might be called Glenn Gould's eccentricity for the sake of eccentricity (not that I agree with this view, but some hold it). Coltrane, it was said, was intentionally making his music hard to follow, and taking obscurity as an end in itself. There is perhaps one kind of "avant-garde" sensibility that might respond to this by saying, "so what?" But there is more to the story than just the inability or unwillingness of some people to follow musical explorations wherever they may lead. And the "inability" does not necessarily have to do with some sort of mental incapacity, but also the question of having the time and energy to devote to the kind of music that makes extreme demands.

In his earlier recordings, Cecil Taylor was more "in" than he was later on, but he was basically "out" from the start. (In these scarequotes there is a certain irony that will be understood by readers who are familiar with Taylor.) In the early 1950s Taylor was still using chord changes and standard 12- or 32-bar structures, but by 1957 he was playing in the "experimental" session at the Newport Jazz Festival. As the subtitle to her pathbreaking book, *As serious as your life*, Valerie Wilmer gave "John Coltrane and beyond." It is easy to forget that Coltrane and Taylor were contemporaries—the former was born in 1926 and the latter in 1929. Taylor's recording career began with *Looking Ahead* in 1958, and that same year he recorded an album with Coltrane, *Hard Driving Jazz*. Unfortunately, Taylor was overshadowed in the early sixties by another great innovator who was born a year after him, Ornette Coleman. Perhaps the idea was that free jazz could have only one major voice at a time. Indeed, the 1960s, especially the first five years, were lean times for Taylor, and he spent much more time playing the piano at home than he did in concert venues. One might wonder if the elevation of Coleman (for instance, Leonard Bernstein took Coleman to a rehearsal of the New York Philharmonic and introduced him as "the future of jazz;" on the other hand, Coleman's brilliant symphonic composition, *Skies of America*, was only released in a much-abridged version by Columbia in 1972), and the relegation of Taylor to years of struggle and obscurity, might have had to do with the intensity, fire, harshness, and *anger* of the latter's music.

Incidentally, and perhaps surprisingly in light of what was just said, Taylor was influenced in his early years by Dave Brubeck. The latter was treated as some sort of "great white hope" for some years, especially thanks to a *Time* magazine cover story. The same issue had a little story in the back about a nutty pianist named Thelonius Monk. About Brubeck there was the whole air of "jazz goes to college," not unlike the way that Gershwin was said to have "made a lady out of jazz." That's a lot of racist crap, of course, and as a result the pendulum went the other way for some years. The *Rough*

Guide to Jazz, for instance, barely gives Brubeck the time of day. What was lost in this is that Brubeck never asked for the great white hope mantle (nor did Gershwin or, for that matter, Larry Bird in the NBA), and he is a fine musician. Besides the great music in odd time signatures (especially 5/4, 7/4, and 9/4), Brubeck stands out for his strong left hand, placing him in the company of other great "two-fisted" pianists such as Mary Lou Williams and McCoy Tyner—and Cecil Taylor, of course. Another major contemporary figure who admires Brubeck is Anthony Braxton, which does tend to reinforce the "college" bit. Other influences on Cecil Taylor were Duke Ellington, Bud Powell, Erroll Garner, Horace Silver, and Thelonius Monk.

Starting in the early 1970s there was a succession of books on free jazz—it took ten to fifteen years for writers (of book-length studies, at any rate) to catch up with what was also called the "New Thing." In 1971, A. B. Spellman published *Black Music: Four Lives in the Be-Bop Business*. One of the four musicians discussed was Cecil Taylor. *Free Jazz*, by Ekkehard Jost, first appeared in 1974, followed by Valerie Wilmer's *As serious as your life* in 1977, and John Litweiler's *The Freedom Principle: Jazz After 1958* in 1984. A crucial gap is bridged by David H. Rosenthal's *Hard Bop: Jazz and Black Music 1955-1965*. Taken together, these books articulate what is even today the most recent significant trajectory in jazz—against the background of which occurred other important developments, such as interaction with rock music (for example, Miles Davis) or a turn toward more "European" structures (for example, Anthony Braxton).

Perhaps another way of making the point about hard bop is that the crucial bridge is John Coltrane, who had his first "big-time" gigs with Dizzy Gillespie (first the big band, then the sextet, where Coltrane finally made the permanent switch from alto to tenor), then with Miles Davis. Coltrane's first recordings with his "classic quartet" (McCoy Tyner, Elvin Jones, Jimmy Garrison), as well as *Giant Steps* (1959, a year before the formation of the quartet) are still in the be-bop universe, though progressively harder and more intense. The increasing intensity certainly owes a great deal to drummer Elvin Jones—here's a great line from the *Rough Guide to Jazz*: "The driving, and psychologically driven, quality of his work was especially appropriate to the emotional climate of the new jazz in the 1960s, and it is difficult to imagine the eviscerating explorations of mature Coltrane without Elvin's percussive outpourings playing a simultaneous, indeed equal role" (Brian Priestley, p. 338). Indeed, in live performance, Coltrane would often have the bass and piano sit out for a spell, and duet with Jones—the point being freedom from chord structures and, ultimately, to make a statement about *freedom* itself.

This "psychologically driven" intensity, even when formally still within the structures of be-bop, broke through more and more toward the "new thing"—and the new things in jazz were motivated just as much politically as aesthetically. This is made clear in the title of another work that crosses over from bebop to new thing, Max Roach's *We*

Insist!: Freedom Now Suite. Consider the resonance of this title, from 1960, with Charlie Parker's "Now's the Time." First recorded in 1952 (with Max Roach on drums), the record company would not release it—the title by itself was too inflammatory. Then, however, there came a point when freedom could no longer be contained. Does this mean that the difficult changes of bebop gave way to pure wailing? It sounded that way to some; the rebuttal is that the changes in the music were both political and structural. While not focusing on the political questions, Ekkehard Jost's remark at the beginning of his chapter on Coltrane says something important about what it meant to come out of the background.

> At the end of the Fifties, Ornette Coleman made the programmatic statement, "Let's play the music and not the background." By "background" he meant the general framework of jazz improvisation which had established itself soon after the birth of jazz as a more or less incontestable norm. With an aura of inviolability , it had survived all the stylistic upheavals that followed—swing, bebop, cool jazz and the rest. This framework consisted of a code of agreements which made up . . . the "musically universal" in jazz, and remained constant throughout the years of jazz evolution, while the "musically particular" changed. Earlier stylistic upheavals in jazz were triggered primarily by the extension of technical resources, or else by increasing complexity in the structure of the background. Around 1960, however, the background itself started to disintegrate. The evolution of jazz, which until then had followed a straight line, took a sudden turn. (p. 17)

Now, I don't know if it is quite right to say that the development of jazz until that point "had followed a straight line." Certainly figures such as Louis Armstrong and Sidney Bechet, Duke Ellington, and the pioneers of bebop, had each represented qualitative changes in the music, and in each case the politics of race had played a significant role. Even so, as Jost argues, the idea of having musicians "comp" behind the soloist was done with when the new thing emerged. Indeed, we can take this "sudden turn" as also being emblematic of what occurs in a good deal of avant rock. The rock music in which a soloist or singer performs *on top of* a "rhythm section" (bass guitar, drums, perhaps "rhythm guitar," perhaps some keyboard instruments and/or a horn section) will tend to be both tied to blues form, and not liberated, not free. Perhaps this is why avant rock today finds its opposite in a pap culture that is completely oriented toward singers—singers who must be photogenic before all else.

As Jost explains, Coltrane played a dual role in this emergence of freedom. First, Coltrane encouraged the rising generation of formal innovators who, arguably, were starting at a place that he was still working toward. Not only did Coltrane make a record with Cecil Taylor in 1958, in 1960 he recorded a piano-less quartet album with the other members of Ornette Colman's group (*The Avant-Garde*). Then, after bringing along the "second generation" of free jazz, as Jost puts it, "from 1965 on—at the latest—he was regarded as 'head of the school' . . . 'the central figure of post-1965 free jazz'" (p. 11). These giant steps were not taken in isolation; in particular credit has to be given—and Coltrane gave it—to Miles Davis. The irony of this where free jazz is concerned will become apparent in the next section. When Coltrane rejoined Davis's group in 1958, the latter was in the midst of a shift from chord-based to modal improvisations. Except for the troublesome fact that these developments occurred at the same time, it would make sense to say that Davis played "Schoenberg" to the "John Cage" of Ornette Coleman, Cecil Taylor, Albert Ayler, and the later John Coltrane. (If you consider Coltrane's "world music" dimension, especially in albums such as *Africa Brass* and *Kulu Se Mama*, and in his admiration for Ravi Shankar—after whom Coltrane named one of his children— then perhaps Stravinsky is there as well.) John Litweiler writes of two "transitional generations" in jazz, the first being the bebop innovators of the early 1940s.

> The second transitional generation appeared twenty years later, when young musicians followed the lead of Miles Davis into modes. They subjected Free discoveries to the perceptions of hard bop and at times almost managed to bridge the two idioms. But modes were only a step toward something new and different, whereas the Free directions of Coleman, Dolphy, Cecil Taylor, and Coltrane were a leap into the unknown. So modal musicians and Free musicians did not, as a rule, perform each other's music.
>
> Instead, in the sixties modes became a parallel idiom. (p. 105)

Indeed, as Litweiler argues, the modal turn was "to some extent . . . a reaction against Freedom" (p. 105). For Davis, freedom from regular chord changes allowed the development of long, melodic lines:

> When you go that way, you can go on forever. You don't have to worry about changes and you can do more with the line. It becomes a challenge to see how melodically inventive you are. When you are based on chords, you know at the end of thirty-two bars that the chords have run out and there's but to repeat what you've just done—with variations. (Miles Davis quoted by Jost, p. 20)

It is not hard to see that, for Davis, modal playing represented the next step in form, while free jazz would seem to be the refusal of form. Certainly many post-Schoenberg musicians (Glenn Gould would seem to be among them) had a similar view of John Cage. To be sure, it could be argued that part of what Cage was saying is that it does not matter, at least as a question of musical intention, what note is played and what note is played after that, and so on.

Is this what "freedom" means to Cecil Taylor and the later Coltrane? Certainly freedom for either does not mean the refusal of form. Perhaps though, and this applies more, I think, to Taylor than Coltrane, there is an energetic interrogation of form and the meaning of form. (This goes for Cage as well.) Even in the final years, Coltrane was relating, even if in an extremely abstract and complex way, to chord changes. This does not mean that he was *following* the changes, necessarily! But they are there, at least in the distant background, and their faint echoes can be heard. Coltrane and Taylor can both be ferocious, but their music is not one unmitigated wail. And in fact a substantial part of Taylor's music is either notated or at least planned out in some fashion.

For something more like the "wail," there is Albert Ayler. Even here it would be wrong to say that the music is formless, whatever that means. It is common in the analysis of very abstract poetry or song lyrics to say that these words are simply taken from the "stream of consciousness." Similarly, it is sometimes said that words or sounds "well up" from the subconscious (or unconscious, but I don't want to get into a discussion of psychoanalytic ideas here). With Albert Ayler (1936–1970; he died under mysterious circumstances), certainly one feels that the connection between his inner being and what becomes manifest through the tenor saxophone is very direct, unmediated. But why are *these particular* sounds coming out, even if they are manifestations of something subconscious? Coltrane admired Ayler, and, after recording *Ascension*, he told Ayler "I found I was playing just like you" (*Rough Guide*, p. 23).

Ayler came from a church and gospel-music background, and indeed returned to this background in the last years of his life. This raises an interesting point, which also goes to the roots of rock music—given that figures such as Little Richard and Jerry Lee Lewis also came from charismatic and Pentecostal backgrounds. We might consider the relationship between free jazz, especially at the more "unmediated" end of the spectrum, and speaking in tongues. If free jazz (when it is working, let's say) seems to depart from structure, perhaps it is attempting to speak a language from beyond. I would argue that this form of the "break" with structure as was hitherto known is once again political as much as it is "spiritual" or "aesthetic." The politics of this break are somehow both sheer negativity and utopianism. Bebop also began as a desire to speak a language that had not yet been assimilated by the system, and especially the system of white jazz musicians who had recuperated swing as the feel-good music of World War Two and its aftermath. Charlie Parker and company wanted to leave the feel-good swingers in the dust with complicated chord changes. Part of the impulse behind free jazz was that the bebop revolution had run its course, and now it was time to inject yet more fire into the music. That's the negativity. But anyone who rejects this world—or perhaps anyone up until Johnny Rotten sang "I don't know what I want but I know how to get it"—also longs for another world, a world quite unlike this one. And the language for that world does not yet exist, and therefore one must reach beyond and listen at the limits and try to give some form to what comes through. To me that is the essence of free jazz, keeping in mind the particularities of the politics of race and the history of Black music, especially in the United States (but very quickly reaching out beyond American borders). Free jazz claims the right to attempt to say some things that perhaps cannot yet truly be said, and this attempt is what structures the music.

One of the things that Coltrane and Taylor have in common is epic scope. With the latter this comes through whether the format is solo piano, duet (for instance the extraordinary *Historic Concerts* that Taylor performed with Max Roach in 1979), trio, small group, or orchestra. The ten to twenty minute journey that Coltrane could take you on, with "My Favorite Things" or "Impressions" becomes an hour or more with Taylor; when you listen to a highly complex work such as *3 Phasis*, you will be taken to many places, and, for sure, you will be exhausted at the end of the trip. Though it is very hard to choose, among my favorite Taylor recordings are the afore-mentioned *3 Phasis* (sorry, I don't know the story behind the spelling) and *For Olim*. The former features a sextet, the standout members of which are, in my view, Ramsey Ameen on violin and Ronald Shannon Jackson on drums. Jackson had previously played with Ornette Coleman, and he would go on to play with James "Blood" Ulmer and in a quartet with Bill Laswell, Sonny Sharrock, and the frightening tenorist Peter Brötzmann. Though certainly capable of subtlety and a light touch, what is especially stunning is the way Jackson begins the second part of *3 Phasis* with a hard-rocking backbeat, really whomping along in a way that no Taylor group or record had before.

For Olim is a more mature solo piano recording, beyond even the great solo performances of 1975 and 1976, released as *Silent Tongues* and *Air Above Mountains*. *Olim* is a good example of where you might think, on first listening, that there is a good deal of "random" playing going on, but, on the tenth, or the fifteenth, or the twentieth listen, you realize that, instead, there is an immense order.

Musicians such as Ornette Coleman, and Gerry Mulligan before him, formed "piano-less" groups in part to avoid the strictures of Western tonality. ("Piano-less" came into common usage in the early 1960s, just as "acoustic piano" became a term in the later 60s when Bill Evans, Chick Corea, Herbie Hancock, and others began making much use of the Fender Rhodes electric piano. More recently, "guitar-less" came to be used to describe groups such as the Ben Folds Five.) With the piano, it seems that you can only play the notes that are right there in front of you. Cecil Taylor's mode of dealing with this is to understand the piano for what it is, namely a percussion instrument. "Eighty-eight tuned drums" is an expression often applied to Taylor's approach to the piano. This does not mean that Taylor is always banging away. Though no one can play harder, there are also delicate and airy ways of playing the drums, and Taylor's albums have many moments of lightness and space. But, to say the least, this is not the norm:

"In white music the most admired touch among pianists is light. The same is true among percussionists," says Taylor. "We in Black music think of the piano as a percussive instrument: we beat the keyboard, we get inside the instrument. Europeans admire Bill Evans for his touch. But the physical force going into the making of Black music—if that is misunderstood—it leads to screaming." (Wilmer, pp. 49–50)

It is telling that Taylor has often struggled to find drummers who could really play with him, perhaps because there is already a "drummer" in the band, and the great drummers who have managed to fill the bill, such as Dennis Charles, Andrew Cyrille, and Sunny Murray, have transformed their playing in the process of coming together with Taylor (on this point, see Wilmer, pp. 160–61). But it was also exhilarating to hear the recordings of Taylor's duets with the great Max Roach, because here Cecil also had to come to terms with another major voice and to make a few adjustments of his own— and what he showed was that these adaptations could be made without compromise of any sort.

Unfortunately, another pairing did not go as well, the performance with Mary Lou Williams. She was a great pianist with a great spirit, someone who lived through many eras in jazz and made herself at home in almost all of them. (If you have the good fortune to be able to listen to the often-excellent radio program, *Piano Jazz*, with Marian McPartland, the program with Williams is one of the best, as is the program with Alice Coltrane.) Of her later recordings, 1975's *Free Spirits* is wonderful, with a fine rendering of Miles Davis's "All Blues," and the very subtle and sweetly-titled "Baby Man." The duet (with double-bass and drums accompaniment) with Cecil Taylor, however, despite the best of intentions, does not really come off, except perhaps as a study in extreme contrasts—not even ships passing in the night, more like a submarine and a flying saucer. But they tried; they tried.

The "eighty-eight drums" idea conjures the image of a percussion orchestra, and the technique that Taylor brings to this symphony is scary and comprehension-defying. For this reason, as much as I like many of Taylor's group projects—the more recent (1988) duet with someone who might even be called his British counterpart, Derek Bailey, is fascinating, as is a trio recording from 1998 with Dewey Redman and Elvin Jones—on the whole I prefer the solo piano albums. If there are others who agree with me on this point, we will have to think further on how this would make Cecil Taylor different from other major jazz musicians. Taylor can do great things with a group, but there is a sense in which he does not need anyone else, because he *is* a group all by himself—to paraphrase Walt Whitman, he contains multitudes.

Of the five musicians discussed in these sections devoted to European and African-American classical musics, only Cecil Taylor remains among the living. As far as I know, he is still going strong. Let us treasure him.

Miles Davis, electric period (and a few from before)

The Complete Birth of the Cool (Capitol LP, 1950).

Kind of Blue (Columbia LP, 1959).

Miles Smiles (Columbia LP, 1966).

In a Silent Way (Columbia LP, 1969).

Bitches Brew (Columbia LP, 1969).

Jack Johnson (Columbia LP, 1970).

Live-Evil (Columbia LP, n.d.—early 1970s).

On the Corner (Columbia LP, n.d.—early 1970s).

At Fillmore (Columbia LP, n.d.—early 1970s).

Big Fun (Columbia LP, 1974).

Get Up With It (Columbia LP, 1974).

Water Babies (Columbia LP, 1976).

Agharta (Columbia LP, 1976).

Tutu (Columbia LP, 1986).

Electric Miles

Some critics and other listeners thought that Coltrane and Taylor had gone into outer space, as far as jazz practice is concerned. Jazz, in their view, has to riff off of certain structures, and those structures ultimately have to find their grounding in the blues. After Cage, we might question what a "structure" is, exactly, and argue that, in fact, the music of Coltrane and Taylor is indeed grounded in the blues, at least somewhere down the line, just as Cage's and Gould's music is "grounded" in the Western classical tradition. One can just as well argue for this proposition negatively: to think otherwise is to reject the "next step," which in turn is to claim either that the jazz and classical traditions are exhausted or that, in any case, it would be better for these traditions to become museum cultures than to develop in the directions set out by the aforementioned. In terms of these mentalities, the music of Cage, Gould, Coltrane, and Taylor is in fact anti-music, a traitorous assault on music—and certainly there have been those among critics and other listeners who have claimed this. Now we will turn to a fifth "traitor," Miles Davis in his period of using electric instruments, from the late 1960s until his passing in September 1991. What Mr. Davis did with jazz bears some relation to Coltrane, of course—the latter was part of the group for the great *Kind of Blue* (1959), where Miles introduced modal structures. Davis did not have much good to say about Cecil Taylor. (It is easy to forget that all three men were contemporaries: Davis and Coltrane were born in 1926, and Taylor in 1929.) *Downbeat* magazine created a famous institution known as the "blindfold test," where musicians are challenged to guess who made a certain recording and to comment on it. (*The Wire* has a similar institution called "Invisible Jukebox.") In his biography, *Miles Davis*, Ian Carr reports on the blindfold test of June 1964, administered by jazz critic Leonard Feather.

> And finally, when Feather plays him a Cecil Taylor piece, Davis says: "Is that what the crit- ics are digging? Them critics better stop having coffee. If there ain't nothing to listen to, they might as well admit it." (p. 141)

Noting that, of all of the offerings in the test, the only one that appealed to Davis was "Desafinado" by Stan Getz and Joao Gilberto (from the same session that produced the hit record, "The Girl from Ipanema"), Carr continues,

> Miles is generally disgusted with his contemporaries, and also totally disaffected by the avant-garde. At the same time, there is no doubt that during this period, he was equally dissatisfied with himself. The reexamination of his own immediate past . . . had not yet resulted in any new vision. Meanwhile, retrospective views of him were starting to classify him as a man of the 1950s. (p. 141)

The period of flux lasted for several years, and its resolution took place in two stages.

The first of these has to be associated with Herbie Hancock. The groups that Miles put together in the mid-1960s contained some of the great young musicians of that period, including drummer Tony Williams (who would later form the fusion group Lifetime with John McLaughlin and Larry Young, and who would do some of his final work with Bill Laswell), bassist Ron Carter, and tenor saxophonist Wayne Shorter. Pianist (and later, "keyboardist") Hancock was tremendously broad in his musical interests. As Carr puts it, Hancock "was, for a jazz musician, remarkably unprejudiced and never made a generic condemnation of music of any kind, preferring to listen to and judge any piece on its own merits." Thus, while the Miles Davis group that made the mid-1960s albums *ESP*, *Miles Smiles*, and others was still somewhat more in the vein of "straightahead" jazz—with, however, the startling rhythmic complexity that came from Williams' inno- vative "free drumming" and with basic departure from chord structures—Hancock introduced Davis to musicians ranging from James Brown, the Beatles, the Byrds, and the Fifth Dimension.

The second stage occurred when Miles Davis, having had his head turned by the psychedelia and funk of the Beatles, Jimi Hendrix, and Sly and the Family Stone, jumped ship, so to speak, and became a traitor to "jazz"—at least to the jazz of a certain critical establishment. Perhaps the final lines in the entry for Miles Davis in the *Illustrated Encyclopedia of Jazz* (1978) tell this story well enough:

> Miles' new conception was derived from West Coast acid rock, riff dominated with the trumpeter more economic than ever over a brocade of electric ripples. Using an enlarged personnel, Hancock, Chick Corea, and Joe Zawinul on electric pianos, Dave Holland on bass, John McLaughlin on guitar, Shorter on soprano saxophone and Tony Williams on drums (all of whom went on to lead their own units), Miles cut what, from the jazz fan's viewpoint, was to be his last album (*In a Silent Way*). Although labels are arbitrary, Miles Davis' subsequent output is of little interest to the jazz record collector. (p. 59)

One cannot help but get an image here, of the purely "archival" personality, some sort of jazz librarian who is almost certainly white and who has formed an academic, museum-culture notion of what jazz is and should be. Miles Davis's sensibility, in his new direction, was formed by something else.

By the middle sixties, jazz seemed to be faced with two possibilities. One possibility went in the direction toward which avant-gardes typically go. The parameters of the existing music are pressed to the breaking point. This sounds rather formulaic, and so one might ask what is "avant-garde" about this—but the "parameters" of any reasonably sophisticated music leave lots of room for expansion, and avant-garde gestures bring about transformations of quality to quantity. This reworking of the received material of a tradition describes, in oversimplified terms to be sure, the music of Cage, Gould, Coltrane, and Taylor. Another possibility is to open the music to "outside" influences. (Certainly there is some element of this in the other four as well; the conceptual connection is that musical traditions pressed to their limits generally encounter ideas that have been developed in other traditions.) Miles Davis took this path, at a time when labels were being made arbitrary not first of all by innovative artists, but rather by history and society. Social upheaval led to category flux, and Davis rode that wave.

One thing that is funny, I suppose, though perhaps only in twenty-twenty hindsight, is that it is not as though Miles Davis moved over from jazz encyclopedias to similar compendia of rock music in the late 1960s. Nor does the term "fusion" entirely describe what Miles was up to, though a good deal of jazz-rock fusion was to come from the musicians involved in the seminal *Bitches Brew* (1969)—the Mahavishnu Orchestra, Weather Report, Return to Forever, Lifetime, and Herbie Hancock's "Mwandishi" sextet and, later, the Headhunters. Miles gravitated toward rock music, to be sure—it has long been rumored that Davis's hope was to record with Jimi Hendrix and Sly Stone; when the former died suddenly, his replacement was John McLaughlin—but in the process of linking up with rock, Miles created his own milieu. The best music from the aforementioned groups was generally closer to rock than what can be heard on the Miles Davis albums of the *Bitches Brew* era, with perhaps one exception, the very groovy and rocking *Jack Johnson*. This album was named for the first Black heavy-weight boxing champion—in fact it was the soundtrack for a film, *Tribute to Jack Johnson*. Significantly, it was Johnson's ascendancy to the heavyweight title that gave rise to the racist term, the "great white hope." Paradoxically, just as Miles was bridging jazz and rock in the late sixties, and playing with various non-Black musicians, he was also creating a current that linked up culturally with Black nationalist aspirations in the United States.

Although there are brooding moments in the electric period, most especially the haunting "He Loved Him Madly" from *Get Up With It* (the "him" is Duke Ellington, who passed away earlier that year, in May 1974), there is also a brightness that stands in con-trast to Davis's trumpet on the phenomenal *Kind of Blue*. There Davis used the Harmon mute to create a lonely, existential vibe; heard late at night, it brings tears to your eyes. If there was any other color than black in this music, it was blue; the later, electric music is every color, and especially bright, splashy, funky colors—red, green, yellow. Some, such as John Litweiler, argue that this expansion of instrumental colors has the contrary effect of actually narrowing the emotional range of the music.

> Thus the content of his music declined to a search for the new idea or effect, and innova-tion became valueless. It is ironic that having chosen to play trumpet through a guitar amplifier, with a consequent narrowing of sound, in pieces such as "Ife" [from *Big Fun*] he further alters his sound with a wah-wah pedal—this device had been invented to enable guitars to imitate plunger-muted trumpets! In 1975, after the vamping back-grounds of percussion and electric instruments were dominating his music completely, he retired from performing. (p. 224)

This is an assessment from the perspective of the early 1980s; I wonder what Litweiler would say now. The reason I raise it this way is that it took a good twenty years for some people to get in the groove with what Miles was doing in the period from 1969 to 1975, and now there are many listeners who tell me that they like this stuff more and more. *Bitches Brew* was the turning point. Until then, Davis might have made an elec-tric record or two, but still gone back to playing in acoustic, modal bop groups. It's interesting that Litweiler focuses on the "Fender bass" as the dominating feature of the electric groups—sure, blame the bass player! (I think the two main bass players in Davis's groups in that period, David Holland and Michael Henderson, did actually play Fenders—sometimes that term is used generically.) Litweiler's charge is that the bass guitar, as Davis employs it, provides a thumping, thudding continuo that is mindlessly repetitive. Again, I wonder what he would say now, because it seems to me there is a bit of it-all-sounds-the-same syndrome here, which is sometimes overcome with hindsight. And, using a wah-wah pedal and amplifier to imitate the sound of an electric guitar imi-tating a trumpet, well, that seems kind of ingenious to me.

If I may interject a little personal history: although *Bitches Brew* was the turning point, the electric Miles album that first pulled me in was *At Fillmore*. To be honest, something about the album cover pulled me in. This was one of the gigs where Davis and group opened for rock groups, in front of large audiences. Reportedly, when it was first suggested to Davis that he could enlarge his following by supporting rock groups, he was outraged. He accused the people at Columbia Records (in particular, vice-president Clive Davis) of racial bias, and threatened to break off relations with the company. In the end, however, Davis got hooked up with concert promoter Bill Graham, and played at both the Fillmore East and Fillmore West, supporting such artists as the Steve Miller Blues Band, Neil Young and Crazy Horse, and Laura Nyro. (Later he also opened for The Band and Santana—those were the days, incidentally, when concert bills were put together with little attention to musical coherence. For example, in 1974, I saw Poco—the country-rock group—open for King Crimson. But then, coherence isn't all it's cracked up to be, either.) *At Fillmore* was based on four nights at the venue, with each side of the double album representing a slice of each night. As a result, there is a beginning-and-ending-in-the-middle feel to each side, which works with that music. The album was one of perhaps ten in that personally-formative period (the early 1970s) that changed not only the way that I heard music, but also the way I understood life and tried to live it. (A very detailed account, which I draw upon here, of how Davis moved toward not only rock music but also rock audiences, can be found in *Miles Beyond: The Electric Explorations of Miles Davis, 1967–1991*, by Paul Tingen.)

Not all of the albums from Miles Davis's electric period are uniformly good, and some of them are not good at all. Three that simply continue to gain in reputation are *Big Fun* and *Get Up With It*, both released in 1974, and the live album, *Agharta*, from 1976. There is a good deal of excitement to this music, largely because of its brassy, big sound, but there is also harshness and a sort of burbling swampiness to a good deal of it. It isn't quite the case that this swampy background is just there for Miles and some other horn player (such as Steve Grossman, Wayne Shorter, Dave Liebman, and Bennie Maupin) to solo over. Often the horns (I mean trumpet and sax, or, in the case of Maupin, bass clarinet) are down in the swamp also. Sometimes there is no guitar, and sometimes there are three guitarists—which must have been the inspiration for Lynyrd Skynyrd. Kidding aside, I could see the three-guitar set-up in "He Loved Him Madly" as inspiring some of Sonic Youth's more meditative work, such as the haunting title track from the recent *nyc ghosts & flowers*. There is always a lot of percussion, and, yes, there is that bass, and sometimes more than one bass (sometimes both bass guitar and double bass). The structures remain modal, and the lines tend to be very long.

After *Agharta* and the similar *Pangaea*, and after period of retirement lasting about five years, Davis released a number of real duds, what seem to be blatant attempts at commercialism. Among these are *The Man with the Horn*, *Star People*, *Decoy*, and *You're Under Arrest*. The period was the early to middle 1980s. I remember something funny that a critic said at the time (what I cannot remember is which critic). This critic pointed out that Davis had said that one of his hobbies at home was to listen to white people on the radio and make fun of them. With these new records, the critic said, it seemed that Davis had now moved on to listening to Black people on the radio and making fun of *them*. I suppose there were two good sides to this period. First, even if it was not a good comeback, at least Miles was on the scene again; many did not expect to hear any more from him. Second, the live album from that period, *We Want Miles* (1982), is actually pretty good, especially the twenty-minute long version of Gershwin's "My Man's Gone Now." Part of what made the album worthwhile was the bass playing (yes, Fender) of Marcus Miller, and it was Miller who helped, perhaps led, Miles Davis into a final fruitful period, beginning with the 1986 album, *Tutu*. Miller played many of the instruments on the album, which basically consists in electronics plus trumpet. The structures are very "blocky," and the trumpet parts are often simple, but the album anticipates some of the experiments with techno and electronica that would heat up a few years later. But it is the period from *Bitches Brew* to *Agharta* and *Pangaea* that is animating many musicians now, from the remix projects of Bill Laswell, to the recent offering from Tortoise (*Standards*, discussed in the final chapter), to young people just coming to experimental rock. That six-year period, very fruitful for Miles Davis, may very well continue to be fruitful for experimental musicians well into the twenty-first century.

A stray comment: it is interesting to contemplate Cecil Taylor's response when told of John Cage's view of jazz and improvisation: "What does John Cage know about Harlem?" (Also recall Taylor's comment about "white music.") Apart from the derision evident in Taylor's comment, we might also take it as a warning that music does not come from abstract principles alone, but instead from localities, traditions and counter-traditions, and real people who live their real lives under definite social conditions. Music theory will only take you so far; you have to live, and live with music, and *live musically*, too. Theory in general will only get you so far; on the other hand, it would be a big mistake to try to do without it.

What kind of narrative about rock music goes from Yoko Ono to John Cage to Cecil Taylor? The answer has to do with both earth and sky. If we are going to be able to understand the experiments that have taken place in rock music, if we are going to be good listeners, and if some of us are going to contribute experiments of our own, we need a good grounding, and a good grounding for an experimental rock musician means one that is not only in rock music itself. We can also think of Yoko Ono, John Cage, Glenn Gould, John Coltrane, Cecil Taylor, and Miles Davis as a six-stage booster rocket that will take us toward the stratosphere of experimentation.

So, let's turn to some grounding in rock music.

PART 2

....

Forests and trees

Noisy New York: The Velvet Underground

Although he described himself as someone who preferred breathing to working, Marcel Duchamp did a lot for chess. He did not only play, but also took responsibilities as an organizer. He was a member of the board of the French Chess Federation and a delegate to the meetings of the International Chess Federation (FIDE). He designed beautiful chess sets and in New York he organized exhibitions such as The Imagery of Chess (1944/45) and Hommage a Caissa (1966).

This last exhibition in particular was quite impressive. At the vernissage on the roof of the building on 978 Madison Avenue, Duchamp played a game of chess against Salvador Dali, and Andy Warhol had the band Velvet Underground sent to provide background music. After the game, chess pieces were sent into the air by balloons.

—Hans Ree, *The Human Comedy of Chess*, p. 321

As with the Beatles, we tend to forget that the Velvet Underground was a band—they seem more like a scene or a happening, in that argot of the late 1960s. Certainly a good deal of their fame or artistic cache came from certain associations, with Andy Warhol, John Cage, LaMonte Young, Nico, Delmore Schwartz, and others of the New York avant-garde cultural milieu.

Like Yoko Ono, for the most part the members of the Velvet Underground were ambivalent about being involved in rock music. They only made three albums, each with somewhat different personnel, and the music tends to be as imagistic as the lyrical content. The group only achieved recognition within a narrow circle during its existence; then, starting especially with the punk revolution, their influence has grown every year, and shows no sign of abating. And, if any group was to be the model for the second wave of the New York art-underground rock scene, for example, Lydia Lunch, Tom Verlaine and Television, and especially Sonic Youth, it is the Velvets.

At the same time that the working-class lads from Liverpool were making their music more sophisticated, and, with the exception of a few songs from the *White Album*, creating a very clean, often crystalline sound, some of the Velvets were graduating from college with degrees in literature and mathematics, and heading in just the opposite sonic direction. Sometimes the Velvet Underground's music was severe, especially on their first album, with Nico on board, but it was never "cleaned up." Musically, the Velvets pursued primitivism, though with sophisticated lyrics.

It is commonly said that the Velvet Underground were ahead of their time in terms of attitude, and this was reflected in their orientation toward drugs. They were not a band for the Summer of Love, that's for sure. In the blissed-out, psychedelic era, they were already strung out. Personally, I have a hard time valorizing this, but certainly it could be said that the Velvet Underground were the first "alternative rock" group.

Unlike much of what was to later come under this heading, however, what made the Velvets "alternative" was their connection to the larger arts scene—and to the seedier side of life, not only in the form of drugs, but also prostitution, transsexuality (before this became just one of the subjects for campus lesbian and gay groups), sado-masochism, and longing taken to bizarre and deadly lengths, as in John Cale's song, "The Gift." In respect of this last, if there was a philosopher who would go nicely with the Velvets, it is probably Georges Bataille.

Musically, one of the most interesting "primitivist" elements came from Maureen ("Mo") Tucker's drumming. She plays standing up, with the bass drum set on its side. Her sound is a wonderful combination of the orchestral tympani player and chunky jungle drums. It is an approach with certain in-built limitations (though Eddie Prevost with AMM, the experimental improvisation ensemble that at one time included the late Cornelius Cardew, also sets his drums out this way), but working with limitations, sometimes by violently assaulting them, was what the Velvets were all about.

The heart of the band, however, was the interaction between Lou Reed and John Cale. The latter came over from Wales in 1963, having had a classical-music education on viola and cello in London, and eventually studying with John Cage, Aaron Copland, and LaMonte Young. He performed with Young in the legendary Dream Syndicate (which also included violinist and minimalist composer Tony Conrad), the legal status of whose recordings remains under dispute more than thirty years later. With this pedigree in European classical and experimental musics, and having attached an electric pick-up to his viola, Cale encountered Lou Reed at Syracuse University, where they were both majoring in literature. Reed's rock aesthetic beats even Pete Townshend's for economy of chord use (Reed once said that one chord is best, and, if you're going to play three chords you've moved over into jazz territory). The resulting synthesis—What if John Cage started a garage band with surrealist and beat lyrics?—was often strikingly original, at least for the first two albums. After that, thanks to tensions between Reed and Cale, the latter left the group. The two subsequent albums had some good moments—for example "Sweet Ray" and "Rock and Roll," two of Lou Reed's best songs—but the music suffered from the loss of creative tension. Better to burn out than fade away? In any case, it remained for other groups to extend the potential first demonstrated by the "classic" Velvets, though in a world quite different from New York at the end of the 1960s. Indeed, sometimes it is hard to imagine that the world of Andy Warhol and "Popism" ever existed at all.

The Velvet Underground and Nico (Polygram LP, 1967).
White Light/White Heat (Polygram LP, 1967).
The Velvet Underground (Polygram LP, 1969).
Loaded (Cotillion LP, 1970).

Iannis Xenakis, *Electro-Acoustic Music* (Nonesuch LP, n.d.; pieces from 1957–1962).
James Brown, *Live at the Apollo, Volume One* (Polydor LP, 1963).
Pauline Oliveros, *Outline for Flute, Percussion, and String Bass*; Nancy Turetzky, flutes, Ronald George, percussion, Bertram Turetzky, contrabass; from *The Contemporary Contrabass* (Nonesuch LP, n.d.; composed 1963).
Elliot Carter, *Orchestral Music*; SWF Symphony Orchestra, Michael Gielen, conductor; Ursula Oppens, piano (Arte Nova CD, 1995; works composed 1964 –1989).
Terry Riley, *In C* (Columbia LP, n.d.; composed 1964).

Beach Boys, *Pet Sounds* (Capitol LP, 1966).

Glenn Gould's famous and caustic remark on Terry Riley's *In C* was, "And you thought Carl Orff had found an easy way to make a living?" Part of the Xenakis album is an amplified recording of the crackles and pops made by a burning piece of coal. By comparison, even the spare instrumentation of Oliveros's *Outline* is fairly cluttered—but not really. Bertram Turetzky is the champion of experimental music for the double bass. James Brown, on the other hand, is the champion of other bass grooves. As heavy as the Godfather of Soul can be, however, there is often a simultaneous lightness to his music, something that keeps rocking in your skull long after the record is over. "Papa's Got a Brand New Bag" is the epitome of this, the initial two-note bass figure dropping a fifth from B to E, and then the horns sailing ever so lightly on top. You could be at sea forever on just a few notes, and if that is an easy way to make a living, so be it. Then the Beach Boys came along to make it all complicated again, opening the path in rock music that went from *Sgt. Pepper's* to *Close to the Edge* and beyond. The ethic in rock is to make it simple when you can. Sometimes you can, but you don't, and that violates the ethic. Sometimes you make it simple, "primitive" even, and that turns out to be complicated after all and against your will. Perhaps that is the situation the Velvet Underground found themselves in.

Psychedelic blues: Jimi Hendrix

Most likely you just had to be there. By "there" I do not necessarily mean one of Jimi Hendrix's actual performances, but I am probably saying that because I did not have the privilege of attending one. No, by "there" I mean 1969. Anyone who was there—or *then*—will at least know what I mean by the idea of being in awe of Hendrix, sometimes even *frightened* by the things he could do with the electric guitar. Rock form was extended in the late sixties by two main methods, one more calculative and "intellectual," the other taking blues form to its limits and beyond. Hendrix, like John Coltrane and Cecil Taylor in jazz, mainly followed the second route—which is not to say that these musicians were unschooled or unaware. Even while it is the Paganini of the

Stratocaster who will be most remembered and celebrated, Hendrix was also a very good songwriter, singer, and arranger. Indeed, many of his songs are underrated as such. This is one of the things that separates him from the more recent slew of masturbatory electric-guitarism. The other thing was his commitment, the way that he gave himself over to being an opening and a transit point through which *something other* cried and howled.

Hendrix's songs were not, for the most part, just vehicles for guitar solos. This can be seen in his appreciation for Bob Dylan. In his singing, Hendrix aimed for the quality of "breathfulness" that Dylan exemplified at his best—possibly nowhere better than in "Like a Rolling Stone." (Allen Ginsberg, no stranger to artful breathing in the long line, often spoke to this quality of Dylan's music.) But this combined art and science of breathing can be heard in Hendrix's guitar solos as well. Sometimes this striving for the long breath, at least in live performance, led to tiresome wanking—as much as I am awed by Hendrix, I am not of the orthodox church that takes his every note and screech for revelation. The element of risk, however, of letting the guitar get "out of hand"— and we are talking about some of the great hands and fingers of history here—was, of course, a major part of allowing music to speak for itself, in a way both transcendent and as concrete as crosstown traffic or the cry of love. As with John Coltrane, two things were necessary for Jimi Hendrix to make music the way he did: tremendous ability with his instrument, and vision, the drive to transcend. What the first, *virtuoso*, element brings to vision is the ability to develop a complex musical logic. Not all such logic is that of the long line; within the latter, however, Hendrix is part of an elite group that includes Coltrane, Ravi Shankar, and Carlos Santana (anyone who is skeptical about the last of these is urged to listen to—and study—the Santana *Lotus* album). Inverting the biblical formula, we might say that Hendrix's long lines were often *of* blues form, but not always *in* it.

Hendrix's earlier background was not only in blues, but more specifically in rhythm and blues. His first bit of professional fame was as the guitarist for the Isley Brothers, and he also toured with Little Richard. But it was his move to London, at the behest of Animals bassist Chas Chandler, that opened him up to the larger possibilities of the electric guitar: hard blues met psychedelia. Hendrix was a master of the electric guitar, it goes without saying—but he also allowed the guitar to speak its own mind, in ways that are perhaps not possible without high-voltage amplification. The Velvet Underground also allowed the guitar to do its own thing, and Sonic Youth would take up their approach on the other side of the 1970s, but here is where vocabulary and musicianship come into play, because Hendrix was able to engage in a more active sense of "letting" the guitar speak, and the words that came out had not been heard before. There was also an epic quality to Hendrix's explorations, and even though the Velvets could let the noise unfold for long periods (for example, *White Light/White*

Heat's "Sister Ray," at almost eighteen minutes), the feeling is more that of being strung out than of a psychedelic vision. Hendrix was obviously no stranger to being strung out, but his sixties ran the spectrum from the Summer of Love to the Black Panther Party, a very different world from the Andy Warhol scene. The science fiction influence was important, too—Hendrix was an avid reader of the genre.

As manipulated and controlled as Hendrix was by various overseers—management and record company people, he at least was able to do much of his music the way that he wanted to do it. While some of the live performances that have been released are spotty, to say the least, one sees a growing maturity in each of Hendrix's solo albums, right up to *Cry of Love*. In many ways, while folks of a certain generation can undoubtedly still catch a buzz by going back to the first album, *Are You Experienced?*, Hendrix went on to even greater things with *Axis* and *Ladyland*. Give the rest of the band some, too. Mitch Mitchell was phenomenal, a real powerhouse—those opening drum breaks in "Fire" can still inspire, and they probably always will. Noel Redding, while not originally a bass player (of course, that can be said of about eighty percent of bass players, at least), gave the group the grounding without which it would have flung itself into another galaxy. When Hendrix left us for worlds beyond he was only 27. What he or John Coltrane might have been like in the time of cyberpunk is anyone's guess—unfortunately, in our postmodern period, we have to worry about what the commodification of everything would have done to them. Even in his own time, commodification and heaven knows what else went into overdrive trying to contain and control Hendrix. The doors he opened remain open, but it might be argued that the legacy of Hendrix has not been fully taken up or fulfilled. The electric guitar virtuoso has to be very careful about what muses he or she listens to these days. Some of the more thoughtful ones, such as Buddy Guy or Stevie Ray Vaughn, went deeper into the blues, but with a full awareness of what Hendrix contributed. Other virtuosos who came out of progressive rock, such as Steve Howe or Robert Fripp, have little or no connection to the blues. Perhaps it is the case, in the Cecil Taylor-ish sense of "blues into fragments," that the true inheritor of Hendrix is Derek Bailey.

▲ Jimi Hendrix

Are You Experienced? (Polydor LP, 1967).
Axis—Bold as Love (Reprise LP, 1967).
Electric Ladyland (Polydor LP, 1968).
Band of Gypsies (Capitol LP, 1970).
Cry of Love (Reprise LP, 1971).

● 1967

Pink Floyd, *The Piper at the Gates of Dawn* (Capitol LP).

Red Crayola, *The Parable of Arable Land/God Bless the Red Krayola and All Who Sail With It* (Decal CD, 1990; orig.1967/1968).

Rolling Stones, *Their Satanic Majesties Request* (London LP).

Ravi Shankar, *Live at the Monterey International Pop Festival* (One Way CD, 1993; performance from 1967).

1968

Grateful Dead, *Anthem of the Sun* (Warner Bros. LP).

Pink Floyd, *Saucerful of Secrets* (Capitol LP).

The United States of America, *The United States of America* (Edsel CD, 1997; orig. 1968).

Just as many classical composers tried to write their own *Rite of Spring*, so many rock musicians wanted to make a *Sgt. Pepper's*. Two such attempts are represented here by the Rolling Stones and the Grateful Dead. *Satanic Majesties* is the dark side of *Sgt. Pepper's*, with its fuzzier guitars, stray percussive sounds, primitive synthesizers, harmonies that are slightly off and strained in ways that make them highly effective. Loads of people reportedly stopped by to help with the album, including the Beatles (who are pictured on the cover; the *Sgt. Pepper's* cover, you will recall, had the words "Rolling Stones-Nice Guys" on it) and Keith Moon. It's a very eerie album—not just "2000 Light Years from Home," but also songs such as "Citadel," which conjure the grotesque notion of a prison planet—and I love it; I would probably be more likely to listen to it now than to the album that inspired it. *Anthem of the Sun* transposes this vibe to the San Francisco Bay scene, with a key role played by Tom Constanten. Like John Cale, Constanten had studied with experimental composers—in his case, Luciano Berio, Pierre Boulez, and Karlheinz Stockhausen. Subsequent Dead albums have not featured the prepared piano. Joseph Byrd likewise brought hippie music together with experimentation, in a group that featured not only fretless bass guitar, electric violin, and harpsichord, but also ring modulator and electric percussion. *The United States of America* is completely loopy, and it may not hold up all that well, but as a document of an attempted meeting between rock music and the New York classical avant-garde, a meeting that actually took place in Los Angeles, the album is an interesting artifact of its time. As bookends we have space-rock and the transition from Syd Barrett to Dave Gilmour—it's so very lonely, when you're 2000 light years from home. "Ethereal" is the word for it, this combination of outer space and inner madness. The Red Crayola were even more obscure than the Velvet Underground, but they also did their part for the garage band meets all manner of experimentation idea. And in the middle, Ravi Shankar, whose influence by this time was everywhere, from the Beatles to John Coltrane.

The passage through progressive

. . . an installation in [Yoko Ono's] New York apartment in which she had posted statements on furniture, ceiling, and windows that encouraged viewers to effect an imaginary transformation of the space . . . . One of the texts was the single word YES installed on the ceiling. *Ceiling Painting* is a work in Ono's series of Position Paintings, which seek to alter the viewing experience by requiring an unorthodox relationship between the body and the work of art.

When Ono prepared for her exhibition at Indica [in London] in late 1966, she made a framed version of this text, rendered in tiny letters on a large sheet of paper. The text was nearly impossible to read from the floor; the addition of the ladder was an invitation for viewers to ascend and complete the piece by reading it with the magnifying glass hanging from the frame. When this was done, the open-ended affirmation of the word YES became the viewer's reward for making the climb. At least one viewer—John Lennon—remembered feeling relieved to find that the text was not an example of the "negative . . . smash-the-piano-with-a-hammer, break-the-sculpture boring, negative crap" that he associated with avant-garde art of the period. "That 'YES' made me stay . . .."

—from *YES Yoko Ono*, p. 100

Now for the music that, seemingly, everyone in the rock critical establishment loves to hate. Despite this, I would make some rather large claims for progressive rock, by which, of course, I mean the best of it. First among these would be the claim that almost everything that is interesting and creative in rock music that comes after about 1970 is influenced in one way or another by progressive rock. Among the ways that musicians were influenced affirmatively are: improvement in musicianship, broad eclecticism, utopianism, romanticism, a commitment to experimentation. On the flip side, as a reaction to progressive rock, some rock musicians went back to basics and to a reassertion of blues form. All of this, however, was already the dynamic by the time of the later Beatles. The difference with progressive rock was perhaps that what had appeared as novelty in the Beatles had become something of a "language" or a norm with groups such as Yes and King Crimson. When we heard sitars and harpsichords alongside one another on *Sgt. Pepper's*, we were stunned by the novelty of the combination; by the time of Yes's *Close to the Edge*, only about five years later, we had the sense that *of course* rock music should draw from every point on the globe. In this, progressive rock anticipated what we more recently call "world music." However, my larger point is that, if you don't like progressive rock, blame it on the Beatles.

The Beatles were the ones who put rock music decisively on the path of experimentation. The latter can take many forms, and there were certainly others who were experimenting with the larger possibilities of rock music somewhat apart from what the Beatles were doing. Certainly the scene around the Velvets represents a somewhat different line of inquiry. The Englishness of the Beatles resonated with some California groups, especially in the San Francisco Bay area, more than it did with the New York scene. In part this has to do with the way that California must have seemed like a utopia to four working-class lads in gloomy Liverpool. More directly, there was a kind of friendly competition between the Beatles and Brian Wilson of the Beach Boys, with attempts at going one better with each album, from *Pet Sounds* to *Revolver* and beyond. Albums by the Byrds, The Band, Bob Dylan, and others also played a crucial role in this energetic and creative time, and these efforts were channeled in a certain direction by progressive rock.

The later Beatles established the *album* as the unit of artistic production. The usual provisos apply—such as, there were others doing similar things—but the point is that, after albums such as *Revolver* and *Rubber Soul* and especially *Sergeant Pepper's Lonely Hearts' Club Band*, there were basically two kinds of rock groups: those that were making integrated, sustained statements, and those who were still concentrating on individual songs. The latter divides into two as well. Certainly there were plenty of good songs produced by artists and groups who did not gravitate toward the album sensibility. But in that period, of the late 1960s and early to middle 1970s, it also seemed that the "song" artists were the ones most often providing pop drivel and product in the midst of the attempt, on the part of others, to conceive of musical projects of epic scope. The Velvet Underground remains the strange exception to this bifurcation. Not only progressive rock groups from Great Britain and elsewhere, but also groups such as the Doors, Jefferson Airplane, the Grateful Dead, Santana, and even the Allman Brothers Band were creating albums that attempted to sustain a larger vision. Like some of the aforementioned, Led Zeppelin and The Who also worked with expansive forms, even while staying closer to the blues roots of rock. All of this activity, from the extraordinary "Good Vibrations" to Dylan's *Blonde on Blonde* to *Quadrophenia*, was "progressive," in the sense of trying to take rock music to new places, and to do experimental and creative things with it, and to create something that would "stand up" musically, that would endure as good and significant music. Even at the time there were critics who thought such efforts could not help but be "pretentious"—which has been *the* watchword of the anti-progressive rock critics from then until now. I discuss all of these issues at length in my two books on progressive rock, but it seems to me that two things are paramount as regards this last question.

First, we ought to ask where this "anti-pretentiousness" argument ultimately leads. I think it leads back to the idea that all rock music can really be is pop entertainment for adolescents and those who wish to remain adolescent in their sensibility—which is most rock critics. Then one has to analyze how this fits in with the culture industry and the niches that it has for various functions that need to be performed in the production and advertisement of its products. (Simply look to the film industry and the various "critics" who are always raving about some clearly inferior and stupid film—some film that is indeed meant to be stupid—for the paradigm of how such a system works.)

Second, most creative musicians have not been swayed by the critics; most creative rock musicians have respect for what the best of progressive rock achieved. Perhaps this is because musicians have more of a sense of what that achievement consisted in, at least in terms of its technical aspects.

Progressive rock, at its worst, got carried away with some of its "technical aspects." But why judge a genre by its worst? What characterizes progressive rock at its best? I just used the term "genre," and this is the term that I have come to think of as properly describing what progressive rock is—there were all sorts of things in rock music in the late 1960s that were "progressive," including Progressive Rock, but there are particularities of the latter that set it apart as a stream within rock music. Like most forms of creative rock music, progressive rock has one foot in rock music and one foot out. Progressive rock seems to break with blues roots more than most other forms of creative rock music either before or possibly even since the time of its greatest strength, roughly 1969 to about 1974 or 1975. Significantly, some of the recent music that is perhaps most like progressive rock in its eschewal of what I call "blues orthodoxy" is techno or what some call "electronica" (the jury is out on what exactly to call this genre, if indeed there is a larger unity to it). And, like progressive rock, some of the recent electronica involves large-scale conceptually-driven explorations—think of *Saturnz Return* by Goldie (and featuring the voice of Björk), as the techno equivalent of Yes's *Tales from Topographic Oceans*. Critics were hard on both albums, and for similar reasons.

Other particularities of progressive rock include the high level of instrumental skill that many of the players demonstrated and a generally visionary or romantic sensibility that could be seen to be rooted in what literary theorist Raymond Williams called "the green language." Alternatively some of the groups more often displayed the other side of this sensibility, a gothic dystopianism that was especially concerned with technology (and sometimes urbanism) run amok. One sees this in the founding statement of progressive rock, King Crimson's *In the Court of the Crimson King* (1969), but also in Emerson, Lake, and Palmer's *Tarkus* and *Brain Salad Surgery*, and in the early albums by Genesis. The latter, as well, presented some scathing send-ups of the British class system, especially with what I consider to be their best album, *Selling England by the Pound* (1973). (Another very good album in this genre that deals with class is *Three Friends*, by Gentle Giant. Jethro Tull's *Thick as a Brick* might also fit in this category.) Critics in recent years have harped on the idea that these preoccupations with technology and class (or, more abstractly, with utopian-hippie visions of an egalitarian and cool society) are hypocritical, coming as they did in some cases from musicians who depended on a good deal of advanced technology and who came from fairly well-off backgrounds (sometimes very well-off, as with, for example, Robert Wyatt). Taking the latter question first, two things ought to be said. There were in fact progressive rock musicians who did not come from the lap of luxury, among them members of what I consider to be the two most important groups of the genre in that period, King Crimson and Yes. (Obviously there were many other important groups, and I am happy that we have them all to listen to, but I see Yes and King Crimson as both pillars and bellwethers of the genre.) The other thing is that progressive rock emerged in the time of the 1960s counterculture, and was reflective of at least one wing of that counterculture, what again might be called the hippie-utopian wing, where boundaries of all kinds were being crossed—class, gender, the color line to some extent (in that genre, I mean), and musical boundaries especially. Philosopher Alasdair MacIntyre, in his critique of Herbert Marcuse's political solidarity with the young radicals, referred to "the parent-funded middle-class student movement." MacIntyre's point was that well-off students in the first world do not really know anything about the real lives of Third World peasants or possibly even first world working class people. The whole point of solidarity, however, is that people try to break through barriers and find common humanity. Certainly, to do this from a certain background might reveal some limitations, and critics of progressive rock, in a way that I would say parallels MacIntyre's critique of Marcuse, focus on these.

What interests me more, however, are the real strengths of this striving. In the video retrospective that was made around the twenty-fifth anniversary of Yes, there is a telling interview snippet with Jon Anderson, the singer and composer of many of Yes's pieces. Anderson, it should be mentioned, comes from a lower working-class background, and from the gritty industrial town of Accrington in the north of England. He has sometimes spoken of the way that this background has given him a bit of a chip on the shoulder, and how he has tried to use this in productive ways. In the interview, Anderson is addressing the fact that some reviewers were very hard on Yes's 1973 album, *Tales from Topographic Oceans*. *Tales* was a very ambitious album, an eighty-one-minute symphony in four parts. Overall, I would say the album is a flawed masterpiece (the fact that the band members themselves were somewhat divided over the music led to some of the flaws). But I don't think that the flaws have to do with the music having been "overambitious." Perhaps the conception was overambitious, but that part I have the greatest respect for. In any case, Anderson remarks in the interview that some critic had said, "What's Yes going to do next, set the Bible to music?" Anderson said that his response at the time was to think, "I'll show you suckers—it *can* be done." The result was a piece of music, "The Gates of Delirium" (on the 1974 album, *Relayer*), one of the group's strongest works. But my point has more to do with this quality of striving and stretching, and of confronting and surmounting boundaries, of opening rock music up to all of its possibilities.

That progressive rock did not always have something worthwhile to say with this expanded language should not blind us to the fact that the language did indeed expand. And even if the sources of this expansion or even what was made of these sources was not always exactly avant-garde, this passage through progressive made it much more possible for rock to open itself up to the entire world of music. Steve Howe of Yes, for example, draws heavily on the guitar stylings of Wes Montgomery and Chet Atkins. Anyone who knows anything about the guitar will certainly recognize these two as important stylists and, of course, great practitioners of the instrument. I doubt that anyone would say that Montgomery or Atkins are "avant-garde." Likewise, some of Yes's epic works, pieces such as "Close to the Edge" or "Awaken" or the more recent "That, that is" (*Keys to Ascension I*, 1996) or "Mind Drive" (*Keys to Ascension II*, 1997) might arguably contribute no more to the sonic world of harmony, rhythm, and timbre in a purely abstract and analytic sense than, say, the works of some minor but significant classical composers such as Sibelius or Dvorak or Villa-Lobos. But this line of reasoning (which ultimately leads to the old saw about progressive rock musicians wanting to be the new Beethovens, and everyone knows that is not possible) does not recognize the ways that progressive rock expanded the language of rock in general. This expansion can be seen in microcosm in the way that individual musicians, such as Steve Howe, Robert Fripp, Chris Squire, Bill Bruford, or Christian Vander (of the French group, Magma) expanded the possibilities of rock guitar, bass guitar, and percussion.

Take the bass guitar, for example. This is my own instrument, and I feel that I know something about it by now (having played the bass guitar for about thirty years as of this writing). It is also a somewhat marginal instrument in various ways—for example, it is something of a hybrid of two other instruments, the contrabass violin (double bass or "stand-up bass") and the guitar; in addition, the bass guitar does not rise to the level of consciousness in the way that many people think about music. Many people love the Beatles, of course, but could not tell you that Paul McCartney was the bass player of the group. Even many people who are aware of that do not see how the bass lines make crucial contributions to the music. (Likewise, consider the wonderful bass lines in "Good Vibrations," which were written by Brian Wilson and played by the superb Carol Kaye.) In rock music up through the early 1970s there were five or six waves of the expansion of the role of the bass guitar—roughly Motown (James Jamerson, Carol Kaye) and James Brown's bands (Bootsy Collins and others); the Beatles and Beach Boys; late '60s and early to middle '70s funk (Larry Graham, Anthony Jackson, Verdine White, Bootsy again, with Parliament/Funkadelic and Bootsy's Rubber Band); late sixties "hard rock" (Jack Bruce with Cream, John Entwistle with The Who, John Paul Jones with Led Zeppelin, Tim Bogert with Vanilla Fudge, Cactus, and Jeff Beck) and also Bay-area psychedelic rock (Phil Lesh with the Grateful Dead, Jack Casady with Jefferson Airplane); and finally late '60s to middle '70s progressive rock.

Chris Squire absorbed all of these previous waves and took them to another level, mixing in his background as a chorister in what was regarded as the best English church choir of his time. Squire's bass lines are very "Bach-like" to me, in their counterpoint and linearity, and he brought a new timbre to the way the instrument was used with his often extremely trebly and yet somehow quite meaty Rickenbacker 4001 sound. Consider especially Bach's six suites for cello. But, one might say, "well, what's avant-garde about Bach? What Squire was doing with the bass was creative and experimental because it opened rock to an extended linearity, a developmental logic to the music that broke with the way that most rock music cycles around and around on fairly simple chord progressions. In most rock music, the bass "holds down the bottom" and anchors some cyclical progression that is built on three or four verses and a chorus and perhaps some sort of instrumental break (often a guitar solo). In microcosm we can see here how progressive rock, in incorporating elements from the Western classical tradition, jazz, and other world traditions, forged a new language and in a sense forced certain issues for rock musicians. In my book, *Listening to the future*, I call this the "generous synthesis." By the first part of this term I mean not only an openness, but also a way of generating new rock music, of pushing it forward. And, again, to extend the microcosm argument, I would wager that there are very few bass guitarists (at least of a certain generation, before the idea that rock music should develop and progress came under attack from the culture industry) who do not know about the innovations of Chris Squire, and who do not take them into account in some fashion (even if perhaps by attempting to negate them). At the same time, it would not surprise me if many rock critics would not have a clue about this sort of thing.

Incidentally, sometimes the sort of thing that Squire does is called "lead bass," indicating that there is a departure from the usual thing, which is "rhythm bass"—just like "lead" and "rhythm" guitar. But part of what happens in progressive rock is that you get groups that are firing on all cylinders, so to speak. This is a departure not only from the bass guitar's usual role, but also from the whole idea of the "rhythm section," and therefore also with a certain aspect of blues orthodoxy. But in most blues of the classic sort, the drums and bass are relegated to a purely supportive role; they are not supposed to be independent voices in the music. (In classical music the comparison might be made to the harpsichord or viola da gamba *continuo* in baroque works.) The emergence of all instruments in the band as independent voices, or as voices that each contribute equally, changes the music and liberates it, opens it to other possibilities that cannot be realized under the regime of blues orthodoxy.

To have this sort of liberation also requires a certain level of musicianship. This was also a contribution of progressive rock, even if, admittedly, sometimes the musicians got a bit too wrapped up in their own technical abilities. In the best progressive rock these abilities served the music, however, not the other way around (as with, for example, the wave of wanking guitarists of the Yngwie Malmsteen/Edward van Halen notes-per-second school). To go back to the Lou Reed statement about a period when some musicians were trying to get a lot better on their instruments while others were trying to forget what little they already knew, both approaches can be valid on the face of it, *if* there is some interesting musical idea that is being served in the process. But, on the whole, if a musician wants to be able to experiment with form, then it helps to have the chops to be able to do that. If one wants to experiment with 11/8 time, or with chords beyond the straightforward majors and minors and sevenths, well then, it helps to be able to actually play those things. One of my frustrations with Sonic Youth, even as much as they are somewhat the "heroes" of this book, is that they sometimes do not have the musicianship to carry some of their ideas as far as they might go. As a result, they often fall into certain ruts that simply represent what they are able to do with their instruments—perhaps the most common example in the music is the steady eighth-note guitar figures that seem to emerge sooner or later in many of their pieces. (More on this in due course.) There was a generation or two of rock musicians who heard "Twenty-first Century Schizoid Man" and "Heart of the Sunrise" (Yes, *Fragile*) and other progressive rock works, as well as music by Frank Zappa and others, and who figured they'd better get down to work. Although punk can be seen as one kind of reaction to this orientation toward better musicianship, I see this orientation working itself out in some of the more recent avant-garde rock that is played by very good musicians, from Bill Laswell to Björk, Jim O'Rourke, and Ikue Mori. These are people who have both ideas and chops—their conceptions are not limited to what they can do with their instruments.

Already one saw this opening up of the rhythm section with the Beatles and Beach Boys, and then with Mitch Mitchell's superb drumming with Jimi Hendrix and the brilliant bass guitar work of John Entwistle and the quantum drumming of Keith Moon of The Who, not to forget Jack Bruce and Ginger Baker of Cream—all of these being groups that remained closer to blues roots.

To return to the technology question, I think the way this played its biggest role in progressive rock—and in a way that has continued to have a great deal of influence on the way that experimental rock music is made—has less to do with the development of electronic instruments (especially the synthesizer) and more to do with multitrack recording and relatively sophisticated mixing boards. Starting with the Beach Boys and Beatles, these developments allowed musicians who were not "schooled" in the classical sense to create extended and complex compositions. Indeed, recording was and is "composition" for many rock musicians. (Theodore Gracyk explores this issue thoroughly in his valuable book, *Rhythm and Noise*.) Though some progressive rock groups did contain the occasional "ringer"—a conservatory-trained musician such as Rick Wakeman—this was actually rare. Most of the really good progressive rock musicians were basically self-taught, as were most rock musicians in general. But they were teaching themselves in a time when it was the cool and hip thing to do to treat the whole world and society as a school, and to draw from every corner. The utopian sensibility was also reflected in the group composition process that bands would then carry out in the studio, each member bringing ideas and working on the ideas of their mates. Yes carried this procedure to an extreme with *Close to the Edge*, where apparently there would be endless discussion over whether the next bass note should be F or F# (according to various interviews with Bill Bruford)—something like an SDS meeting. Brilliant producers and recording engineers, such as Eddie Offord, following in the footsteps of George Martin's work with the Beatles, played a large role as well, preparing the way for figures such as Brian Eno, Bill Laswell, and recent electronica artists for whom the studio is their instrument. "Tape" artists and earlier electronic composers such as John Cage, Pauline Oliveros, and Morton Subotnik also opened this path, but the point is that rock was developing its own possibilities, out of its own eclectic language.

Progressive rock was, in its time, a very diverse phenomenon—so diverse that various wings of it are attempting to rewrite the history of the early seventies and to say that they were not really a part of the trend. What unifies a genre that has a group of very harsh Brechtians such as Henry Cow at one end, and sometimes syrupy-sweet plagiarists of late Romantic (especially Russian) classical music such as Renaissance, at the other? Although I find the idea that a clear distinction can be made on the basis that one was listening to Stockhausen and Orff while the other was listening to Tchaikovsky and Rachmaninov a bit ludicrous, there is something, I think, to Brian Eno's argument that progressive rock was not the start of something new but instead the completion of something old, the nineteenth century project of epic Romantic music. I do not think this is the whole picture, but there is something to this. The shortcoming of the claim is that the expansion of rock music's material resources had to come from somewhere and would undoubtedly have affinities with other traditions. Part of what characterized progressive rock was the idea that the affinities might as well be self-conscious—but many critics do not like that sort of thing, because it supposedly undermines the "authenticity" of a rock musician's expressiveness. I would say instead that such critics have a Cartesian, phonocentric notion of authenticity at work, one that only recognizes the supposedly self-constituted subject. It seems to me that, on the contrary, all good rock musicians know that their materials come from somewhere else. In any case, though I find Henry Cow's music more interesting and challenging and enduring than, say, Renaissance's (which to me is more just a guilty pleasure, though I have found myself especially appreciative of Jon Camp's bass lines in recent years—but there I go again on the bass), I still think there was a core phenomenon that included, from about 1969 to about 1975 or so, a diverse range of groups from King Crimson to Soft Machine to Henry Cow to Yes to Jethro Tull to Emerson, Lake, and Palmer, to Magma, to Genesis, Gentle Giant, and Gong, to even the Mahavishnu Orchestra with John McLaughlin, and to a whole series of very good Italian groups such as PFM, Banco, Le Orme, and Area. They were groups playing complex, extended compositions (and sometimes extended improvisations that went beyond mere rock jamming), expanding the possibilities of rock, and basically letting certain cats out of the bag that, thankfully, have not been reined in to this day.

There are many works of progressive rock that I am quite fond of for themselves (a short list of which appears in the discography; a much longer account appears in *Listening to the future*—see pp. 245–46 especially), but my larger point here is that such works (meaning albums, basically) constituted a passage through which rock came, and that avant-garde rock music of more recent years is very much on the other side of that passage. Progressive rock rethematized the whole question of playing rock music as "music." I do not mean to go into the whole "is rock music *real* music?" non-question. All music is a kind of social negotiation, or "social text" (as John Shepherd argues in his insightful book, *Music as Social Text*), and perhaps the "popular" forms of music that are also developmental (where there is a tradition that attempts to progress) are simply those that are more aware of this social/musical intertextuality. (I'm thinking of rock and jazz, predominantly.) But there are trends in these genres and traditions where the musicians do seem to ask what can be done that develops musical form in a more concentrated and aware way. That is what I think progressive rock, following in the footsteps of the later Beatles, did for rock music.

That was the first half of the 1970s, and, arguably, the second half represented the other pole of a dialectic—a progressive/punk dynamic that I have also characterized as the "YesPistols" dialectic (see *Music of Yes*, pp. 186–89). Indeed, in some sense the most important claim of the present text is that *almost everything in experimental rock music since the late 1970s comes out of this dialectic.*

In some sense it is the dialectic of the time when rock music became "mature," but when it also asked whether becoming mature was really a good or appropriate thing for rock music. And, of course, this corresponds to a generational shift where rock musicians had to confront the fact of adulthood and no longer being able to fake it as a teenager. Perhaps this internal struggle is best played out in the passage of The Who from *Tommy* (1969) to *Quadrophenia* (1973), with *Who's Next* (1971) coming in-between.

What of progressive rock after its time? If you look at the albums of some of the core groups in the interval from about 1975 to 1978, it is clear that a period of indirection set in. King Crimson took a sabbatical in 1974, reincarnating in a very different form seven years later. Yes made a couple of very good albums, *Relayer* and *Going for the One* (1977), and then entered a period of transition that was resolved with the emergence of a band that was sort of an amalgam of new wave, progressive, and mainstream rock, best known for the hit single, "Owner of a Lonely Heart" (from *90125*, 1983). A very good song, in my opinion—I think Rick Wakeman was right to call "Owner" a "Roundabout for the eighties." I and others have had a running argument with Robert Fripp over the question of whether King Crimson is a "group" in the same sense that a band such as Yes is a group, or if instead Crimson is something more like a "project" that has maestro Fripp as its director. I will return to this question, but one distinction that might be made is that Yes works out of something like a "language," and the question is whether they find more or less new and creative things to say in that language, while King Crimson is perhaps more motivated by an ur-concept of creativity, one that expresses itself in numerous languages. In the case of Yes, I would say that it has been a real struggle, since their period of immense creativity from *The Yes Album* to *Going for the One*, for the group to go forward with its utopian-romantic-green language in far less utopian times, when the radical spirit of the sixties (taken as a political unit of time from the mid-sixties to the mid-seventies) has receded and has been bashed with wave after wave of cynicism. Their recent efforts, since reforming with Steve Howe in the mid-1990s, have been a bit spotty, though there are some very good examples of the Yes language—the aforementioned epics from the *Keys to Ascension* albums, as well as the other three longer, new songs from the second *Keys*, and a few of the songs from the 1997 album, *Open Your Eyes*. However, the band's most recent outing, *The Ladder* (1999), exudes too much of Jon Anderson's sugary new-ageism, which can be tolerable if it is leavened with some sort of edge supplied by the other band members—but that has not happened here. There is *some* good music on *The Ladder*, and I was opened further to this by watching a recent concert video by the group, *House of Yes*. There I got a better sense of what the group is up to with pieces such as "Homeworld" and "The Messenger." But there is too much white-note prettiness and stylizing of elements that at one time had the ability to jar sensibilities.

Yes's status as a "supergroup," where the members live all over the place, also does not help to get the sort of communal dynamic going that led to their most creative music. The question might be raised as to whether the "Yes language," as I am calling it, still has something to say in these postmodern times—or was it the exhaustion of that language that opened the way to punk in the first place? Yes represented, even in their very name, a radically utopian spirit that comes out of the sixties counterculture. Certainly it can be argued that a moment was reached in the late seventies, especially with the ascendancy of Margaret Thatcher and then Ronald Reagan (who embodied the anti-sixties), when it was time for radical negativity instead. What bothers me quite a lot in this "post-punk" world is the idea that radical affirmation was somehow always simply naïve and certainly has no place in our supposedly much more sophisticated world now. That strikes me as mere cynicism, especially when the language of the Pistols is also not something that can be straightforwardly taken up in the present situation.

Before leaving Yes, let us note that their 1971 effort, *The Yes Album*, where they made the transition to playing progressive rock, features "Your Move," a song based on chess imagery. Underneath the final chords of the song, deep in the mix, the group can be heard singing the chorus to "Give Peace a Chance." Alan White, member of the Plastic Ono Band for the *Live Peace in Toronto 1969* concert, joined Yes in 1973. And, referring again to the progressive/punk dialectic, please note the following.

> The Flaming Lips have always found freedom in failure. The beauty of the accidental career is that when nobody knows who you are again, you can be anyone you want to be—even yourself. If they were a fluke at bubblegum radio pop, why couldn't they be a hit as a high-concept art-rock band? "We had all been secretly listening to Yes in private," says [Michael] Ivins. "But it was only a couple years ago that we could finally look each other in the face and say, 'I like Yes—there, I said it'." (Jonathan Valania in *Magnet*, June/July 2000, p. 60)

The musicians know, even if the critics often do not, that there is a power in that language that will keep speaking to us.

As for other torchbearers of progressive rock, there are perhaps three or four trends. A band such as Rush, which falls somewhere between progressive rock and heavy metal (it has become a cliché, but not necessarily false, that up to a point Rush was a cross between Led Zeppelin and Yes—which is also interesting because at one point there was an attempt by Chris Squire and Alan White of Yes to form a band with Jimmy Page and Robert Plant of Led Zeppelin), carried forward the genre up to a point, especially from *2112* (1976) to *Grace Under Pressure* (1984). To the extent that Rush can be associated with progressive rock, *Grace* is their best album. It is uncool to like Rush, critically speaking, but it is interesting how many techno and turntable artists sample riffs from the band. I would not make any claims for Rush being "avant-garde," but I do think they have often done a good job of speaking a certain "prog" language, and, like the classic progressive bands, they have pretty much done the music that they want to do, and commercial pressures be damned. (And, any bass player is going to be impressed with Geddy Lee.)

Another way that progressive rock has manifested itself more recently is through the so-called "neo-progressive" or neo-prog trend. There are an amazing number of groups to choose from, and a kind of DIY underground, on the punk model, has emerged around this trend. Neo-prog is covered extensively in well-produced but marginal and sometimes hard to find magazines such as *Progression* (United States), *Big*

Bang (France), and *Lunar Waves* (Spain). Some of the new bands are made up of younger people who found Yes and King Crimson albums in their parents' record collections. An archetypal neo-prog band might be Spock's Beard—perhaps first of all because their name comes from an episode of *Star Trek*, and the neo-prog scene somewhat resembles (and in some cases actually overlaps) that of the Trekkies. Their 1997 album, *The Kindness of Strangers*, is a good example of the transmutation of material from the 1969 to 1975 period, not only from Yes, Gentle Giant, and Genesis, but also from the Beatles, Pink Floyd, and Crosby, Stills, Nash, and Young. Like much neo-prog, there is much in Spock's Beard that simply takes one to another time, on a pleasant journey down memory lane, without doing anything that is especially new. They are very good at speaking a certain language, much as Lenny Kravitz is sometimes good at speaking the languages of Curtis Mayfield or Jimi Hendrix, or perhaps as Leonard Bernstein, in his three symphonies, recapitulated the classical discourse from Mozart to Stravinsky. Apart from considerations of the "avant" status of such gestures, we might also consider the idea that such music has a certain validity inasmuch as there are still things to be said in these languages. Indeed, we might also hold this consideration up as a standard for more intentionally avant-garde efforts, and wonder if the latter are sometimes even more naively reinventing the wheel.

What remains as a project is to do something of a "Glenn Gould" on progressive rock—to do what Gould did with the languages of Bach, Beethoven, and more recent classical composers (Sibelius, Schoenberg, Hindemith). I am not sure that that this project has fully manifested itself yet, but I see something of it in the work of groups such as the 5uu's, from Los Angeles, Ghost, from Tokyo, and TriPod, from New York City. The 5uu's must be especially annoying to writers who would prefer to have nothing good to say about progressive rock, since they quite clearly draw from a whole range of progressive groups (that themselves would prefer to be mutually exclusive), from Yes to King Crimson to Henry Cow. Bass guitarist and singer Bob Drake (who has a number of solo albums as well) plays in a style clearly influenced by Chris Squire, and his voice is not unlike Jon Anderson's (as is often remarked in reviews of 5uu's albums). And yet the 5uu's are also very much in the Henry Cow school of whimsy and fragmentation, sometimes also with the biting quality that characterized the Cow's Brechtianism. This side of the 5uu's music opens them to other marginal, experimental trends in rock music since the progressive era. (By contrast, the question is raised as to whether a language such as Yes's does not reach the point where it is sealed up, and all of the edges come off—as in their recent music, as much as they have also tried to incorporate bits of reggae, world music, and New Age material.) Ghost is interesting for their medieval influences, both Western and Asian. In some respects Ghost go back behind progressive rock, to the latter's psychedelic roots, and they also partake of the more recent rock avant-garde. Significantly, their albums are available from Drag City, the Chicago avant-rock label that is associated with Jim O'Rourke and others. Finally, TriPod finds itself between King Crimson and Painkiller (the reeds, bass guitar, and drums trio featuring John Zorn and Bill Laswell), not only because of their instrumentation, but at least partly for that. Updating the progressive rock "power trio" idea, á la Emerson, Lake, and Palmer—or, better yet, Back Door, the little-known sax-bass-drums group that was briefly called "the new Cream" in the U.K., TriPod employ tremendous musical skills rather than overdubs to achieve a large sound. Clint Bahr's main axe is the 8-string bass, which he uses to amazing effect. Along with alto and tenor saxophones, Reed player Keith Gurland adds not only flute but also the rarely-heard (in rock, that is) clarinet to his arsenal. And percussionist Steve Tobin seems to combine the syncopation of Bill Bruford with the drum-set-as-orchestra approach of Keith Moon. Part of the excitement of their self-titled album is that it was produced by the great Genya Ravan (who also sings on one song); she was the singer for one of the best "horn" bands of the 1970s, Ten Wheel Drive. Some of TriPod's lyrics are wonderfully whimsical, and there has been a debate in this household over whether the line (which you have to hear in context, really, to appreciate) "danger is danger—it is not safe!" is brilliant, moronic, or somehow both.

(In the final stages of writing this book I was informed that TriPod will now have for its percussionist the great Pierre Moerlin, formerly of Gong.)

None of these last three groups constitutes the progressive rock trend of today; instead, these are examples of groups that come out of progressive rock and still feature aspects of that music. But they are also just as contemporary as anything else out there, and in that sense they are carrying forward a truer sense of "progressive" rock than what is found in most of the neo-prog groups.

What remains is to discuss King Crimson. It is perhaps not sufficient to speak of the intermittent existence of this group. Instead, the correct term might be "incarnation" or perhaps "manifestation." King Crimson, as Robert Fripp has said, reappears when there is King Crimson music to be played. At every stage, at least in my opinion, this has been music that expands the frontiers of rock and that is very much of the present—whenever that happens to be. Thus a section is reserved for the Crimson King later in this narrative.

King Crimson, *In the Court of the Crimson King* (Atlantic LP, 1969).
Soft Machine, *Volume Two* (MCA LP, 1969).
Caravan, *In the Land of Grey and Pink* (London LP, 1970).
Gentle Giant, *Acquiring the Taste* (Vertigo LP, 1971).
Yes, *Fragile* (Atlantic LP, 1971).
Jethro Tull, *Thick as a Brick* (Warner Bros. LP, 1972).
Mahavishnu Orchestra, *Inner Mounting Flame* (Columbia LP, 1972).
Yes, *Close to the Edge* (Atlantic LP, 1972).

Emerson, Lake, and Palmer, *Brain Salad Surgery* (Manticore LP, 1973).
Genesis, *Selling England by the Pound* (Charisma LP, 1973).
Jethro Tull, *Passion Play* (Chrysalis LP, 1973).
Magma, *Mekanik Destruktiw Kommandoh* (A&M LP, 1973).
Premiata Forneria Marconi (PFM), *Photos of Ghosts* (Manticore LP, 1973).
Yes, *Tales from Topographic Oceans* (Atlantic LP, 1973).
David Bedford, *Star's End* (Virgin LP, 1974).
Henry Cow, *In Praise of Learning* (Virgin LP, 1975).

Rush, *2112* (Mercury LP, 1976).
————, *Grace Under Pressure* (Mercury LP, 1984).

5uu's, *Hunger's Teeth* (Recommended Records CD, 1993).
Ghost, *Ghost* (Drag City CD, n.d.—mid-1990s).
————, *Second Time Around* (Drag City CD, n.d.—mid.-1990s).
Spock's Beard, *The Kindness of Strangers* (Radiant CD, 1997).
Yes, *The Ladder* (Beyond CD, 1999).

Can, *Tago Mago* (Spoon LP, 1971).
————, *Ege Bamyasi* (Spoon LP, 1972).
————, *Future Days* (Spoon LP, 1973).
————, *Soon Over Babaluma* (Spoon LP, 1974).
————, *Landed* (Spoon LP, 1975).
————, *Peel Sessions* (Strange Fruit CD, 1995; live performances from 1973–1975).
————, *The Can Box* (Mute CD/Video/Book, 1999).
Holger Czukay, with Jah Wobble and Jaki Liebezeit, *Full Circle* (Spoon Records LP, 1981).

There has been a debate in recent years concerning the relationship between progressive rock and so-called "Krautrock." Some who are interested in the former want
to include the latter within progressive rock; while most who are mainly interested in
the latter do not. Certainly both genres come from a time of general experimentation in
rock. With Can, as with Henry Cow and Magma, we see groups that were listening to
more recent trends in classical music and jazz than were many of the progressive rock
groups. As has been remarked here and there, musicians and others who wouldn't be
caught dead listening to a Yes or Jethro Tull album practically worship at the feet of Can.
Their influence in the current avant-rock scene is undeniable. What makes their music
interesting is the combination of extremes: composed sections, played with great skill,
alongside spontaneous, "freak-out" jams; space rock alongside raw passages not unlike
the Velvets; very strong musicianship in the standard sense (especially in the case of
percussionist Jaki Liebezeit) alongside indifference to musicianship and the use of ran-

domizing elements, radios, and tapes á la John Cage. I cannot do justice to Can here; there are three or four books that deal with the group at some depth, but a full-scale analysis is still needed.

1969
Captain Beefheart, *Trout Mask Replica* (Straight Records LP).
Alexander "Skip" Spence, *Oar* (Columbia LP).
The Tony Williams Lifetime, *Emergency!* (Polydor LP).
Larry Young, *Mother Ship* (Blue Note LP, recorded 1969, released 1980).

1970
Musica Elettronica Viva, *Leave the City* (Spalax CD, 1997; orig. 1970).
Steve Reich, *Four Organs* (Angel LP, 1973; composed 1970).
Santana, *Abraxas* (Columbia LP).
Frank Zappa and the Mothers of Invention, *Weasels Ripped my Flesh* (Rykodisc CD, 1990; orig.1970).

Trout Mask Replica was both one of the most influential albums of its time, and yet then and still now an underground classic. Skip Spence was originally the drummer for the Jefferson Airplane, and he recorded his one and only solo album in three track—how or why, I don't know. Spence had originally switched from guitar to drums for the Airplane, then he switched back and joined Moby Grape. Both *Trout Mask* and *Oar* explore insanity, or perhaps it is more correct to say that they represent madness, but the latter for real, more in the manner of Syd Barrett. The Tony Williams Lifetime, which featured John McLaughlin on guitar and Larry Young on organ, might be called the first true "fusion" band. Larry Young was the person who would have carried the jazz organ to the next phase beyond the great Jimmy Smith, if he had not been the victim of racist medical negligence. Of his several albums, *Mother Ship* is the best, in part because of its instrumentation: organ, drums, trumpet, and tenor saxophone. The compositions are spare, sometimes stark.

As progressive rock was heading into a period of maximalism, Steve Reich was composing one of the key works of minimalism, *Four Organs*. Played on four electric ("combo") organs, plus maracas, the piece builds very gradually from intermittent, single notes to a full, sustained chord, about twenty-four minutes later. Like progressive rock, this is primarily music for patient listening—though criticism from the "you can't dance to it"-quarter is often motivated, I think, by a rather narrow conception of dancing. Reich's major in college was philosophy, incidentally. Musica Elettronica Viva, or "MEV" as they were usually called back in the day, were a woollier Tangerine Dream, with more improvisation—hippies playing synthesizers, inspired as much by rock and free jazz as by their roots in the classical avant-garde.

Abraxas was as much an album of progressive rock as anything else in 1970, at least in terms of extended pieces that featured exemplary musicianship and an other-worldly feel. There is no greater rock guitarist than Carlos Santana. His sense of the long line even rivals, at least at times, that of John Coltrane. Frank Zappa combined serious knowledge, if not seriousness itself, of contemporary classical and jazz trends, with an irreverence of and toward rock.

Intimations of postmodern rock: Steely Dan

Even Cathy Berberian knows there's one roulade she can't sing.

—"Your Gold Teeth"

Angular banjo sounds good to me.

—"Aja"

After about nineteen years of no studio albums and no new music, Steely Dan released *Two Against Nature* in early 2000. There is the usual cleverness, lines such as "How about a kiss for your cousin Dupree," and "What a shame about me," more or less what Donald Fagen, Walter Becker, and their assembled cast of highly skilled studio musicians were doing throughout the 1970s. If they could have made the same album twenty years before (Fagen said that they made *Two Against Nature* so that the band would have something new to play in concert), doesn't this tend to undercut any claim that Steely Dan might have on avant-rock status? Not necessarily, though it is unlikely that Becker and Fagan would particularly care whether or not they are "avant"—then or now. So, why include Steely Dan in a discussion of avant rock?

One temptation is to see Steely Dan as what the Beatles—or was it progressive rock, or even Supertramp—might have sounded like if the music had been made by Woody Allen-ish wiseass Jewish kids from New York, instead of witty lads from the U.K. There is a level of craft in Donald Fagen's compositions and arrangements that is superior to that of at least ninety-five percent of rock music, but craft alone does not make for important music. Salieri had craft; Mozart had craft and something else. Indeed, most of the Steely Dan albums are populated with studio musicians, whose chief contribution is to make difficult music seem effortless. The group sometimes crosses the line between the ironic use of smooth playing and "lite" jazz—or, at least, some of Steely Dan's fans do not seem to be in on the joke. ("Hey 19," from *Gaucho*, would be the perfect example.) My guess is Fagen and Becker figure that, if you are going to mess with this line in the first place, you might as well cross it every now and then—and in this Steely Dan has set the stage for "avant-lounge" experiments such as Stereolab and Jim O'Rourke's albums *Eureka* and *Halfway to a threeway*.

What really makes the Steely Dan vision, however, is a synthesis of jazz-rock with a sound from the first decades of the twentieth century, a sound that I associate with Cole Porter, the Gershwin brothers, and Duke Ellington—I would call this sound "music deco." As with the art deco movement in design and architecture, music deco is innovation developed from popular materials. And, as with art deco, there is a definite Jewish side to music deco, or a synthesis of Jewish and African-American influences, as seen especially in George Gershwin's *Rhapsody in Blue*. For many years, this piece was simply heard as a meeting of "orchestral music" and jazz. In recent decades it has been recognized that Eastern European Jewish influences are there as well—for instance in the opening clarinet figure, which comes out of Klezmer music. There was a peculiar way, in the Gershwins' music, in which heartbreak and irony were combined, culminating in *Porgy and Bess* (with lyrics by Ira Gershwin and DuBose Heyward). Cole Porter also captured this quality in some of his songs, but perhaps the greatest example of this combination, as expressed in a single song, was the extraordinary jewel by Duke Ellington's protégé, Billy Strayhorn. "Lush Life" (c. 1938) could legitimately lay claim, in my humble opinion, to being the finest example of the songwriting craft. The song is intimidating in its cleverness; indeed, it elevates wit to the level of supreme genius. And yet there is nothing of mere artifice in the song. Especially in what many, myself included, take to be the most compelling version of the song, by Johnny Hartman and John Coltrane (1963), "Lush Life" can leave one gasping for air.

I would be remiss if I failed to mention that George Gershwin, Cole Porter, and Billy Strayhorn were gay. Although arguments for how sexuality and creativity interact are still being developed, especially as regards music, it seems that an investigation into this "heartbreak and irony" school of songwriting might prove quite fertile.

Nothing in Steely Dan has the emotional depth or intensity of "Lush Life," but there is a kind of melancholy under the witticism. Songs such as "My Old School" (*Countdown to Ecstasy*, 1973), "Any World" ("any world that I'm welcome to is better than the one I come from," *Katy Lied*, 1975), and "Deacon Blues" (*Aja*, 1977) expand the emotional range of rock music, though sometimes by injecting a large dose of cynicism.

One aspect of Steely Dan's music that most likely makes a subconscious impression on many listeners, but that is rarely remarked upon, is the quality of the guitar solos found in many of their songs. I'm ambivalent about the electric guitar, and even more ambivalent about guitar solos. One of the liberating features of punk was to get rid of these often self-indulgent and musically-thin interludes. It is hard to imagine rock music without the electric guitar, however, and a well-constructed solo can be a wonder to behold. Steely Dan employed a legion of guitarists, among them Larry Carlton, Hugh McCracken, Denny Dias, Jeff "Skunk" Baxter, Elliot Randall, Dean Parks, Rick Derringer, and Walter Becker himself, so it would require a major work of scholarship to sort out who played what. Still, the guitar work on the second album, *Countdown to Ecstasy*, performed entirely by Jeff Baxter and Denny Dias, stands out as especially good—and it comes from a time when Steely Dan was more of an actual group. Two great performances from the "post-group" Dan are Steve Gadd's drumming and Wayne Shorter's tenor saxophone playing on the title track from *Aja*. Jazz listeners will know that Shorter played in the great Miles Davis Quintet that also included Tony Williams, and he went on to be the co-leader, with Joe Zawinul, of Weather Report. The interaction between Gadd and Shorter is thrilling, in part because of the element of role-reversal: here Gadd, rather than simply laying down a beat, orchestrates a series of very precise, stop/start patterns, against which Shorter paints with a broad brush. A whole album developing this framework would have been welcome, perhaps as something to set alongside the duet album by John Coltrane and Rashied Ali, *Interstellar Space*.

For whatever cosmic reason, the best Steely Dan albums are numbers two, four, and six: *Countdown to Ecstasy*, *Katy Lied*, and *Aja*. Each shows Steely Dan (I hesitate to say "the group," because there wasn't really such a thing after the second or third album) in a different phase of development—and, no mean feat, each is filled with songs that are little gems, really up there with the Gershwins and Cole Porter, but also representing subsequent developments in harmony and rhythm. Yes, timbre as well, which has increasingly become a preoccupation "after Eno," but in a way that remained subordinate to the song. So, to return to where I started: What is so avant about songcraft? I don't have an adequate answer to that question, but it sure seems as though the loss of such craft would be a very bad thing.

Cathy Berberian (1925–1983) was a classically-trained vocalist who devoted herself to avant-garde works. She was married to composer Luciano Berio, who wrote a number of works for her. Funny line from Brian Sweet's book on Steely Dan, *Reelin' in the Years*: "Many fans and critics thought that Cathy Berberian was a figment of Fagen and Becker's imagination, but she actually did exist" (p. 59). According to Sweet, Berberian said that she was "terribly flattered by the tribute from Steely Dan," and she bought copies of *Countdown* for family members. A roulade is "a musical embellishment consisting of a rapid succession of tones sung to a single syllable" (*Webster's New Unabridged Universal Dictionary*); secondarily, it is some sort of dish that involves meat wrapped around more meat. If Berberian didn't sing the latter, perhaps she was a vegetarian?

In a bizarre twist, *Two Against Nature* won a Grammy. Becker and Fagen were introduced by (militant vegetarian and philosophy major) Moby; not having heard of him, the Steely duo asked if he was connected to Moby Grape.

Steely Dan

Can't Buy a Thrill (MCA LP, 1972).
Countdown to Ecstasy (MCA LP, 1973).
Pretzel Logic (MCA LP, 1974).
Katy Lied (MCA LP, 1975).
The Royal Scam (MCA LP 1976).
Aja (MCA LP, 1977).
Gaucho (MCA LP, 1980).

1971

Anthony Braxton, *For Alto* (Delmark LP).
Cornelius Cardew, *The Great Learning*; Brian Eno, vocal (Deutsche Grammophone LP).
George Crumb, *Ancient Voices of Children* (Nonesuch LP).
Stomu Yamash'ta, *Red Buddha* (Vanguard LP, 1973; orig. 1971).

1972

Faust, *Faust So Far* (Virgin LP).
Stomu Yamash'ta, *Henze/Maxwell Davies/Takemitsu* (L'oiseau-lyre LP).
Stomu Yamash'ta and Come to the Edge, *Floating Music* (Island LP).

1973

Harry Partch, *The Bewitched* (CRI LP).
Iggy and the Stooges, *Raw Power* (Columbia LP).

Almost in the manner of players of the Japanese wood flute (shakuhachi), Braxton's alto saxophone is suspended in thin air, alone—but *For Alto* is rarely meditative, often busy and urgent, and it has pieces dedicated to Cecil Taylor and John Cage. The final piece is more percussion than woodwind, as it consists in playing the saxophone's buttons without blowing. Cornelius Cardew attempted to turn the sonic innovations of the European avant-garde toward more explicitly political ends; famously, he wrote a tract under the title, "Stockhausen Serves Imperialism." Note the Eno connection. Against the background of atonality, George Crumb's music shocks by moving into tonality (and explicit quotations from the canon, from Bach to Schubert to Chopin). He stands just to the left of the point where the categories began to break down altogether. *Ancient Voices of Children* is a setting of poems by Federico Garcia Lorca, haunting and for the most part very quiet. One of the strangest aspects of the piece is its use of "tuned stone slabs" as part of its expanded percussion section. Stomu Yamash'ta is an expanded percussion section all by himself, as evidenced by the multi-tracked solo performance, *Red*

Buddha. I wish that Yamash'ta's name was in more evidence these days; back in the 1960s and 1970s he was regarded by many as the best percussionist in the classical avant-garde, and he crossed over into jazz and rock as well. His best album in the latter vein was *Floating World*, with his group, Come to the Edge. Yes, come very close to the edge. Furthest out, beyond the edge, is the 1972 solo (and not multi-tracked) performance of works by Toru Takemitsu, Hans-Werner Henze, and Peter Maxwell-Davies.

Faust and Iggy and the Stooges make a nice, existential pair, the one gloomy and loopy, the other insane, rude, and nude. Both transcended technique by trashing it, more or less, and both revel in monotonal singing, though the one is more like a chant and the other is often a scream. Harry Partch fits in here more than one might at first expect, with strange, new, acoustic instruments of his own design. The descriptive phrases in Alan Rich's *American Pioneers: Ives to Cage and Beyond* are both informative and amusing: born in 1901, "[t]he son of apostate missionary parents,

> Partch grew up in Arizona, where by the age of six he had already mastered several instruments: reed organ, harmonica, cornet and violin among them. His musical education was gleaned from readings in public libraries and by associating with native American Indians in nearby villages; he once listed his influences as 'Yaqui Indians, Chinese Lullabies and music-hall songs, Christian and Hebrew hymns, Congo puberty rites . . . and Mussorgsky's *Boris Godunov*.
>
> During his time of self-education the young Partch developed a personal philosophy of Western music which, he decided, had begun to go wrong about the time of the Crusades. (p. 199)

The passage through punk

> Glenn was always going on about nice things, like the Beatles."
> I was always making up my own words for "Substitute" [by The Who], but Glenn said, "You can't do that, it's a classic."
>
> —John Lydon, in the film *The Filth
> and the Fury*, commenting on
> Pistols' bass player Glenn Mattlock

Was punk rock musically significant? Punk opened a new era in DIY music-making, similar perhaps to the activities of "outsider" artists in the world of painting and other plastic arts. Little record labels sprung up all over the place, locally- or regionally-popular groups made cassette-tape albums, and *Maximum Rock 'n' Roll* magazine, roughly produced on newsprint, along with many other more obscure *'zines*, publicized this new underground that was also very much in the public eye and ear. The impact of punk is undeniable. Along with hip-hop, the effect that punk has had on general fashion and cultural sensibilities has been lasting, as perhaps most manifest by a new generation that was not even born by the time the Sex Pistols imploded. Indeed, as someone who played in punk bands in the early 1980s, I wonder if others of my generation (I was born in 1956) who were part of that musical-political movement are also amused by the way that we are often treated like old fogeys by the new "punks" of the Limp Bizkit generation?

Having opened an autobiographical side of the question, I wonder if a personal narrative might shed some light on punk's significance. Like many people, I first became aware of punk around 1977, when sensational accounts of the British scene, especially around the Sex Pistols, were published and broadcast in the United States. As a musician and someone who tried to be aware of what was going on in music, I was in something of a limbo district around that time. My enthusiasms from my high school and college years, which covered most of the 1970s, were for progressive rock, avant-garde jazz, and avant-garde "classical" music of the post-John Cage type. With the waning of progressive rock in the middle-1970s, it didn't seem as though much was going on in rock in general. At first I just saw Bruce Springsteen as a greaser throwback, a recapitulation of rock'n'roll as it was already fully known, so that bandwagon did not appeal. Later, around the early 1980s, I came to respect him as a very good songwriter and chronicler of the underside of the American dream, and I still hold that view of him. (One of the many virtues of Greil Marcus's writing on punk, by the way, is that he is able to see through fashionably hip views of Springsteen as a merely "commercial" rocker.) But even with good songwriters out there, my worry in that period had to do with the fate of experimental trends—and most likely this could be called a "musical-political" worry, in that the more properly musical issues could not be separated from the sense that the political energy of the sixties was being eclipsed. I had even made a pact with my good friend from college and since, Chelsea Snelgrove: we were not going to become the sort of people who did not move forward with the music and who then became merely backward-looking, reveling in the music that we enjoyed as teenagers. Only in hindsight could it be seen that we made our pact at a time when the culture industry was carrying out a massive effort to recuperate the wilder side of rock music, such that trends that were both adventurous and popular were once again relegated to the margins.

The first time I heard snippets of the Sex Pistols' music, and saw the band performing, it was on one of the "news magazine" television shows, perhaps *60 Minutes*. Hearing just a few seconds of the music, and seeing scenes of Sid Vicious gobbing (spitting) on spectators (who gobbed back) did not make a good impression. My main thought was something along the lines of, What a load of crap, another indication of the bankruptcy of capitalist society. (And yes, I realize how politically backward and narrow that judgment was, and how ridiculous it was to allow my sense of a cultural phenomenon to be informed by a capitalist institution.) However, only two or three weeks later (as best I recall), my sense of what was going on was changed when I heard a radio news report concerning the Sex Pistols. They had come to the United States to begin a tour and then been denied access. It was very clear that the reasons for the lock-out had more to do with politics and less with gobbing. The same can be said about the aesthetic innovations of punk. That is, it is because punk is politically significant that it is aesthetically significant: punk begins not as "return to basics, stripped-down" rock and roll, but as a reinvention of radical negativity. Punk's rejection of musical technique is first of all a rejection of the orientation of the aesthete, and possibly of the idea of staying in one's room to practice playing an instrument for hours on end. Once you have the minimal musical ability to make a statement, get out there and make it—and "minimal" in rock music can be reduced to the most basic elements. Of course, you might get better at playing the guitar or drums, but that can happen while you are out there making the music and making a statement. Or, as John Lydon put it, "I'm not a musician"—you have to hear this last word, especially, in his sneering voice—"I'm a noise structuralist."

Sex Pistols, *Never Mind the Bollocks* (Virgin LP, 1977)
The Clash, *The Clash* (Columbia LP, 1977).
Richard Hell and the Voidoids, *Blank Generation* (Sire LP, 1977).
Wire, *Pink Flag* (Harvest LP, 1977).
The Clash, *Give 'Em Enough Rope* (Columbia LP, 1978).
——, *London Calling* (Columbia LP, 1979).
Gang of Four, *Entertainment* (Warner Bros. LP, 1979).
The Pretenders, *Pretenders* (Sire LP, 1980).
The Clash, *Sandinista* (Columbia LP, 1980).
Bad Brains, *Rock for Light* (Abstract LP, 1983).
Black Flag, *Damaged* (SST LP, 1981).
Dead Kennedys, *In God We Trust Inc.* (Alternative Tentacles EP, 1981).
The Clash, *Combat Rock* (Columbia LP, 1982).
Gang of Four, *Songs of the Free* (Warner Bros. LP, 1982).
Hüsker Dü, *Everything Falls Apart* (SST LP, 1982).
R.E.M., *Murmur* (IRS LP, 1983).
Black Flag, *My War* (SST LP, 1983).
Hüsker Dü, *Zen Arcade* (SST LP, 1984).
Meat Puppets, *Up on the Sun* (SST LP, 1984).
Minutemen, *Double Nickels on the Dime* (SST LP, 1984).
Bad Brains, *I Against I* (SST LP, 1986).
Living Colour, *Vivid* (Epic LP, 1988).
Nirvana, *Nevermind* (Geffen CD, 1991).

Public Image Ltd.

Public Image (Virgin LP, 1978).
Metal Box/Second Edition (Virgin LP, 1979).
Flowers of Romance (Warner Bros. LP, 1981).
Album (with Bill Laswell) (Virgin LP, 1986).

This "punk discography" gets strange very quickly. The Clash messed up punk by neither burning out nor fading away, by learning to play their instruments better, and by expanding their range of musical styles. Wire's first album, punk lore has it, was recorded within a few days of the acquisition of instruments by the band members. The Gang of Four had a more "cooked" ideology, part Situationism, part Adorno. Certainly their example makes us wonder about the "primitivism" of punk in hindsight. Even at the beginning, R.E.M. was never exactly a punk band—perhaps the bass-playing was too good! Still, the first years of its existence when you could only make out every fifth or sixth word in the song, if that, were magical in a way that seemed connected to punk, at least via the Southern gothic sensibility that is in some part an offshoot of Albion's seed. Also key for its quality of voice was the first Pretenders album. Chrissie Hynde— what a great, great singer. The songwriting is excellent too, combining harsh, trebly, Telecaster chords with more melodic, "Britpop" elements from James Honeyman-Scott's Gibson, and the perfect, Ringo Starr goes punk, big-beat drumming of Martin Chambers. Hüsker Dü and the Minutemen also expanded the range considerably. *Zen Arcade* might be called the *Quadrophenia* of punk. In a brief conversation with me just before the release of *Double Nickels on the Dime*, Mike Watt mentioned that the next album would be a double—why?—"because the Hüskers did one!" The Bad Brains combined frightening shred ability with hard, fast reggae and very pointed stabs at U.S. imperialism. The Meat Puppets, at least musically, went in the other direction, and were positively "laid back," at least as much as this could be said of a punk band. Certainly a Puppets/R.E.M. comparison, for example, reveals the regional influences in punk. The largest and most important distinction, however, is that between English and American bands—in the former, the class element stands out much more explicitly, as it does in the different cultures more generally.

An album that was very controversial at the time was *My War* by Black Flag. This was for three reasons specifically: some of the songs were as long as five to seven minutes (when three minutes seemed the upper limit); some of the songs were very slow, with big, blocky chords; some of the songs featured long, manic guitar solos. In that time, Greg Ginn was one of the more interesting guitarists going, something that could not be said of anyone else in punk. When I saw Black Flag on the tour for *My War* Henry Rollins said at one point, "Ladies and gentlemen, Tony Iommi," by way of introducing a Ginn solo. Already in 1983 Black Flag was leading the rapprochement between punk and heavy metal that was taken to another level by Rage Against the Machine ten years later.

Who carried on the spirit of punk, beyond the time when the music was very directly connected to the events of the day, which is to say, beyond the timeframe of about 1977 to 1982 or so? Living Colour and Nirvana are worthy examples compared to which the whole Green Day to Limp Bizkit scene is just a cartoon (and some of the other grunge/Seattle sound stuff, while pretty good, is simply something else; it doesn't have the harsh edge and true fury that Kurt Cobain did). There was also more to be done with Lydon's sneer, best aided by the overwhelming bass of Jah Wobble. Lydon's book, *Rotten* (from whence the "noise structuralist" remark comes) is also a significant document of punk.

I haven't mentioned the Ramones, who strike me as having been a cartoon from the start. Still, there is an interesting discussion to be had about where the true spirit of punk lies. I doubt that any of the Ramones ever read Guy Debord or were influenced by anyone else who actually did the reading (Malcolm McLaren, in other words). It could be argued that not reading is more punk than reading (I don't recall a lot of reading being done at the Rock and Roll High School), and that stitching the Pistols into a narrative such as Greil Marcus's in *Lipstick Traces* isn't punk either. The question can be resolved, at least to a large extent, by returning to the politics/aesthetics distinction. Were the stripped-down musical elements in punk simply ends in themselves? The Ramones took this paring down to the point of dumbing down—represented very well by the idea of only playing downstrokes on the bass (which strikes me as just plain stupid).

There is, however, something to be said for the idea that punk was not this or that famous band or album, but instead the countless bands and little shows covered in *Maximum Rock'n'Roll* and other 'zine publications. In this sense, it doesn't matter so much that there are perhaps only ten or fewer "real" punk albums that hold up beyond the period of the late 1970s/early 1980s (recognizing that a number of the listings in the discography are not "real" punk albums), records that you could get much out of now that their time has passed, because instead the deeper effect of punk was to bring about a reorientation in music, culture, and politics. This reorientation is still very much with us, for better or worse.

● **1974**

George Crumb, *Makrokosmos, v.1: Twelve Fantasy-Pieces after the Zodiac for Amplified Piano* (Nonesuch LP).
———. *Night of the Four Moons/Voice of the Whale* (Columbia LP).
Fred Frith, *Guitar Solos* (Carolina LP).
Kraftwerk, *Autobahn* (EMI LP).

Nico, *The End . . .* (Island LP).
Robert Wyatt, *Rock Bottom* (Virgin LP).

1975
Anthony Braxton, *Five Pieces 1975* (Arista LP).
George Crumb, *Music for a Summer Evening (Makrokosmos III), for Two Amplified Pianos and Percussion* (Nonesuch LP).

1976
Jan Steele/John Cage, *Voices and Instruments* (Antilles/Obscure LP).
Tashi, *Plays Messiaen, Quartet for the End of Time* (RCA LP, 1976; composed 1940).

With his *Makrokosmos* series, George Crumb both pays tribute to Bartók and seems to presage the New Age. Frith, using "preparations" on his electric guitar, along with various dangerous objects (for example, pieces of glass) for plectrums, and painfully dissonant tunings, not to mention fine technique, builds a bridge between John Cage and free jazz—which is also to say that he ventures into Derek Bailey territory. *Autobahn* became one of the most influential records of all time, probably the source from which almost all techno music flows. With the help of John Cale and her ever-present harmonium, Nico produced one of the creepiest albums of the decade, *The End*. In a similar vein is Robert Wyatt's *Rock Bottom*, especially in terms of its spare instrumentation and the plaintive-yet-alienated quality of voice. Substance abuse is a major issue in both cases, ultimately killing Nico and leading to a fall from a third-floor window in Wyatt's case. *Rock Bottom* was his first album on the way back up, and thank heaven he is still with us.

Braxton's *Five Pieces* featured one of the most interesting "piano-less quartets" in jazz history, in some ways a nice cross between the format's roots in Gerry Mulligan and its subsequent development by Ornette Coleman. As has been said by many commentators, there is something very mannered in Braxton's music, and there are ways in which his work is more like classical music than jazz. The music is well-served here by Kenny Wheeler on trumpet and flugelhorn, Dave Holland on double bass (a classically-trained bassist and cellist who was also a member of the great Miles Davis group with Tony Williams, and later a part of the electric experiments), and the ambidextrous, polyrhythmic brilliance of Barry Altschul on drums. Braxton is one of the most important composers of the second half of the twentieth century, and he's a very good chess player, too.

The Jan Steele/John Cage album is listed here in part because it appeared on Brian Eno's Obscure Records label. The album features a lovely setting of a poem by James

Joyce. Tashi, the group convened by pianist Peter Serkin to perform Messiaen's *Quartet for the End of Time*, is something of a forerunner to the Kronos Quartet—a classical ensemble with something of a rock sensibility. The unusual instrumentation of the *Quartet*—piano, clarinet, violin, cello—reflects the fact that Oliver Messiaen composed the piece while a prisoner of war in a German Stalag, performed by himself and fellow inmates for an assemblage of five thousand prisoners on a grim winter day in January, 1941. The idea of the "rock and roll survivor" is shown for the load of rot that it is, by contrast.

Punk meets the Godmother: Patti Smith

Before punk emerged as a full-blown trend, there was Patti Smith. And, after all but a handful of punk albums have receded into obscurity (in many cases, deservedly so), there still is Patty Smith. Indeed, part of what Smith, along with Sonic Youth, serves to remind us is that there were punks before punk—they were called beat poets. Again, too, we see the dynamic that drove much rock music in the 1970s—just to be fashionably structuralist about it, we can now call it "the raw and the cooked." Like the Velvets, Smith aimed at refinement of the word combined with three-chord rock. The first words from her first album, "Jesus died for somebody's sins, but not mine," are fitting for someone raised by a Jehovah's Witness mother and an atheist father. A childhood bout with scarlet fever also gave Smith the gift of hallucinations without recourse to psychedelic drugs. In the early 1970s, Smith began giving poetry readings that were backed by the noise-guitar stylings of journalist-cum-musician Lenny Kaye. Only a couple of years before, Yoko Ono and John Lennon had done something similar in London, before an audience of avant-garde music listeners who were put off by the presence of the bespectacled Beatle. Smith made the transition from "reader" to rock singer, though often oscillating within the parameters of speech and singing—what Schoenberg had pioneered in *Pierrot lunaire* as *Sprechstimme*, though he didn't have the benefit of Stratoscasters and Marshall amplifiers.

Struggle with Christianity and its attendant ghosts and spirits is a significant part of Smith's music and poetry. *Radio Ethiopa*, my own favorite Smith album, opens with "Ask the angels"—"who they're calling . . . I believe they're calling for me." The LP contains a booklet, with a long poem/autobiographical ramble, opening with lines from the Book of Revelation. Soon enough she mentions being raised a Christian, though she doesn't remark on the distance between the Jehovah's Witnesses and more mainstream or fundamentalist Christianity. The Witnesses' brand of apocalyptic religion is especially noteworthy for taking seriously Jesus's admonition regarding rich people, that they have even less chance of being saved than a camel has of going through the eye of a needle. (It is interesting to hear fundamentalists, Evangelicals, and others engage in semantic gyrations in order to get around this.) In 1977 Smith was performing the intense second song from *Radio Ethiopia*, at a concert in Tampa, Florida. The song is a challenge to God to talk to her. Dervishly whirling, singing the line, "Hand of God, I don't get dizzy, hand of God, I do not fall," she fell off the stage and broke her neck.

When Smith returned in 1978 with *Easter*, her sound was more polished (though the button-down shirt and tie of *Horses* was replaced by a sleeveless camisole and centrally-featured armpit) and her former rebellion against God seems to have led to "the warm and infinite love of Christ." And even while she had become the priestess of punk at New York's CBGB club, she continued to sing rock and roll anthems on her albums, in this case, "Because the Night," written with Bruce Springsteen. On her first album (produced by John Cale, and for which she was photographed by her friend, Robert Mapplethorpe) she gave a spirited rendition of Van Morrison's "Gloria" (adding to the title, "in excelsis deo"), while 1979's *Wave* opens with the Byrds hit, "So you wanna be a rock and roll star." Unfortunately, the overly slick production by Todd Rundgren was emblematic of the fact that Smith seemed to have buried for the time her more interesting self, which was and is a bundle of contradictions, and to have found some tidy resolutions.

These, however, may have kept her alive. Smith largely disappeared from public view for much of the 1980s and early 1990s. The harsh assertion of mortality, however, in the form of the deaths of her husband, her brother, and Mapplethorpe, spurred her to create one of her strongest works, *Gone Again*.

▲ Patti Smith

Horses (Arista LP, 1975).
Radio Ethiopia (Arista LP, 1976).
Easter (Arista LP, 1978).
Wave (Arista LP, 1979).
● *Gone Again* (Arista CD, 1996).

● 1977

Robert Ashley, *Private Parts*, with settings for piano and orchestra by "Blue" Gene Tyranny (Lovely Music LP).
David Bowie, *Low* (RCA LP).
———, *Heroes* (RCA LP).
Kraftwerk, *Trans-Europe Express* (Cleopatra LP).
Tashi, *Plays Stravinsky, L'Histoire du soldat* (RCA LP).
"Blue" Gene Tyranny, *Out of the Blue* (Lovely Music LP).

1978
Kraftwerk, *The Man Machine* (Cleopatra LP).
Pere Ubu, *Dub Housing* (Chrysalis LP).
Steve Reich, *Music for 18 Musicians* (ECM LP).
Throbbing Gristle, *20 Jazz Funk Greats* (Mute CD, 1997; orig.1978).

If you haven't heard Robert Ashley, then you probably haven't heard anything like his work, either, even if the elements of it are simple enough—spare instrumentation and rambling stories told by individuals in ordinary voices. Ashley's music is its own form of minimalism, set against all contrivance and pretension. The "orchestra" here, by the way, consists in a string synthesizer and some rudimentary tabla-drumming. In this period David Bowie made what are considered his most experimental albums, with the help of Brian Eno and Robert Fripp. Bowie was in his "Berlin" period, at a time when the city stood at the Cold War crossroads. (At the same time, Helsinki was a major center for punk. The Sibelius influence was at something of an ebb.) Kraftwerk continued to make pocket-calculator music, while Steve Reich also achieved a clockwork minimalist masterpiece with *Music for 18 Musicians*. This left room for more raucous noise-making, in the form of Pere Ubu and Throbbing Gristle—teaming with more than their fair share of madness and perversion, respectively. Members of both groups continue to be active in the experimental rock scene.

Funk beyond the Godfather: George Clinton and P-Funk

A book ought to be written on what might be called "progressive soul," music that begins with Ray Charles, Motown, and James Brown, and culminates in Stevie Wonder's great trilogy (*Talking Book*, *Innervisions*, and *Songs in the Key of Life*) and such albums as War's *All Day Music* and *The World is a Ghetto*. Whether George Clinton and his two-bands-in-one (or is it the other way around?) groups Funkadelic and Parliament would belong in such a book is open to debate, but I would put them in there. P-Funk, as the musical approach of the whole conglomeration is called, takes the James Brown on the one hand, and the Motown/Detroit legacy, on the other, to the next stage, primarily through the infusion of psychedelia.

P-Funk bassist Bootsy Collins, famous for the star-shaped bass, the Mutron effects pedal, and the longest, slipperiest fingers on the planet, had in fact been a member of James Brown's band; mainstay of the JB horns, Maceo Parker later lead the P-funk horn section. Like the JBs, P-Funk could rock hard and intensely, but the forte of the Clinton vision was seen, as in the albums listed here, when the groove was loose and subservient to an album-length musical voyage. The narrative is never especially coherent or consistent, and indeed every possible countercultural theme makes its appearance sooner or later. It would be easy to make comparisons to the Grateful Dead or Frank Zappa and the Mothers of Invention (especially albums such as *We're Only in It for the Money*), and then to say, "but imagine a Black twist on that." There's something to that, but then you have to take account of the idea, as John Corbett puts it, that there were already "brothers from another planet," especially Sun Ra, who developed visions of symphonic scope. In other words, sure, Clinton was ready to take sounds from wherever, from Bay Area psychedelia to Jimi Hendrix, but he had his own freaky thing going, too. Funkentelechy, after all, invokes not Jerry Garcia, but a warped reading of Aristotle.

Although the Funkadelic albums are hilarious in their sheer nastiness and compulsive danceability, Parliament's *Mothership Connection* is the album I always go back to. "Good evening," the DJ intones at the start, and you know that you're in good hands. If Funkadelic's music is often about the (justifiable) anger within, *Mothership Connection* is about that voice of redemption that speaks from beyond: "Swing down sweet chariot, stop, and let me ride." As Peter Shapiro put it in the *Rough Guide*, this "most moving moment on any Clinton record yields the entire Parliament concept."

Funkadelic, *Maggot Brain* (Westbound LP, 1971).
Parliament, *Mothership Connection* (Casablanca LP, 1975).
———, *Funkentelechy Vs. The Placebo Syndrome* (Casablanca LP, 1977).
Funkadelic, *One Nation Under a Groove* (Warner Bros. LP, 1978).

1979
James Blood (Ulmer), *Tales of Captain Black* (Artists House LP).

1980
Captain Beefheart, *Doc at the Radar Station* (Virgin LP).

1981
Fela Anikulapo Kuti, *Black President* (Arista LP).
Meredith Monk, *Dolmen Music* (ECM LP).
James Blood Ulmer, *Are You Glad To Be in America* (Artists House LP).

Besides James Brown, from Barnwell, South Carolina, we have James Blood Ulmer, native of the small town of St. Matthews. Though coming from a varied background that included gospel and blues, he was propelled into innovation through his stint with Ornette Coleman. Through his adaptation of Coleman's "harmolodic" concept, Ulmer developed one of the most distinctive guitar sounds of the 1980s, and he channeled this sound, along with a good singing voice, into pointed (but not propagandistic) commentary on racism in the United States. In doing so he has created music that is both experimental and primal.

Though I am not a Beefheart aficionado, *Doc at the Radar Station* really stands out as a powerful album. Here, too, the guitar makes a major impact, in a way not unlike Ulmer's approach to the instrument—at times trebly to the point of tinniness, harsh and screeching, like an angry bird. Trombone, Mellotron, and Chinese gongs also form an interesting part of the tableau. The singing and songwriting are brilliant, especially on songs such as "Ashtray Heart." The cover allows you to enjoy Don Van Vliet the painter, so look for the LP.

Fela Kuti was legendary in numerous ways, whether for his opposition to American and European imperialism in Africa, his voracious sexual appetite (he claimed that he had to have sex at least three times a day, every day) and legion of "wives," his concerts that would sometimes last eight hours or more, or the song titles that he would reduce to initials—perhaps the funniest of which is "I.T.T.," standing for "International Thief Thief." In his native Nigeria Kuti was known as the "black president," hence the album of that name. For much of his life he was a "president" in exile. Kuti's music resembles P-Funk in some respects, especially in the size and scope of the groups he would use—generally about fifteen or more musicians, which included horn and percussion sections, often two bass players and two or three guitar players, himself on electric keyboard, tenor sax, and vocals, four or five background singers, and five or six dancers. In front of the group, to Kuti's left, would be a man playing the afuche, a gourd wrapped with beads—always this sound underlying everything else. So, like P-Funk, Kuti put a small village on stage. But Kuti was not much about partying, and many of his concerts ended with a Pan-Africanist chant, "Africa must unite!" The music is hypnotic and intoxicating, almost always starting with a very small figure in the bass or the keyboard, eventually developing into overwhelming crescendos from the horns. Kuti made lots of albums, some better than others. *Black President* is one of the best.

Meredith Monk's *Dolmen Music* is much more spare in its instrumentation, and it is rarely overwhelming. But there is something primal about it also, in a Druid or Stonehenge way that thankfully does not invoke either Spinal Tap or the sappier side of New Age music.

Progressive times punk equals New Wave

In recent years there have been a series of "period" television shows, sitcoms for the most part, that play on some of the funnier or kitschier aspects of their target decade. "The Wonder Years" was perhaps the start of this trend, though it did not seek to be silly at every moment, and the music it featured was some of the best, as opposed to the more embarrassing, of the period it portrayed, the early and middle 1960s. More recently we have seen "That 70s Show," which I find hilarious, and which features typical jock-rock bands of that period, such as Kiss, Foreigner, Cheap Trick, and the like. This opened the door to an "80s show," called "Freaks and Geeks." In "That 70s Show," you wouldn't know, for the most part, about progressive rock or Pink Floyd or Frank Zappa, and in "Freaks and Geeks" there isn't much about punk or new wave. We might not forget about punk, because there was a social movement aspect to it (which was often more interesting than the actual music), but I could easily see new wave falling through the cracks.

Many "real punks" didn't know what to do with new wave when it emerged around 1977 and 1978, but they tended to denigrate the music as "punk lite," a version of the new, more streamlined rock music, but safe enough for nice college kids to dance to. Certainly new wave did bear some relationship to punk and the desire to make rock music hard and powerful and not overly baroque and frilly. It was typical of many of the young punks to claim a break from everything else in rock music that happened before them. Everything else, in their view, was fatally compromised with the existing order of things. From Elvis to the Beatles to Pink Floyd, it was all bollocks. Rock music, in their view, had to consist in the most basic musical building blocks, and with those blocks it needed to remain. Anything beyond this would be a concession to the supposedly bourgeois values of craft and aestheticism. The risk would be one of making something less ugly than it ought to be if one is to make a powerful statement against a prettified reality. (Not every punk could or would spell this aesthetic out in so many words, of course, but these formulations capture the basic sensibility, I think.) A larger discussion of this issue could do with a bit of sociology or demography, because I tend to think that the people who made new wave music might have been on the whole a few years older than the punks, and possibly from backgrounds where they were exposed to a wider range of culture. New Wavers seemed more aware of the kinship between punk and early rock'n'roll. Furthermore, they did not harbor the animosity toward the Beatles or some of the progressive rock groups that was typical of many of the punks. This was evidenced in the various crossovers that one saw in the later 1970s—the circle around Brian Eno, Robert Fripp, David Bowie, and Talking Heads, for instance, or the merger between Yes and the Buggles (Geoff Downes and Trevor Horn; the latter went on to create *The Art of Noise*) that resulted in the prog/new wave album, *Drama*.

There was also an element of whimsical humor to some of the best new wave music; there was social critique, too, but this often took the form of satire, as opposed to the more scowling, snarling, in-your-face approach of punk. Did this make the music "lite"? Only if you take distorted major chords on the guitar and downstrokes on the bass as the epitome of what it means to be heavy.

Talking Heads, *77* (Sire LP, 1977).
———, *More Songs About Buildings and Food* (Sire LP, 1978).
———, *Fear of Music* (Sire LP, 1979).
XTC, *Drums and Wires* (Virgin LP, 1979).
Talking Heads, *Remain in Light* (Sire LP, 1980).
Martha and the Muffins, *Metro Music* (Virgin LP, 1980).
The Method Actors, *"This Is It"* (Armageddon 45, 1980).
———, *Rhythms of You* (Armageddon EP, 1981).
———, *Little Figures* (Armageddon LP, 1981).
Martha and the Muffins, *This is the Ice Age* (Oved LP, 1981).
XTC, *English Settlement* (Virgin LP, 1982).
Talking Heads, *Speaking in Tongues* (Warner Brothers LP, 1983).
Martha and the Muffins, *Danseparc* (RCA LP, 1983).

Of the many interesting new wave groups, only four of them are represented in the list of albums cited above. Two of these groups are broadly familiar. If punk was in part the music of the outcast ne'er-do-well, new wave of the Talking Heads variety was the revenge of the nerds. Much punk eschewed, supposedly, any aspect of "performance"—this is just *me* and my authentic rage! What it meant to actually have that rage on demand, at any given show, created existential difficulties—in sports they call it putting on your game face. David Byrne went the opposite route, toward unabashed self-consciousness. Of course, that is performative as well, but part of what made Talking Heads so refreshing was the anti-attitude attitude: "I am doing this and I know that I am doing this." When wearing black was the only cool way to dress, both XTC and Talking Heads seemed to say, gee, this wastes an awful lot of colors—and this went for their music as much as their album covers. Something of the punk sensibility was there, in that the music was not overly loaded with artifice, and the songs started with basic structures and some of the directness of punk. But where punk was in a quandary as to what to do on the second album, new wave in the hands of its more adventurous advocates began the process of building up and fleshing out the musical materials. For sure, this was true in the case of a few punk groups as well—Husker Du and Black Flag stand out as good examples. What is interesting in all four of these cases is that the articulation of the basic elements of punk and new wave required going back into some of the most creative currents of "classic" rock: The Who (Hüsker Dü), Black Sabbath (Black Flag), the Beatles (XTC), and even progressive rock (Talking Heads). The affinity between XTC and the Beatles is not only in Andy Partridge's melodic-but-pointed songwriting, but also in the McCartney- and Starr-like structures created on the bass and drums by Colin Moulding and Terry Chambers, respectively.

The first Talking Heads album will always be remembered for songs such as "Psycho Killer" and "Don't Worry 'Bout the Government," but the group really made a leap with its second effort, *More Songs About Buildings and Food*. Brian Eno, already an enthusiast and friend of the band, came on the scene as producer, a role in which he would continue for two additional albums. The third of these, *Remain in Light*, would be an easy candidate for one of the top two or three albums of the new wave genre, along with XTC's *English Settlement*. Three years passed before the fifth Talking Heads album was issued, years that saw the release of three side projects, all of high quality: Jerry Harrison's *The Red and the Black*, Tina Weymouth's and Chris Frantz's *Tom Tom Club*, and the excellent collaboration between David Byrne and Brian Eno, *My Life in the Bush of Ghosts*. The tour which followed the release of 1983's *Speaking in Tongues* yielded one of the best concert films ever, *Stop Making Sense*.

These were bands that were taking rock music in new directions, even while clearly working out of the dynamic of the 1970s—*both* the directness of punk *and* the subtleties and complexities of the trajectory that led from *Revolver* to *Close to the Edge*. XTC continues to make albums, as do the members of Talking Heads, in various combinations. New wave also consisted in many creative groups that did not become as famous. One of these was a group from Athens, Georgia, called The Method Actors. Athens, as is well known, was a hotbed of music in the early 1980s, giving us not only R.E.M. and the B-52s, but also groups such as Pylon and the Flat Duo Jets. Indeed, it was at an album release party for Pylon that the members of R.E.M., before they had decided for sure that they wanted to make a go of it as a group, and before their name had been chosen, assembled to play some Byrds and other cover songs. (As fate would have it, I was at that party.) The Method Actors pared rock minimalism down to the most basic components: the group consisted of Vic Varney on guitar and vocals, and David Gamble on drums and vocals. Although their sound was full, especially thanks to some very clever syncopation, Varney and Gamble did not employ any tricks to "compensate" for their instrumentation. Their output was at first minimal too—a 45 rpm 7-inch with three songs on it, a 10-inch EP with seven songs, but then a double LP (all released on the London-based Armageddon label) with seventeen songs. In concert Varney would sometimes play bass guitar, which presaged the Japanese bass/drums duo The Ruins by a good many years. It may sound like a cliché, but what I really liked about the Method Actors was the way their instrumentation and little gems of songs stripped rock right down to its essence, without a single wasted or superfluous motion.

Martha and the Muffins had a radio hit with "Echo Beach," which many people will remember if you bring it up, but otherwise they don't get the credit they deserve for their role in the new wave. For one thing, they were not only a band with two women members—both named Martha—but they were also feminist, and increasingly so, in the orientation of their songs. They had smart arrangements, in many ways like Talking Heads but without the self-conscious quirks, and often their songs dealt with the alienation of urban life and the difficulties of gender relations. Perhaps future editions of the

Rough Guide could find a place for the Muffins (and the successor group, M+M)—it would be a shame if they were lost to rock history.

1982
Laurie Anderson, *Big Science* (Warner Bros. LP).
James Blood Ulmer, *Black Rock* (Columbia LP).
Robert Wyatt, *Nothing Can Stop Us* (Rough Trade LP).

1983
Game Theory, *Pointed Accounts of People You Know* (Enigma EP).
James Blood Ulmer, *Odyssey* (Columbia LP).
Tom Waits, Swordfishtrombones (Island LP).

Laurie Anderson had a big hit with "O Superman," which then introduced millions to her combination of musical minimalism and performance art. Among my favorite of her innovations is a violin on which tape playback heads are mounted, and where the horse-hair on the bow is replaced with recording tape. By using different bows and tapes, she created a form of sampling that still has unexplored possibilities. Robert Wyatt's *Nothing Can Stop Us* runs the gambit from radically pared-down covers of "At Last I am Free" (Chic) and "Strange Fruit" (the song about racist lynching made famous by Billy Holiday), to the Cuban revolutionary song "Caimanera," to the World War 2 folk-song, "Stalin wasn't Stallin'" and, finally, a reading of the poem "Stalingrad," by its author, Peter Blackman. From funk to agit-prop, in other words—though the poem is not propagandistic, and is quite moving. Game Theory was another smart new wave group that deserved a larger audience—of course, their name and the presence of chess imagery on the album cover is endearing to me. Tom Waits integrated his beatnik and late-night diner schtick with Harry Partch-like instrumentation, and created something new. Similarly, James Blood Ulmer found a way to rock out even while articulating his harmolodic chops, and thereby added a new chapter to rock music—again, a chapter that ought to be revisited.

Before and after Eno

Those who have reached the top in both fields [music and chess] include [Francois-Andre Danican] Philidor, who played chess and composed music, and Rudolf Heinrich Willmers (1821-1878), who played music and composed chess problems. While playing Schumann's "Carnival" in a piano recital in Copenhagen, Willmers stopped suddenly, wrote on his cuff, and then continued. He explained afterwards that he had been struggling for a week to solve a difficult problem when the solution came to him in a flash. "I had to jot it down to get it out of my head and let me concentrate entirely on my playing."

—David Hooper and Kenneth Whyld, *The Oxford Companion to Chess*

If you are looking to be frustrated, perhaps infuriated, on any given day of the week, talk to someone who is fully ensconced in the academic discipline of music. Some of these folks have a way of using the term, "musician," such that it only applies to those who are academically trained to play Western classical music. That's silly, of course, and hardly worth the ink that it would take to discuss it. I raise the issue here only to thematize the fact that the "non-musician" has played a significant role in the transformation of music in the avant-gardes of classical music, jazz, and rock—I am thinking especially of John Cage, Cecil Taylor, Ornette Coleman, and Brian Eno. Of course, anyone who is reading this book will almost certainly recognize these figures as musicians. But in each of their respective genres and beyond, their status as musicians has been put into question. Each has been called a charlatan, early and often. Indeed, when I was first formulating the idea for this book, a fellow music theorist wrote me and said words to the effect that he hoped that I was not planning to set up Brian Eno as some sort of "John Cage of rock." Another theorist, who is a classically-trained musician and who writes on both classical music and rock, wrote to say that there was a reason why Cage is smiling or laughing in many photographs—he's having one over on us. Some people said that Ornette Coleman couldn't play in tune, and some said that Cecil Taylor couldn't play at all. Only very ignorant people could think that Taylor and Coleman are not "real" musicians, but the question gets a bit more interesting in the case of Cage and Eno. The distinction between musician and non-musician in Cage goes the way of the distinction between music and "noise." As for Brian Eno, he readily embraces the label "non-musician." Eric Tamm wrote an interesting book about Eno; published in 1989, it was actually his doctoral dissertation in music at Berkeley. The section titled, "Craft and the Non-Musician" (pp. 44–50) contains some interesting and sometimes amusing remarks from Eno, as well as some insightful observations from Tamm.

Tamm maintains that "[a] full understanding of [Eno's] often quoted assertion that he is 'not a musician' is crucial to a grasp of his music." Before grappling with this idea, Tamm argues that Eno "is in fact a talented and versatile, if intuitive and marginally skilled, multi-instrumentalist: he has played synthesizers, piano, organ, other electronic keyboards, electric guitar, electric bass guitar . . . , and assorted traditional and 'found' percussion instruments, such as ashtrays and plastic pipes" (p. 45). The ellipses after "bass guitar" conceal the remark: "which he called in 1985 'the only instrument I have the remotest hope of learning to play before the end of my life—though I don't know what I'll do with it once I've learned" (p. 45). Ouch! My guess is that, at the turn of the millennium, Eno isn't a whole lot further along in his bass-playing skills. As irksome as this might be to a bass guitarist, however, there is more to Eno's approach to craft.

In response to a journalist's comment about not having any formal training in musical theory, Eno responded: "No, I don't. Well, let's say I know many theories about music, but I don't know that particular one that has to do with notation" (p. 45). Cute answer. Tamm comments: "One aspect of the rock tradition—indeed, part of the significance of the rock tradition—has been its refusal to let arbitrary technical standards of musicianship interfere with the music-making process" (p. 46). But Eno went even further in his formulation: "I'm an anti-musician. I don't think the craft of music is relevant to the art of music" (p. 47). Significantly, in the same period (from around 1979 to 1981, when Eno was clearly sorting out exactly what it was he thought he was doing), Eno remarked that he did not consider himself a professional musician, but he did consider himself to be a "professional composer" (p. 47). Interesting distinction. Tamm wonders if "composer" is the right word, either, for someone who has avoided that troublesome "notation theory." In this connection, Eno does note that a good deal of his music deals with "sound texture," which notation would not capture even if he was conversant in this particular "theory." And, indeed, one of the many ways in which Eno is connected with almost everything that is happening in experimental rock music in more recent years is in this turn to texture and timbre. This, however, points to the way in which Eno has no shortage of craft, it's just that his craft does not lie in the areas of either notation or skill with traditional or rock musical instruments. The two related forms of Eno's craft can be seen in his response to an interviewer's question about his instrumental abilities: "Do you ever practice things on a keyboard or a guitar in order to be able to execute them to your satisfaction?" "Not very often. . . . If I have a phrase that has a fast set of notes, I might break the phrase down into three simpler ones, and do them as overdubs" (p. 48). In other words, craft is in the fields of what might be called "conceptualism," and in the use of the recording studio as an instrument in its own right. In saying that Eno is a "conceptualist," I don't mean that he is a "conceptual artist" in the way that, say, Yoko Ono is. For sure, some of his work relates to Ono's, but I mean something else, simply that Eno is a person who comes up with ideas. In that way Eno is in fact something of a "John Cage of rock," in that he comes out of the language of rock, but his music is conceptually driven.

To call Eno a "John Cage" in rock might be a way of saying that few of Eno's ideas are absolutely original. But that could be said of John Cage as well—that's how ideas work. In music, and even in philosophy, what ultimately counts is how ideas rise from the abstract to the concrete, to borrow a phrase from Karl Marx. Jim O'Rourke is another figure in this discussion of whom the "John Cage of rock" label might be used. O'Rourke, unlike Eno, is actually a very capable instrumentalist, especially on guitar. Still, they both represent a transition in rock music away from the traditional or rock instructions, and Eno is really the turning point. I would therefore credit Eno with standing at the transition from rock to post-rock.

Roxy Music, *The First Roxy Music Album* (Island LP, 1972).
——, *For Your Pleasure* (Island LP, 1973).
Brian Eno, *Here Come the Warm Jets* (Island LP, 1973).
——, with Robert Fripp, *(No Pussyfooting)* (Editions EG LP, 1973).
——, *Taking Tiger Mountain (By Strategy)* (Island LP, 1974).
——, with Kevin Ayers, John Cale, Nico, *June 1, 1974* (Island LP, 1974).
——, *Another Green World* (Island LP, 1975).
——, with Robert Fripp, *Evening Star* (Editions EG LP, 1975).
——, *Discreet Music* (Obscure LP, 1975).
——, *Before and After Science* (Island LP, 1977).
——, with Cluster, *Cluster and Eno* (Sky LP, 1977).
——, *Music for Films* (Editions EG LP, 1978).
Devo, *Q: Are We Not Men? A: We Are Devo!* (Warner Bros. LP, 1978; produced by Eno).
Brian Eno, with Moebius and Rodelius, *After the Heat* (Sky LP, 1978).
——, *Ambient 1: Music for Airports* (Editions EG LP, 1979).
——, with David Byrne, *My Life in the Bush of Ghosts* (Sire LP, 1980).
——, with Jon Hassell, *Fourth World Vol. 1: Possible Musics* (Editions EG LP, 1980).
——, *Ambient 4: On Land* (Editions EG LP, 1982).
——, *Apollo: Atmospheres and Soundtracks* (Editions EG LP, 1983).
——, *Thursday Afternoon* (Editions EG CD, 1985).
U2, *The Joshua Tree* (Island LP, 1987; coproduced by Eno).
Brian Eno, *Nerve Net* (Opal CD, 1992).
——, *The Shutov Assembly* (Opal CD, 1992).
——, with Jah Wobble, *Spinner* (Gyroscope CD, 1995).
Bang on a Can, *Music for Airports/Brian Eno* (Point Music CD, 1998).

1984
Butthole Surfers, *Live PCPPEP* (Alternative Tentacles EP).
Einsturzende Neubauten, *2X4* (ROIR Cassette).

1985
Kronos Quartet, *Plays Music of Thelonius Monk*; with Ron Carter, bass (Landmark LP).
Tom Waits, *Rain Dogs* (Island LP, 1985).

1986
Big Audio Dynamite, *No.10, Upping Street* (Columbia LP).
Kronos Quartet, *Sculthorpe/Sallinen/Glass/Nancarrow/Hendrix* (Elektra Nonesuch LP).
James Blood Ulmer, *Live at the Caravan of Dreams* (Caravan of Dreams Productions LP).

Noise asserts itself: the wack-punk of the Butthole Surfers, turntables and tubas in Big Audio Dynamite and Tom Waits, jackhammers in Einsturzende Neubauten, "Purple Haze" in the Kronos Quartet. All right, it isn't all noise, but clearly the shape of rock music is changing. Music is just as much its time congealed in sounds and silence as philosophy is its time captured in thought, as Hegel put it. Eno's function, if it can be put so bluntly, is to ask whether rock music will simply continue to play out dynamics from the past, or will it invent new things. It's interesting to look at what others were doing when Eno made certain of his albums—especially *Here Come the Warm Jets* (1973), *Another Green World* (1975), *Before and After Science* (1977), *Music for Airports* (1979), *My Life in the Bush of Ghosts* (with David Byrne, 1980). Eno's first solo album, *Warm Jets*, comes at the point when progressive rock is peaking in Great Britain and North America, and in that period before punk but where Bruce Springsteen and Patti Smith were taking rock back to a more direct sound. *Warm Jets* manages to combine basic rock and roll with some of the sonic innovations of progressive rock and the gender-bending of glam. Much of the music is very manic. *Another Green World* is much more mannered, by contrast, and it benefits not only from Robert Fripp's "restrained lead guitar," but also the bass playing of Percy Jones and, indeed, Eno's innovation of having "lead" and "anchor" bass on some tracks. Among Eno's own instrumental credits are: snake guitar, desert guitars, treated rhythm generator (one of Eno's roles in Roxy Music was to supply "treatments"), castanet guitars, synthetic and Peruvian percussion, tape, and uncertain piano. We need an album of just those instruments (plus Percy Jones on bass, something to hold it together). Eno was applying his famous "Oblique Strategies" at this point, the deck of cards that contain vague or very general sorts of instructions. You shuffle the deck, pick a card, and see what it suggests as regards the activity that you are involved in.

Before and After Science, also a relatively subdued album, comes upon us at the same time that punk explodes on the scene. In some sense, Eno was already there, though perhaps more in sound than in politics—on the latter he remains a sort of pragmatic, left-liberal. Indeed, at one point journalists noted that Eno was often seen with his copy of Richard Rorty's book, *Contingency, irony, and solidarity* (this had to be some years later, as the book was published in 1989). The album with David Byrne along with the collaboration with John Hassell, *Fourth World, vol. 1*, represented a real transformation, a kind of "Third Stream" music that the jazz/classical syntheses were never quite able to pull off. But this might be said of Eno's first post-Roxy album, the collaboration with Robert Fripp, where treatments and electric guitar plus effects replace tambura (the drone instrument in Indian classical music) and sitar. Collaborations are Eno's strong point, and, of his "non-rock" albums, the best one is *Spanner*, with Jah Wobble. When you consider that Eno's real money-making career is in the field of production (Talking Heads, Devo, U2, Russian progressive-rock group

Zvuki Mu, David Bowie, Terry Riley, and many more), perhaps what he really discovered—before the remix track and album became an everyday occurrence—is the "treatment."

Of course, let us not forget Eno's brilliant clarinet work with the Portsmouth Symphonia!

One of the things I most like about Brian Eno is that, in his work, and in the way he operates as an artist, there is always an attempt to forge connections to the larger culture. This is not an easy thing to do, these days, despite all of the opportunities for communication—and perhaps it takes a "non-musician" to forge connections beyond music, to the other arts, philosophy, technology, and politics. To me, some of the most exciting times in the arts have been when there have been broad movements—when one feels that there are connections between Einstein, Wittgenstein, and Gertrude Stein, for example. These days, artists are often ensconced in one scene or another, the worst examples of which are found in academic visual arts and music, where the last thing that many of the artists and musicians want to get near is an idea, and they probably wouldn't know an idea if it bit them on the proverbial backside. Eno's academic training was in the visual arts, and in more recent years he has done a good bit of work in that field, specifically in the genre of the installation. Beyond this, he is a reader, a discussant, a thinker. He says interesting things in interviews, even if they are not always things that one such as myself would agree with. There are some out there who want to beat up on Eno a bit, since, after all, he's been at this stuff for around thirty years now. That's too easy. Instead, I want to thank Brian Eno for his major role in making it clear that rock music can also be about ideas.

The transition to post-rock

In the 1970s rock music came of age—for better or worse. One might argue that this new "maturity" leaves rock with a basic problem, because much of the great rock music of the fifties and sixties comes from the adolescent experience, where one is not yet expected to be "all grown up." A good many rock music critics cling to this time, though it does not take much to show why that is a bad idea. This is not so much a matter of turning our backs on the best music of the first generations—there is no reason to do that—but instead a question of not wanting rock to become a museum culture, and feeling that rock still has a good deal to give. The culture industry has come up with at least four normalizing responses to the developments in rock after the 1960s.

The first of these was the emergence of so-called "adult-oriented rock" in the mid-1970s. The idea here was to say that, yes, rock music has matured, and that means setting aside whatever rebellious impulses you had coming out of the sixties. By and by,

"AOR" was primarily aimed at the new class of yuppies. What was said, repeatedly, was that this class had now come to a new political realism and was ready to get back to work. As so often is the case, the group that this music was aimed at were people who for the most part had never been Yippies or sixties radicals (extra points if you know what "Yippie" was the acronym for), but instead what we used to call the "good do-bees." (Obviously, if all of the people who became yuppies had really been out there with Abbie Hoffman, then the sixties might have turned out differently.) AOR might be called the music of political stultification and quietism—the "big chill." If I had to pick the ultimate musical document of AOR/yuppie rock, it would probably be the 1977 album by Fleetwood Mac, *Rumours*.

Secondly, toward the end of the seventies, record companies stopped funding musical experimentation. (Significantly, these companies continued to fund all other sorts of rock star excess, at least for some time—someone to take all of the brown M&Ms out of the bowl for Van Halen or whatnot.) You might say that the record companies—which at that point were beginning the process of merging into giant media conglomerates—viewed rock musicians, whether of the experimental sort or not, as having been too long without adult supervision. "Growing up" means finally bringing rock music under the control of business people and accountants, with key roles played also by lawyers and, in the music-making process itself, the people in "artists and repertoire," the notorious "A&R men." Coming to grips with this assertion of control is instructive. The adventurous music of the preceding period actually made plenty of money for the record companies—so why did they seek to kill that goose? The answer is that, adventurous music is by its nature unpredictable, and capitalism, especially in the form of capitalist corporations, seeks to plan its ventures. This means normalizing "product." (I always find it amusing when some enthusiast of the existing state-corporate order claims that economic planning does not work. If you were to make a list of the largest economies in the world, gigantic corporations begin to enter that list in the latter half of the top ten, and appear regularly thereafter. Would anyone like to argue that these corporations, which have larger economies than most countries, do not *plan?*) At this point rock music becomes even more assimilated to the culture of advertising—what is "revolutionary" and "new" is how the music is promoted. In order to know whom to promote the music to, it becomes necessary to minimize any real originality. Hype and celebrity begin to play a very large role. Well, weren't these elements present in the scene around the Beatles or the Rolling Stones? Yes, but with this difference: the Beatles and Stones were actually talented—there was some musical reason for all of the excitement in the midst of the manias. There comes a point in the 1970s where the promotion of certain artists was *pure* hype, even in the case where there might have been some actual talent buried underneath. The obvious representative document of this phenomenon is the 1975 album, *Frampton Comes Alive*, which used ecstatic, dubbed-in applause to create the impression that people were going nuts over some quite mediocre songs. Soon enough, people were indeed crazy for Peter Frampton. Since that time, although there are talented people in the mainstream of rock, and although rock music since its earliest roots was connected with a recording "industry," the integration of hype and rock music-making has become progressively more complete. The emergence of the media and entertainment megacorporations has regularized this hype further through the integration of the music, television, and film industries.

A specific way in which A&R has shaped rock music is the reassertion of what I earlier called "blues orthodoxy." As the first form of rock music that fully broke with this orthodoxy, progressive rock bears further examination. Indeed, it might be said that it was first of all to bring the experiments of the more interesting progressive rock groups to heel that was the driving aesthetic impulse behind the new, "adult" imperatives. Notice here, also, progressive rock's own claim to "adult" status—we can mark, then, the middle 1970s as a time when there opened up a bifurcation regarding what it meant for rock music to come of age.

Thirdly, an important, particular mechanism of the normalization of rock has been the rendering of the radio dial into a series of niches. The two niches that have the most to do with making rock music into a museum culture are "oldies" and "classic rock" stations. When it comes to rock music, most cities or towns of any size have either three or four options: the two aforementioned categories, "today's hits," and, in the case of some cities with universities, "college radio." These latter are the main source of experimental rock music on the airwaves in the United States. (*The Wire* provides "playlists from the outer limits of planet sound" on p. 65 each month, and these cover stations in the U.S.—WNUR, the excellent station at Northwestern University, is often included— as well as stations in the British Isles, continental Europe, Australia, New Zealand, and elsewhere.) The distinction between "oldies" and "classic rock" is weird—somehow, under the latter, schlock-rock bands such as Journey or Foreigner are "classic," while Chuck Berry is not. I could easily imagine a *great* classic rock station that plays the best of rock music from its earliest days until, say, Bruce Springsteen in the seventies, but I have yet to hear it. Meanwhile, the oldies stations tend to lean toward the silly stuff— the idea being that this is "fun" rock music, before it got so "serious," either musically or socially. Serious music, of course, is for poindexters and eggheads and street radicals—and here avant rock is seen in the same light as jazz and classical music. Fun rock is, instead, something in the background, and something to remind one of formative experiences in life. It would be presumptuous to say that the latter is such a bad thing, really, and most everyone has their set of songs that have become significant for them because of an association with particular personal experiences. But, clearly, a rock music that has become mostly backward looking cannot remain an aesthetic or social force. Increasingly, "today's hits" reflects this situation, in the form of gushy sentimentality, purely formulaic songwriting, or thinly veiled and uninteresting plagiarism of hooks that worked before (as opposed to the interesting forms of plagiarism one hears in, for example, Beck).

Another way to come at this point has to do with the post-sixties *generational* orientation of niche marketing. This is the fourth strategy of normalization. The strategy works in two ways, ways that may at first seem in contradiction with each other. The point can be put provocatively with a pair of examples. On the one hand, we have generations coming to rock music who were born after the Sex Pistols broke up. Niche marketing has effectively destroyed, for the most part even if not yet absolutely, the sense that rock music has a trajectory, a dialectic, a dynamic—that it can develop and grow and go in new directions (which means having an idea of what the earlier directions were). In this context, it does not matter if Cream was already doing a million times better twenty-five years ago what the Spin Doctors are doing now, because the key consideration is that the Spin Doctors are "my" band, of "my generation," now. So, significantly, what began to open up in the seventies was a scene where rock music became a more universal culture but where particular niches within it were tied to generations. On the other hand, to the extent that some music is promoted more universally, much of this is the more juvenile and insipid stuff. The example I have in mind is the Spice Girls. I don't really have a problem with a phenomenon such as the Spice Girls, insomuch as this is basically music for young girls, somewhere in the range of ages nine to fourteen. (And clearly there are worse things in the world than "girl power.") The Spice Girls and Hanson and the Backstreet Boys are fine for this age group, just as Barney the Dinosaur is fine for two- and three-year olds, and the Teletubbies are great for the age one-and-a-half set. But adults don't stay up late to see the Teletubbies on *Saturday Night Live*, and it is hard for me to see why the Spice Girls or Backstreet Boys are on there, either. Now, is this merely old-fogeyism, "in my day we had the Beatles and Jimi Hendrix"-ism? Perhaps. Certainly, we had our silly stuff in the late sixties, too, and not all of the music in the contemporary rock mainstream is by any means bad or insipid. Some of it is even very good, and it remains a strength of rock music that it does not have, on the whole, the sort of Leonard Bernstein/John Cage dichotomy that one sees in the classical scene. Neither is mere snobbism very helpful when it comes to real creativity—and elitism and cliquishness are contrary to the spirit of rock in any case. But what has changed, and this is not something that primarily has to do with the people who make up these generations themselves, is that, by the end of the late sixties, adventurousness and originality in rock music was something of the norm, even demanded by people, whereas the post-seventies dynamic has been toward the marginalization of avant-garde trends.

For the avant-garde to be marginalized and underground is, of course, the historical norm. Indeed, the late 1960s and early 1970s was a time unique in history. I realize that I have said this repeatedly, but I think it bears repetition, and, even more, understanding and study: the "sixties" (in the political and cultural sense) was a time when the marginal, radical, and avant-garde came very close to being the mainstream. Avant rock is music that has this period as one of its aspects, one of its continuing formative inspirations, and yet that is also at least part of the way back to where avant-gardes have generally found themselves, in the smaller spaces rather than the arenas. We might return to a broader and better definition of "classic rock," one that includes the best music from Chuck Berry or thereabouts to Springsteen or REM. In this period, from the early or middle 1950s to the middle or later 1970s, more adventurous groups were not for the most part "set aside" from the more "mainstream" groups, for the simple reason that the overall climate of social upheaval and rebellion made it possible for experimentation to be *cool*—and not in the more jaded sense in which the term has been more recently used. At the height of this period, experimentation was everywhere and seemed to be the dominant trend. Most avant rock today still has one foot in this period, in the sense of taking inspiration from it or working out of its ideas and energies, or even by attempting to negate or escape the classic period. But there would be nothing avant-garde about more recent experimental rock if it did not also have one foot somewhere else, and it is this attempt to go beyond the classic period that makes this music "post-rock."

What we find if we try to actually define avant rock is two sorts of things. There is a historical relationship to the dynamic just described. And there is, in the matter of form, and sometimes in the matter of content, a series of gradations from, to put it simply if crudely, the far out, the further out, the really far out, to the extremely far out. I do not believe there is a determinable point where something simply becomes "beyond the pale" of what might be considered art, at least in a pre-defined sort of way, but there may be a point where avant-garde experiments in rock music are no longer "rock." Everything discussed in the previous sections in this part remains clearly within the bounds of rock, I think, except perhaps for some of the work of the "bookends" to that narrative, Yoko Ono and Brian Eno. Even there, the work either "comes out of" or has some historical intersection with rock. In the rest of Part 2, in addition to dealing with more recent figures, I deal with some figures who, though they have spent considerable time and effort on the borderlands of rock, clearly cross into other territories as well. Often, however, these territories are undefined, they are new or they are places where the lines drawn on earlier maps are under dispute. In some sense I am claiming these territories for rock; the reason is the sensibility with which these new explorations have been undertaken. Definitions here, ultimately, are a matter of what Wittgenstein called "family resemblance."

1987
Game Theory, *Lolita Nation* (Enigma LP).

1988
Game Theory, *Two Steps from the Middle Ages* (Enigma LP).

1989
Rhys Chatham, *Die Donnergotter* (Homestead LP).
Steve Reich, *Different Trains/Electric Counterpoint* (Nonesuch CD).

1991
Jonas Hellborg, *The Word* (Axiom CD).
Slint, *Spiderland* (Touch and Go CD).

1992
Kronos Quartet, *Pieces of Africa* (Elektra Nonesuch CD).
Zoviet France, *Collusion* (The Grey Area CD).

Game Theory's Scott Miller is a very good songwriter, and the band entered a period of prodigious output (*Lolita Nation* is a double LP). The music is witty and funny, with titles such as "All clockwork and no bodily fluids makes Hal a dull metal Humbert." (Humbert Humbert was the licentious professor in Nabokov's *Lolita*, while HAL 9000 was the computer in Kubrick's *2001: A Space Odyssey*. What connects them? Humbert and HAL both play chess—and, in "real life," Vladimir Nabokov and Stanley Kubrick were bona fide chess nuts.) The first song on *Lolita Nation* is titled, "Kenneth—What's the frequency?" Didn't this turn up a few years later as a song by R.E.M.? And wasn't the occasion of that song the accosting on the street of CBS anchorman Dan Rather, by someone who said, repeatedly, "Kenneth, what's the frequency?" Who was that man, and what strange chess game was he playing?

Slint is often associated with a trend called "math rock," which sounds like the reemergence of progressive rock. There are some similarities, but they occur in a world where punk had happened and couldn't be made to un-happen. Like many artists and musicians from towns such as Louisville, Kentucky, or Cleveland, Ohio, at least a couple members of Slint made their way to Chicago, and guitarist David Pajo became a member of Tortoise. Part of the importance of *Spiderland* is that it gave permission to musicians who were in their teens or twenties in the early 1990s to think again about making more complex music.

Rhys Chatham was another composer who experimented with orchestras of loud, electric guitars. Kronos expanded their world music outreach, and Steve Reich wrote a piece for Kronos and also for guitarist Pat Metheny, "Electric Counterpoint." Jonas

Hellborg is a bass guitarist whom many rock musicians do not know about—but they should. *The Word* has some very nice writing on it, but even better is the playing and instrumentation: in addition to Hellborg on acoustic bass guitar, Tony Williams plays drums, and the group is filled out by a string quartet. A "power trio" with string quartet instead of electric guitar seems like a very cool idea to me, and it works well. Zoviet France represents well the emerging trend of those who bear some relationship to rock music, even though they are not playing standard rock instruments, and even if the music is beyond classification. One might say that it is "electronic" music but by 1980, at least, this label really did little to explain anything. In any case, it is unclear where many of the sounds come from. They are a true example of a group of people who came out of rock but who are more in the territory of John Cage.

Symphonies of hellacious electric guitars: Glenn Branca

As reported by Alec Foege in his book on Sonic Youth, the New York "No Wave" art rock scene was composed of people who, while inspired by the raucous energy and intensity of punk, were less impressed by what punk amounted to as a way of making music. Indeed, the initial impression of punk was, as Lydia Lunch put it, "Chuck Berry on speed." This group, which includes the aforementioned as well as Glenn Branca, in some sense wanted to combine two things that may or may not go together: the intensity that comes from the best of punk's in-the-moment/in-your-face anti-aesthetic, and a largeness of musical project. And what could be more symbolic of the idea of the "project," with all of the appropriate Sartrean resonances, than to write symphonies? In Jean-Paul Sartre's philosophy, to be human is to have a project, which in turn is to have a future—to *pro-ject* oneself. The symphony stands with the novel as the archetypal form of the project in modernity, because it generates an extended narrative. The Beach Boys with *Pet Sounds*, the Pretty Things with *S.F. Sorrow*, The Who with *Tommy*, and others wrote their "teenage symphonies to God" (to borrow an album title from the group Velvet Crush), expressions of this epic sensibility that seems to repeatedly return in surprising places. Whether there came a moment when rock musicians, say in the form of *Sgt. Pepper's*, *Quadrophenia*, or Yes's *Tales from Topographic Oceans*, transcended adolescent rock or rock's adolescence is a debate that will most likely continue forever. When punk made its contribution, however, it seemed as though noise and fragmentation had finally triumphed over narrative, at least in the larger sense.

Glenn Branca started off in music as one of those people in the New York scene that Greil Marcus finds annoying—someone really just using music as a vehicle toward becoming something else, an actor, performance artist, painter, or all-round character and celebrity. That tendency, since the days of Andy Warhol's association with the Velvet Underground, looms large in that city. Coming from a background in experimental theater in Boston, Branca moved to New York City in 1976 and formed a band that eventually became the Theoretical Girls. Over the next four years, Branca experimented with ways to make the electric guitar more noisy and uncontrollable, all the while *composing* for this wildness. Among his innovations are dissonant tunings, the replacement of standard guitar strings with various kinds of wire, the construction of crude guitars—really just wooden planks with frets and pickups—that allowed for nonstandard fret placement, and, of course, the use of very loud amplifiers and outrageous levels of feedback. What Jimi Hendrix sometimes did with one guitar, Branca would do with six or more guitars, ultimately creating his Guitar Army. This group included, at one point, Lee Renaldo and Thurston Moore, who later formed Sonic Youth. (In fact, Renaldo and Moore piggybacked a Sonic Youth tour onto a tour by the Guitar Army, and this led to a falling out with Branca.) If you take the larger ensemble sound of Branca's guitar orchestra, streamline it, and focus more on songwriting, you would be following the formula for creating Sonic Youth. (There is more to Sonic Youth than this, of course, and we will soon come to that.) But first there were some symphonies to be played.

Experimental rock, has ambivalent feelings about the electric guitar. For one thing, the electric guitar is the central instrument in rock music, it's the *axe*, it is the instrument that makes the statement that is rock. To be experimental then, one might want to get far away from this instrument. For another thing, there is obviously a strong element of machismo involved in a good deal of classic rock axe-wielding. As with everything in this book, ten other lists can be given for any of the lists presented here, so it is most likely that a more guitar-heavy list of the precursors to more recent avant rock can be generated. To be sure, ambivalence about the electric guitar shaped the choices I made in this part, though there is a section devoted to Hendrix and a good many other important guitarists are included as well. But even such an outstanding practitioner of the instrument as Steve Howe—who is as good as anyone who ever played the instrument, in any genre—did not make the music of his group guitar-oriented. Progressive rock, which also tended to downplay or even contravene the macho tendencies of the rest of rock, produced players who were musicians first and guitarists second. What is interesting is how the guitar has made something of a comeback in more recent experimental rock. Again, this may have to do with the historical contingency of who did what and when they did it. However, I do not think there is any denying the role played by Sonic Youth in the post-seventies scene, and the electric guitar is integral to not only their sound but even to their ethos. Lee Renaldo and Thurston Moore had their own ideas about the guitar before hooking up with Glenn Branca, but, on the other hand, something crystallized around Branca that set the stage for Sonic Youth.

Punk and the DIY aesthetic played an important part, as well. Although I reject the idea that punk was mainly a reaction to progressive rock—instead both were reflections of their times—still, there was justifiably a reaction in the later seventies to the banks of keyboards that were associated with musicians such as Rick Wakeman and Keith Emerson. These keyboards more and more seemed set against the spirit of rock on several levels: they cost a lot of money, a good deal of time was necessary to learn how to play them, one of their main roles in the music was to generate some sort of ersatz orchestra, they displaced the central position of the guitar, and they took up a lot of room on stage. A guy such as Rick Wakeman, brooding onstage behind his nineteen keyboards, having his picture taken on the lawn behind his castle or with his fleet of Rolls Royces, is a bit much—and comes across as rather medieval. In the pre-digital age, synthesizers in rock at least had the virtue that one never quite knew what would come out of them. As digital, polyphonic instruments became widely available, especially with their cheesy pre-set voices, yet another element of wildness went out of rock. Punk recovered this wildness, and Branca and then Sonic Youth set about integrating it into larger visions—with co-thinkers such as Hüsker Dü and the later Black Flag also taking punk into a new expansiveness.

One might even see a dialectic in post-seventies avant rock that has to do with the guitar, for there seems to be almost a bifurcation between groups that really feature the instrument, such as Sonic Youth or King Crimson or Fushitsusha (the extraordinarily intense Japanese trio with Keiji Haino), and those groups or artists who run the gambit from downplaying the guitar (Stereolab would be in that camp), not having a guitar player (for example, the Painkiller trio with Bill Laswell, John Zorn, and Mick Harris—though Keiji Haino appears on some of their recordings; Björk's solo recordings also tend to not feature guitar), to not having any of the instruments typically associated with rock music at all (much electronica and turntable music). A group such as Big Audio Dynamite, formed by ex-Clash member Mick Jones, did a nice job of bridging this gap, and effectively combined punkish guitar and hip-hop. There may be still more to be done in this vein, though this means continuing to recognize the centrality of the electric guitar to rock. In any case, in a 1996 interview where he was asked about the future of rock guitar, Branca commented,

> This may sound inconceivable, but I think the potential of the guitar is almost untouched. Sonic Youth has been revolutionary in terms of what it does in rock with guitar tunings, but they still haven't touched on microtonality, really writing carefully worked-out pieces based on microtonality. And I think that's too bad, because rock guitar seems to have stopped completely with Nirvana. . . . (H. P. Newquist, "Glenn Branca: The Devil's Choirmaster," p. 51)

Well, that may be overstating the case a bit, or it may be that things have opened up more in the time since that interview (Sonic Youth's amusingly titled "Musical Perspectives" series on their own SYR label bears examination on this point, and several others), but clearly Branca's own music makes a case for the relevance of the electric guitar to avant-garde music-making.

One other thing about Branca's approach was hard to take, initially. In the 1970s it became almost an orthodoxy to see the displacement of the electric guitar (at least as the central instrument) as key to going beyond rock'n'roll and toward experimental rock. To have more than one guitar in a band was seen as going back toward the Rolling Stones/blues-rock side of the Beatles/Stones dichotomy of the late sixties. What was even worse was to have "lead" and "rhythm" guitarists, which was simply taken as a sign of poor musicianship. Perhaps a group might use electric and acoustic instruments to create more colors, but this was generally done in a way that did not foreground the guitar per se. What struck many of us in the early and middle seventies as especially retrograde was to have *three* guitar players in your band, as some of the Southern rock groups did—this just seemed to have to do with the laziness of warmer climes or drinking problems or drinking buddies who played guitar. And, in fact, some of those "several- guitar" bands did look pretty lazy—I recall a TV performance by the Eagles in about 1976 or so, where they were set up in some sort of ranch or corral scene, sitting on covered wagons and haystacks and gnarly wooden fences, with each player contributing a note or two every now and then and the whole band pretty much nodding off. Nowadays I feel a little more kindly to some of the Southern rock bands—mainly Lynyrd Skynyrd (I always liked the Allman Brothers Band, and what they did with two guitars was more akin to Trane and Pharaoh). In the late seventies, however, whether one came out of the progressive scene (or Frank Zappa's music), where the guitar was expected to play a musical part that downplayed its more "guitar-rock" aspects, or whether one came out of punk, where the guitar made something of a comeback, but again not in a way that "featured" it (no long solos or other pyrotechnics), it seemed bizarre that not only would one bring the guitar back to the center of experimental rock music, but, indeed, assemble a whole orchestra of very loud, obnoxious electric guitars. When Branca does it, the result is the diametrical opposite of heavenly. *Götterdämmerung*—twilight of the gods—doesn't do it justice: bloody massacre of the gods is more like it.

● **Glenn Branca**

  The Ascension (99 Records LP, 1981).
  Symphony No.5: Describing Planes of an Expanding Hypersphere (Atavistic CD, 1996).
  Symphony No.6: Devil Choirs at the Gates of Heaven (Blast First LP, 1989).

Symphony Nos.8 and 10 (The Mysteries) (Blast First CD, 1994).
Symphony No.9: L'eve future; Polish Radio National Symphony, conducted by
    Christian von Borries (Point Music CD, 1995).
Selections from the Symphonies (Atavistic CD, 1997).

1993
Einsturzende Neubauten, *Tabula Rasa* (Mute CD).
The Loud Family, *Plants and Birds and Rocks and Things* (Alias Records CD).
Robert Wyatt, *mid-eighties* (Gramavision CD).
Frank Zappa, Ensemble Modern, *The Yellow Shark* (Rykodisc CD).

1994
The Best of Eurodisco (Rebound Records CD).
Portishead, *Dummy* (Mercury CD).
Gary Lucas, *Bad Boys of the Arctic* (Enemy CD).
The Red Crayola, *The Red Krayola* (Drag City CD).
The James Blood Ulmer Blues Experience, *Live at the Bayerischer Hof* (In & Out
    Records CD).

Someone must have thought it would be pretty interesting, or at least funny, to
commission Branca to write his Symphony No. 9 for a standard orchestra, with the violins and cellos and such. Number 9 is of course the most significant number for sym-
phonists and *White Album* revolutionists. Branca's 9 is a dark and brooding affair, and
for the most part he did not attempt to translate what happens with the electric guitars
to the classical orchestra. One comparison that comes to mind is the dirge-like second
(and final) movement of Shostakovich's No. 15, his last symphony and final large-scale
statement. Terror, danger, destruction, and yet also a frightening beauty characterize the
music of Einsturzende Neubauten. This is a group that made industrial music for real—
with power tools and other heavy equipment. But they are also people who know how
to play instruments (in the ordinary sense) and sing, and here, with a "blank slate"
before them, they combine both sides of their activity into a very interesting synthesis.
Quite a career these fellows have had for more than twenty years; if only Bakunin and
Bataille could have heard them.

The Yellow Shark is by far one of the more satisfying Frank Zappa recordings, at
least to me, and the reason is the careful reading of the music presented by Ensemble
Modern, which maintains Zappa's whit and whimsy, but doesn't stray into his sillier side.
But then, I really go for those contemporary chamber ensembles, whether it is Arthur
Weisberg's group or a more recent ensemble such as Eighth Blackbird—they are like
the rock groups of classical music, and a band such as the *Lark's Tongues* edition of
King Crimson are something like the correlate on the other side. Ensemble Modern
plays Zappa is a nice meeting place of the two sides.

Loud Family was Scott Miller's project after Game Theory. Gary Lucas was one of several innovative guitarists who participated in Captain Beefheart's Magic Band (or endured membership, as the case may be). Lucas has some worthwhile ideas of his own, and more recently he has done some recording as part of the Jewish Alternative Movement (see the Laswell/Zorn section). Robert Wyatt's *mid-eighties* collects two LPs worth of simple recordings made with a Casio keyboard and a basic drum machine. (One of my favorite films, John Sales's *The Brother from Another Planet*, has a fun little scene where a street vendor is selling these keyboards: "Step up and play a Casio! Anyone can be a musician!") Among the gems on the album is a version of Charlie Hayden's tune, "Chairman Mao," with lyrics by Wyatt.

I used to know someone (a philosophy graduate student) who claimed that the Beatles stole all of their later ideas from the Red Crayola. The group, which started in Austin and made its way to New York, London, and Dusseldorf—or at least core member Mayo Thompson did—teamed up with some of the Chicago avant-rockers for the 1994 album listed here. Portishead's great trick is to use turntables in "both" directions, so to speak: the undercurrent of scratchy-vinyl crackle invokes the 1940s (especially that of postwar England), while other forms of scratching add a hip-hop element. They have a good singer, too.

Sonic truth

Sonic Youth can be pretentious, they can be embarrassing, and yet for all the corn in their music it's never merely corny. Cliches are almost always present, and so is the sense that whatever is set before you can blow up at any time. Corn is not unstable; Sonic Youth's music is.

—Greil Marcus, *Artforum*, Summer 1986

Alex Foege writes in his 1994 book about Sonic Youth, *Confusion is Next*: "Rock music has changed an awful lot in the last decade and a half—for one, it seems a lot closer to an immanent [sic] wane. Never again will sounds emerging from an electric guitar provoke terror" (pp. 8–9). Now, I don't know that I follow this, exactly, because a big part of Foege's overall argument is that Sonic Youth rescued rock music by making the electric guitar interesting again. But leaving aside the "imminent wane" issue, perhaps there is something to the idea that Sonic Youth made the electric guitar a force again, and then they made it a spent force for once and all. Is terror what it's all about, though? Greil Marcus concludes another of his *Artforum* pieces (where he had also mentioned Sonic Youth) with the claim that "[w]hen rock'n'roll no longer produces a version of itself worth banning, none of it will be worth listening to" (in *Ranters and Crowd Pleasers*, p. 362). We might as well throw in Laurie Anderson's famous statement about terrorists being the true artists now, because they are the only ones who can still surprise us. On some level I sympathize with these sorts of claims, in the sense that they say something about music in a time of cultural exhaustion. But, on another level, these prescriptions and formulas seem to come down to the idea that rock music can only stay alive as long as it finds a way to always make itself louder, louder, and louder. At the end of that road is also exhaustion, and given that it is a road where each segment, after awhile, is only quantitatively more and never qualitatively different from the last—well, we are already at the end of that road; we already know what happens when you turn the amps up to eleven. So, fortunately, Sonic Youth found other, different things to do, even while developing their language of chaos and contingency, of imminent explosion.

In this connection, it is interesting to note that two of Sonic Youth's members, Thurston Moore and Kim Gordon, are the children of academics, in philosophy and sociology, respectively. (Moore's father, who was also a pianist and composer, died of a brain tumor in 1976, when Thurston was a senior in high school.) Sometimes there is a bit of the "preacher's kid" attitude in the children of professors—a rebellion against the sometimes prissy and very middle-class world of the university, but a rebellion that eventually has to come to terms with the fact that such kids have been exposed to worlds of culture that others haven't had the opportunity to experience. Whatever connection the Sonic Youths may have had to punk rock, and bands such as the Ramones therefore, has been worked through many other influences. In fact, if you consider the years of birth of the three original Sonics—Kim Gordon in 1953, Lee Ranaldo in 1956, and Thurston Moore in 1958—you can readily see that punk would come to them as an "influence," rather than as something that came of age about the same time they did. It's interesting and funny to look at what some of the earlier, pre-punk influences were—as witness, for example, this vignette about Thurston Moore.

> In high school, Moore's favorite rock star was Alice Cooper, an allegiance that didn't exactly win the rangy teen many friends. His classmates were primarily interested in the popular British supergroups of the day: Yes, Pink Floyd, and Emerson, Lake and Palmer. "I remember sitting in the cafeteria and those kids came around to me, the music kids, the Yes fans," he recalls. "They sort of wanted to find out where I was coming from, and I could tell that's what they were up to." They had seen Thurston wandering around the school halls with tattered issues of *Cream* magazine under his arm. So, they wondered, was Thurston into Flash, the new Yes spinoff group?" (Foege, pp. 51–52)

That Flash would get a mention in a narrative about Sonic Youth is hilarious, at least to a Yes fan like me. Moore's response to the prog-heads was that he was more into "theater rock" (Foege, p. 52). I'm not sure that, in the early and middle 1970s, the distinction among different kinds of creative rock music had opened up so fully—teenagers who listened to Yes and King Crimson might also have listened to Alice Cooper and David Bowie and Black Sabbath. Alice Cooper may have become something of a cartoon later on, but the band did something to attract the interest of Frank Zappa in 1969 (he signed them to his Straight label), and albums such as *Killer* (1971) added to the range of expression available in rock music at that time. Indeed, Alice Cooper was a forerunner not only of eighties Goth groups, but also of the Goth side of Sonic Youth, as heard in songs such as "Death Valley '69" and "Expressway to Yr Skull."

Amusingly, the Sonics would go on to create a three-part, epic-length work with the title, "Trilogy." Even if by parody, there seems to be some connection to the Emerson, Lake and Palmer album of the same name. "Trilogy" is from 1988's *Daydream Nation*, itself a two-LP epic album. In the Japanese duo The Ruins, we will see the third stage of the dialectic, equal parts progressive rock and Sonic Youth. We might even say that the current (*construKction of light*) version of King Crimson has elements of Sonic Youth but with more *precise*—shall we say—musicianship, and here's the rub. If you want to really do ELP-style *Trilogy*, you have to have a certain facility with your instruments. The secret of Sonic Youth, or one of them, anyway, is that they find themselves caught in a triangle, the three-sides of which are: Velvet Underground-like orientation toward noise and the refusal of technique, a striving toward epic and even profound vision—at least some of the time, and perhaps much more influenced by the scope of a work such as *Kaddish* or *Howl* by Allen Ginsberg than by progressive rock, and, finally, *longevity*. By this last I mean our old friend, the question of what to do when you hope for the band to be an ongoing concern, even if it has punk roots and attitude. What we have to say about Sonic Youth in the end is that it is all there: Neil Young, punk, progressive, John Cage, Cecil Taylor, and much more, but still the influence of the Velvet Underground remains overriding.

There is an additional element that ought to be noted, namely the feminist element that Kim Gordon brings to the band. Please do not misunderstand, it isn't simply that she is a female member of a major band. Lots of bands have female members (though more and more thanks to women who play instruments in bands, such as Gordon and Tina Weymouth with Talking Heads). Gordon's contribution is significant, first, because she is an equal member in a rock band. Second, Gordon has written many songs with feminist themes, for example "Tunic (Song for Karen)," "Kool Thing," and "Swimsuit Issue." Third, and most intriguing, when Gordon sings, she is willing to explore, as Foege puts it, "non-melodic vocal timbres." Doing this, Foege writes, is "nothing new for men . . . , but previous to Kim Gordon, women in rock were more likely to find a vocal style and stick with it than to play with the different, dark personas implied by shifting deliveries" (p. 226). Another way to put this is that there is tremendous pressure on women singers in rock to sound (and look, of course) "pretty," and Gordon instead sings in a way that is unsettling. Finally, especially in the period of *Dirty* and

Experimental Jet Set (1992–1994), Gordon gave many interviews where she talked about misogyny and sexism, and she became something of a feminist icon for teenagers and young women especially.

One of the lovely things about Sonic Youth is that, as much as there were gems in the first ten years of the band's existence, the second decade has been even more interesting—there are not many musicians in rock about whom this can be said. One of the strangest things about Sonic Youth, which must come from the combination of punk and "art" sources (both the background in arts that Kim Gordon and Lee Ranaldo had in college, as well as that New York Art Scene thing), is the way that carelessness (again, nonchalance) and integrity coexist in the music, thus the unevenness of the early albums, and even an album or two that were outright duds. But some of what sounds like carelessness comes from the group's willingness to experiment with extreme contingency—not just through jamming, but through the use of a huge array of different guitars (often cheap electrics that have been—ahem—*modified*, or, to put it more colloquially, heavily messed up), and through extremely dissonant, and often unrepeatable, tunings. Besides their desire to move forward, this is another reason that Sonic Youth rarely (now, in fact, never) revisit old material—"we [would] have to relearn our songs, and the songs are really unorthodox. They're in different guitar tunings, we use weird guitars . . . which guitar was I using? What the hell notes are those?" (Thurston Moore, in Steve Appleford, "Come on, feel the noise," *Option*, March/April 1998). Probably all of this could be digitized now, so that Ranaldo, Moore, and Gordon could just use one guitar each and input some data that would give them different sounds. No one who is into rock music can afford to be a purist—it goes against what the form is all about—but I for one am happy that the Sonics have not taken this step, because it would remove something that is really essential to their music: to take care with contingency. In this, perhaps the leading lights of Sonic Youth's work are not to be found in music first of all, but instead poetry and painting. I'm thinking again of Allen Ginsberg, but also Mark Rothko. Some other abstract expressionist once told Rothko that there was more to painting than just choosing the colors. Rothko responded that, no, that was pretty much it. Let the paint do the work—that approach goes just as well with the sound field as with the color field. Then, sometimes one can attempt to build songs in and through these fields—and sometimes they work and sometimes they don't, which can also be said of Ginsberg's cosmic transmissions.

A turning point can be seen in the period from around 1995 to 1997. The band headlined the 1995 Lollapalooza tour; despite having inspired many a lesser "alternative" band, many in the audience stayed for their more popular and easier to listen to favorites, and then left partway through the Sonics' set. My edition of the *Rough Guide to Rock*, published in 1996, even speculates that there might not be any more Sonic Youth albums after *Washing Machine*, as the group seemed mainly involved in side projects. But in that period Sonic Youth did three things that have opened a whole new chapter in their explorations: they set up their own recording studio in Manhattan, they began to issue some of their most experimental recordings on their own SYR label, and they began working with other musicians, especially Jim O'Rourke and (percussionist) William Winant. Indeed, the presence of O'Rourke makes SYR3 the most interesting of the series thus far.

Asked by Biba Kopf in *The Wire* where he sees things going after the spring of 1998, Thurston Moore gives the following, amusing answer:

> Everything's allowed now and those who are enlightened enough know there is no hierarchy here. So what can we do? We just do what we do and it's kind of beautiful, and we owe a debt to free improvisation, which is, like, the bedrock here. But what's going to happen? Who cares? You shouldn't have any anxiety about it. Once I saw a contemporary composer who used to record for Glenn Branca's Neutral label stumbling around the street late at night, and I asked, 'What are you doing?' And he answered, 'I can't sleep, I don't know what is going to happen to 20th century music.' He was just freaked out by this anxiety: where is composition going? And there I was, 18, saying, I don't know, I'm just looking for this girl. I never want to reach that level of anxiety. (May 1998, p. 32)

And yet, a couple of sentences later Moore mentions that he had played with Cecil Taylor the previous year, as well as with Merce Cunningham's dance company, and that, at present, he was working with free-jazz drummer Milford Graves. One gets the impression that these sorts of things for the Sonics are simultaneously heavy and not heavy.

Sonic Youth, *Confusion is Sex* (Geffen CD, 1983).
——, *Evol* (Geffen CD, 1986).
——, *Sister* (Geffen CD, 1987).
——, *Daydream Nation* (Geffen CD, 1988).
——, *The Whitey Album* (Ciccone Youth) (Geffen CD, 1988).
——, *Goo* (Geffen CD, 1990).
——, *Dirty* (Geffen CD, 1992).
——, *Experimental Jet Set, Trash and No Star* (Geffen CD, 1994).
——, *Washing Machine* (Geffen CD, 1995).
——, *SYR1* (Sonic Youth Records CD, 1997).
——, *SYR2* (Sonic Youth Records CD, 1997).
——, with Jim O'Rourke, *SYR3* (Sonic Youth Records, 1997).
——, *Silver Session for Jason Knuth* (SKR CD, 1998).
——, *A Thousand Leaves* (Geffen CD, 1998).
Thurston Moore, *Root* (LO CD, 1998).
Thurston Moore, with Tom Surgal and William Winant, *Piece for Jetsun Dolma* (Victoriaville CD, 1996).

Lydia Lunch, *13:13* (Line Records LP, 1982).
——, *Honeymoon in Red* (Atavistic CD, n.d.).
——, and Clint Ruin, *Stinkfist* (Atavistic CD, 1996).
8 Eyed Spy, *Luncheone* (Atavistic CD, 1997).

Lydia Lunch is a leading figure in the New York "No Wave" scene, which formed part of the background for Sonic Youth. (The main elements of this scene, including the also notable James Chance and the Contortions, are captured on the "No New York" album, compiled by Brian Eno.) Indeed, she was the frontperson for what is considered the cornerstone No Wave group, Teenage Jesus and the Jerks. Lunch, whose real last name is Koch, is prolific as singer, performance artist, and writer (she is the author of several books). She also plays a frightening slide guitar. Teenage Jesus was known for their short, jagged songs, and for manic live sets that would sometimes last as little as ten minutes. Like almost everyone who comes in the wake of the Velvet Underground, Lunch's main inspirations are more literary than musical—especially running the gamut of French writers from Sade and Jean Genet to Georges Bataille and Michel Foucault. Strangely, another writer who caught her attention was the Florida-based Harry Crews. Playing guitar, Lunch formed a power trio with Kim Gordon and professional wrestler Sadie Mae on drums. Their mayhem ("We could have profited from a bit more structure . . .") was captured on the live album, *Naked in Garden Hills*. Lunch describes herself as "obsessed by my obsessions . . . there were certain things based on adrenal overload that I repeatedly sought out as an adrenal junkie" (David Keenan, "I was a teenage Jesus," *The Wire*, July 1998, p. 39). Some of this stuff is harder than Henry Rollins.

1995

Laurie Anderson, *The Ugly One With the Jewels* (Warner Brothers CD).
Peter Blegvad, with John Greaves and Chris Cutler, *Just Woke Up* (Recommended Records CD).
Caveman Hughscore (with Hugh Hopper), *Caveman Hughscore* (Tim Kerr Records CD).
Michael Giles, Jamie Muir, David Cunningham, *Ghost Dance* (Piano CD).
Meridian Arts Ensemble, *Prime Meridian*, works by Frank Zappa, Captain Beefheart, Milton Babbitt and others (Channel Crossings CD).

The "spoken word," incredibly, became a part of alternative music in and through the punk period—with the aforementioned Henry Rollins and Lydia Lunch leading the charge. At a punk gig around 1982 or so, I remember an 18- or 19-year old guy mentioning "spoken word album." I remember thinking, "does this mean the same thing as poetry?" Not exactly. In fact, without the element of performance in the presentation—for example the menacing anger of Henry Rollins—often the words do not stand up very well by themselves. But perhaps that can be said of a few of William Blake's ditties, too! Telling stories to an ethereal or somewhat oddball musical accompaniment has been a major part of Laurie Anderson's stock-in-trade more or less from the start of her public career. *The Ugly One with the Jewels* captures a London concert that consisted primarily of these stories.

Peter Blegvad was a part of the Henry Cow/Slapp Happy agglomeration that created *In Praise of Learning*, a love it or hate it Cow album that is my personal favorite. Blegvad appears as a singer/songwriter, along with the bassist and drummer from Henry Cow. The album closes with a sweet rendition of "Catch a Falling Star." This isn't "out-there" stuff, just very well-done and not overdone music making.

Hugh Hopper is the legendary fuzz-bass player for Soft Machine, and Caveman Hughscore is the Oregon-based transmogrification of a band called Caveman Shoestore, playing Hugh's music. Two bass guitars (one played by longtime Hopper fan and excellent bassist in his own right, Fred Chalenor), accordion, drums, and singing—great combination. There is even a snippet of Hopper's great tune, "Dedicated to you, but you weren't listening" (which was also given a fine reading on a Keith Tippett album of the same title). *Ghost Dance* is a soundtrack for a film that featured a scene with, of all people, Jacques Derrida. Strangely, the album also features liner notes that go off on a ridiculous screed against deconstruction. However, the music is worthwhile and especially noteworthy because two of the great percussionists from two different eras of King Crimson, Michael Giles (*In the Court of the Crimson King* and *In the Wake of Poseidon*) and Jamie Muir (*Larks' Tongues in Aspic*), resurface after some years of absence from public activity. In Muir's case, part of his time away was spent in a Buddhist monastery. Meridian Arts Ensemble, like the Ensemble Modern, bring out the chamber-music potential of Zappa and Beefheart.

The Laswell/Zorn nexus

The amount of musical activity going on around Bill Laswell and John Zorn is staggering, almost as difficult to keep up with as everything that might fit under the umbrella of experimental rock itself. Neither one is exactly a "rock" musician, but nowhere else does the double negative apply so appropriately—not "rock," but not "not-rock," either. Laswell's main instrument is the bass guitar, and his first solo album (1983's *Basslines*) features that instrument, so this alone perhaps brings him closer to rock. Zorn is a reed player, his primary horn being the alto sax; when all is said and done, the temptation is to think of him as a jazz musician. Listening to Painkiller, however, the power trio that Laswell and Zorn formed with drummer Mick Harris, one would think that categories are unimportant in their intense mixture of free jazz and hardcore punk.

But this is not the case. In experimental rock music, the "channeling" of diverse influences takes many forms. In critical circles there can still be found the background assumption that all of the eclectic concatenations being assembled (sometimes thrown together) out there must still be the result of some "natural" or "authentic" affinity for all of these musical forms on the part of the musicians. Why the crossing of social and aesthetic boundaries needs to be a "natural" thing—or why some critics or listeners feel the need to think that such authenticity is possible or desirable—would make for an interesting study in itself. What strikes me about the border crossings that have occurred in the post-Beatles era, however, is that musicians tend to be very self-conscious about them, and I think this is eminently true of Laswell and Zorn. They know where their musical materials are coming from and why they are combining them.

If we were to trace this kind of self-consciousness about musical materials back to anyone in particular in the post-Beatles period, I would propose Brian Eno. (Eno and Laswell worked on several projects together in the early 1980s.) Like Eno, Laswell and Zorn are also no strangers to using the recording studio as an instrument. What distinguishes them most of all is that both are more purely oriented toward music as such. Where Eno works with very general ideas and then tries to find expression for them in music or other artforms, Laswell and Zorn are both players with no shortage of chops. If Eno is more like John Cage (or even, in the earliest incarnations, something like Cage meets sophisticated glam-rock), with not much of John Coltrane or Cecil Taylor, all three of these figures, and Glenn Gould and Miles Davis too, figure into the musical vocabularies of Laswell and Zorn. Then, of course, there is the wider world. I don't know that I accept Laswell's claim that his involvement in world music or in diverse musical cultures is more "authentic" than that of, say Peter Gabriel (Laswell made a comment to this effect in a *Wire* interview from some years ago), but certainly connections are being forged. Albums such as Sola's *Blues in the East* are reminiscent of Japanese pop-rock records from the 1970s, where eclectic borrowings from the West find themselves more side-by-side than mixed up or synthesized. More successful is Zorn's group, Masada, which combines Klezmer and harmolodic (Ornette Coleman) elements, while also remaining quite recognizably a jazz quartet.

Painkiller (John Zorn, Bill Laswell, Mick Harris), *Collected Works* (Tzadik CD, 1997).

Bill Laswell and Laswell projects
——, *Basslines* (Elektra LP, 1983).
——, *Silent Recoil* (Dub System One) (Low CD, n.d.).
——, *panthalassa: the music of miles davis, 1969–1974* (Columbia CD, 1998).
——, *Invisible Design* (Tzadik CD, 1999).
Bill Laswell, Yosuke Yamashita, Ryuichi Sakamoto, *Asian Games* (Verve CD, 1993).
Material, *Live from Soundscape* (DIW Records CD, 1991; concert recorded 1981).

Praxis, *Transmutation* (Mutatis Mutandis) (Axiom CD, 1992).
Arcana (Laswell, Tony Williams, Pharaoh Sanders, et al.), *Arc of the Testimony* (Axiom CD, 1997).
Umar Bin Hassan, *Be Bop or Be Dead* (Axiom CD, 1993).
Nicky Skopelitis, *Ekstasis* (Axiom CD, 1993).
Hakim Bey, *T.A.Z.* (Axiom CD, 1994).
Sola, *Blues in the East* (Axiom CD, 1994).
Material, *Intonarumori* (Axiom CD, 1999).

Painkiller might just as well have been called "Paincauser," so much of their music being on the order of Ozzie Osbourne with a dentist's drill. Let 'er rip, as they say. I have a special fondness for trios that do not include guitar or keyboard, but instead some "single note" instrument such as the saxophone or violin. There is a tradition of these trios in both jazz and rock (more in the former, which means there are still some interesting things left to do in the latter), from Ornette Coleman's trio with David Izenzon (double bass) and Charles Moffett (drums) to the Revolutionary Ensemble, which consisted in Leroy Jenkins on violin, Sirone on double bass, and Jerome Cooper on drums. An especially neat trio album is *Bush Baby*, by alto saxophonist Arthur Blythe, accompanied by Bob Stewart on tuba and Ahkmed Abdullah on conga drum—*one* conga drum. These trios, especially the last, tend toward the austere. In rock the tendency is in the opposite direction—though there are far fewer examples. It is almost as if, even though the "lead" instrument might be a saxophone or a synthesizer, the spirit of Eric Clapton or Jimi Hendrix hovers, and the question is whether this trio can *rock*. The best such trio in rock, in my opinion, was Back Door, especially their first (eponymous) album. They were not much known outside of the U.K., but there they were compared to Cream. The apt comparison for Painkiller might be more on the Experience side, perhaps with a little Led Zeppelin thrown in. Is it "jazz" or "rock"? Well, again, part of the significance of the Zorn and Laswell projects is that, without playing jazz-rock fusion, they render the question fundamentally moot, and ultimately irrelevant.

Bill Laswell has a special place in his heart for dub music, represented here by not only *Silent Recoil*, but also elements of several of the other listings, including the Miles Davis remix project, as well as the Hakim Bey album. Dub presents that rare context that is heavy without being overbearing—indeed, dub tends instead to be ethereal. The effect owes something to the romance of the radio, but Third-World style—and, of course, especially Jamaica. A voice whispers to you at night over the radio, but the reception is bad, and other signals float in and out. It's "mood music," in a way, and yet also subversive—what is the secret message that some understand and others do not get at all?

Far less subtle is the music of Material and Praxis, where thrashpunk and funk come together. What is perhaps most impressive here, as well as in the Arcana project is Laswell's amazing abilities as an impresario—he is able to pull people together from every corner of the globe, and from the great heights of music, whether we are talking about Fred Frith or Herbie Hancock or Tony Williams (Arcana was his last album, I think) or Pharaoh Sanders. But here lies both a blessing and a curse. It's great to get certain people together in a room to make music, especially if these are people who have already made great music on their own. But they still have to deliver the goods. Peter Shapiro, who often has a sharp word in his reviews, writes at the end of his entry for Laswell in the *Rough Guide to Rock:*

> Laswell treats music as pure sound to be manipulated any which way. It's an idea that has the potential to be incredibly exciting. Unfortunately, his music often fails to deliver because the culture mix he conjures up is not an organic one. His music is the product of a brilliant mind which often forsakes the pleasures of the body for exercises of the intellect. (p. 498)

As much as it pains me, I have to agree with this assessment to some extent. The problem is not so much that the mix is not organic—rather Laswell seems to think that the synthesis will simply arise of its own accord if you just throw the right people or elements into the musical blender. This is where a little more exercise of the intellect might help, actually. (Techno types like Shapiro expect the body to dance its way to musical truth if the mind can just be gotten out of the way.) As with Zorn, the discography for Laswell is only a tiny part of an immense oeuvre. It has been argued, convincingly, that both are (somewhat? vastly?) over-recorded at this point. However, there are ultimately two things to be said about Laswell's enterprise. First, while it is true that his many recordings or productions have a hit or miss quality, the hits are really good, if you have the patience to find them. Second, apart from what he has done as a musician or producer, it is Laswell's *role* in music that stands out—he is someone who opens doors.

Ironically, then, the most satisfying of recent Laswell albums for me has been *Invisible Design*, which he made for Zorn's Tzadik label. Made primarily with bass guitar and electric upright bass (sometimes multitracked), and occasionally little percussion instruments (Pharaoh Sanders plays bells on one track), this is a quiet album that is something like what you would get if you did some dub on dub, about four times removed. There are little musical references here and there, my favorite of which is from Charlie Hayden's "Song for Che." *Invisible Design* just has a nice, stand alone quality to it, and I hope that Laswell pursues this direction further.

John Zorn, *Elegy* (Tzadik CD, 1992).
———, *Kristallnacht* (Tzadik CD, 1992).
———, *Angelus Novus* (Tzadik CD, 1993).
———, *Duras: Duchamp* (Tzadik CD, 1997).

————, *Aporias* (Tzadik CD, 1998).
————, *The String Quartets* (Tzadik CD, 1999).

Masada, *Live in Jerusalem 1994* (Tzadik CD, 1999).

This smattering from Zorn's immense catalogue is mainly representative of his work as a "classical composer," in settings ranging from string quartet and other chamber ensembles to orchestra. Not a great deal has been written about this side of Zorn's multifaceted work, beyond short reviews. For present purposes the point is simply the amazing breadth of Zorn's project, which he has increasingly associated with Jewish themes (seen here, for example, in *Kristallnacht* and *Angelus Novus*; the latter is a famous painting by Paul Klee which inspired some famous lines from Walter Benjamin, lines that acquired a qualitatively more ominous meaning after the Holocaust). Perhaps the most persistent quality of Zorn's notated music (yes, "that particular theory") is its contrast of harshness and humor. In this respect, one of his more satisfying works here is "69 paroxysms for Marcel Duchamp." The instrumentation for this piece—violin, cello, and percussion—reminds one that, even in his "classical" guise, Zorn is one of those musicians who transmutes everything—so that here we have a bit of a rock band as avant chamber ensemble, or perhaps vice-versa. These "paroxysms" come awfully quick—sixty-nine of them in a little over thirteen minutes (that's an average of one paroxysm per every eleven or twelve seconds, folks!). Duchamp is a good subject for Zorn—the former was a great chess player, and the latter has composed works using not only chance operations, á la John Cage, but also game theory. *Elegy* and *Kristallnacht* feature groups that are more like rock ensembles, using turntables on the former and electric guitar and keyboards on the latter, thereby showing once again the limitations of received categories.

Masada, the jazz quartet with Dave Douglas on trumpet, and what is now regarded as one of the best rhythm sections in jazz, Greg Cohen on bass and Joey Baron on drums, is captured to stunning effect at a 1994 concert in Jerusalem. This was, in fact, the group's first visit to Israel, and the intensity of Jewish jazz meets Jewish nation is palpable. A question: does the power of the music transcend the political questions that such a meeting raises?

Radical Jewish Culture/Jewish Alternative Movement

New Klezmer Trio, *Melt Zonk Rewire* (Tzadik CD, 1995).
Uri Caine/Gustav Mahler, *Primal Light* (Winter and Winter CD, 1997).
Hasidic New Wave, *Jews and the Abstract Truth* (Knitting Factory Works CD, 1997).
————, *Psycho-Semitic* (Tzadik CD, 1998).
Jewish Alternative Movement, *A Guide for the Perplexed* (Knitting Factory CD, 1998).

Naftule's Dream, *Smash, Clap!* (Tzadik CD, 1998).
Jewish Alternative Movement, *Knitting on the Roof* (Knitting Factory Works CD, 1999).
The Uri Caine Ensemble, *Gustav Mahler in Toblach: I Went Out this Morning Over the Countryside* (Winter and Winter CD, 1999).

As a coda to this discussion, let us take a moment to explore a very fascinating off-shoot of John Zorn's activities as both musician and impressario—a trend that has taken on a life of its own. Under the umbrella of his Tzadik label, Zorn has initiated a number of fecund imprints, including a series for new avant-garde composers (in addition to Zorn's own recordings in this category, the reader might be motivated to check out Annie Gosfield's 1998 album, *burnt ivory and loose wires*, and Zeena Parkins's 1999 album, *Pan-Acousticon*), and a series for new music from Japan (which figures into the penultimate section of this part). Perhaps the most interesting of all of these is the Jewish Alternative Movement. This is a diverse grouping of artists and bands, not all of which are releasing recordings through Tzadik, but which finds its core in the "Radical Jewish Culture" imprint. I am attracted to this culture because I see in it the kernels of historical materialism, which, apart from whatever else might be said of it in terms that are drawn from a more specifically Marxist political economy, holds that it matters that we human beings live in this material world, and that we have a story to tell, and that the story is one of the struggle for redemption. Philosophers such as Walter Benjamin (whom Terry Eagleton once labeled the "Marxist rabbi") and Theodor Adorno bring forward the radicality of this Jewish vision. The Jewish Alternative Movement, accordingly, attempts to capture this vision in music. As with Zorn himself, most of the music found under this heading cannot really be called "rock," and yet, as with Zorn's and Laswell's music in general, it is most definitely post-rock, and a rock sensibility informs a good deal of it. Narrowly speaking, most of this music is "jazz," but I think it would certainly be of interest to the kind of listener who follows the avant-garde wherever it leads.

Among my favorite works in this genre are the albums *Melt Zonk Rewire* by the New Klezmer Trio (of course, it's the trio thing again, this time with clarinet/bass clarinet), the live recording of Uri Caine's bizarre and fascinating attempt to make jazz with Mahler (*Gustav Mahler in Toblach*), and *Jews and the Abstract Truth* by Hasidic New Wave. Jazz listeners will know that this last title is a takeoff on the great album by Oliver Nelson, *Blues and the Abstract Truth*. The brilliance of Hasidic New Wave is to resonate with the profundity of Nelson's title, even while adding a little Jewish humor. A good starting place with this music is the sampler, *A Guide for the Perplexed*; perhaps some readers will know from where this title has been lifted? Finally, let it be said, if only because it is fun to say it: Ben Goldberg of the New Klezmer Trio is the Jimi Hendrix of the clarinet. It is doubtful that anyone ever leaned on the licorice stick so hard.

1996

Beck, *Odelay* (Geffen CD).
Evelyn Glennie, *Drumming* (Catalyst CD).
Kronos Quartet, *Howl, U.S.A.* (Nonesuch CD).
Mondo Exotica: Mysterious Melodies and Tropical Tiki Tunes (Capitol CD).
Porcupine Tree, *Signify* (Delerium CD).

Beck may be "Björk lite," but he does some things that ought to be appreciated. It's retro-rock with an eye to the future (unlike some of the neo-classical types, like Lenny Kravitz) that is also very funny. Beck's grandfather was a member of Fluxus, as was Yoko Ono. Evelyn Glennie is widely regarded as one of best classical percussionists playing today—I see her as a successor to Stomu Yamash'ta. Part of the fascination, though one also need never know this, is that she is deaf. *Drumming* is a good introduction to her work. Glennie was part of the percussion orchestra assembled for Björk's excellent MTV-Europe Unplugged concert. As with Kronos, Glennie is a classically trained musician with something of a rock sensibility; the Quartet demonstrates this once again with a performance of Allen Ginsberg's great poem, with the author reading. *Mondo Exotica* is a silly album, by turns highly amusing and highly annoying, that is useful for seeing where some of the more recent "space-age bachelor-pad music" (Stereolab, Jim O'Rourke) is coming from. Some of those guys back in the 1950s and 1960s, Serge Gainsbourg and crew, were pulling a few fast ones—let's leave it at that. Porcupine Tree could also be accused of merely looking backward. They are one of the leading exponents of the still-growing and yet destined to remain underground neo-psychedelic trend, along with such bands as Ozric Tentacles and The Bevis Frond. If you think that psychedelic is a musical language that still has some life in it, then *Signify* will appeal. For my part, the best work of these bands indicates that there is a living legacy to Syd Barrett-era Pink Floyd—but please, be careful with that axe.

Avant-retro: Stereolab

The core members of Stereolab, Laetitia Sadier and Tim Gane, seem to have Marxist sympathies. Maddeningly, the music journalists whom I've read on the group are content with the idea that there is something called "Marxism" in there, never going so far as to inquire as to what kind. Somehow I want to think that Louis Althusser is in Stereolab's music, given the unlikelihood of rock music of an Althusserian persuasion. And yet I also want to coin the term "the soft Brechtians" for the group. They take a great deal of what is weirdly familiar, like an ambience from the elevator almost, and make it strange again, without making it harsh. Is it a meeting of the generations? Think of kids growing up in suburbia, the never-ending struggle over the car radio, the parents wanting some sort of easy-listening pap, the teenagers needing something that rocks. Stereolab gives us the funny contradiction, rock that is avant-lounge. They unearth what was never truly so easy to swallow, the soundtrack for alienation in the time of "Camelot," when we watched reports from Vietnam at the dinner table. Henry Mancini and Serge Gainsbourg provided cool music for an intense time, that first effort to bring back the 1950s and its discourse of the "normal" as the 1960s drew to a close. That is a perspective from these American shores, anyway, but meanwhile the core members of Stereolab are from England and France, and their sound is certainly "European" if anything is.

The lounge thing can be taken too far. Tim Gane is yet another good example of an avant-rock musical transmuter, with a record collection upwards of five thousand vinyl LPs. But it is not simply a matter of "luxuriating in the retro chic of these totems" (as Jonathan Valania puts it in his article on Stereolab in *Magnet*, "The Now Sound," Nov./Dec. 1997, p. 53). Instead, says Gane,

> [t]he problem I have with this whole lounge thing is it's getting stuck in the past a bit
> . . . . I like loads of the music it came from, it was very out of the mainstream music with
> a lot of futuristic ideas. The point is to take the interesting ideas and mix them up with
> something now. I don't see the point in dressing up like the 50s and going to cocktail
> bars. Why not take the things that have relevance now instead of just copying the whole
> thing lock stock and barrel?
>
> I believe you have to take the best of the past and best of the present to get the best.
> (p. 53)

Gane's obvious frustration here is connected to the way that not only the music business, but even the fans for an innovative group form certain expectations, and try to lock their favorite musicians into a set way of doing things. For example, along with reviving the Farfisa combo organ, Stereolab is famous for using analogue synthesizers. Valania writes

> there was a time when 'synthesizer' was a very bad word, evoking unpleasant memories
> of the cokehead new-wave eunuchs of the New Romantics, those mincing mid-'80s Brit
> bands with silly names and sillier haircuts. But for many, Stereolab caused a total re-think
> of what could be done with electronic music. (p. 53)

Having allied itself somewhat with the analogue set, however, the band found that there were those for whom the retro obsession "has devolved into elitism and tunnel vision" (Valania, p. 53), even to the point of "a new Puritanism that dictated that if you work with analog gear and [messed-up] Farfisas that you have to use two-inch tape" (Gane, quoted by Valania, p. 53). Instead, with 1997's *Dots and Loops*, Stereolab moved away from tape altogether, and recorded on hard disk.

What will such a shift do to Stereolab's aesthetic of accidents? This aesthetic was announced in the titles of their first two albums, *Peng!* and *Transient Random Noise Bursts with Announcements*. Sadier and Gane express an idea that goes back to John Cage and that has become a mainstay of avant rock, especially thanks to Brian Eno and Jim O'Rourke, the giving up of control, especially as concerns the final outcome of a musical project. Sadier calls this the ability to "surprise yourself." Gane explains at some length:

> Clashes and accidents in the music are the things that make me most happy . . . . I like to come out of a record and have it sound nothing like I expected it would. I want to divorce the fact that we made it. I want the least control as possible. To me, it's more empowering, because you're reaching points that formally you can't put into context— that you can't write down. You reach complexities that you can't normally achieve. Things that are unexplainable, or the element of X-unknown.

> The core parts of the song that you start with are the ones that you want least represented, least in the fore . . . . It's the aspect I don't want to be seen. I'm much more interested in color, a montage, someone who puts together elements and shows something new. (Lorraine Ali, "Mistakes were made: Stereolab's accidental pop," *Option*, Nov./Dec. 1997, p. 77)

Of course, the point and click possibilities of recording to a hard disk are especially amenable to the montage aesthetic, but they also point to the Cagean paradox of intentionally refusing intentionality.

If a person had not heard any actual Stereolab records, she or he might suspect from the discussion thus far that they are very chaotic affairs—random noise bursts more like the music that Japanese noise artist Merzbow is known for. Instead, there is often a driving beat in the Lab's music, and the organ and synth sounds are very inviting, often quite warm. Laetitia Sadier sometimes sings words, sometimes in French, and sometimes she simply vocalizes sounds, often simply "ba ba ba. . . ." To me there is a wistful side to this; not to be too sappy about it, but her vocalization suggests the barest reminiscence of a simpler time, set in contrast to the emerging cyberworld. Sadier says something very interesting in a formulation that speaks both to what seems like the wistful quality in Stereolab music (and especially in her voice) and to the question of where this music stands in terms of the avant-garde:

> Instead of churning out defiantly experimental music with no regard to the listener, Gane and Sadier leave enough space for audiences to comfortably observe their unorthodox

approach without feeling left out. "In our music, there is something that is definitely missing that is left to be filled out by the listener," says Sadier. "That's why we're not solely making music for ourselves. There is a part of it that is unfulfilled unless it's heard. I think there are musicians who make avant-garde music, and it doesn't really matter if anyone likes it or listens to it in great quantities. Our music is certainly more addressed to people." (Ali, p. 79)

One might say this is the Marxist or at least the populist speaking; beyond this, however, what Sadier says thematizes once again the question of just what the "avant-garde" is or can be in our time. Obviously there is a very "pop" side to Stereolab, but that's not the end of the question. Even if one is looking up music on amazon.com or whatever, one still feels trapped in the dichotomy of Theodor Adorno's Beethoven on the one side, or "popular music" on the other. The real dichotomy seems to be between those who are exploring new sounds and developing craft in music, and those who are doing no more than repackaging pap for quick sales. I love Sadier's idea of a space in the music that has to be fulfilled by the listener—and it seems to me to be both a musical and a psychological space. Part of what is cancelled when "popular music" is nothing more than a marketing category is the idea that *the people need new sounds*, new art, new ways of thinking, new ways of organizing their thoughts. This is a necessity, not a mere luxury. To the extent that Stereolab is exploring this space, and struggling with these questions, including the problematization of the idea of the avant-garde, it is showing itself to be one of the most interesting experimental groups today.

Stereolab

Peng! (Too Pure CD, 1992).
Transient Random-Noise Bursts with Announcements (Elektra CD, 1993).
Jenny Ondioline (Duophonic CD EP, 1993).
the groop played "Space Age Batchelor Pad Music" (Too Pure CD, 1993).
Mars Audiac Quintet (Elektra CD, 1994).
Emperor Tomato Ketchup (Elektra CD, 1996).
Dots and Loops (Elektra CD, 1997).
Cobra and phases group play voltage in the milky night (Duophonic CD, 1999).

1997

John Fahey and Cul de Sac, *The Epiphany of Glenn Jones* (Thirsty Ear CD, 1997).
William Hooker, with DJ Olive and Glenn Spearman, *Mindfulness* (Knitting Factory Works CD, 1997).
Arto Lindsay, *Mundo Civilizado* (Bar None CD, 1997).
Radiohead, *OK Computer* (Capitol CD, 1997).

John Fahey was a remarkable figure (he died in the spring of 2001), a guitarist who both preserved old-style fingerpicking and blues playing, and who reached out to newer developments in rock and electronica. Perhaps the term would be "avant-preservationist"—Fahey traveled the Southern states in the 1960s, rediscovering country blues artists such as Skip James, engaging in what might be called "living musicology." Fahey preserved, but he also carried forward. *The Epiphany of Glenn Jones* represents the last phase of Fahey's work. Ironically, Fahey was himself rediscovered, by a generation of young avant-rock musicians that includes Jim O'Rourke. William Hooker is a jazz drummer with a rock sensibility, generally found in the vicinity of the John Zorn and Sonic Youth scenes in New York. On *Mindfulness* he assembles an interesting combination of drums, turntables, and saxophone. Another fixture of that scene is Arto Lindsay, guitarist with exceedingly noisy DNA and the ever-clever Lounge Lizards. Lindsay was born in Brazil, and here he connects New York noise with the politically charged Tropicalia sound. *OK Computer* is either one of the most brilliant rock albums in many a year—or it isn't. At least, that seems to be the critical consensus: either they are the messiahs of rock, or the heck with them. (This issue is reprised in the final chapter.) *OK Computer* is a very good album for our time—it would be a fitting soundtrack for a film version of William Gibson's *Neuromancer*.

Mom, can I take turntable lessons? or, Nobody here but me and my sampler

Someone who sets out to organize a closet arranges the things in it. If you are told not to organize the shoes or shirts, but the closet itself, you would be bewildered.

—Donald Davidson

■ was reminded of this amusing passage from Davidson's essay, "On the Very Idea of a Conceptual Scheme," when I thought about the moment when it became widely accepted that a musician might not just play something on the turntable, but indeed she or he might play the turntable itself. When I wrote my book on progressive rock, *Listening to the future*, I knew that I was setting myself up for at least a few critical lashings in the conclusion, when I discussed music in these postmodern times. I referred to what we quaintly used to call "musical instruments," and I had a few questions about music made with turntables and samplers. John Cage and others—perhaps most of all Christian Marclay—had been using the turntable as an instrument for many decades by the time DJ Qbert came along, but they had not dedicated themselves to perfecting an instrumental technique with it.

Two basic questions occurred to me, to be specific, and the questions have to do not only with turntables, but also samplers and other ways of making music electronically or with computers.

The first question has to do with what sort of instrument a turntable or sampler might make. Although I have not undertaken a thorough study of this question (it might be worthwhile to do so), I have discussed it with a good many people, and there seems to be a fundamental divide between musicians who are open to new ways of making music, instrumentally speaking, but who came up playing a more traditional musical instrument, and, on the other side, those whose only experience of making music is with turntables or samplers. Now, of course, in the realm of rock music, this sounds like a very retrograde distinction to make—after all, Andres Segovia had nothing good to say about the electric guitar, so a master of the Stratocaster such as Jimi Hendrix did not even count as a musician in his narrow conception. Whether the electric guitar is capable of the subtleties of the classical instrument, or whether a seemingly bastard and marginal instrument such as the electric bass guitar is capable of the subtleties of whatever "traditional" instruments it is most like (part of its marginality is that it is like at least three other instruments in some respects, the guitar, the double bass, and the cello), is in itself an interesting question. Still, the Les Paul, Stratocaster, Rickenbacker 4001, or Fender Jazz Bass have in common with their more traditional cousins that the player has to *touch* them in certain ways, the player has to acquire a certain familiarity with the feel of the instrument. Most of all, there is a certain intimacy and element of eros involved in playing a more traditional instrument—you *embrace* it (which is what eros has to do with in its root meaning), you work with it, it is a musical partner and you have to come to terms with it. You may quite rightly come to *love* the particular instrument, and certainly then you know that it is irreplaceable.

Speaking as a bass guitar player who prefers instruments that have a good deal of their own character, and that are not especially pliable (in the sense that a Rickenbacker 4001 or a Fender Jazz each have their own sound and feel, and each is quite unlike the other), I am very familiar with the intimacy that comes from working with an instrument over a period of years. One time I was standing around talking with friends, with my Rickenbacker 4001 bass on the strap around my shoulders. Stupidly, I was not holding onto the instrument with my hands, and, in the blink of an eye, the bass came off of the strap and fell onto the concrete slab that I was standing on. Until the day I die I will remember the sound that the instrument made, and I could do nothing but stand there for several minutes. I was badly shaken and on the verge of crying. This was not mainly because I was worried about replacing the instrument—Rickenbackers are not cheap, but neither are they extraordinarily expensive (certainly not as compared to a Stradivarius or a 1959 Les Paul goldtop; in any case, I had bought the instrument used, as is the case with most of my basses). Replacement might have been what I was looking at, because Rickenbackers, as some readers will know, have necks that go through the body; if the neck is seriously damaged, that is pretty much the end for the instrument as a whole. But that isn't what had me so upset. Instead, I felt that I had betrayed a good friend, and carelessly so; a friend who had only ever done me good, and who deserved to be taken good care of. I felt like a real jerk, not because of some harm I had done to myself by harming "my property," but instead because I had done harm to a partner who embodied the possibility of creating music.

(Miraculously, the instrument, though it fell about four feet, landed flat on its face, and the whole blow was taken by the strings, the control knobs, and the pick guard—the body and the neck were not damaged at all. I do not intend to tempt fate in this way again.)

Now, turntables have to be touched in order to play them, and I can even see some degree of intimacy being involved. The *Turntable TV* videos released by the Invisibl Skratch Piklz (the group that includes DJ Qbert) certainly show some amazing feats of digital dexterity. But it is hard to imagine that a broken turntable would be much more than a matter of mere replacement, and it is hard to imagine that one Technics SL1200MK3D turntable is a whole lot different from another one. Indeed, there seems to be an aesthetic of replacement that is at work in music from about the time that the turntable gains wider acceptance as an instrument. More on that in a moment. Whatever intimacy and partnership is possible with a turntable, however, I find it unlikely that this extends to samplers, computers, or mixing boards. Or, at the very least, the form of intimacy is radically different. As I said, I get one set of opinions on this question from people who play more traditional instruments, and another set of opinions from people who have only played turntables, samplers, drum machines, computers, and mixing boards.

None of this says anything about the "validity" of the music that is made by these different means; on the other hand, if we could not mark differences such as these, we also would not be having a discussion about this new music in the first place—and it is clear that there are some new sounds here that ought to be grappled with.

Just to take the "intimacy" question one step further, we might take recourse to the original turntablist, or at least one of them, John Cage. In Cage's music, it is often the case that anything can be an "instrument." Cage was one of the composers who started the trend of bringing a good deal of percussion into classical music, even to the point of writing pieces for percussion ensembles or orchestras. These ensembles often included such well-known percussion instruments as racks of brake drums, silverware, and the "water-gong" (a gong under water, naturally). Percussion is anything that can be banged on—a trombone or a large sheet of tin, perhaps. Percussionists dedicate themselves to finding things to bang on, to be sure, but it is very unlikely that a percussionist is going to *completely* throw her- or himself into achieving virtuoso skills with the various brake drums (specialist articles could be written in music journals comparing the brake drums from various types of cars, trucks, or what-have-you). There is a reason why the tympani or the trap drums or the vibraphone have achieved a certain status as percussion instruments, and this has to do with the range of expression possible with them. John Cage was *anti-expression*, in the sense of the idea that what music is about is the expression of some inner state of the musician or composer. This he opposed. Brake drums and the like were a part of his campaign against expressivity in music—as were turntables, tree branches, conch shells, contact microphones, kitchen utensils, and anything else under the sun. But he was also engaged in the search for new sounds, and this search also included finding unorthodox ways of playing the "old" instruments.

However, this leads to my second question, precisely concerning the character of the "new" sounds of turntablism and electronica. A good deal of the new music that is made with these new instruments (or old things now used as instruments) consists in the discombobulation and remixing of found sounds. Some of these found sounds are already pieces of music, or snippets of such pieces, in the conventional sense. I think that concerns ought to be raised about this, and I do not think that it is merely a retrograde gesture to raise such concerns. We have now reached the point where some artists put out an album, remix it, and then the remixes are further remixed by still other artists. There is a bit of a "nice work if you can get it" aspect to all of this, and one has to wonder how much of a future there can be for the various forms of "plunderphonics" out there. At the same time, remix and sampler music might legitimately have its moment just as punk did—especially insomuch as this music is intensively *of* its moment. Sampler music calls into question the "originality" of any music. Even more, as my former teacher Houston Baker argued in his book about hip-hop, there is a *redemptive* aspect to some turntable and sampler music, in that the old sources and sounds are rewoven into new tapestries, creating a vital sisterhood and brotherhood of sound. Still further, the resources for making this music are broadly accessible. Lots of people can get into the act, and if not all of the music produced in this way is great, so what? The same can be said for garage bands down through the years, but this does not diminish what might be one of the most avant-garde things about rock music, that it can be a kind of experiment in democracy and popular participation.

In other words, the times they are a'changin', and it behooves us to try to understand what appears to be a millennial shift in music making.

There are various schools of turntablism, and even more so are there many different trends within the new electronic music—from ambient to jungle to trip-hop and on and on. Some have suggested the term "electronica" to cover all of it, while others have immediately leaped forward to say that any umbrella term is no more than a marketing device. For my part, I know that I am a rank novice with this music, and I do not want to pretend that I have the slightest competence in sorting it out.

Therefore, what I will say from this point on should be taken with some very large grains of salt.

Turntablism and the use of more primitive electronics and sequencers (such as the Roland TB-303) originally had to do with making a virtue of necessity. DJs in cities such as Detroit and Chicago were looking for novel ways to keep the music going and to keep the young people dancing. Breakbeats were originally used as a way of keeping an underlying beat running while the DJ segued from one record to another. This is exceedingly potted history, but at some point in the early 1980s, a number of elements came together—street rap, the earlier wave of electronic rock music from Europe, best exemplified by Kraftwerk, disco, some new instruments and new ways of using turntables, and what might broadly be called "club culture." This was a long way from "guitar rock," but it was something else than just a repeat of disco or dance music, in that the DJs, MCs, and producers started to use the elements of production in such a way as to bring them center stage.

Indeed—this is the clincher—in the final analysis we might have to say that this music, by whatever name or family of names it is called, is the first real post-1970s musical paradigm to come out of rock. The proof is that the logic that propels this "coming out" goes so far as to establish a music whose relation to rock is, at the very least, highly questionable. One primer on the emergence of this music, in *Revolution* magazine (Sept. 2000; the magazine refers to itself as "the new music manifesto," and also has the words, "at last, a magazine about music that matters" emblazoned on its cover—which seems a far fetch for a publication filled with adverts for clothing), is titled, "50 Albums That Killed Rock 'n' Roll—And Got Us Dancing." Thank heaven. Sarcasm aside, the implication is that rock music needed to be killed, in part because it was keeping some people from dancing. One of the ironies of this new music is that it wants to focus on the body and the experience of embodiment, which generally means a heavy emphasis on rhythm and beats, but quite often this music is made without a percussionist taking hand or stick to the *skin* of a drum. There is a lesson here about materiality in the cybernetic age, I think. The other implication of the need to kill rock music is that all of this mindful listening that some music called us to is just a real drag, when really what we want to do is party. There might be a more hopeful and less cynical reading of at least some of this new music, however—even if the skeptical reading does apply, I think, to that particular magazine and its approach to the music. There are other creative ways of listening to music than through the ears alone, and there may be other creative ways of thinking than through the brain alone. And, after all, if there can be great music that *someone else* is dancing to—keeping in mind that works such as *The Rite of Spring* and Ravel's *Daphnis et Chloe* were written as ballets—why cannot there be great music that the *listener* dances to?

- Afrika Bambaata, "Planet Rock"/*Don't Stop-Planet Rock Remix* (ZTT CD, 1992; original single 1982).
  Public Enemy, *It Takes a Nation of Millions to Hold Us Back* (Def Jam LP, 1988).
  NWA ("Niggers with Attitude"), *Straight Outta Compton* (Priority LP, 1988).
  Public Enemy, *Fear of a Black Planet* (Def Jam LP, 1990).
  A Tribe Called Quest, *People's Instinctive Travels and the Paths of Rhythm* (BMG LP, 1990).
  Consolidated, *Friendly Fascism* (Nettwork CD, 1991).
  A Tribe Called Quest, *Low-End Theory* (Jive CD, 1991).
  Yo-Yo, *Make Way for the Motherlode* (East West CD, 1991).
  Arrested Development, *3 Years, 5 Months, and 2 Days in the Life Of . . .* (Chrysalis CD, 1992).
  Eric B. & Rakim, *Don't Sweat the Technique* (MCA CD, 1992).
  Eye & I, *Eye & I* (Epic CD, 1992).
  Paris, *Sleeping with the Enemy* (Scarface CD, 1992).
  US3, *Hand on the Tourch* (Blue Note CD, 1993).
  DJ Spooky, *Necropolis: The Dialogic Project* (Knitting Factory Works CD, 1995).
  DJ Spooky, *Songs of a Dead Dreamer* (Asphodel CD, 1996).
  Christian Marclay, *records* (Atavistic CD, 1997).
  DJ Krush, *Milight* (Mowax CD, 1997).
  Invisibl Skratch Piklz and others, *Turtable TV Annual Special vol.1* (ISP Video, 1997).
  DJ Qbert, *Wave Twisters* (Galactic Butt Hair CD, 1998).
  DJ Spooky, *Riddim Warfare* (Outpost CD, 1998).
  Phil Kline, *Glow in the Dark* (Composers Recordings, Inc. CD, 1998).
  D:Fuse, *Psychotrance 2000* (Moonshine CD, 1999).
  DJ Spooky vs The Freight Elevator Quartet, *"file under futurism"* (Caipirinha CD, 1999).
  DJ Vadim, *U.S.S.R.: Life From the Other Side* (Ninja Tunes CD, 1999).
  Ming + FS, *Hell's Kitchen* (Om Records CD, 1999).

The discographies here have no pretense to being coherent; the aim is nothing more than to provide a list of some albums that I have found both interesting and representative of some new vibrations. The "avant" status of some of these records can be debated; the point instead is that they all show emerging, creative dimensions of new ways of making music. The previous comments about dancing and listening do not do much to address the roots of this music in the question of race in the United States, and the hip-hop culture that emerged on the inner-city streets starting around 1980. "Planet Rock," along with "The Message" by Grandmaster Flash and the Furious Five, introduced the world to a sound that might be described as Berlin meets Detroit, or, more specifically, Kraftwerk meets Funkadelic. Public Enemy consistently, and NWA in one apocalyptic burst, represent not only the brilliance of hip-hop, but the militancy as well. Tribe Called Quest, Arrested Development, Yo-Yo, and Eric B. and Rakim, and US3 all represent refinements on the basic form. US3 combines funky jazz à la Herbie Hancock's post-Miles group with hip-hop, and one nice thing about their record is the acoustic sound of the piano cutting across the heavy electronic beats. Eye & I might be called an experiment in Living Colour meets turntables. I thought their record would be huge, but for some reason it didn't take off. Paris's *Sleeping with the Enemy* is one of the most intense rap performances ever—it just builds and builds, in a very subtle way at first, and then you realize that you're caught up in the whirlwind. Great line: "that Aryan is scaryin'."

At least the way my discography posits the narrative, around the mid-1990s things got a good deal more experimental. This is a bit deceptive. Christian Marclay's involvement with turntables goes back to the late 1970s, and relates to his earlier involvement in visual arts, and with a Swiss Fluxus group called Ecart, and the influence of musique concrete composers such as Pierre Schaeffer and Pierre Henry—and of course John Cage. In more recent years he has found allies for his kind of turntable art among some of the more exploratory DJs such as DJ Olive and Erik M, as well as Lee Ranaldo from Sonic Youth. He continues to juggle involvement in music and visual art, even going so far as to say that, "It may sound like a contradiction, but I'm interested in sound, not just for how it sounds, but also for how it looks" (Rahma Khazam, "Jumpcut Jockey," *The Wire*, May 2000, p. 28).

DJ Qbert is the leader of the Invisibl Skratch Piklz. Their *Turntable TV* video is a good introduction to virtuoso scratching. At their level, the degree of control and digital dexterity is undoubtedly comparable to that of any other very good musician. So, their skill stands as a good response on the question of musical instruments.

There are four listings for DJ Spooky. He is a controversial figure. He does stuff that you can dance to, so some question how exactly "heavy" his music is. On the other hand, "Spooky's sets are just as likely to incorporate outre jazz master Sun Ra or electronic innovator Luciano Berio as Wu-Tang Clan," writes Kurt Reighley in his book, *Looking for the Perfect Beat: The Art and Culture of the DJ*. Further, "If any individual best represents the DJ as a filter for organizing information and history to create new connections between cultures and ideas, Spooky is the number-one contender" (p. 80). Also known as That Subliminal Kid, Spooky is Paul D. Miller, from Washington, D.C. The liner notes to his CDs are filled with quotations from Plato, Francis Bacon, Marshall McLuhan, and, of course, Gilles Deleuze and Felix Guattari. *Riddim Warfare*, which some might call his most "accessible" album—but perhaps it is simply his most refined—features guest appearances by Thurston Moore and Ben Neill. Of all of the musicians in this exponentially-expanding scene, Spooky is my favorite—probably because, even if he might not be a "true Deleuze scholar," he is definitely someone who is grappling with ideas.

Future Sounds of London, *Lifeforms* (Virgin CD, 1994).
Mouse on Mars, *Vulvaland* (Too Pure CD, 1994).
Autechre, *Peel Sessions* (EMI CD, 1999; performance from 1995).
Leftfield, *Leftism* (Columbia CD, 1995).
Muslimgauze, *Salaam Alekum, Bastard* (Soleilmoon CD, 1995).
In Memoriam Gilles Deleuze (Mille Plateaux CD, 1996).
In the Nursery, *Deco* (ITN Corp. CD, 1996).
to rococo rot, *veiculo* (Emperor Jones CD, 1996?).
Autechre, *Envane* (Warp Records CD, 1997).
Chemical Brothers, *Dig Your Own Hole* (Virgin CD, 1997).
Roni Size/Reprazent, *New Forms* (Mercury CD, 1997).
Trancespotting: Music from the World of Trance (Hypnotic CD, 1997).
Goldie, *saturnzreturn* (FFRR CD, 1998).
Grooverider, *Mysteries of Funk* (Columbia CD, 1998).
Ben Neill, *Goldbug* (Antilles CD, 1998).
Photek, *Form and Function* (Astralwerks CD, 1998).
Talvin Singh, *OK* (Island CD, 1998).
Reich Remixed (Nonesuch CD, 1999).
Unknownwerks: the new crop of american electronic artists (Astralwerks CD, 1999).

Again, the entries listed in the discography above are in the "try it, you might like it" category. Fortunately there are now *Rough Guides* for techno, drum 'n' bass, and house music, which are an enormous help in navigating this now extremely far-flung and sometimes confusing scene. The new electronica, especially as represented by the present discography, is often quite understated. Paradoxically, in some of these works there is more than a smidgen of the epic vision of psychedelia and even progressive rock. Goldie's 1998 album, *saturnzreturn*, with its main track, "Mother," clocking in at an hour long, might be called the *Tales from Topographic Oceans* (Yes's 80-minute epic) of the genre. Opinion is divided as to whether this is good or not. There are some nice connections here: *Lifeforms* by Future Sounds of London features a guest appearance by Robert Fripp, while Björk is somewhere in the mix on *saturnzreturn*. Talvin Singh, who has also appeared with Björk, combines his skill as a classically trained tabla player with electronica. Ben Neill achieves a similar synthesis, though in his case using a wild-looking three-belled trumpet. Autechre, to rococo rot, and Photek, are all on the austere side of electronica, shading into minimalism. *In Memoriam Gille Deleuze*, in addition to the interest it holds as a set of attempts at "rhizomatic" music, is also a good sampler of the new electronic music, featuring artists ranging from Mouse on Mars and Zoviet France to Oval and Jim O'Rourke.

Often I wonder about the politics of some of the recent music. Some of the new electronica can be said to have taken over for disco, insofar as dance and club culture goes. In recent years it is common to hear the argument that this is a culture of ethnic minorities (primarily Blacks and Latinos) and gays (primarily men)—or, at least, club culture serves as a refuge or island of freedom for folks who are not always appreciated in the mainstream culture. The relationship to hip-hop carries some political resonance too, seen especially in albums such as Leftfield's *Leftism* (where John Lydon appears as a guest). In the Nursery is at the other end of the aesthetic/political spectrum. The duo is from Sheffield, sometimes maligned as one of those northern industrial wastelands— it was the steel city of England, but the automation of the industry led to the layoff of nine out of ten workers (meanwhile more steel is produced there than ever). Def Leppard is also from that city—but so is one of the great avant-garde musicians of our time, Derek Bailey. The members of Mouse on Mars, from Cologne, Germany, make an interesting political connection with their music, triangulating among "minute sound events," Deleuze's rhizomatics, and the Third World. Group member Jan St. Werner explains:

> I think it will happen, that the Third World will come. And I know this causes the highest fear in the First World. But in a way this music is also about what happens when you mix those things, and if those opposed forms come together. This is a real big idea now, brought into a very tiny system of music and aesthetics, but it's not to make a better version of these genres and styles, or to do a revival of this kind of style or make poopy-pap music, to be more famous, or any of this. It's a deterritorialisation idea, to move on from your own territory. (Rob Young, "The Mouse That Roared," *The Wire*, October 1999, p. 42)

Rock is dead? Long live rock?

1997

Paul Schutze, *Deus Ex Machina: The Soundtrack Panic Heat Vengeance* (Tone Casualties CD).
———, *Nine Songs from the Garden of Welcome Lies: improvisations for organ and percussion* (Tone Casualties CD).
James Blood Ulmer, *Music Speaks Louder than Words: James Blood Ulmer plays the music of Ornette Coleman* (Koch CD).
Robert Wyatt, *Shleep* (Thirsty Ear CD).

Paul Schutze is a composer who comes out of progressive rock but also embraces many of the elements associated with the new electronic music. Paul Stump, in his book on English progressive rock, argues that Schutze "perhaps best represents the contemporary manifestation of Progressive ideology mediated through postmodernism" (*The Music's All that Matters*, p. 344). Schutze identifies especially with a film aesthetic: "the piece defines a space . . . . I imagine a space and then position things at certain points in that picture" (p. 344). Many musicians these days profess to a film aesthetic and to the imaginary soundtrack, from Eno to Zorn and beyond. Schutze is one of the few (along with the aforementioned) who applies himself to this aesthetic with depth, and with the encyclopedic grasp of many genres of music that ought to be expected of the avant-rock musician. His appreciation of progressive rock has led to some insights regarding the new electronic music. For instance, he worries that some of the new music is not the work of what he calls "signature players"—"which is what a lot of Progressive musicians were. . . . In the space of a few bars, you'd know it was Carl Palmer playing or Alan White playing. Signatures. That's what Progressive was all about. Individuality" (p. 344). Furthermore, "[s]ampling has fundamentally changed the way we relate—all of us—to sound. . . . A lot of Progressive tricks can be reproduced now by non-musicians—the feeling can't" (p. 345). Additionally, Schutze is critical of what he calls the "narrative-free" slant of much recent music, though he sees narrative coming back in under new guises, for example in the music of Tricky and Portishead (p. 345). (I would like to hear his comments on Radiohead in this respect.) What Schutze hopes for, in his own music and that of others, is an updating of some of the key elements of progressive rock. In some sense, a big part of the argument over the new electronic music will be over whether this is being done in some cases (again, I find Goldie's *saturnzreturn* to be a stellar example, and it turns out that those who truly despise progressive rock despise that album as well), and whether this a good thing. There is a perfectly plausible argument that genres of music that go beyond what might be called progressive rock's modernism will also necessarily break "signatures" and individuality. Perhaps some brave soul could plot the changes in rock music from, say, the Beatles and Yes to Radiohead and Björk and Autechre, against the transitions in French philosophy from existential Marxism (Sartre) to structural Marxism (Althusser) to postmodern anarchism (Deleuze, Foucault, Lyotard)—yet another dissertation in search of a graduate student! Schutze is forging a different path, against the grain of postmodernity; his music (only two of his many albums are listed here) will bear attention accordingly.

James Blood Ulmer's guitar-oriented rendition of Ornette Coleman's music restores the hard-edged country-blues roots whence it originally came. In the manner of Jimi Hendrix, Ulmer shows how a musician can burn intensely, in a way that still relates essentially to the blues tradition, and yet be innovative at the same time.

Robert Wyatt created yet another melancholy masterpiece with *Shleep*, an album that recapitulates some of the sound of 1974's *Rock Bottom*, but with greater refinement and maturity. Among the musicians who helped out were Brian Eno, Phil Manzanera, Paul Weller, and one of England's greatest jazz musicians, saxophonist Evan Parker.

King Crimson exists when there is King Crimson music to be played

King Crimson yesterday, today, and tomorrow, but never the same—never the same group of musicians, even. What is a "band" when there is little or no continuity of *members*—members in the plural, that is. Robert Fripp is always there, of course, and yet he maintains that he is *not* King Crimson, nor is King Crimson simply his "project." *When* King Crimson exists, it is a *group*, Fripp maintains—and King Crimson exists when there is King Crimson music that needs to be played. It is this music, Fripp claims, that calls forth the group, even if he might play a special role as leader or what might be called "convener." What is the meaning of all this when, when all is said and done, there are more discontinuities to not only the groups that make up King Crimson, but also the music itself, than there are continuities? Perhaps most of all this: King Crimson has existed in every decade from the 1960s forward (which now means more than thirty-three years since King Crimson first formed—and also *five* different decades), and in each of these decades King Crimson has created music at the cutting edge of the possibilities of rock. I would even go so far as to say that an aspiring student of experimental rock music ought to take King Crimson as the most consistent guidepost to the forward edge of rock. Paradoxically, it is the discontinuities of King Crimson that makes this the case.

King Crimson has a special place in the hearts of those who came to musical awareness in the late 1960s. Robert Fripp has described the effect that hearing "A Day in the Life" had on him, the way that it showed the open-ended potential of rock music. *In the Court of the Crimson King* was one of those life-changing, knock-your- head-off albums that still resonates these many years later. It is often called the album that started progressive rock. At this juncture, I don't want to get into the whole debate; suffice it to say that the progressive rock aficionados out there certainly claim Crimson as one of their own, and it would be hard to see that ever changing. Then again, there is a "wandering" side to the music that is absent from many of the other mainstays of progressive rock. Part of this is the strong jazz influence in Crimson, and part of it is the absence of the whole "multiple keyboard" thing (nineteen of them stacked in banks of six, six, and seven, or whatever) that is characteristic of bands such as Yes and Emerson, Lake and Palmer. The main keyboard in Crimson music up through *Red* was the Mellotron, the notoriously finicky instrument that used segments of recording tape to play back the actual sounds of orchestral strings, flutes, and choir voices. Most often used to give the impression of a string orchestra in the background, Fripp and company (generally Fripp and one other band member alternated on the instrument) played the Mellotron as though it was an instrument in its own right, instead of a substitute for other instruments. Other progressive rock groups had gothic elements (Genesis and

Van der Graaf Generator, for instance), and jazz elements (Yes guitarist Steve Howe, for instance, was heavily influenced by Wes Montgomery and later by John McLaughlin), but few, if any, could invoke true heavy-metal thunder the way King Crimson did from the very first measure of "Twenty-first Century Schizoid Man." What I referred to as the "wandering" quality—most apparent in *Lizard* and *Islands*, though partly because the group structure was not especially secure in that period—is instead a manic careening in the guitar and saxophone solos of "Schizoid Man." The impression is of a brilliant Grand Prix driver pushing things to the absolute limit, where the line between control and loss of control can no longer be seen.

In the Court introduced a generation of rock musicians and listeners to frightening instrumental difficulty—if you were going to play music like this, you had to spend a lot of time in your room practicing. Obviously, a good many musicians and listeners rejected this, and the question of whether this was mainly out of mere laziness or an alternative aesthetic has been with us ever since that time. (In the final chapter I return once again to the technique question.) Part of the genius of King Crimson was to be able to combine musical parts that required everyone to play very difficult passages together—in a way akin to that "notation theory" that Brian Eno talked about—with other parts that were completely open and quite a bit like free jazz.

On *Lizards* and *Islands* these parts really are free jazz, as played by some of England's best musicians, especially the brilliant Keith Tippett. The pianist had already made an essential contribution on what might qualify as one of rock music's all-time great whimsical moments, "Cat Food," from the second King Crimson album, *In the Wake of Poseidon*. The *Ovary Lodge* trio album from 1973, with Tippett, percussionist Frank Perry, and contrabassist Harry Miller, has not been reissued on CD, as of this writing, but fortunately the 1971 album, *Septober Energy*, is available. This is Tippett's composition for a fifty-person jazz orchestra called Centipede. Robert Fripp produced both records. (Many other Tippett albums are available, including several with his wife, vocalist Julie Driscoll, a wonderful singer who was a member of Brian Auger's Trinity back in the 1960s, and who made a good album with Jack Bruce back in the 1970s.) Debate rages over which of the first two King Crimson albums is better. They were both cut from the same mold, and the second features some significant recapitulations of the first. But *In the Court of the Crimson King* is the more essential of the two; it launched not only the project of King Crimson, but also significantly widened the possibilities of creative and complex rock music.

It is easy to get lost in the labeling system for the many versions of King Crimson (KC MK I, MK II, and so on; see the website "Elephant Talk" for information on this issue, from maestro Fripp and others). The third album, *Lizard*, represented one of the many major swerves that typifies the group. Andy McCulloch took over the drum chair from the superb Michael Giles; this was the beginning of a succession of remarkable percussionists—someday there ought to be a King Crimson Percussion Ensemble featuring all of them. Keith Tippett brought along three of his friends from the jazz world to play various horns, and Jon Anderson of Yes supplied vocals for one song. Whereas *In the Court* had a good deal of what I like to call "sci-fi medievalism," that peculiar combination of pastoral and space-age utopianism that manifested itself in a number of progressive-rock groups (especially British ones), *Lizard*'s imagery was more solidly feudal. For the first seven albums, King Crimson had a full-time lyricist, and for the first four albums this was Peter Sinfield. As with a number of other progressive groups, the lyrics demonstrate the influence of John Milton and English Romantic poetry. An interesting line of examination would be to compare the influence of the English Romantics on groups such as King Crimson and Yes to the influence of the American Beats on Sonic Youth, given that the Beats were themselves influenced by the Romantics. A later, very different version of King Crimson recorded an album called *Beat* (1982).

By the fourth album, *Islands*, the group concept is wearing a bit thin—one could say that *Islands* is a B or possibly a B+ album in comparison to the first three, which does not mean that it doesn't have some A-grade material here and there. Tippett and the horn players remain from *Lizard*, with the addition of Paulina Lucas on soprano sax, the only woman to have appeared on a King Crimson album. Bass and vocal duties were taken over by Boz Burrell (here listed simply as "Boz"), who was later to join the dreadful Bad Company, a move that is perhaps only exceeded by Ian McDonald, from the original group, who later joined the even more execrable Foreigner. Boz was a good singer for Crimson, but unfortunately he continued the weakness at the bass station already established by folksinger Gordon Haskell on the previous album. For the most part King Crimson has had bass players in the range of good (Greg Lake) to very good (Peter Giles, an under-appreciated musician who supplied fine lines on both the second King Crimson album, as well as the excellent album that he made with his brother Michael and the aforementioned McDonald) to great (John Wetton, Tony Levin, Trey Gunn). The group has also had some wonderful singers. And yet one sometimes gets the feeling that bass and vocals are secondary to the larger mission of the band—just a little observation that the legions of "crimheads" can debate endlessly, no doubt. Fortunately, *Islands* also features another Tippett associate, South African double-bass player, Harry Miller. The bass guitar often plays the role of holding down a pedal point, while Miller supplies a countermelody that generates a powerful tension.

The *Lizard* band tended to lack something that Robert Fripp values highly, namely discipline. The version of King Crimson that convened for *Larks' Tongues in Aspic* was a radical departure from what had come before. Even though the sound was often full and rich even to the point of being overwhelming, the music also seemed more streamlined, going more directly "to the point," so to speak. Improvisation was emphasized, but in a fully collective way; listening was essential. The musicians were stellar. Bill

Bruford jumped ship from Yes, accomplishing the feat of being the drummer on what in my opinion are the two most creative progressive rock albums, *Larks' Tongues* and *Close to the Edge*. John Wetton came aboard from Family, and for the first time made the bass guitar an equal voice in the mix—which not only strikes a blow for bass equality (not that there's anything wrong with that), but also opened up new contrapuntal possibilities in the music. Wetton is also an excellent singer. A classically trained musician, David Cross, added a previously unheard sound in King Crimson, violin. The vocal aspect was further de-emphasized (*Larks' Tongues* has only three, short "songs," surrounded by three, longer, instrumental pieces), but once again Crimson had someone whose job it was to supply lyrics, Richard Palmer-James. There is a bleakness to his lyrics that makes a nice contrast to Sinfield's. The coup de grâce however, was the inclusion of percussionist Jamie Muir, something of a mad genius who added a dimension hitherto not present in King Crimson, what might be called a cross between free jazz and John Cage. The *Larks' Tongues* band did not deal in the *refusal* of intention, but rather the *disturbance* of intention—a constant spanner in the works. What made the music of this period different from some of the free playing of Derek Bailey or AMM or the Spontaneous Music Ensemble—improvisors who relate to the classical avant-garde as much as jazz—is that King Crimson did employ composition as well, they played pieces with parts where everyone needed to be together at a certain time and place, and they also played songs where the instruments supported the vocalist. In other words, their music was still rock, even while dramatically expanding the idiom in a way that remains a paradigm of experimentalism.

This basic group made three albums, but Jamie Muir left after *Larks' Tongues*, apparently to enter a Buddhist monastery. He was a percussionist who was as likely to blow a horn or whistle, or, reportedly, swing a large bag of fall leaves around his head as to bang on a drum, and he made a big impression on Bill Bruford. The latter, I would say, is the most creative drummer to play rock music, and one quality that makes him so is the ability to make refraining from hitting the drum—in other words, silence—a powerful force. This ability is a natural extension of the fact that Bruford syncopates like there's no tomorrow, and his brilliant and quirky "beat divisions" can be heard not only on King Crimson albums, but also on such Yes classics as "Heart of the Sunrise" from *Fragile*. He is a genius at setting up expectations and then confounding them; to wax Derridean, it's a case of the absence that is felt as a presence. There are many great rock drummers, of course (half of them in King Crimson at one time or another!), but none who subdivide the beats and silences quite so subtly. The subsequent Crimson albums of this era, *Starless and Bible Black* and *Red*, are very good too, even if not as innovative as *Larks' Tongues*, but the real excitement was in the band's live playing. Fortunately, this is now extensively documented, most dramatically on the *Great Deceiver* 4-CD box set. I had the great fortune to see King Crimson in that period and

I can say without exaggeration that it was a life-changing experience. Truly, the likes of that band was never heard before and most likely will never be heard again.

Red is an outstanding album, from beginning to end, and one of the strongest albums in the whole Crimson corpus. Many Crimson aficionados—including Eric Tamm, the author of books on Robert Fripp and Brian Eno—regard the closing piece, "Starless," as the finest piece of Crimson music ever. There is an aggressive and muscular quality to much of the album—as Tamm puts it, "It seems almost impossible that this was the same Fripp who had made the delicate *Islands* a few short years previously" (*Robert Fripp*, pp. 78–79). Of course, one might say that whether or not this was the "same Fripp," it was *not* the same King Crimson. One of the harshest and most striking aspects of two of the pieces on the album, "Red" and "One More Red Nightmare," is the use of the tritone. As Tamm explains, the tritone,

> so named because it spans three whole steps or tones, . . . is classed among the most dissonant of the thirteen fundamental intervals in music. (If you turn in your college harmony assignment and have idiotically included a tritone in the final chord, you'll get it back marked in red.) Because of its searingly harsh, problematic sound, the tritone was called the *diabolus in musica* ("the devil in music") by medieval theorists, and some forbade its use entirely. The King Crimson metaphor—it goes deeper than one might think. (p. 78)

The melancholy tone of Wetton's voice on "One More Red Nightmare" and "Starless" captures well the feeling that an era was coming to an end.

After this period, the Crimson King was silent for about seven years. The story of Robert Fripp's "sabbatical" is a dramatic tale in and of itself, involving feelings that the world was coming to an end, that the lifestyle of a touring rock musician was no longer sustainable (for Fripp and perhaps not for anyone), encounters with the thought of G. I. Gurdjieff and J. G. Bennett ("I had a glimpse of something . . . the top of my head blew off"—Tamm, p. 76), and then the gradual re-immersion in music in the form of projects with Peter Gabriel, David Bowie, Daryl Hall, and a solo "Frippertronics" concert at the Kitchen in New York in February 1978. (A fascinating, detailed account of the sabbatical period is found in Tamm, pp. 75–129.) In 1979, having quite substantially remade his life, Fripp launched what he called "the drive to 1981." The intervening period involved the making of a very strong solo album, *Exposure*, and the formation of a "dance band," The League of Gentlemen. (One member, bassist Sara Lee, would later join the Gang of Four and then the B-52s.)

Finally, upon the arrival of the magical year 1981, once again the call of the Crimson King was heard by Fripp, and the new group was once again a radical departure. After all, if you've said something, why say it again? (Incidentally, one might be excused for having an apocalyptic view of 1981, since that was the beginning of the bizarre and now almost unbelievable Reagan administration in the United States.) Bruford came back as part of the new quartet, along with two Americans, bassist Tony Levin and guitarist and singer Adrian Belew. For the first time in its history, King Crimson had a true "frontman," someone who would make such over-the-top comments from the stage as "good evening" and "thanks." Such frivolity had never been heard before from a King Crimson stage! Fripp encountered Levin, a top studio player, and Belew, an alumnus of Frank Zappa's group, in his work with Bowie and Gabriel (and Levin was the bassist on *Exposure*). It might be argued that this was the most carefully put-together Crimson ever. In addition to playing bass, Levin also plays the Chapman Stick, a ten-stringed instrument that is played by tapping the strings with both hands—in this way one can play two independent lines.

The new music had almost nothing in common with any previous King Crimson sound, in at least four ways. For one thing, the new Crimson had two guitarists, something unimaginable in the previous formations—and, with Levin on Stick, the effect was sometimes that of three guitarists. A second element was the use of repetition. Whereas the idea in the previous formations was to always try to play something new with each measure—a strategy especially appropriate for Bruford, who rarely plays a straight beat or stock fill—now the idea was to work with minute changes, developed through many repetitions. In this the music was not unlike some of that of Philip Glass and Steve Reich.

Third and perhaps most important was the texture of the music, based as it was in interweaving lines, truly a musical fabric. In the spirit of the times, and even somewhat ahead of the times—into the 1990s, perhaps—there was an emphasis on the vertical, though not to the point of the sort of pure "cloud" of timbre associated with ambient music. Significantly, part of the subtitle of Eric Tamm's book on Eno is "the vertical color of sound." Clearly, the experiments that Fripp had undertaken with Eno, which resulted in the albums *No Pussyfooting* and *Evening Star*, had a lasting effect on both musicians. In some sense, or in part, the music that King Crimson played from 1981 to 1984 reflects an expansion of these improvisations and timbres to a group context. (Another path from that same context is Fripp's work with soundscapes.) However, what differentiates the interwoven "cloud" of 1980s King Crimson from some techno and electronica—with which it shares some similarities—is the horizontal aspect, the propulsive forward movement that in the end makes this rock music.

One theory about King Crimson is that the band could be understood in each of its periods as, at least in some sense, taking the music of a dominant trend or even a particular group and raising it to the next level. Clearly, there is much more to King Crimson than this, but it's a fun theory to think about. So, the first four King Crimson albums relate to the Beatles. The *Lark's Tongues* period has something to do with John McLaughlin and the Mahavishnu Orchestra. (Significantly, Yes's *Tales from Topographic Oceans*—which I would call an audacious, if flawed, masterwork—was also made under the influence of Mahavishnu.) The *Discipline* era relates to new wave and even disco, and perhaps especially to Talking Heads. (Amusingly, concert videos from this period show disco dancers in the audience.) Just to complete the picture, the *Thrak* formation (about which I will say more in a moment) has some connection to grunge and even Nirvana, while the most recent version, the band that made *the construKction of light*, might even have something to do with Sonic Youth—except the Crims have a lot more chops!

Well, that's just a little provocation to have fun with. If anything, the influence of the Beatles seems resurgent in the *Thrak* and *construKction* formations. But let it be said—before I get into a lot of trouble—the primary factors in King Crimson music are creativity and craft, and though there is a bit of transmutation going on, this music has been at the forefront of experimental rock for more than thirty years.

Staying with the *Discipline*-era group for one more moment, there is a fourth difference with the music, namely that you can dance to it. Surely followers of the group in the 1970s would never have expected this. The danceable quality of the music demonstrated—along with that of Talking Heads and other of the more creative new wave and punk groups—that creative listening was possible with other parts of the body than the ears.

There must be something about King Crimson music that makes it such that no version of the group can hold together for more than about three years. Furthermore, the pattern since the *Larks Tongues* period has been two- or three-year periods of activity by particular incarnations of the band followed by even lengthier periods of, shall we say, the withdrawal of the King. The *Discipline*-era band made three albums—a King Crimson record for making albums with the initial line-up intact. *Discipline* was really good, with some great songs such as "Elephant Talk" and "Thela Hun Ginjeet." Although there was always more humor and wit in earlier Crimson music than most people gave it credit for, some of the new music was even funny—for example "Elephant Talk" (which reintroduced young people to such excellent expressions as "argy bargy" and "brouhaha") and "Indiscipline." The second album from this group, *Beat*, was also good; part of the fascination was to see how "American" this previously very English group had become, with references to beat writers Jack Kerouac and Allen Ginsberg and the manic, urban scene. The lyrics for *Beat* are some of Belew's best. The third album, *Three of a Perfect Pair* has some good moments, but it is considerably weaker than the first two. The problem with episodic incarnation is that, in human form, one encounters the forms of decay that affect all flesh—if one isn't simply crucified outright. This has been a continuing problem for King Crimson, how to keep it going and not peter out. There is something about the initial Crimson idea, each time it incarnates, that seems unsustainable over the long haul. But one also has to recognize that Robert Fripp, as the convener of the group, knows how to walk off the stage if necessary. He is the best guide to when a particular incarnation has played itself out, and, arguments about what sort of thing King Crimson "really is"—a "real" group or an episodic project of one individual—aside, for sure Fripp is the leader. It is not unusual to hear Fripp called eccentric—but the way he deviates from the mainstream is by making decisions about playing rock music that have to do with the music and with ideas. It is sad that Fripp's commitment to these things is treated by some as though it is nutty.

After the *Discipline* era, Fripp took an even longer sabbatical from "Crimsoning" (as I once heard him put it), this time for about ten years. Though he participated in a few musical projects during this time, one of the main things he did was to develop a new system of playing the guitar (and even for tuning it) and a school for teaching this method, both called Guitar Craft. (Eric Tamm provides a substantial and sometimes humorous account of Guitar Craft in *Robert Fripp*, pp. 150–209.) In 1994 yet another version of King Crimson emerged. This new formation included the 1980s group *en toto* plus two additional musicians: Pat Mastelotto on percussion and Trey Gunn on various "touch guitars" (offshoots of the Chapman Stick idea, but made by other manufacturers). The new group of four string players and two percussionists aimed to constitute a kind of "double trio," with Fripp, Bruford, and Levin as one "unit," and Belew, Mastelotto, and Gunn as the other. By Fripp's own account, the double-trio idea never completely jelled, and the main studio recording of this group, 1995's *Thrak*, is something of a mixed-bag. There are some powerful moments, however, and I would especially single out "One Time" as a lovely song, possibly the best piece that Adrian Belew has contributed as a member of Crimson, and certainly the most subtle. The really great thing about this formation was its live playing—though Fripp had espoused the "small, mobile, intelligent unit" since reformulating his musical philosophy in the late 1970s, and though he has mostly kept to this idea ever since, the *Thrak* group was King Crimson as "orchestra." They made one hell of a sound. Even without completely realizing all of the possibilities, the intertwinings of doubled guitar lines (often not sounding at all like guitars, thanks to the digital revolution in effects—to deal with all of the sounds that Fripp has been able to coax out of the guitar would make a book in itself), doubled bass and Stick lines, and doubled percussion lines, and the further intertwining of *all that* led to a music not hitherto heard. This miraculous intervention can be experienced on two live double albums. *B'Boom* represents the entire concert that the group performed on tour. Even better, though, is *THRaKaTTaK*, a selection of improvisations from different concerts on the *Thrak* tour. This album shows what the six-headed beast was truly capable of, which doesn't mean that it is unremittingly heavy—as always, the emphasis is on listening within the group, and on complex interplay, dynamics, and subtlety, as well as the periodic unleashing of overwhelming and frightening power.

There was some possibility of going further with this version of the group, but Bill Bruford and Tony Levin had their own projects and commitments to get on with. Thus the sextet became a quartet once again, with the remaining members releasing *the construKction of light* in 2000. However, this was no mere "remainder" of the *Thrak* group; instead it is yet another incarnation of the Crimson idea. This is the best King Crimson since the *Larks' Tongues* era. (I discuss the *construKction* crew at some length in the last part of this book.)

I hope this sketch will entice those not familiar with the Crimson King to explore this essential chapter in creative rock music. In the liner notes to the live album from the *Discipline*-era group, *Absent Lovers*, Robert Fripp responded to some points I made in *Listening to the future*, especially the issue of whether or not King Crimson is a true "group." There are a few points in Maestro Fripp's essay that I would still take issue with. (For instance, Fripp says that the essential point is whether or not the money from albums and concerts is shared out equally—as it is in King Crimson; well and good, but there is also the additional and perhaps even more fundamental question of *who decides* that this is how things will be done. Of course, this question cannot be divorced from that concerning the decision that there will be a group to begin with. But hey, this can be grist for the mill for further liner-note essays.) None of these issues is very important in the long run—what is instead important, and the real reason why King Crimson has remained such a force for over three decades (during which the group has actually been "incarnated" for much less than half of that time) is the idea of hearing a *call*, feeling the force of a conception, and even a philosophy, and responding to that philosophy with music. Robert Fripp has been the one with his ears open to that call, and, when appropriate, he has convened and led the very different, discontinuously different, manifestations of the King. But I think Fripp is both sincere and right when he says that King Crimson exists when there is King Crimson music to be played—ultimately, the music speaks itself.

▲ Giles, Giles & Fripp, *The Cheerful Insanity of Giles, Giles & Fripp* (Deram LP, 1968).

King Crimson
In the Wake of Poseidon (Atlantic LP, 1970).
Lizard (Atlantic LP, 1971).
Islands (Atlantic LP, 1972).
Larks' Tongues in Aspic (Atlantic LP, 1973).
Starless and Bible Black (Atlantic LP, 1974).
Red (Atlantic LP, 1974).
The Great Deceiver: Live 1973–1974 (Discipline CD, 1992).
USA (Atlantic LP, 1975).
Discipline (Editions EG LP, 1981).
Beat (Editions EG LP, 1982).

Three of a Perfect Pair (Editions EG LP, 1984).
Absent Lovers: Live in Montreal 1984 (Discipline CD, 1998).
THRAK (Virgin CD, 1995).
B'Boom: Live Bootleg (Discipline CD, 1995).
THRaKaTTaK (Discipline CD, 1996).

Robert Fripp, *Exposure* (Virgin LP, 1979).
——, *A Blessing of Tears* (Discipline CD, 1995).
——, *The Gates of Paradise* (Discipline CD, 1997).
PROJEkCT TWO, *Space Groove* (Discipline CD, 1998).

1998

Beck, *Mutations* (Geffen CD).
John Cale, *Dance Music for Nico, the ballet* (Detour CD).
Diamanda Galas, *Malediction and Prayer* (Asphodel CD).
Kev Hopper, *Spoombung: New Music for Electric Bass* (Thoofa CD).
Portishead, *Roseland NYC Live* (London CD).

With *Mutations*, Beck continues on his path of the three Fs: freaky, funky, funny. This is probably overreaching, but there is something of The Who meets Parliament in his music—it sounds crazy, but it just might work. Although they are almost purely derivative, the songs "Nobody's fault but my own" and "Tropicalia" are very entrancing.

John Cale demonstrates that the avant-garde classical impulses that led him to rock music are still very much alive in him in *Dance Music for Nico, the ballet*, a series of sensitive sketches for the Dutch chamber ensemble, Ice Nine. The music was composed for "Nico, the ballet," and is appropriately austere and astringent. Even more harsh is Diamanda Galas's *Malediction and Prayer*. It can truly be said that there is no voice like hers, and that to listen to an extended piece by Galas is to stare into the gates of hell.

Experimental bass guitar is in its ascendancy. Kev Hopper's album, *Spoombung*, is a good example of what some of the younger bassists are doing. On *Roseland NYC Live*, Portishead gives a strong live reading to their sound, with the help of a small orchestra.

Land of the rising noise: Ikue Mori, Keiji Haino, Ruins, Merzbow

There is a risk of chauvinism in presenting a selection such as this, given that, of the three artists and one group in the title, only Merzbow is primarily a "noise" musician and the true commonality is that they are all Japanese. No chauvinism is intended, and the risk is worth taking in order to point out the important place that Japanese musicians have in the experimental rock scene today. Indeed, these four, though they would most likely make anyone's list of major figures, are only a part of a scene that has grown by leaps and bounds in the last twenty years.

Some introductions are in order. Ikue Mori is a percussionist who played drums in the band DNA with guitarist Arto Lindsay and keyboardist Robin Crutchfield (and, later, bassist Tim Wright). They were part of the No Wave scene, and appeared on Brian Eno's compilation, *No New York*. She also played drums on the *Death Ambient* album with Henry Cow guitarist, Fred Frith, and brilliant Japanese bassist Kato Hideki. But now Mori rarely plays the drum set, and instead she concentrates on drum machines of various types, often several at the same time. In other words, she is not a "beat programmer," such as one might find with some of the new electronic music, but rather someone who uses chance and improvisation in conjunction with an array of drum machines, from the primitive to the more sophisticated. Mori is also a graphic designer whose work can be seen on the CD covers from John Zorn's Tzadik label.

Keiji Haino is known primarily as a guitarist, though another instrument that he often records with is the hurdy gurdy. He also sings, or sometimes wails, the latter being what he is famous for on the electric guitar. Haino is most often found in a trio setting with bass and drums, often with his longstanding group, Fushitsusha. Intensity is the key element in his music—though occasionally Haino backs off a little bit. It will not sound very complimentary in the context of experimental rock to say that "outrageous shredding" is Haino's stock in trade—that's the sort of thing that metalheads are impressed by. For sure, despite the way that some probably want to see Haino's playing, his music cannot be dissociated from heavy metal—not that there's anything wrong with that. But this heavy metal thunder is further intensified with the influence of the hard tenor saxophone playing of John Coltrane, Archie Shepp, Pharaoh Sanders—and perhaps most of all Peter Brötzmann, who also specializes in unbridled overdrive (check out *Machine Gun* from 1968, and *The Berlin Concert*, 1971). Jimi Hendrix is also a major part of the picture. One of the funnier comparisons is with American group Blue Cheer, who were the loudest group in the world for awhile (in the late 1960s, before, as I recall, Deep Purple took over that dubious title), and who were called, even before Grand Funk Railroad (a Frank Zappa discovery!), the worst rock band in the world. Blue Cheer have gone from being goats to heroes in some circles these days (so, can Grand Funk be far behind?). The difference is that, even at its loudest and most frantic, Haino's guitar playing has a logic to it that is more Coltrane than Blue Cheer, even if the latter deserves credit for showing what overdriven amplifiers can do.

Ruins are a duo of drummer/vocalist Yoshida Tatsuya and either Sasaki Hisashi or Masuda Ryuichi on bass guitar and vocals. Sometimes there are guests on keyboards, sax, or guitar, but sometimes they record with just bass, drums, and singing. Very few have pursued this combination, as one might imagine, though the Method Actors (discussed in the new wave section) and a little-known group from Atlanta, called Oh OK, used this set-up (though the latter was composed of a drummer, bass player, and singer, and they only ever released a three-song single). What Ruins do with it is much more harsh and manic, and they are influenced by progressive rock and Can.

A good account of the Japanese noise scene can be found in the book, *Japan Edge: The Insider's Guide to Japanese Pop Subculture*, edited by Annette Roman. Mason Jones, the author of one of the two extensive chapters on noise, argues that the scene in Japan initially sprang from two European sources. One was those Manchester (England) purveyors of terror and the grotesque, Throbbing Gristle. No doubt the Gristles have been unfairly ignored in this book. Strangely, Greil Marcus did not hear the call of Gristle in *Lipstick Traces* either, even though his orientation toward dada, surrealism, and situationism would seem more predisposed in that direction. Perhaps Marcus thought that a band whose live act so often featured soiled diapers, used tampons, and the like was another example of people who are more into celebrity outrage than music. However, starting out in 1975, anticipating punk as well as reenacting Artaud's Theater of Cruelty, Throbbing Gristle is certainly a good example of what at least one side of avant rock is all about. Rather than inventing something new out of the basic elements of music, or even learning to play their instruments especially well, they instead took some elemental impulses of rock and pushed them to one kind of extreme. As with many experimental rock musicians, the source of inspiration is the Velvet Underground.

The other big influence in Japanese noise, according to Mason Jones, is "a combination of free jazz artists, modern composers, and so-called Krautrock bands, such as Neu!, Faust, Can, and Amon Duul" (p. 77). (I'm pleased, by the way, that Jones says "so-called Krautrock"; it is not a term that I care to use either.) Jones explains that these influences also led emergent noise artists to find out about John Cage and Karlheinz Stockhausen, and also to form an informal network of experimental musicians who shared their work by means of cassette tapes. One of the first of these musicians in Japan was Masami Akita, who named his project "Merzbow" after a work by German collage artist Kurt Schwitters (*Japan Edge*, p. 77). Sometimes Masami has collaborators in his recordings, but often Merzbow is just Masumi and various forms of sound generation. Like many sound artists of the recent two decades, Merzbow is inclined toward the film aesthetic, especially the idea of the soundtrack—real or imagined. What sets him apart from most other such artists, however—though what connects him to John Zorn—is his interest in Japanese bondage films. Indeed, he has written essays for books on the subject of *kinbaku*—Japanese rope bondage—and created the albums *Music for Bondage Performance* volumes 1 and 2 (see *Japan Edge*, pp. 87–91).

The Japanese noise scene in recent years is both extensive and marginal. Among the major artists are Masonna (a name concocted by combining masochism and Madonna), Mne-mic, Aube, Solmania, Government Alpha, Building of Gel, and Yukiko. When Sonic Youth has toured Japan, they have often included one or more of these artists on the bill.

Jones concludes his chapter on noise with some interesting reflections on whether this music can be assimilated, the way that the rawer forms of industrial music (of which Throbbing Gristle was one of the first examples) were taken up into "more beat-driven music, which later helped spawn the techno craze" (p. 97). Significantly, Jones makes a comparison with free-jazz artists. Though he does not mention him by name, I think it is unlikely that Cecil Taylor's music will ever be assimilated into some sort of jazz mainstream.

Is the issue one that is absolutely crucial for avant-garde music? There are some forms of music that are very far out to begin with, but by and by a sizeable part of the listening public comes around to them, or at least there is some kind of "acceptance." The avant-garde musician, or for that matter, any creative musician, cannot be motivated first of all by the desire for acceptance—but does this mean that an element that is defin-itive of the avant-garde is that it does everything in its power to resist eventual accep-tance or assimilation? In the case of Merzbow, or for that matter, Throbbing Gristle, is the attachment to the music of other "extremes"—of the grotesque, or of "strange" sex-ual practices—a somewhat artificial means of achieving and maintaining status as art that will forever remain on the outside of common tastes, or is it simply an extension of what led to this unholy noise in the first place? Mason Jones says of Merzbow's interest in bondage, and the use of bondage photographs on his album covers, "Personally, I find the connection between noise and that sort of imagery embarrassing. [Noise artist] Hijokaidan's choice of beautiful, pastoral photographs is far more interesting as a con-trast to music that some people find ugly" (p. 87). One might wonder if there is a con-nection between sexual practices that are not only "extreme," but that also seem mainly to involve tying up women (in a culture where gender inequality runs very deep), and forms of music where one's subjectivity is pulled into a maelstrom so intense that ethi-cal bearings are impossible to come by. I have a similar worry with the way that some techno music, often associated with "club culture," is played so loud that prolonged exposure would certainly harm one's hearing. The idea is that one "listens with the whole body," and one achieves a state of ex-stasis, often helped by a substance similarly named. I suppose there is a rationalist side to me that is highly skeptical of such things (and we might keep in mind that, by contrast, Gilles Deleuze—the patron saint/philoso-pher of some of these musicians—called himself a "radical empiricist"). Without hav-ing any definitive answers to these questions to propose, it might at least be important to have them on the table. At any rate, Mason Jones is inclined to think that the gap between "music" and "noise" is large enough to absorb the impact of the occasional contact between noise and the musical mainstream. Additionally, the sheer intensity of noise artists keeps the noise vision alive. In any case, I believe there will always be, somewhere in the deepest underground, noise artists at work, happily oblivious to the latest musical trends. (p. 97)

Ikue Mori, *Garden* (Tzadik CD, 1996).
——, *B/Side* (Tzadik CD, 1998).
Ikue Mori, Kato Hideki, Fred Frith, *Death Ambient* (Avant CD, 1993).
Ikue Mori, Tenko, and guests, *Mystery Death Praxis* (Tzadik CD, 1998).

Keiji Haino, with Greg Cohen and Joey Baron, *An Unclear Trail: More than This* (Avant CD, 1998).
Fushitsusha, *Withdrawe, this sable Disclosure ere devot'd* (Victo CD, 1998; live performance from 1997).
Purple Trap (Keiji Haino, Bill Laswell, Rashied Ali), *Decided … Already the Motionless Heart of Tranquility, Tangling the Prayer called "I"* (Tzadik CD, 1999).

Ruins, *Refusal Fossil* (Skin Graft CD, 1997).
Derek Bailey and the Ruins, *Saisoro* (Tzadik CD, 1995).
Ruins, *Symphonica* (Tzadik CD, 1998).

Merzbow, *Pulse Demon* (Release CD, 1995).
——, *Pinkream* (Dirter CD, 1995).
——, *1930* (Tzadik CD, 1998).

Kato Hideki, *Hope and Despair* (Extreme CD, 1996).
——, *Turbulent Zone* (Music for Expanded Ears CD, 1998).

By now, all of the folks discussed in this section are heavily recorded. Indeed, like a lot of people these days, and perhaps especially in the Zorn/Laswell universe, there is a bit of overrecording. What is offered in the discography here, therefore, is just a smattering. Among Ikue Mori's recent projects has been a trio recording with Kim Gordon of Sonic Youth, and DJ Olive, as part of the Sonic Youth Records series. Being fond of music that is spare and produced by only two or three people playing "small" instruments, I was impressed with Ikue's collaboration with Zeena Parkins on the latter's album, *Isabelle* (Disk Union CD, 1995). The second of two pieces on the album, "Hup!", is a duo for Parkins on electric harp, sampler, and "East Berlin toy," and Ikue on electronic percussion. According to the liner notes, the piece was inspired by "Wonder Woman and Super Heroes from English and American comics of the Forties and Fifties." Parkins figures significantly into Björk's album, *Vespertine*, about which there are a few comments in the concluding chapter. A good example of what Ikue Mori does in a group context is *B/Side*, where she performs with a group that includes Parkins (on accordion in addition to harp and sampler), Kato Hideki (bass), Anthony Coleman (organ), Erik Friedlander (cello), David Watson (guitar), Andy Haas (didjeridu), and Tenko (vocals). The album is a collaboration with film-maker Abigail Childs, for whom Ikue has done a number of soundtracks. The album that provides the essence of Ikue Mori, however, is the solo effort, *Garden*. An entire album of drum machines might sound like the ultimate basis for a nervous break-down. For some it will be, but not because the album is wall-to-wall beats, but instead because the main elements of the music are economy and silence. To say the music represents the Zen sensibility in the cybernetic age would be one of those phrases that has always already been a cliché, but still. In a profile of the artist in *The Wire*, appro-priately titled "Cyborg Manifesto," A. C. Lee gives an excellent description of what Ikue Mori is all about:

> Treating her drum machines as a prosthetic extension of her own mental and physical processes, Ikue Mori embodies just such a (wo)man-machine interface [as represented by the figure of the cyborg]. On stage, barely visible above stacks of black boxes and their intestinal knots of cables, she taps out a broadcast of pulsing textural helixes in bright stereophony. In the flurry of coding and decoding passing between her mind, fin-gers and microchips, as she processes and patterns her beats and pulses, Mori and her machines merge as a single system, a biomechanical network of flesh and metal. But for Ikue, the merging of mental and mechanical processes preceded the drum machines that facilitated the cyborg evolution. "Even back when I was playing a drum set, I was playing it like a drum machine," she recalls, "I would program the patterns in my brain and then repeat or change them in performance." (June 1998, p. 20)

Donna Haraway wrote an essay that has become rather famous in some circles, with the title, "A Manifesto for Cyborgs" (in her book, *Simians, Cyborgs, and Women: The Reinvention of Nature*). Her central claim is that we have now entered a period where the human species has to be considered as part of a continuum, with apes on the one side and intelligent machines on the other. The more sophisticated the machines get, the more humanity is stitched into the continuum.

The question remains as to how close the machines have really come to us, or how close they can ever come, in terms of language. If language is mere symbol manipula-tion, then the machines are getting ever closer. If language is fundamentally something else—"world-disclosiveness" is Heidegger's proposal, and the point here (to oversim-plify, for sure) is that no *quantity* of the ability to move symbols or words around will amount to the *quality* of "being-in-the-world"—then our "conversations" with com-puters and the like will necessarily be limited. But is the limitation the same as that for any musical instrument—a violin is not a trombone—or is there an additional dimension, something to do with the new possibilities of technology? In some sense, Ikue Mori's music is about what sorts of conversations are indeed possible, and therein lies its interest.

Returning to the useful and enjoyable book *Japan Edge* (which also deals with anime, manga, and film in addition to noise/music) for a moment, the author of the chapter on music, Yuji Oniki, uses a wonderful phrase to describe the music of Fushitsusha: "the annihilation of the comprehensible" (p. 112). The record with Greg Cohen and Joey Baron—the "rhythm section" for John Zorn's Masada quartet, and among the most highly regarded musicians in the New York scene these days—is deeply strange. After many albums where there is no release from the unrelentingness of Haino's full-bore guitar, here he seems to be deconstructing the quiet fire that one hears in more mainstream jazz guitarists such as Joe Pass or Bucky Pizzarelli. I'm not sure it works in its own terms; instead, it makes a fascinating chapter when sandwiched between a live Fushitsusha album (such as the one listed), and the Purple Trap album, where Haino is playing with Bill Laswell and former Coltrane drummer Rashied Ali. The album and song titles sound a bit like the wacky rap that Hendrix would sometimes do from the concert stage, so one wonders if the idea here is that hard, psychedelic rock has gone from "haze" to "trap"—whatever that means. This is acid rock reinvented and extended. (Again, there are many recordings of Haino and his various groups—I just picked three of the ones I find most interesting.) There is subtlety in Haino's playing, appearances sometimes to the contrary—but it is often found in that just *slightly* less raucous moment, a moment that passes quickly. In that respect it would be appropriate to call this *absolutely urban* music—the "quiet" of the gigantic city is not the quiet of the countryside, nor could it be.

Ruins are a vastly more versatile band than one would ever expect from a unit consisting in bass guitar and drums. For one thing, they have outrageous chops. For another, they are transmuting a large array of influences through those two instruments and vocals, the latter almost always in a "language" of their own invention. In this they show one of their many progressive-rock connections, namely that of Magma, the French group that sounds like Mahavishnu Orchestra meets Carl Orff (led by the extraordinary drummer/composer Christian Vander). Ruins shows the influence of Magma in its music, too, but then it also shows the influence of Yes and King Crimson. One of the funny things I came across that was said about Ruins on an internet site was, "they sound like atonal King Crimson, but way more obnoxious." *Refusal Fossil* is a good example of Ruins with and without guests. On the more recent *Symphonica* they add two vocalists and a keyboardist and basically make their own progressive-rock album, updated to the millennium for sure. The discography entry for *Saisoro* is slightly inaccurate; actually, the album cover says "Derek and the Ruins," clearly a twist on Derek and the Dominoes. There's no rendition of "Layla," however—more's the pity. Ruins turn out to be a fine foil for the angularity of this Derek.

Bailey's aim is to always do something different, not to repeat himself. That is probably a goal impossible to attain, and yet Bailey comes close, and his playing can be especially provocative when other musicians are trying to triangulate with it. In 2000, Tzadik released another interesting grouping for Bailey, *Mirakle*, with progressive funksters Jamaladeen Tacuma (bass guitar) and Calvin Weston (drums). Put *Sairsoro* and *Mirakle* together with the Purple Trap album, and the message to the makers of all of those guitar-wanker CDs out there, to quote Robert De Niro's line from *Taxi Driver*, is "suck on this!"

Knowing where to start or stop with Merzbow is another impossibility: Masami Akita has released more than one hundred albums, including the fifty-disk *Merzbox* set. The best written introduction to Merzbow is Edwin Pouncey's excellent overview in *The Wire*, "Consumed by Noise" (August 2000, pp. 26–33; this includes a survey of ten Merzbow albums by David Keenan), from which I draw in what follows. One of Masami's funny comments about his productivity: "Initially I used to believe that Sun Ra released more than 500 albums . . . so my goal was 500 releases. Later I learned that it was not that many, around 120 something, or even 200. So now I aim for 1000" (p. 28).

Masami, born in 1956, came of age in the late 1960s. He was influenced by many of the same groups that his contemporaries were, including the Rolling Stones and Beatles, but with a twist: when they were listening to the Stones' more blues-oriented music, Masami was into *Their Satanic Majesties Request*. And the Beatles' music that Masami was especially attracted to was George Harrison's *Wonderwall* and Yoko Ono's and John Lennon's *Unfinished Music No.1* ("Two Virgins"). Among the other trends of that time that played a role in Masami's early formation were progressive rock, Frank Zappa, and Captain Beefheart. It may be difficult to see these influences in the albums or concerts of Merzbow, but I think there is a connection in terms of an epic approach to composition. Indeed, for all of the many Merzbow albums, it might be possible to hear Masami's music as a single, open-ended project, the full-dimensions of which will never be heard. In this respect, Pouncey provides a helpful bit of advice: "The knee-jerk response that 'all Merzbow recordings/performances sound identical' is a theory that only those with neither imagination or patience will adhere to. The fact is that to understand, enjoy and eventually reach noise nirvana through Masami Akita's work, you have to listen to a hell of a lot of it" (p. 28). In other words, one has to devote oneself to Masami's oeuvre, or at least one has to have some expert help in sorting through the noise.

There are many colors in Merzbow's music, many influences—and the final product hardly resembles any of them. At one point in his conversation with Pouncey,

Masami says that heavy metal is the biggest influence in his music. At another point he mentions having done a collaboration with a Japanese hard-rock band called Boris, where the aim was to reproduce what was already a reproduction: the cover version of the Beatles' "I am the Walrus" by British hard-rock group Spooky Tooth. Is there a dialogue with Plato going on here? Plato, those who took Philosophy 101 will recall, was skeptical of art that was merely a copy of a copy—for instance, sculptures that are copies of the human form, which is itself a copy of the *form* of the human. While we're with Plato, we might recall, too, that he believed that music is very important, especially as a preparation for understanding mathematics. Mathematics, in turn, gives us a sense of the eternal forms. But some things are so *base*, so low, that there is no ideal form for them. Examples would be excrement and dirt—but surely *noise* would also be in this category? Of course, Merzbow, like John Cage, does not make a distinction between "music" and "noise." (One funny comment he makes on this subject is, "If noise means uncomfortable sounds, then pop music is noise to me"; Pouncy, p. 26.)

To return to the question of all of the influences in Merzbow's music, Masami talks about the role that feedback and the ability to control it played in his early music. One of the people who made feedback a part of hard-rock music was Jimi Hendrix—he was both a pioneer in using feedback as an integral part of music, and he was the one who made feedback popular. Merzbow uses just the feedback, without the "source," so to speak (whether it is a heavily amplified electric guitar or what-have-you), and this is a method in much of his music. He uses radios, but he especially uses static. And, again, there are many non-musical influences too, from dada and surrealism to Japanese bondage stuff, and he is likely to associate all of his influences in one way or another with "the erotic." As Masami puts it, "Noise is the most erotic form of sound, that's why all of my works relate to the erotic" (Pouncey, p. 29). Now, if you take all of this stuff and, so to speak, mix it very hard in a cauldron where the aim is to create noise, isn't it likely that the result will be similar to what you would get if you mixed every color in the spectrum? In other words, isn't the result the sonic equivalent of black—the point where all colors turn into the lack of color—or at least very, very dark shades of brown or gray? Even the noise artist must confront this question—especially the noise artist who hopes to issues a thousand albums! In principle, however, isn't it this sort of line that it is the whole point of the avant-garde (in whatever art form) to explore and push? I have only heard a small part of Merzbow's output, but what I have heard thus far is impressive in the way that it explores the different possibilities for going to the very brink of incomprehensibility.

Is this "rock," even if "avant rock"? At one point in the interview with Edward Pouncey, Merzbow likens his approach to "punk and not like academic electroacoustic music." Perhaps more than any other artist discussed in this book, Merzbow underlines the idea that rock can be the unlimited basis for experiment, just as much if not more than any other kind of music—even if the result of the experiment is not recognizable as rock.

1998

Thinking Plague, *In Extremis* (Cuneiform CD).
Tom Ze, *Fabrication Defect: Com Defeito de Fabricacao* (Luaka Bop CD).

1999

The Ananda Shankar Experience and State of Bengal, *Walking On* (Real World CD).
Cibo Matto, *Stereo Type A* (Warner Bros CD).
The Olivia Tremor Control, *Black Foliage* (Flydaddy CD).
Os Mutantes, *Everything is Possible!* (Luaka Bop CD; best of collection).

Thinking Plague is carrying forward at least one thread from the days of progressive rock, namely that associated with Henry Cow and Rock in Opposition. As some readers will know, there is now a large, though somewhat underground, trend called "neo-prog." These are bands such as Spock's Beard and The Flower Kings, and by some accounts Dream Theater, that are more in the vein of Yes and Genesis—and often the lighter side of these bands. The music of Thinking Plague is much more harsh and jagged, in the spirit of hard Brechtianism, and, unlike some of the new bands that are relating to progressive rock, they have their own things to say. Deborah Perry has the kind of sharp-edged voice that goes substantially beyond what is taken for "astringent" these days, and the lyrics are in the acidic tradition of the great Henry Cow/Slapp Happy album, *In Praise of Learning*. The superb Bob Drake, from the 5uu's, plays bass and violin on several tracks.

Like Arto Lindsay—and the best of neo-prog, for that matter—Tom Ze is also updating a previously established language, in this case in the form of a wacked-out Tropicalia refracted through Funkadelic and a No Wave sensibility. *Walking On*, the collaboration between Ananda Shankar and the State of Bengal, might seem like a gimmick at first look: classical Indian music, especially sitar, meets heavy-beat dance electronica. In England—and in Asia, of course—such combinations are becoming more common, thanks to the blowback from colonialism. In this case it works quite well, thanks to the sensitivity of the musicians.

The Olivia Tremor Control is one of a group of bands from Athens, Georgia, that are referred to as "Elephant 6." (Another of the better-known groups is Neutral Milk Hotel.) *Magnet* magazine has been keen on these groups, and especially on *Black Foliage*, which is being set up as something like the *Sgt. Pepper's* of current indie rock. Well, there are indeed some similarities: strong, McCartneyesque melodies, psychedelic scaffoldings and even the occasional freakout, and then moments of alienating,

John/Yoko collage. If the *White Album* had had greater continuity, like *Sgt. Pepper's*, with bits and pieces from everything that has happened in the meantime, then the result would be something like *Black Foliage*. It sounds like a great idea, and the realization *is* mostly great—though, like the *White Album*, and at seventy minutes in length, there are moments where the project goes a bit off course. And yet, as with the Beatles' epic, the journey is very much worth taking.

While we are on the subject of the Beatles and their lasting influence, two other albums are worthy of note. Os Mutantes actually started out on TV, in the Brazilian show, *The Small World of Ronnie Von*. This was in the late 1960s, during the period of military rule in Brazil, and musicians associated with the Tropicalia movement (the best known in the United States being Gilberto Gil) were often suspected of engaging in subversive communications in their songs. Os Mutantes combined Tropicalia with influence from the Beatles, John Cage, and Frank Zappa and the Mothers of Invention—and they anticipated Devo by some years as well. The band broke up in 1971 (having previously left the TV/Rio scene to form a commune in the hills), though a couple of the solo albums that came from members of the group in subsequent years are essentially Mutantes efforts. David Byrne has had a longstanding interest in Brazilian music, and he compiled *Everything is Possible!* for his Luaka Bop label. Some have questioned both the choices and the pacing on this 2-CD album, but it is a good introduction to the group, and all of the Mutantes albums have now been reissued.

From Beatles and Tropicalia to Beatles and hip-hop/electronica—actually, Cibo Matto is more Yoko Ono than the Fab Four, and there are elements of funk, bossa nova, and even country music here as well. The core of the group is singer Miho Hatori and sampler, sequencer, and keyboard player Yuka Honda. They are obsessed with food to the point that the name of their group is Italian for "food madness." Actually, their earlier effort, 1996's *Viva! La Woman*, was more food-saturated, with every one of the ten songs dedicated to that subject. *Viva!* is a lot of fun, but *Stereo Type A* is a significant advance—and still a lot of fun. This is an album that stays in my car stereo for weeks at a time (although I don't drive the car every day or even most days), not the place where I am as likely to listen to Cecil Taylor or John Cage. The other members of Cibo Matto are Timo Ellis and Sean Lennon—son of Yoko and John, playing drums, bass guitar, various guitars, and contributing vocals. The lyrics are often very funny, with a beat slant. Like many of the albums and even groups discussed in this book, the question arises once again regarding what is really "avant." Much of the originality in creative rock music is in the particular mix of eclectic elements that are combined. There are sounds *in* the music that we have all heard before, but it seems to me that the overall sound is striking and original, and the fact that it is fun, funny, and often good for dancing, makes it even better.

Björk, O'Rourke, and beyond

A song on the 1984 album by Prefab Sprout contains the chorus:

> When Bobby Fischer's plane—plane, plane—
> Touches the ground—plane, plane—
> He'll take those Russian boys and play them out of town,
> Playing for blood,
> As grandmasters should . . .

> —"Cue Fanfare," from *Swoon*

Two years later, in 1986, Reykjavik, Iceland, would be known as the site of a failed summit between Ronald Reagan and Mikhail Gorbachev. As Graham Burgess reports in his *Chess Highlights of the 20th Century*, news coverage of the summit mentions "the Fischer-Spassky match in 1972 as the last event of global importance in Reykjavik" (p. 177). Unless you are over forty years of age at the time of this publication, or unless you are a chess enthusiast, this last bit may not mean very much to you. Reykjavik, a town on the margins of the Earth, also has the world's longest functioning parliament, established by Vikings a thousand years ago. Iceland has one hundred percent literacy, and all Icelanders learn two other languages in addition to their own. Reykjavik is a sophisticated place, a crossroads of world culture where a young girl could hear Stockhausen and Jimi Hendrix and Miles Davis. Reagan and Gorbachev met there to continue the Cold War; ten years earlier Britain and Iceland settled a dispute over fishing rights, a dispute that included a brief episode of actual gunfire, which came to be known as the Cod War.

The population of Iceland is about a quarter of a million. In 1972, the *New York Times* published a book under the title, *Fischer/Spassky*, and they opened the book with a short essay on Iceland by Katherine Scherman. Her opening paragraph reads as follows:

> The World Championship match has been held on an obscure island of which, before Mr. Fischer and Mr. Spassky put its name on the front pages of the world's newspapers, perhaps only four facts were generally known: some priests there a long time ago wrote some sagas, there are a lot of volcanoes, there is no darkness in summer and it rains all the time. Now for the first time in its thousand-year history Iceland is exciting curiosity beyond its own rocky shores. A look at the backdrop against which the champions played shows a land quite as extraordinary as the dramatic match just finished. (New York: Bantam Books, 1972; p. 1)

If you were born before 1960, and if your memory still functions serviceably, you probably associate Reykjavik with Bobby Fischer and Boris Spassky. If you were born after

1970, you are more likely to associate Reykjavik with Björk Gudmundsdottir, more commonly known as Björk, citizen of the world.

Björk was born in 1967. There are various "first-name only" pop stars out there, Madonna, Cher, Prince, and so on. Björk has many of the surface qualities of a pop star, perhaps—she is both lovely and interesting to look at, she has a provocative personality, she is often reinventing herself. The association that springs to mind, even before Madonna, is someone I referred to as a "psychedelic opportunist" in my book on progressive rock, namely Donovan. Now I am not sure if such a charge is really fair, or, even if fair, such a bad thing. Donovan had a nice song about an enlightened island, "Atlantis." Meanwhile, Katherine Scherman says of Iceland that "[t]he extraordinary clarity of the air is the first impression a newcomer has" (p. 5). Following the chain of references in Scherman's portrait leads to a significant claim:

> Even on a foggy day Reykjavik's many-colored houses shine as clear and bright as the flowers of the fields. Everything looks new. It is as if the city, and indeed the whole country, had come up out of the sea, clean-washed and fully formed, only this morning.
>
> The reason for the remarkable absence of smog and grime is that Iceland has no heavy industry. A nation of farmers since its founding, the end of the last century saw Iceland change to a nation of fishermen. The country has no resources of minerals, chemicals, timber, any of the raw products on which an industrial economy must be based. So the industrial revolution passed her by. Having no industry, Iceland has no overconcentration of population, no slums, no unemployment, no mine-blighted areas, no crime (there is less than one murder a year) and—this is the pleasantist—no classes. (pp. 5–6)

It is as if Atlantis had resurfaced, at least in this rosy portrait.

I cannot help but comment that, even if Ms. Scherman's claim about "no classes" might be a bit overdone, it is still a very pleasant thing to read the words of someone who at least thinks that it would be the "pleasantist" thing of all for a society to not have classes. (Perhaps there are at least two basic classes in the Icelandic economy: humans and fishes.)

What kind of band was the Sugarcubes? Outside of Reykjavik, at least, it was through this band that the larger world caught its first sight of Björk. The band seemed to have something to do with punk, even if a bit on the new wave side—the music was raw and energetic. The *Rough Guide* to rock calls them "odd, spiky, avant-garde pop" (p. 856). Listeners in Europe and North America became aware of the group in 1987, when they released the single, "Birthday," which was followed in 1988 by the album, *Life's Too Good*. Björk stood out, of course, especially in the concert video performance of the single, which was shown on MTV. There was a feral quality projected not only from her appearance or her movements, but seemingly from her very being, a quality that remains today. Alongside Björk in the band was a whole other spectacle,

Einar Orn. He's the fellow whom I imagine many Sugarcubes fans, or perhaps people who would otherwise be fans, found quite annoying. Orn plays the pocket trumpet—an instrument previously most associated with jazz musician Don Cherry—and raps a kind of beat poetry in the background of Björk's vocals, sometimes joining in with full voice for the chorus. Although I have not devoted myself to Sugarcube-ology, I still go back and forth on the issue of whether Orn's contribution was an ornamentation that was sometimes welcome and sometimes not, or in some sense integral to the structure. For sure, he was the one adding a good deal of the "odd, spiky" to the aforementioned characterization. Even so, Björk was clearly more than just the "singer" for a neo-punk band, and a good deal of what is special about her instrument—that is, a voice infused with a powerful sensibility—already comes through in the Sugarcubes' albums.

If this music was meant to have some relationship to punk, however, at least in its rawness, it was a generally happy, trippy, and even utopian punk. Punk in the early years, around 1977 to 1980 (and, at least in the United States, for a few more years into the eighties), tended to be very "anti-hippie." (In the United States, the anti-hippie orientation of some punks made them, in a way that was both amusing and annoying, the counterparts of the Alex Keaton character on the TV show, *Family Ties*—in other words, cocky little twirps from privileged backgrounds.) Björk came along at a time when she could be in punk but not exactly of it. She was raised by hippies (her parents), and with grandparents who were immersed in classical music and jazz. Born in 1966, by age eleven she had already recorded an album of Icelandic folk songs, and then proceeded to participate in a number of anarcho-punk collectives: Exodus, Tappi Tikarass, and Kukl. From the last of these Björk and Einar Orn emerged to form the Sugarcubes. By 1987, when the remarkable "Birthday" was released, punk was already ten years old and possibly more than five years gone. Björk got an early start, and in her way she was part of the early wave of punk; but she was not someone who eschewed musical sophistication, and, even better, along with the energy she brought to the Sugarcubes, Björk also brought a quality generally missing from punk—exuberance. The Sugarcubes albums are sweet and fun—with titles like "Life's Too Good" and "Stick Around for Joy," their spirit is worlds away from *Never Mind the Bollocks* or *Plastic Surgery Disasters* (Dead Kennedys), though comparison with the B-52s might stand up. But then, that's not "punk," per se, and neither are the Cubes, really. Maybe it comes from growing up in a classless society? Just kidding, sort of, but as much as I like the Sugarcubes, there is the fact that this is post-punk music with very little of the political edge of the first wave. What Louise Gray calls the "Icelandic occult anarchopunk syndicalism" of Björk and her band is mainly manifest in the communal artistic endeavor that is manifest in the Cubes. The members of the band were writers and poets as much as musicians, and the art collective they formed, Bad Taste, continues its work today.

Significantly, Gray titled her *Wire* (November 1998) profile of Björk, "The Idea of North." That's a bit of serendipity, recalling as it does the title of one of Glenn Gould's contrapuntal radio documentaries. Like Gould, Björk is a self-avowed hermit; unlike Gould, Björk has quite another side, what might be called the "shy exhibitionist" (a term inspired by Molly Shannon's hilarious "Mary Katherine Gallagher" character on *Saturday Night Live*). One of the interviews Björk did upon the release of her 2001 album, *Vespertine*, was with fashion designer Donna Karan (of DKNY fame). Responding to Karan's query regarding what the album is "about," Björk speaks to this side of her artistry, as well as a number of other issues:

> This album is slightly nostalgic in the sense that it's basically about being an introvert. It's sort of about hibernation and being in a cocoon. I call it a winter album, because in winter you cocoon yourself and prepare for next spring. On a lot of levels, the sounds are kind of frozen. It's also like a love affair with a laptop. I wanted to make modern chamber music. And it's a love affair with two things: the home and laptops, basically saying that a hundred years ago the most ideal music situation was in the home, where people would play harps for each other, or tell each other stories. And in the middle of the century it became the opposite, the most ideal music situation was something like Woodstock, with many hundreds of thousands of people hearing the same song in the same mud pit, having the same euphoric experience, and the target, sonically, was to make a stack of amplifiers that could reach China. I think we've come full circle and the most ideal music situation now, through Napster and through the Internet and downloading and DVD, is back to the home. (*Interview*, Sept. 2001, pp. 191, 195)

That's some history and theory! Björk often has her interviewers on a bit. Still, to put the laptop computer (the program of choice for most musicians, including Björk, is Pro Tools) together with more intimate settings, where the point is to actually listen to the music, certainly expresses a nostalgia for Glenn Gould. To facilitate isolation through forms of technology that require an extensive, social infrastructure—that's Gould to a T. It is also a nice connection to Jim O'Rourke, also a shy fellow who makes much use of the laptop (more on that in a moment).

This winter album finally came out of its cocoon in the heat of summer (I will have more to say about *Vespertine* in the final chapter), reminding us that this supposed homebody is not averse to morphing in all kinds of ways. There is an erotic quality to Björk's music and performance—which is more than obvious—but it is an eros that runs from a sexuality that can suddenly seem strange, indeed alien, to the larger sense of embracing the world, even the cosmos. And yet, a fundamental fragility also comes through, expressed especially in the chances that Björk takes with what might be called her overall "presentation." Her *person* is in her music, and she is an interesting person—but does that necessarily make the music interesting? Does the music become interesting because Björk uses her persona to get us back into the old nature/culture debate again? She even seems to foreclose the debate, since it is difficult not to experience her as some sort of raw force of nature. But that is both the trick and the charm: Björk knows very well what she is doing.

The Sugarcubes made some plenty good music, especially on their first and third (and final) albums. *Stick Around for Joy* ends on a delightfully feral note, with the song "Chihuahua." Although the format of a rock band with the standard guitars and drums is a constraint on the possibilities that Björk has pursued since the disbanding of the Cubes, the group had a very good sense of syncopation; although the guitars were occasionally hard or jangling, most often there was a lot of space and interweaving single-note lines, and the drummer concentrates on the toms, for that jungle feel. At the very least, you can make a great 90-minute tape from the three Cubes albums—although that may sound a bit backhanded, I mean it as a compliment. The videos are good, too (a collection is available), especially for earlier songs such as "Motorcrash" and "Delicious Demon." The victim in "Motorcrash" finally makes it home, only to have her jerk husband yell, "where have you been all this time?" Björk's singing here is a prime example of the primal quality that she can infuse into a line.

For the most part, there was a definite Sugarcubes sound that came across on all of their records (the comparison to the B-52s is again apt). Björk's solo albums, on the other hand, are close to being just the opposite. Although there are now a zillion remixes and alternative versions of Björk's songs and pieces, for any given one of them, the sound and approach is close to unique. Louise Gray has a better term for what Björk is doing than mere eclecticism: "Her compositional method is more a *connective* activity than crossover fusion" (p. 46, my emphasis). In one interview after another, Björk describes herself as a total music fan, a "trainspotter," and, thankfully, someone dedicated to music to the point where a lucrative film career does not interest her. She has maintained her interest in composers such as Stockhausen and Messiaen—"experimentalists with soul," and meanwhile she also collaborates with some of the most innovative people in electronica today: Graham Massey, Mark Bell, Howie B., and Talvin Singh, among others. Björk has her own "cyborg manifesto" going:

> I'm really interested in blending together electronic music with everyday life to prove that's actually how we're living . . . . I guess my attempt is to take just the life we're leading every day and make magic out of that. Just to be honest, those are the sounds [of life]; it's what we hear all the time
>
> . . . I like extremes, I guess: very raw acoustic things and then very pure electronic beats. To me, electricity comes from nature. Like acupuncture—something several thousand years old triggers the electricity that's inside us within our nerve system. (Tamara Palmer, "A different sort of bird," *Urb*, September 2001, p. 125.)

Indeed, Björk's explorations have led her to a highly refined and idiosyncratic electroacoustic chamber rock, perhaps taken to their furthest point on 1997's *Homogenic*, where several tracks featured the combination of electronic beats and string octet. The effect of this combination is both raw and sophisticated at the same time.

And yet, for all of the electronica in Björk's solo music, all of the advanced beat science and digital synth textures, I don't think the music is dependent on these things at all. The proof is found in a wonderful video that I would recommend to all sentient beings, the MTV Europe Unplugged concert from 1994. The concert features nine songs from *Debut*, and the instrumentation ranges from harpsichord ("Human Behaviour") to percussion orchestra plus tuba ("One Day" and others), to saxophone trio ("The Anchor Song"). Among the excellent percussionists in the orchestra are Talvin Singh and Evelyn Glennie. This is really chamber rock at its finest, and the instrumentation allows the craft of Björk's songwriting to shine through. What comes through is that Björk is really a songwriter in the European *Lieder* ("art song") tradition. Her albums represent orchestrated song cycles, not so far removed from Schoenberg's *Pierre Lunaire*—a work that, according to Louise Gray, Björk has performed. It can also be argued that Björk, for all that she came of age in the time of punk, owes something to the time of progressive rock—clearly she has an epic approach to her albums, even if she is not given to pieces that last fifteen or twenty minutes. In the end, of course, Björk is a paradigm avant-rocker, because she transmutes music from everywhere, and then she adds to this her very distinctive voice— by which I do not mean only her vocal chords, but, let's face it, her vocal chords are not to be denied.

While on the subject of concert videos, I would also highly recommend another offering from 1994, *Vessel*. This is a concert from London, with a band that also features Talvin Singh (the entire line-up is two keyboardists, two percussionists, a bass guitarist, and a fellow playing saxophones and flute—there is very little guitar to be found in Björk's solo music). There is such a lovely feeling to the concert, it gives me hope that London might just make it as a multicultural metropolis. Perhaps my affection for that city and its seeming vibrancy and comfort with its many colors and cultures is the same sort of naivete that would lead one to think that Iceland is a classless society— but perhaps we have to have a few dreams to get by on. Björk made London her home for a number of years, and indeed her English leans toward the Cockney, but she soured on the city after a racist lunatic from Florida attempted to send her a mail bomb there. That is hardly London's fault, of course, but the episode led Björk to retreat once again to her beloved and sacred Iceland. In the most recent period, Björk has been living in Manhattan. A very sweet moment in the *Vessel* concert is a song titled, "Atlantic," a song that does not appear on the solo albums. "Atlantic" is not sung in English and, as best I can tell, it is not in Icelandic, either. It is not in any language that I recognize, but in any case understanding the words (or sounds) does not detract from the sense of having received a communication.

The paradox of Björk is that she has all of her communes, all of the collaborative work that she does, and she opens her mouth wider than one might think humanly possible in order to project a sound, and yet she truly does have that hermit side to her as well. She often comments that engineers have a difficult time capturing her voice, because she tends to move about as she sings—music seizes her. Even when she is relatively still, she looks a little possessed. Her range is not only difficult for engineers to capture, but she is also possessed of a wide assortment of squeals, gasps, even hiccups, and other vocal tricks that remind me of what Pharaoh Sanders has developed on the tenor saxophone. "I learnt to sing . . . acoustically," Björk told Louise Gray (p. 47)— by which she means she learned to sing by screaming and wailing in the woods, a five-minute walk from Reykjavik.

At either end of this discussion of experimental trends in rock music stand two "strange" women, at least as far as mainstream tastes are concerned. And yet Björk has a large audience among music listeners whose other tastes may not necessarily run toward the avant-garde. This is a key element of avant rock, that it is not so absolutely set off from "mainstream" rock—as, say, John Cage is set off from Leonard Bernstein, or Cecil Taylor is from Wynton Marsalis. Whether these divisions are completely necessary in classical music and jazz is another question. The onus there is on the "mainstream." It is not as important that another symphony be written in the language of the classical or romantic traditions as that there be a forward edge to the music, so that it doesn't become simply a museum culture. Part of the significance of avant rock is that it is also capable of reconstituting the other traditions in such a way that we can have Beethoven and Bernstein and Berio—because rock is open to all of it. The Beatles started that! By the same token, avant rock is not committed to thinking that everything that is closer to the mainstream is necessarily bad. Perhaps this ought to be called the "Springsteen principle"—if the core of the work of someone like Björk is still songwriting craft, albeit overlaid with far out, difficult, complex textures and rhythms, and so on, then we had better recognize that someone like Bruce Springsteen is a fine practitioner of that craft as well. Avant rock, then, for all that it may be the re-creation, in a post-sixties way, of the "underground"—with appropriate political consequences drawn from the fact that it *is* a re-creation and it *is* post-sixties—does not disdain (except in the case of the sorts of culture snobs who are more likely to be critics, writers, or fans, rather than actual musicians) the idea of poking its head above ground here and there, perhaps most anywhere. As Tamara Palmer points out in her profile in *Urb*, Björk is a paradigm here:

> Björk is so unequivocally underground, she knew the discography of some of electronic music's most innovative producers before you even dropped the needle on one of their

records. She's so incredibly above ground that immigrant cab drivers, dentists, construction workers and Joan Rivers all have an opinion of her looks and style. (p. 125)

I don't know what Joan Rivers had to say about Björk's looks and style, but we can all probably guess. Ono and Björk, these two strange women at either end of this discussion, have had to make it in spheres that are overwhelmingly populated by, and largely dominated by, men. When a woman raises her head in such spheres, she will generally be called every name in the book, and almost as often by other women as by men—this has certainly been the case with Yoko Ono and Björk.

Tamara Palmer raises this issue in her profile of Björk; in so doing, she mentions something that I was delighted to learn:

Speaking of odd ducks, the fact of the marketplace is that Björk is a minority as a female involved in the creation and arrangement of electronic music. As a tomboy who was not only good at math in school, but *on the chess team as well*, it's clear she never let stereotypes of gender limit her field of interest. (p. 130, my emphasis)

Right on! Iceland has a strong chess tradition, and its place in chess history is secure because of the Fischer/Spassky match. Chess has been even more male-dominated than music—and yet, improbably, a narrative of avant rock has unfolded that involves as pivotal moments the work of two chess-playing women from Tokyo and Reykjavik. Jim O'Rourke's 1999 album, *Eureka*, begins with the chant, repeated over and over, "Women of the world take over, 'cause if you don't the world will come to an end, and it won't take long." Perhaps we are heading for a convergence of Ono, Björk, and Judit Polgar. The latter is the brilliant Hungarian chessplayer who, in 1991 and at age fifteen, surpassed Bobby Fischer's record and became the youngest grandmaster to that date. There is such an energy in these associations, there has got to be a lot more music here as well.

Is avant rock the revenge of the nerds? Despite all her glamour, Björk describes herself that way, and now we turn to a precocious musician who is even younger—barely over thirty at the time of this publication. It's a much longer walk to the woods from the working-class neighborhood in northwest Chicago where Jim O'Rourke grew up, so I doubt that he came by his music "acoustically," at least in Björk's sense of the term. There are some nice parallels between Björk and Yoko Ono, and also between Brian Eno and Jim O'Rourke. Eno initiates what might be called "bedroom music," by which is meant not anything too racy, but instead the young person who spends his or her teen years sitting in their bedroom, listening to music, learning to play the guitar or sampler (!), "making stuff up"—songs or little pieces or grand ideas for some new kind of opera—and now (more and more, thanks to Eno) setting up a studio there, which may mean a four-track cassette machine, a personal computer, or a disk or dig-

ital tape recorder. More and more young people are doing these things, and Jim
O'Rourke is one of those who emerged from the bedroom to have perhaps as great an
impact on experimental rock music as anyone has had.

Unlike Björk, however, O'Rourke does not have much of an "above ground" presence, nor does he seem to care about such a thing—bless his heart. In 1998, I attended
a day-long new music festival in Sheffield, England that featured electronica artists such
as Autechre and Boards of Canada, as well as members of Tortoise, Stereolab, and the
High Lamas. O'Rourke performed a strange duet with Tortoise drummer John McIntyre,
which began with both musicians on combo organs (playing at an excruciating volume,
I might add), after which McIntyre switched to drums and O'Rourke added some sam-
ples to the mix. But otherwise O'Rourke was very much behind the scenes, by which I
mean not just as someone who has produced groups such as Stereolab and Sonic
Youth, but rather as someone who was helping to move equipment. For someone who
is a major part of a scene that has its share of pretentious people, O'Rourke is a humble servant to the music. The term I would use is "ubiquitous anonymity," or perhaps it
should be "anonymous ubiquity."

One place of contact between O'Rourke and Björk is that, while the latter very
much likes for her music to be remixed (for example, there is a CD that features four
different mixes of one of her finest songs, "Isobel," and the *Telegraph* album is basically an alternative, remixed version of *Post*), the former has said that remixing is his
"absolutely favorite thing to do."

> Everything I like doing is in one thing: I get material that's already culturally loaded, so I
> can deal with it in that regard; I get to do [*musique*] *concrete* stuff, which I love to do;
> it's always something different, so I have to really reconceptualise it every single time; I
> get to sit in my studio for two weeks working on a remix. I love it. (p. 40)

This quotation is from a fine article on O'Rourke by philosopher and music theorist
Christoph Cox ("Studies in Frustration," *The Wire*, Nov. 1997), from which I will draw
liberally. The solo and group albums (with Brice Glace and Gastr del Sol) listed in the
discography are really only a very small part of O'Rourke's resume; to take full account
of his impact, one must look to the remixes and the production credits. Like Eno,
O'Rourke is a person with ideas, and he is a person who excels just as much in collaborations and "treatments" (to use Eno's word) as in his own solo compositions. In
either case, as Cox argues, for O'Rourke, "every sound brings into question the meaning of life."

> Jim O'Rourke is a sonic semiotician, a musical materialist, a digital deconstructionist. He
> describes his work as a series of "research reports" that investigate the socially fixed, yet
> ultimately arbitrary, nature of musical meaning, interrogating established relationships

between sounds and their social value in order to produce new relationships and allow these sounds to be heard again differently. "The whole basis of almost everything I'm interested in," O'Rourke explains, "is to point out things that are taken for granted. (p. 37)

Cox mentions that O'Rourke's discography already had 120 entries in late 1997; the number is probably at least double that now. Among his remix projects are those for Tortoise, The Sea and Cake, and Merzbow. In recent years he has especially been associated with Sonic Youth, with whom he is now a full-time member, contributing not only production but also bass guitar, guitar, synthesizer, percussion, and the instrument with which he is increasingly associated, laptop computer. This is another Björk connection, but whereas she carries her laptop all over the world in order to compose and mix on it, O'Rourke *plays* the thing, he jams and improvises with it.

O'Rourke's associations go beyond the world of avant rock—such going beyond being an integral part of experimentation in rock music—to organizations such as the Merce Cunningham Dance Company and the Kronos Quartet. In fact, O'Rourke has a master's degree in music composition from DePaul University. There he studied with George Flynn, composer and performer of the extraordinarily complex and dense work, *Trinity*. Flynn, who has also recorded piano works by Charles Ives, Oliver Messiaen, and John Cage, and also composed works for chamber ensembles and orchestras, doesn't pay much attention to rock music—though, amusingly, he was once asked to audition for the keyboard chair in Yes. O'Rourke, on the other hand, found the path toward contemporary classical music through reading the liner notes of King Crimson and Frank Zappa records that he checked out from the public library. There he learned about Stockhausen and Pierre Boulez. In his own way he came to experiment with preparations to the guitar, even before encountering John Cage's music for prepared piano.

While we are on the subject of Chicago, let me mention that it is one of the cities where the avant-rock trend, as well as important new developments in jazz and the classical avant-garde, are strong. There is a tiny discography at the end of this section that includes just a very few of the more recent avant-rock albums—a complete discography of experimental rock in Chicago would run to hundreds of records.

O'Rourke is quite a good guitarist, it ought to be said, and there is evidence of this on some of the solo albums, as well as on the Gastr del Sol albums (especially *Crookt, Crackt, or Fly*). But like many associated with experimental rock, O'Rourke is at least ambivalent about the guitar, and perhaps even has a love/hate relationship with it. (I would even include so fine a practitioner of the instrument as Robert Fripp in this category; he has as much technique as anyone who ever played the guitar, but as often as not his sound is modified to come across as something else.) For O'Rourke this has to do with the musical value of abandoning those contexts where one is comfortable, and where one has already done what can be done with a given approach. I have said this before in different ways, but here is another formulation of the "guitar problem." The electric guitar has dominated rock music to the point where the "that ain't rock and roll"-crowd feels it necessary every few years to reassert the primacy of "guitar rock." Rejecting this primacy, experimentalists have tended to bifurcate into two camps: either to transcend the guitar through the guitar itself (King Crimson and Sonic Youth would be prime examples), or to just leave the instrument out of the mix altogether (Björk is a good example here, though there are many others). As with other areas of his work, and as befitting a musical deconstructionist, O'Rourke has struggled with the problem from both sides, recording albums such as *Remove the Need*, which consists in solo prepared guitar improvisations, and *Eureka*, which features some very sweet finger-picking, to "Cede" (an extended composition from *Terminal Pharmacy*) and *Happy Days*, which have no guitar at all.

If all of O'Rourke's work were assembled into one marathon listening experience—a difficult project, not only in terms of what is out there already, but even more so because the *oeuvre* expands daily—we would most likely hear some significant continuities, but the discontinuities might stand out even more. (Part of the dynamic here, certainly, is the fact that grappling with fragmentation is one of the most significant aspects of all experimental music since Schoenberg and Coltrane.) One of the major discontinuities in O'Rourke's work is between his "pop" albums, and his more straightforwardly avant-garde experiments. The pop albums are a deconstruction of the genre, in part because they will never be all that popular, and even more because they represent what the Situationists called a *detournement* of everyday materials—which is to say that the music on these albums is warped and twisted, though often in a very subtle way. There are pretty tunes on *bad timing*, *Eureka*, and *Halfway to a Threeway*, indeed a lot of hummable stuff. It isn't that, all of sudden, these nice tunes turn on you and become ugly or harsh. On the contrary, in some cases they become sweeter and sweeter. After you've heard "Women of the world," you'll feel like you've been indoctrinated, you won't be able to get the song's only line out of your head. What's really going on here? After all, these songs are not going to climb the *Billboard* charts, no matter what. Part of the issue here is that it was never all that easy to write a good "pop" song, and that is something every musician, no matter how "serious" he takes himself to be, ought to at least give a little attention to. But I think the deeper effect of what O'Rourke is doing with his "pop" albums is comparable to those electronically enhanced images of conventionally good-looking people, where their most attractive features are pushed to the point just this side of absurdity—which creates an even much more uncomfortable feeling than from the other side. It is a very subtle form of subversion—the application of oblique strategies, to borrow again from Eno.

On the other side of the present dichotomy are O'Rourke's more "conventionally" avant-garde albums, especially *Terminal Pharmacy* and *Happy Days*. These albums have very little, if anything, to do with "rock" music, except perhaps in their sensibility—but that counts for a good deal. The aforementioned piece, "Cede," is a forty-minute long, tape-manipulated "power trio," of clarinet, bass trombone, and drums. Allow me to quote Cox and O'Rourke at length on this piece:

> On one level the piece exhibits characteristic O'Rourke features: slow and deliberate instrumental passages woven with bouts of silence or nearly inaudible sound and complex layers of samples and electronic noise. But "Cede" is intended to explore a particular theoretical issue: whether or not it's possible to recontextualise a set of sounds by continuously deploying them over a single, extended work. With characteristic humor and insight, O'Rourke recounts how the idea for the piece came from his amazed reaction on hearing Foghat's raunchy blues rock classic, "Slow Ride." "The thing I like about that song is that at the beginning 'slow ride' is this thinly veiled reference to some sex act," he says. "But through the continuous use of this in the song, and because the song is the scale it is—it wouldn't have worked it if were shorter—by the end of the song 'slow ride' is referring to the song itself during its actual existence; they're singing about the song. And so in "Cede" there are these obvious *concrete* gestures in it, and I keep hammering these into the ground over and over, so that by the end of it, the final section is about everything that came beforehand and is just this big funeral for it.

> "That's what I wanted to get," he continues, but I don't think it was completely successful. It couldn't be. That's one of the things I learned, of course, while doing it—you can't *make* people think something. The only way I've found that you can completely create your own gesture is by killing somebody else's gesture. Murder is really the only gesture you can make. (p. 39)

There is plenty more to discuss, but it makes sense to stop right here—these two paragraphs are by themselves a textbook for experimental music and avant rock.

Everything else is icing. Gastr del Soul is somewhere in-between the "pop" and the "classical" avant albums, and features another important musician, David Grubbs. (See Christoph Cox's profile of Grubbs in *The Wire*, January 2001.) Their music veers toward King Crimson at some moments, John Cage at others. Stereolab's *Sound-Dust* features production and playing by O'Rourke and John McIntyre. Given Louise Gray's wonderful expression, music as "connective activity," one hopes for a "Stereo Youth" album in the not-too-distant future. Speaking of listening to the future, however, we might conclude that it is not so much a question of Björk and Jim O'Rourke as the future of rock—though I have all faith that they will be a major part of it—but, even more, they are beacons who light up the possibilities for rock to have a future.

Björk

Björk and Tappi Tikarrass, *Miranda* (no label CD, n.d.).
Björk Godmundsdottir and Trio Godmundar, *Gling-Glo* (Smekkleysa CD, 1990).
The Sugarcubes, *Life's Too Good* (Elektra/Asylum CD, 1988).
——, *here today, tomorrow, next week* (Elektra CD, 1989).
——, *Stick Around for Joy* (Elektra CD, 1992).
Björk, *Debut* (Elektra CD, 1993).
——, *Venus as a Boy* (Elektra CD/EP, 1993).
——, *MTV Europe Unplugged* (Video, 1994).
——, *Vessel* (Elektra Video, 1994).
——, *Post* (Elektra CD, 1995).
——, *Telegram* (Elektra CD, 1996; remixes).
——, *Homogenic* (Elektra CD, 1997).
——, *Hammerstein Ballroom, NYC* (Video [Bootleg?], 1998).
——, *Volumen* (Björk Overseas Limited Video, 1998).

Jim O'Rourke

Jim O'Rourke, *Remove the Need* (Extreme CD, 1993).
——, *Terminal Pharmacy* (Tzadik CD, 1995).
——, *Happy Days* (Revenant CD, 1997).
——, *bad timing* (Drag City CD, 1997).
——, *Eureka* (Drag City CD, 1999).
——, *halfway to a threeway* (Drag City CD EP, 1999).
Brise Glace, *When in Vanitas . . .* (Skin Graft CD, 1994).
Gastr del Sol, *Crookt, Crackt, or Fly* (Drag City CD, 1993).
——, *Upgrade and Afterlife* (Drag City CD, 1996).
——, *Camoufleur* (Drag City CD, 1998).

Chicago: City on the make

The Sea and Cake, *The Sea and Cake* (Thrill Jockey CD, 1993?).
Tortoise, *millions now living will never die* (Thrill Jockey CD, 1996).
——, *TNT* (Thrill Jockey CD, 1998).
Isotope 217, *The Unstable Molecule* (Thrill Jockey CD, n.d.—1998?).
Sam Prekop, *Sam Prekop* (Thrill Jockey CD, 1999).

1999

Zeena Parkins, *Pan-Acousticon* (Tzadik CD).
Iggy Pop, *Avenue B* (Virgin CD).
Porcupine Tree, *Stupid Dream* (K Scope CD).
Rage Against the Machine, *The Battle of Los Angeles* (Epic CD).
Solex, *Pick Up* (Matador CD).
Tom Waits, *Mule Variations* (Epitaph CD).

PART 3

....

Rock out

1. Manifesto: Avant rock, the very idea

Make it new and make it rock—are these contrary imperatives?

To talk about an avant-garde in rock music involves one in all sorts of contradictions and confusions. But it might be said that all good art and all good thinking is a matter of grappling with contradictions, because they are there to be dealt with in the world. Here is a contradiction: rock music is music that comes from popular sources (I will deal with the question of "popular music" a little later), while avant-garde music strains the ears and mind and sometimes other parts of the body and the body politic, and is only very rarely popular. Of course, the early recordings and performances of rock music—Louis Jordan, Chuck Berry, Little Richard, Bo Diddley, Elvis Presley, Buddy Holly, and the rest—did indeed bring about these sorts of strains, and all of the normalization and homogenization and absorption into the culture industry since still has not entirely put that cat back into the bag.

However, the contradiction remains. In this large world of music that rock has played a significant role in bringing about, we are finally learning that what seems to really stretch the boundaries in one genre of music may be rather commonplace in another. (Later in this discussion I will turn to the question of what I call "a time of general musical awareness.") A simple and familiar example is that, in its use of rhythm, Igor Stravinsky's *The Rite of Spring* is very adventurous, revelatory even, as a work in the tradition of European classical music. Compared to the rhythmic complexity of many Indian ragas or the playing of African master drummers, though, Stravinsky seems tame. Is it the case, then, that what it means to be avant-garde in art is always to be understood within a certain tradition or genre?

Aesthetic modernism seems to tell against this proposal. For roughly the first fifty or sixty years of the twentieth century, at least in Europe and North America (in other words, a part of the world that—we can see more clearly now—may constitute a "genre" in itself), the idea of the avant-garde was something like this: to be avant-garde meant not only to take the next step in music, literature, or painting, but indeed to take a step that called the different arts themselves into question. This is the period when we begin to hear the "yes, but is it *art?*" question. James Joyce and Gertrude Stein stretched literature to the breaking point, where it was no longer clear that what they were writing could be called "literature." Dadaists, surrealists, and abstract expressionists elicited the "my six-year-old can do that" response. People rioted at the premier performance of *The Rite of Spring* while, at the other end of this period, many called John Cage a fraud. One prominent critic referred to John Coltrane's music as "anti-jazz"; Ornette Coleman and Cecil Taylor were simply beyond the pale.

Much of John Cage's music uses randomizing procedures in its composition. A good deal of this music is scored "for any instrument or combination of instruments." While Cage's music has precedents in the European classical tradition, such that one probably could make the case that his compositions are the next logical step on this or that front, it seems plainly undeniable that Cage explodes both the tradition from which he came and the very idea of music as some sort of experience or activity separable from anything else. If Cage can be taken as giving us a paradigm of the modernist (or high modernist, and some will even say postmodernist) paradigm of the avant-garde, then it seems especially strange, after Cage, to speak of the avant-garde of this or that *kind* or genre of music, for example, rock. In this light, here is another way of coming at the contradiction involved in talking about "avant rock." Up to a point, we can talk about how this or that piece of music, album, or even the body of work of a particular artist or group constitutes *a* next step in rock music. To again take a familiar example, there was clearly a dynamic in the middle and late sixties that drove a kind of friendly competition among the Beatles, the Beach Boys, the Byrds, and Bob Dylan, among others. Each saw the others' albums as a challenge to take the next step. But although there were always some critics or listeners more generally who did not like that next step, each of the aforementioned stayed within the genre that we call "rock," even while stretching the boundaries of the genre and opening it to new possibilities.

What is "rock"? This question is not meant to evoke avant-garde possibilities so much as to point to the fact that rock, at its very roots, is a derivative and synthetic form of music. We might go even further and say that, as an always-already "contaminated" form of music, rock calls into question the whole idea of genre—for surely every kind of music has its roots in something else. It has only been in recent years that the sense of this synthesis and contamination in rock music has been somewhat lost as far as the general public is concerned—thanks to niche marketing. If postmodern capitalism is a form of society and economy where consumerism has fully set in as the cultural ethos, at least in the "advanced" countries (the countries that control industry and information), then the forms of cultural marketing whereby most or all of the traces of an artform's historical resonances are erased may themselves be markers of the postmodern turn. The idea of an avant-garde then becomes difficult to get a handle on—"avant" of what? By the same token, what does it mean for the postmodern work of art to be a "pastiche," as Fredric Jameson would have it, if most people do not have access to the system of references that the work is putting into play? Let us reconnect with the earlier question, What is rock? Rock music has "grown up," so to speak, in a time when the aforementioned issues have troubled art, culture, aesthetics, and social theory.

One might attempt a simple substitution. What is rock? Instead, why not ask, Does it *rock*? If the music "rocks," then you have answered the question, at least by an openness to examples, of what the music is, in its basic form. Of course, this is too simple, and yet—giving a nod to my brother John, for whom this is the only question—I want to hold on to it. The "does it rock?" question could be seen as a transposition of Duke Ellington's famous formula, "It don't mean a thing, if it ain't got that swing." So, does Cecil Taylor "swing"? Certainly the more avant-minded will immediately say, "You'd better believe it!" And I suppose that someone similarly disposed would say that, for example, Henry Cow "rocks." But there were many critics and other listeners who were not willing to swing with John Coltrane, others who would only swing with him up to a point, and still others who, even if they stayed with Coltrane into his final period, are still not going to swing with Cecil Taylor. I choose the example of Henry Cow because the period and sub-genre from which they emerged, progressive rock, represents the post-Beatles beginnings of the time when the condemnation, "that ain't rock'n'roll," began to be heard regularly. Perhaps it is a defining feature of avant rock, if there even is such a thing, that works in this field will evince such a reaction from a significant number of listeners.

Unfortunately, for listeners to react to the music this way, they would first have to hear it—and the time of niche-marketing (for a definition of this, simply work your way up the FM radio dial) ensures instead that one has to seek out music that is far outside of the mainstream of rock. Strangely enough, we have to recover the sense that there was a time when this was not entirely the case. For sure, there was in the late sixties and early to middle seventies the phenomenon of "underground radio," but this refers to stations that were on the same dial as all of the others, generally broadcasting at a similar level of power. Before we can define avant rock, or at least provide a general characterization of what avant rock might be, we can at least recognize that there was a time when experimental trends in rock music were also popular trends. This indisputable fact tells us a thing or two. First, if we look at that period, basically of the late-1960s counterculture, we see that it is entirely possible for large numbers of people to desire, seek out, and appreciate musical experimentation. I would argue (and have done so at length in *Music of Yes*, pp. xix–xxiii, and *Listening to the future*, pp. 1–16) that the social and political rebellions and upheavals of the "sixties" created a window of opportunity for cultural and aesthetic experimentation. This occurred at the same time that rock was emerging as a kind of universal and global musical language. This language was associated especially with youth culture, and yet at the same time rock music was also "growing up." (More on this last point in a moment.) So, to simplify, my first point is that there was a broad audience for experimentation. Although there may have been a very few historical precedents for this moment (perhaps with Dada and Surrealism in Europe, or some of the experimental painters, poets, and architects in the Soviet Union in the 1920s), it seems to me that, in its scale, this time of openness to cultural-aesthetic experimentation was and is unique in history. This fact has been largely overlooked and bears further investigation. Second, for the musicians and audiences that participated in this time of experimentation, there was a broad acceptance of the new music as both experimental and rock.

It is out of this milieu that we will find the roots of post-sixties avant rock. Some sides of this milieu have been affirmed, others forgotten, and still others much denigrated by critics. In that cultural moment, however, perhaps best represented by the social explosions of 1968, there was a general affirmation of the idea that rock music ought to develop and grow. This is an inconvenient idea from the standpoint of marketing. Now, in the time when those "kids" who were "alright" are becoming grandparents, the culture industry has imposed a generational notion of the niche. You are offered a certain array of mostly not very original music as an adolescent, and thereafter you are expected to mainly stay with that music. (Again, check your radio dial—the idea is that there is a station for the music of "your generation," and, in this fundamentally lonely society, you find yourself warming to, or at least tolerating, music that you didn't really like when you were an adolescent, but now at least it feels familiar and as though at least some things haven't changed.) Rock music begins in the adolescent experience of a certain generation, for sure—though the "generation" is a unit complicated by class, color, gender, and geography. Among white musicians both in North America and England, there is the sensibility of the "rebel without a cause"—kids having missed the "good war" and feeling more or less useless in the eyes of their parents. (This comes across especially in the music of English working-class bands such as The Who, the Kinks, the Animals.) But clearly there is a geographical difference; the sensibility is more intense, I think, in England, because there people are surrounded by bombed-out buildings, cathedrals especially, that stand to this day as reminders. In addition, there is much more awareness of class distinctions. In the United States, the postwar ethos was much more geared toward "good times," as perhaps most represented by the "California sensibility." For Black musicians in the United States, however, there was a clear feeling that the war had not ended in 1945, and the forms of dealing with the struggle for basic human rights, even in the terms of bourgeois democracy, make themselves felt through rhythm and blues and the emergence of rock music. (I discuss this issue in terms of Little Richard's "Tutti Frutti" in *Listening to the future*, pp. 34–36; one might see Pat Boone's version of that song as the most insipid form of the journey of rock music from the American South to California.) Rock music begins in certain adolescent experiences but then also has to decide, as the music and the musicians themselves get older, where to go from there.

Some critics do not think there is anywhere to go. This point of view divides into two. There are those who will only affirm rock music in its first generation. They remind me of the philosophers who think that it all went bad with Hegel or perhaps even Kant. (Does this lead to the equation of back-to-basics punks with Bertrand Russell? Not really, but the image is amusing.) In other words, rock music went downhill at the point where it started to grow or try to grow—that is, the later Beach Boys, and especially the later Beatles (to say nothing of the Red Crayola or the Velvet Underground). The argument is basically that rock music, in its essential musical form or material, cannot sustain adult themes—whether this means structural or lyrical complexity or gravity. I suppose that the conservative philosopher Roger Scruton, in his recent *Aesthetics of Music*, is representative of this view (to the extent that he even comments on rock music). We are most familiar with this point of view from folks who affirm the initial impulses of rock music, but who rue the day that rock tried to go beyond these impulses. Then the cry of "that ain't rock'n'roll" must be sounded! At least there is some degree of authenticity to this approach. But this "authenticity" is misguided, for one of the initial impulses of rock music is to disturb authenticity. On the other hand, I have more appreciation for this attachment to early rock than I do for the more purely niche-driven sensibility that fully assimilates rock music to this or that generation, purely as a form of nearly mindless entertainment.

Rock musicians, by the middle sixties, and certainly with great force by the late sixties, made an effort to go beyond such confining perspectives. As a result, we saw a flowering of experimentation. Out of this cultural and political cauldron, if only vaguely at first, there arose the idea that rock could have its own avant-garde.

This general framework helps to define the project of this book, which is to show where this avant-garde came from and what it is doing at the beginning of a new century. Three issues will continue to weigh heavily, however, as we move into this discussion.

First, there is the issue of what "avant rock" is. There will be a necessary arbitrariness to any definition that might be proposed for the concept of avant rock. In my earlier books on music, which concerned progressive rock, I recognized difficulties in the definition of the core phenomenon, and that there could be more or less valid disagreement with the definition that I shaped, but I also thought that I had good arguments for defining progressive rock in the way that I did. My definition excluded, for example, Pink Floyd, on the one hand, and Frank Zappa, on the other. In the former case, this had to do with technical ability, while, in the latter, the question was one of sensibility. While my arguments here can be challenged, at least there are recognizable criteria to be discussed, and these criteria are not wholly arbitrary. In the case of avant rock, however, there are points where the arbitrariness cannot be entirely factored out. The primary difficulty is in putting these two terms together, "avant-garde" and "rock." I bite the proverbial bullet in this book when I focus on music that is either still recognizably "rock" or that at least is "based" in rock or has some "roots" in rock. These terms bring their own slipperiness. Some (probably not readers who appreciate the topic of this book, but, on the other hand, perhaps many of those who do *not* appreciate avant rock, whatever it turns out to be) will say that Cecil Taylor does not play music that is recognizable as "jazz." I think this is profoundly wrong, but, even so, my two other "criteria" would apply—surely Taylor's music is *based* in and has *roots* in jazz, regardless of how slippery these terms are.

There comes a point where creative music somehow connected with rock is so far from rock that it has entered either some other avant-garde (of the European classical or jazz worlds, for instance) or perhaps what might be called the "general" avant-garde. This, too, is a difficult issue, because, by the sixties, there was something like a "general avant-garde" in music and culture that went beyond genres and backgrounds. The experimental rock music of the late sixties and afterwards either came through this general culture or experimentation or at least took a fundamental inspiration from it—whether this was conservatory types turning to rock music, such as Joseph Byrd and his group, the United States of America, and Tom Constantine joining the Grateful Dead, or the Beatles putting a photograph of Karlheinz Stockhausen in the collage on the cover of *Sgt. Pepper's*. These names already present us with some parameters of sorts, though I flesh these out and broaden them considerably beyond the Beatles and the United States of America. However, some of the musicians who are embraced as either progenitors of the more recent rock avant-garde, or as members of this latter category itself, bear a definite relationship to the mainstream of rock.

It seems to me a strength of the rock avant-garde that there remains a dialectic between margin and center—and that the center can mean various things, "popular," "mainstream," closer to the root impulses of rock, and the like. There are many things in the "mainstream" that are very far away from the root impulses, in that they have little to do with rebelliousness. But that is just to say that even the seemingly most harmless terms become difficult where rock music is concerned. That a piece of music becomes popular, for instance, is not the same thing as its being a work of "popular music." If anything, avant rock emerges at a time when the high/low distinction in music and culture seems, at the least, very hard to draw. Rock music comes with the burden that it has some basic relation to "popular music," but the category is itself not very helpful when everything from Top-40 pap and Can's *Soon Over Babaluma* is included (indeed, one would be at pains to actually say what this is, as a "category"). Rock also has the burden of being, at its inception, "commercial music," though the radical culture of the late sixties blew some rather large holes in this category.

On some level I am more than pleased to simply let the term "avant rock" mean rock music that is experimental, very creative, visionary, original, sometimes (but not always) hard to listen to, adventurous, and challenging. Most pieces of popular music are songs, and songs have a long history. Beethoven wrote songs, as did Duke Ellington (and Billy Strayhorn may have written the greatest song of all, "Lush Life"). George Gershwin was a Tin Pan Alley songwriter who then pieced his songs into Broadway productions and from there created jazz- and Klezmer-inflected "classical" works that were perhaps the best musical reflection of that great movement in architecture, art, and design, art deco. Truth be told, there are probably no musical forms (certainly no Western forms, and I mean this to include jazz and its African roots, as well), that do not have their roots in at least one of three things: song, dance, or worship. Why should rock music be any different? Indeed, rock has roots in all of these three. The commercial aspect certainly has the effect of keeping most rock music tied to a "culture" (if that is what it is anymore) of adolescence. (This is not to say that there can no longer be great rock music about adolescent themes, and certainly Brian Wilson and Pete Townshend showed that adolescence can be the subject matter of great music.) But rock *musicians* are for the most part only tied to this culture to the extent that they choose this orientation (not that there are not pressures, mainly monetary, to take up this orientation, but this is just to say what has always been the case with most artistic experimentation—don't *expect* to make a great deal of money doing this). Other kinds of music have experienced their own pressures to conform, commercial and otherwise. The genre of avant rock has to do with those musicians who have resisted these pressures, and who have, in a sense, attempted to imagine what music would be if such pressures did not exist.

One of the debates about terms has to do with whether to call this adventurous rock music "avant rock" or, instead, "post-rock" or some other name. I see the appeal of "post-rock," though perhaps the term signifies an even broader category. In some sense, I would be tempted to call a good bit of the recent electronic music, as well as turntable music, "post-rock." But I would also be tempted, perhaps more provocatively, to call John Zorn's Masada Quartet or the Kronos String Quartet "post-rock," in that both groups play with a musical and cultural sensibility that is very much "after" rock. Zorn, I think, has a closer relationship to rock music and contributes more directly to avant rock, both as a musician and as an impresario. And, clearly, we have to devote attention to electronica, to music made with synthesizers, computers, turntables, and samplers. But my orientation in this book is to the idea that there is a continuing rock avant-garde that incorporates these things. Perhaps there is also a broader category for considering the way that almost all music in the world today has been affected by rock and is in that sense "post-rock." That is another book, although I would be happy to see someone write it.

By the same token, there are almost certainly other definitions of avant rock that would have their own internal validity, and that would lead to the discussion to a somewhat (perhaps completely) different group of musicians than taken up here, and I hope that others will pursue these pathways as well. This leads to the second and third of my weighty issues, namely the selection of a group of progenitors and of musicians who represent the avant rock trend as I see it here around the turn of the century.

Here, I have chosen to look back at some of the predecessors to the recent trends, and then to consider the artists who are creating adventurous rock music now.

In looking at the large musical field from which avant rock emerged, I have been mindful of sources both inside and outside of rock music. In both cases the field could be enlarged. For instance, in the interlude following the discussion of Yoko Ono, where I briefly discuss some developments in European classical music and in jazz, I focus in the former case mainly on what I see as a very interesting dialectic that opens up when one considers John Cage and Glenn Gould in comparison. This leaves aside the influence of a whole range of important composers, from Anton Webern to Karlheinz Stockhausen to Morton Feldman to Steve Reich and Lamont Young, to say nothing of Stravinsky and Schoenberg. In the case of jazz, I restrict the discussion mainly to John Coltrane, Cecil Taylor, and Miles Davis's electric music, largely leaving aside Ornette Coleman, Albert Ayler, Sun Ra, and many other significant figures. But my aim is to reveal a certain dynamic and an emerging cultural ethos—of fragmentation, noise, randomness, intensity, electricity (literally and figuratively), cybernetics, and even what I have now labeled the "rock sensibility" about making music. In recent years there have been record stores, for example in New York and Boston, that specialize in the general avant-garde to which I have alluded, where one could easily imagine Sonic Youth in the rack next to Stockhausen. I favor such an all-embracing approach to music—one is reminded of the old saying that, really, there are only two types of music, "good" and "bad." There is something to be said, however, for attempting to understand better one part of this larger field—so, again, choices have to be made, choices that are sometimes painful or made in recognition that the inevitable "how could you write a book on avant rock and not talk about?" is soon to come. My hope is that the choices—of artists, definitions, and categories—I have made here advance the discussion of experimental trends in rock music.

The other aspect of weighty issue number three that needs mentioning is simply the sheer amount of music that is out there in the world today. Indeed, a great deal of the recent creativity in rock music (as well as, of course, the usual preponderance of stuff that does not add anything to what has already been done) is fueled by, or at least cannot be separated from, the fact that it has never been easier or less expensive to record, produce, and distribute an album. This mainly has to do with the digital revolution in technology. For somewhere between one and four thousand dollars or so, one can obtain recording equipment (digital audio tape, disk recording, or personal computer systems) that has the quality of what used to be only available in very expensive studios. Compact discs can be pressed in editions of a thousand for about five hundred dollars. There are hundreds of independent labels putting out every kind of music, often using web pages, and individual musicians and groups often promote their music using their own sites. Thirty years later, there are at least ten times the number of albums being put out every year as there were in 1969—or perhaps it is more like one hundred times (though it may also be impossible to actually find out the real number). I read magazines such as *The Wire* (on which more in a moment) and *The Magnet* to try to keep up on all of this music, but there are not enough hours in the day (nor enough money in my paycheck) to hear all or even a large part of it. More to the point, the many musicians and groups that, while perhaps making an innovative contribution, are still of the "here today and gone tomorrow"-sort, are more properly the subject of music journalism. I have tried here to focus on artists who have had some sort of staying power. I suppose that one of the holdovers from my studies of progressive rock that has made it into this conversation is my tendency to gravitate toward musicians who are developing their own languages, even while incorporating or reflecting a contemporary *Zeitgeist*. For instance, I see the work of artists such as Björk or Jim O'Rourke very much in this light.

Most recent avant rock (since the heyday of punk and new wave, say) seems to be projects created by individual musicians or by individuals in *collaboration* rather than in "rock groups" as we used to understand that term, though certainly there are important exceptions. Furthermore, there may be a tendency in the recent music toward what might be called "small adventures." Even if there is some interesting sense in which a Brian Eno or a Jim O'Rourke, say, is something like the "John Cage of rock," still, we already have the "real" John Cage. This is once again the "avant, yes, but only in terms of that particular genre" question. But such concerns are also a part of the issue of music in postmodern times, when what appears to be new and innovative is often some new combination of elements that have already been established in musical practice to some extent. And this concern is also balanced by what now seems to me to be the case, namely, that, if one were a young artist with avant-garde inclinations, one might just as likely and just as validly work out these inclinations on the basis of rock music as on the European classical tradition or the jazz tradition. Indeed, for all that the canons of jazz and classical music still may be extended in creative ways, there are also significant ways in which these canons can be stifling. Rock music, on the other hand, tends to admit all comers.

The avant-gardes in classical music and jazz tend to be those movements that, at any given moment in the development of those genres, are the furthest away from the song, dance, and worship roots of all music. These avant-gardes may stretch boundaries in ways that later become part of the culture of songs and dances, but, at first, this is a music that is hard to dance or hum along to. Melody and "common time" (a term that strictly applies to 4/4 time, but that might be stretched to include those time signatures that are not especially hard to tap one's foot to) are either warped beyond easy accessibility or taken to a place where they seem absent altogether. (This wordy way of putting it has to do with a Cagean sensibility about what it means for such things as melody or rhythm to be present or absent.) In rock music, this extreme stretching of song form, sometimes to the breaking point, was first evident in the music of the psychedelic groups, the Velvet Underground, many of the progressive rock groups, and some of the John Lennon/Yoko Ono-conceived music of the later Beatles. And yet it may be that, by the definition of avant rock that I am feeling my way toward, there continues to be, even in the most far-flung examples of the music, a recognizable relation to song or dance. This is very obvious in the case of an artist such as Björk, where a singular vocal instrument meets Stockhausen on the way to the disco.

What seems to be behind such combinations—which are undoubtedly "postmodern" in ways I will discuss further in the next essay—is a dynamic of the avant-garde that exists in rock music but not in jazz or European classical music. Avant rock resists and plays off the mainstream of rock music (which is a very broad category, to be sure, perhaps to the point of meaninglessness), but it may not have the sort of *antagonism* toward the mainstream that one often sees in jazz and classical avant-gardes. Many of us probably remember music appreciation classes or late-night dorm-room debates in which the "validity" of rock music *as* music was debated. (We used to get very worked up over this topic, and I wonder whether this still happens—my worry is that it does not happen very much any more, because the idea of music, or perhaps even much of anything, being *important*, is getting lost in our emergent postmodern capitalist society. The idea that classical music is *important*, as opposed to just something to dress up for, has become the almost exclusive preserve of academic music schools and departments—which is one key factor in the declining significance of this music.) Inevitably, someone would throw out the "Beatles vs. Beethoven" line, and what they would "compare" would usually be some "Yeah, Yeah, Yeah"-type early Beatles rock-'n'roll song with a Beethoven symphony. That is a silly comparison, of course. A more appropriate comparison might be between a Beethoven *song* and a Beatles song. Perhaps a comparison could also be made between what would be a shorter symphonic work for Beethoven and a longer "symphonic" (not meaning "orchestral," necessarily, but instead a work with a broad range of musical colors and elements) work by the Beatles (which might mean something like "A Day in the Life," or perhaps the whole of the *Sgt. Pepper's* album). But then, to compare these different kinds of works would not only be to compare different genres of music, but also different historical times and places. Then one would again be facing basic questions about the "validity" of this or that musical genre.

Perhaps, from the perspective of the European classical music tradition, there is a way to question the basic validity of rock music, as a "way of speaking" musically, in the case where rock music has to do with purely commercial motivations. Certainly, there are those in the European classical music field who know so little about rock music that they believe they can make this assumption of pecuniary motives about all of it. My view of the whole "validity" issue is ridiculously simple and boils down to one question: Are we hearing something that we haven't heard before? Once we get down to cases, the question is not so simple. Perhaps what is original in some works is not so much the result of an experiment in form, but instead in content or the quality of the presentation of the content. (One thinks of the way that some in the post-Velvets New York art rock scene, for instance, Lydia Lunch, initially viewed punk music as just "Chuck Berry on speed.") Be that as it may, I see no inherent limitation in what can be done with rock music, and many ways in which rock can be the basis for profound musical adventurousness.

Part of what makes rock music vital, to return to the earlier point, is the way that its margins interact with its mainstream. In Leonard Bernstein's Norton Lectures (*The Unanswered Question*), there is an antagonism expressed toward outgrowths of the European classical canon that are so experimental that they are not "accessible" to most listeners. John Cage is one of Bernstein's particular targets on this score. To the extent that Cage bothered with such arguments, certainly he thought there was little point in orienting oneself toward the classical canon, given his basic credo: "make it new." Cage carried the sense of a musical "system," á la Schoenberg, to the point where the expressive qualities of music are completely set aside. His approach involves him in the interesting paradox, of which he was completely aware, of intending to set aside intention. In rock music one does not see such a complete antagonism between those parts of the music that are closer to song and dance and those parts that are farther away from it. Certainly, those who are attempting to extend the possibilities of the music will most likely despise the pap and drivel that is the greater part of music industry product. However, except among pure scenemakers, for whom popular appeal is the end of their interest, most experimental rock musicians remain affirmative toward song form and dance music and continue to see these as wellsprings of creativity. Although it is hard to imagine the music of Merzbow (the Japanese noise artist whose real name is Masami Akita), say, climbing the charts, there have been times when more experimental forms of rock music have been both avant and popular. The reason this is possible—again, a very simple reason—is that rock music is tied into the Zeitgeist, both reflecting it and shaping it, in ways that European classical music and even jazz to some extent no longer are. Indeed, whatever relevance classical music and jazz may continue to have may be increasingly expressed through their assimilation to rock music. This is a wild claim, I realize, having everything to do with what "rock music" is in the first place—such that the Kronos Quartet and John Zorn are in some sense "rock" musicians, while perhaps some narrow-minded rock'n'rollers are not.

We can now extend the earlier point about young artists and avant rock, which I think bears repeating in any case. By "young," I mean "young at heart," of course. The creative and adventurous person or group that has some interesting ideas to bring to

music might very naturally gravitate toward rock music, in part because of the very contradictions of avant rock. That is, the largely non-antagonistic dynamic between the
more experimental and the more straightforwardly song- and dance-oriented (and even
"popular," in the better sense of good quality music that has broad appeal) regions of
rock music continues to give the avant-garde rock musician something to play off of.
This dynamic is missing, for the most part, in the contemporary classical scene. To
some extent one can find this dynamic at work in some areas of jazz (though one might
compare the mutual antagonisms of Cage and Bernstein to, for example, those of Cecil
Taylor and Wynton Marsalis).

With jazz, however, there is an additional element that has to be considered, something that complicates the picture—namely technical musical ability, or, more colloquially, "chops." In the experimental rock music of the late sixties, one sees a curious
dynamic whereby one group of musicians is working hard to learn how to play their
instruments better (to become virtuosos or near-virtuosos, even), while another group
is trying to forget what little they already knew. (I think it was Lou Reed who put it this
way; Can would perhaps be the example of musicians who were simultaneously doing
both of these things, which is one key to their originality.) In some sense, one can see
the legacy of John Cage at work here. While some of his music can certainly benefit from
performance by musicians with a high level of technical ability, Cage found that such
"schooled" musicians often let their conservatory-instilled sensibilities get in the way of
grappling with the ideas at work in the music. As a result, Cage's music is sometimes
better performed by people who are open to its ideas *because* they are not inhibited by
canonical conventions. With jazz, on the other hand, and this goes for the jazz avant-
garde as well, it is very difficult for someone to make a contribution to the music if he
or she does not have a certain level of expertise (with an instrument or voice, in writing arrangements, and so on.). The ideas at work in avant-garde jazz are implicated in
the materiality of their expression, through instruments and voice, in a way that goes
beyond either the classical or rock avant-gardes. One cannot separate the ideas of Cecil
Taylor or John Coltrane from their transcendent abilities on the piano and tenor and
soprano saxophones.

In some ways, avant rock stands in the midst of this matrix that is set up among
John Cage, Glenn Gould (who had his own interesting relationship with the materiality
of the piano, his voice, his body, and the recording studio), Cecil Taylor, John Coltrane,
and Miles Davis (where the question of electricity arises), leaning now one way, now
the other. What is the main tendency? I would say the primary orientation is toward
ideas. That is, the people who gravitate toward making avant-rock music are people first
of all with ideas that they want to experiment with, and rock music seems a particularly
welcoming forum for such experimentation. On the other hand, when one considers a
group such as Sonic Youth, one sees that the extreme possibilities of an electric guitar

that has been turned up very loud and generating feedback *is*, in some sense, the "idea." And while there have been and continue to be avant rock musicians who have plenty of chops in the ordinary sense—for example, Jim O'Rourke or Keiji Haino—there are also new forms of virtuosity that are emerging, for example, in the use of the turntable or sampler. There are also refusals of virtuosity that demonstrate their own kind of sophisticated grappling with the materiality of music. My larger point is that rock music is very fertile ground for experimental expressions, and it is hard to see any limitation to what might be done on this basis.

Having said this, the reader might wonder whether the present text risks "academicizing" avant rock. I wonder this as well, and yet any attempt to theorize these experimental trends must encounter this risk—and this in a musical world where techno artists such as Mouse on Mars and DJ Spooky have contributed to an album titled *In Memoriam Gilles Deleuze*, and where it is common for Brian Eno or Stereolab to drop names such as Richard Rorty or Louis Althusser. A major inspiration behind the Velvet Underground was the integration of rock music and literary culture, especially from French and American Beat sources (Lou Reed had been a student of Delmore Schwartz, and Sterling Morrison is today a professor of literature at the University of Texas at Austin). Likewise, a major impulse behind my theorizing of avant rock is the idea of recovering a larger culture that experimental music can be a part of. Again, this has been largely lost in the contemporary classical scene, where music schools and conservatories turn out competent players who often have little or no interest in the world of ideas. Sadly, this is even the case for many composition students, even the ones who lean toward the avant-garde. For sure, the world where Eno meets Rorty or Mouse on Mars meets Deleuze is one of postmodern fragmentation. What "culture" would even mean in this world is up for grabs. Clearly, however, part of the vitality and viability of avant rock has been its resistance to academicizing gestures; in this study I endeavored to remain mindful of this resistance, even while plunging headlong into some of the knottier theoretical issues. In a moment, I will turn to one of the issues that has been given more of a hearing in the academy in recent years, the question of "meaning" in music. The emergence of avant rock sheds some interesting light on this question.

Before turning to this discussion, where I will take up some arguments raised by the analytic philosopher of music Peter Kivy, allow me to introduce two brief points.

It is necessary and important to acknowledge the role that a particular magazine is playing in the discussion of avant-garde music today—*The Wire*, published in London and subtitled "Adventures in Modern Music." Despite what I see as something of a blind spot regarding the progressive rock music of the early 1970s, I see *The Wire* as an invaluable resource. There is no other English-language magazine today of comparable scope in the coverage of experimental trends in music. The strip at the bottom of the cover of the magazine lists the following genres: "Electronica, Avant Rock, Breakbeat, Jazz, Modern Classical, Global"; what I especially like about the magazine is that all of these forms sit next to one another each month. Furthermore, *The Wire* covers both relatively well-known artists (for example, Björk and Sonic Youth, both of whom have been featured on the cover in recent memory) as well as the quite obscure. I have come to depend on *The Wire* to keep me in touch with all of the avant-gardes out there, and avant rock in particular. This being said, one can also see the difficulty in making the selections that have been made in this book. To listen to and write about the albums covered in a single issue of *The Wire*, even just those that fall under some fairly broad conception of "rock," would fill up more hours than there are in the month before the next issue comes.

Two other magazines have also been helpful, *Magnet* and *Urb*. *Magnet* focuses on what it calls "real music alternatives," these being almost exclusively in rock, while *Urb* covers the scene around techno, electronica, and turntablism, as well as the rave and hip-hop cultures. For historical details available at a glance, the *Rough Guides* for rock, jazz, and classical music are also very helpful.

A tip of the hat is offered to *The Wire* not only to acknowledge my immense debt to the magazine, but also to demonstrate a larger point about the current avant-rock scene. In its scope, and in the mixtures of music that one finds between its covers, *The Wire* is exemplary of something that is normative for avant rock musicians and that needs stating as a principle: avant-rock musicians function in a time of and through a sense of what might be called "general musical awareness." The range of musical references for artists such as Bill Laswell, Björk, Thurston Moore, or Jim O'Rourke knows no barriers. Indeed, probably the most stunning demonstration of such awareness was the "Invisible Jukebox" feature in *The Wire* that Jim O'Rourke took part in for the January 1999 issue. (This is a "name that tune" test where musicians are asked to comment on the music that is played for them and their relation to it.) The selections played for O'Rourke were very diverse and many were obscure (Luc Ferrari, Ray Russell, Bernhard Gunter and John Duncan, Christian Fennesz, Kontakta, as well as the better known Robbie Basho, John Zorn, and Slint); as the conductor of the test writes, O'Rourke "identified all selections correctly, to his immense satisfaction." Now, O'Rourke is an extreme example of one of the young avant-rock musicians who seems to know everything that has ever happened in every genre of music, but he is also typical of a generation that has listened very broadly and assimilated very diverse musical histories. This broad listening is attributable to two central social trends of the present time, multiculturalism and the postmodern smorgasbord. It is also a part of what I have called the "generous synthesis" of rock music—a music that, at its best, knows that it is derivative and therefore is always open to new forms of "contamination" (see *Listening to the future*, pp. 21–54). I would contrast this to a previous generation of the academic avant-garde, where one hears such things as, "they tell me that my music sounds somewhat like someone named Cecil Taylor, but I've never heard him."

There were two key moments where this generous synthesis took qualitative leaps in the late 1960s: with the music of the later Beatles and with the emergence of progressive rock. All of this happened in the space of about three or four years, in a time of general cultural and social upheaval. One element of the leaps that were taken was a basic break with blues form, and therefore a departure from "rock'n'roll." If avant rock in more recent years, having passed through not only the progressive period but also punk, does not always or perhaps even often evince much of the later-Beatles/progressive-rock influence (which also owes a great deal to psychedelia and the influence of free jazz), all the same there is a shadow cast by these influences and there is an historical meaning to the passage through the time of *Sgt. Pepper, Abbey Road*, and *In the Court of the Crimson King*. In the simplest of terms, whatever one may think of progressive rock (and Frank Zappa and Pink Floyd, to be sure), it must be recognized that the "rules" for making rock music were radically broken at that point, and they were not to be put back together again. Indeed, there is a backhanded recognition of this point in the fact that a good deal of what goes under the heading of "classic rock" (as played in that niche on the radio dial) is schlocky, adolescent male whining from the period of about 1975 to 1985—I'm amazed, actually, at how often one hears arena rock groups such as Journey or Foreigner on these stations, presented as something "classic," and how rarely one hears, say, the Jefferson Airplane or Jimi Hendrix. This "pop" conservatism and niche-marketing is seen further in the fact that classic rock stations tend to almost exclusively play music made by white people (and *for* middle-class white Americans).

This takes me to my next point, which has to do with the politics of avant rock. If some of the precursors of contemporary avant rock had an essential relationship with the sixties counterculture, it is not at all clear how we might figure the politics of music at a time when it is very hard to know what a counterculture would even look like anymore. "Progressive rock" was really only one part of a larger movement in rock music in the late 1960s that was "progressive," in the sense of musicians trying to expand musical form, to give expression to a general historical sensibility of "progress" or "betterment" or even utopia, and to also become technically better as players.

There are a few significant exceptions to this. There was a significant gothic strain in some progressive rock bands, including King Crimson, Genesis, and, perhaps most of all, Van der Graaf Generator; there was the very often cynical and juvenile outlook of Zappa, which rarely, if ever, matched the sophistication of much of his music. However, the exception to all three of the elements that I just mentioned is the Velvet Underground—they *perhaps* expanded (rock) musical form through their use of noise and drones, and this is important, but their primary innovations were not so much in musical form as in the incorporation of Beat and French Surrealist literary sensibilities. The Velvets did not aspire to become better players, perhaps even on the contrary, and their lyrical focus was usually on the seamier side of life. In speaking of the New York scene in the 1980s, Greil Marcus remarks that "most punks seemed to be auditioning for careers as something else" (*Ranters and Crowd Pleasers*, p. 6). While the "careers" that the Velvets were "auditioning for" were for the most part laudable—as poets, avant-garde musicians, and professors of literature—it could still be argued that their "extra-musical" focus served as precursor for the particularities of the New York scene. On the other hand, there was also something utopian to this focus, in that it reflected the desire to merge "music" with "life," and to transcend inherited, hierarchical categories (composer, performer, spectator).

Apart from the interesting particularities, however, if one looks at the period from the later Beatles (or perhaps from *Pet Sounds*) to the high tide of punk, there is a general dialectic at work, of radical affirmation and utopianism on the one side and radical negation and dystopian visions on the other. In my book on Yes I called this the "YesPistols" dialectic (see pp. 186–89). While on the whole radical affirmation is more prevalent in the late 1960s, and radical negation is more descriptive of the late 1970s, the dialectic runs through the entirety of the experimental current from the middle sixties to today. I call this a "dialectic" because the one side affirms some other world, while the other rejects this one. Neither necessarily has a very direct connection to "politics" in any plain sense, and, indeed, the radicality of either is undermined when the art devolves into mere polemic or agitation. Can the two moments be found together in a single work of art, at least in such a way that is very effective? Such a combination is very difficult, I think, because it tends to undermine the dynamism of the dialectic and what is assumed by it, namely that the affirmation of negation and the negation of affirmation must be unstated to have its critical power. Perhaps one sees some combination of the radically affirmative and the radically negative in the work of Guy Debord, Raoul Vaneigem, and some of the other Situationists, where boundaries between theory and art are also being crossed, which explains the appeal of Situationism for groups such as the Sex Pistols and Gang of Four. A lot of Situationism is pretty half-baked, but perhaps that is just a truism that goes for anarchism in general. Art distilled into "ideology" is perhaps necessarily half-baked, since it is a violation of what art is and can be, a violation of the power that it can have as art. Still, one sees a fairly clear countercultural current to experimental rock music operating up through the high tide of punk. Despite all of the rhetoric about the antinomy between progressive rock and punk, for instance, there is at least the commonality of thinking that music can be important and that, in order for music to be important, one thing it must do is resist commodification. The qualities of radical affirmation and negation, however, are also much more foregrounded in these forms. After the time of this 1970s dialectic, the scene is a good deal more murky—though this is just as one might expect in the time of postmodern capitalism, where all the accoutrements of "rebellion" are already set out for you on the shelves of your local Gap store.

Despite some expressed affinities for political positions on the part of recent avant-rock musicians, the "politics of avant rock," and perhaps the politics of any other than straightforwardly agit-prop music, is most likely a more complicated question than it has ever been. Add to this Theodor Adorno's argument that the politics of the music that seems to tell you straightforwardly what its politics is cannot be radical politics, and things become more difficult still. To take an example, I have to admit that I found it refreshing when the group Consolidated released a series of albums in the late 1980s that were disarmingly direct in their political statements on topics such as imperialism, MTV, vegetarianism, and sexism. For instance, they would quote whole passages from Carol Adams' book, *The Sexual Politics of Meat*. Most often I would agree completely with the positions the band took, and perhaps the saving element was that their directness was sometimes funny. However, while it was valuable to have a kind of musical billboard for the dissemination of views such as Carol Adams's (whose book I also find entirely persuasive), I don't know that it holds up very well as music. Indeed, I have to distrust the use of hip-hop elements in Consolidated's work for this very reason, the idea seemingly being that it might be possible to slide some politics through people's minds if the beat is insistent enough.

For Adorno, the "political energy" of a work of art (this is not Adorno's term) is in its innovative form, not its express content. Still, there must be some point of traction between this form and the form of the existing society. To see the world from the standpoint of redemption, or to create a radical negativity against this world, giving no quarter, means having some critical sense of what *this* world is all about—and it is one of the innovations of postmodern capitalism that it is very hard to generate such a sense. Fredric Jameson calls this the problem of "cognitive mapping." To put it simply, the "system" in our emerging postmodern world is so diffuse, it is increasingly difficult to map, and therefore to find sites of resistance. This is a problem as much for art as for activism, for I take it that the true artist (if I can be indulged this naïve term for the moment) remains just as committed to resisting commodification as ever, but the strategies of commodification have become ever more subtle. "Kill Your Parents Records" could just as easily be a subsidiary of SONY or Warner Brothers as it could be some DIY outfit run out of some punk's bedroom. And although—to address a more purely formal question—reactionary, smarmy tonalities are everywhere in movies and TV shows, people in general have become somewhat inoculated to dissonance as well. Avant rock has developed, in more recent years, in a world where it is very unclear exactly what an avant-garde is anymore; the already difficult relationship between avant-garde art and radical politics becomes even more difficult; to repeat, it is hard to grapple with society when it is evermore difficult to know where to put the hooks in.

We might say that the situation of all forms of avant-garde art, including avant rock, is "post-Warhol." Did Andy Warhol's work represent something of a situationist "detournement" of commodification, employing an ironical strategy for tunneling through a process of reification that could no longer be negated "head on" (and this despite whatever Warhol himself may have said about what he was doing), or was this work no more than an embrace of capitalism as the only way to organize society? My distrust of any commentary that would purport to answer this question quickly and straightforwardly is exemplary of a general feeling that the situation of avant-garde art vis-à-vis politics is at the very least not in any way a simple matter.

Adorno wrote, famously, that "philosophy, having missed the moment of its realization, lives on." This must go for music as well, and there is less and less of a map to navigate by. What remains are experiments with form, though in more recent years I think we have seen that this can also mean a development of form by bringing new content. In some sense, this is what makes avant rock "legitimate" as a form of avant-garde music, that it has taken into itself the experiments with form that have occurred elsewhere in music, in the work of John Cage or Cecil Taylor for instance, but it has also joined these innovations with "contents" that are often not found in Western classical music and sometimes not in jazz either. Hence, again, the vitality of avant rock, a vitality not often found in the "classical" avant-garde these days.

Finally, I would like to conclude this discussion with the question of what sense, if any, can be made of the idea of "meaning" in music. There are two reasons why I do not think this is a mere intellectual exercise. First, I take music-making to be a part of human striving in general, and it is a question of some moment whether there is any point to this striving. Relatedly, meaning itself seems to be embattled in these postmodern times—it is increasingly difficult for productions in the realm of culture to rise to the level of significance in this age when knowledge has been replaced by information, and where "truth" is what sells.

Peter Kivy is an analytic philosopher of music and aesthetics. His provocatively-titled chapter, "It's Only Music: So What's to Understand?" from *Music Alone*: *Philosophical Reflections on the Purely Musical Experience*, will serve as a useful platform for pursuing this question of the significance of music. Kivy opens the essay as follows: "If I were to ask the question, Do you understand music? what kind of question would I be asking, and what kind of evidence might I accept for an affirmative answer to it?" (p. 93) "Analytic philosophy" gets its name from its origins in linguistic analysis—the idea being to recast the basic questions of philosophy in terms of what sense can be made of them (the initiating figures were Frege, Wittgenstein, Russell, the members of the Vienna Circle, and, behind them, Hume and, to some extent, Kant—for example his critique of the ontological argument for the existence of God). Kivy is asking what "sense" can be made of music, and this very quickly takes him toward the linguistic model for what meaning *means*. When I have discussed Kivy's argument with others, either in a classroom setting or elsewhere, I have found people remarkably resistant to this linguistic turn—or, more to the point, to the conclusions that Kivy draws on the basis of this turn. (The resistance is similar to what is regularly offered in response to Donald Davidson's argument about nonhuman animals and consciousness—in the essays "Thought and Talk" and "Rational Animals"—and this will turn out to be a useful reference in the present context.) In this discussion of Kivy, I want to do three things, the first two of them simultaneously. I want to maintain an appreciation for why people resist Kivy's conclusions about the "meaning" of music, while at the same time also appreciating the force of the methodology he brings to the question. After this exercise in contrary appreciations, I will ask how the question bears on experimental rock music, and how this music bears on the question.

Kivy's initial question is followed closely by some remarks that get to the heart of the problem:

> If I asked you, Do you understand German? it is clear what kind of question I would be asking, and that the evidence directly bearing upon an affirmative answer would be your demonstrated ability to provide paraphrases, in other languages, for German sentences. It is equally clear that scarcely anyone who has thought seriously about music is prepared to take this as a satisfactory model for musical understanding. For it is agreed on all hands that music is not a language in any but an attenuated or metaphorical sense, and that it certainly possesses no semantic content. To provide paraphrases in English of pure instrumental compositions would surely be considered musically unsophisticated in the extreme. Such effusions might, under certain circumstances, be charming literary conceits, but not to be taken seriously as musical analysis. (p. 93)

As it turns out, there are really three concerns that unfold from this type of analysis. Perhaps most central to Kivy's inquiry in this particular essay is what it would mean to say that someone does or does not "understand" music, and he goes on to argue that perhaps the defining test of this is whether or not someone can give an account of some particular piece of music. As he develops his position, Kivy is actually quite broad in his appreciation of what might be acceptable as such an account, but he tends to come around again and again to language and discursivity. I am sympathetic to this move, even while I appreciate some of the reasons why some people resist it (however, there are some "reasons" that I do not appreciate—for example, when people just say that music is either to be enjoyed or not enjoyed, but in any case it is not to be analyzed or "intellectualized.") Secondary to this concern, but clearly integral to Kivy's line of inquiry, is the question whether a term such as "understanding" can apply to music, especially when understanding is understood on a discursive model, if indeed "pure music" is not something to which the constituent layers of language—semantics, syntax, pragmatics—apply. To ask, what is the meaning of the forty-third measure of the first movement of Beethoven's Third Symphony does not make sense in the same way—or perhaps not even in a related way—to a similar question about the fifteenth verse of the third chapter of the book of Jeremiah. Finally, Kivy is concerned with the relationship between musical understanding and musical appreciation. In the end he wants to argue that an increase in the former leads to an increase in the latter. This position in aesthetics is called "cognitivism," and it has traditionally been set against "emotivism."

Perhaps the reader can see how all three concerns are bound up together. Appreciating music depends on knowing something about it—but what counts as "knowing something" about music? The issue of "intellectualization" comes right back at the point this question is raised, because people might be rightly suspicious of the "expert knowledge" that the critic might claim to have, knowledge that supposedly entitles him or her to a privileged position with regard to this or that piece of music or genre. (The reader might be amused to know that my own writing on music has been criticized by some because I am not a "trained musicologist.") Kivy does not want to go so far as to say that only those skilled in the intricacies of Schenkerian analysis have an understanding of music. (Heinrich Schenker, 1868–1935, developed a kind of "mathematics" of tonality through which he sees the same basic structure unfolding in the masterpieces of the Western classical tradition from Bach to Brahms.) Indeed, he even allows that "one can, perhaps at times to better effect, say 'the place where the theme goes dum-dum-diddle' rather than 'the place where the theme descends in seconds and thirds'" (p. 121). There might be many ways into a piece of music, and even many levels of understanding—but this does not run counter to Kivy's basic point: "The more I understand a work, the more I hear in it" (p. 115). I have focused on what Kivy says about appreciation, leaving aside the issue of enjoyment. Kivy does, however, draw the necessary conclusions from his cognitivist framework—in particular, that, in some cases, increased understanding and appreciation may lead to decreased enjoyment, because some particular musical work may not turn out to have so much to hear "in it" after all (see pp. 115–17). On the other hand, as one's appreciation of music increases, one will probably have a better sense of where to obtain musical enjoyment. To sum up:

> Any increase in understanding may bring both positive and negative results as far as enjoyment is concerned. And, of course, I cannot back away from musical understanding in order to avoid its possibly negative results, because I could not then avail myself of its positive results either. Understanding (as I understand understanding) is the only game in town. If I don't risk the negative to get the positive, I will never increase my musical enjoyment at all.

Here, then, is what we have to say: musical understanding always increases musical appreciation. But increase in musical appreciation, in any individual cases, may sometimes increase, sometimes decrease musical enjoyment. However, it still might be true that overall, in the long run, increase in musical understanding yields increase in musical pleasure; that in spite of setbacks, the general tendency is for increase in understanding to bring increase in enjoyment. (p. 117)

I accept this argument, on the whole, because, despite my sympathies for people who want to resist any move that would seem to "discursify" music or life, the universe, and everything, and who perhaps resonate with that great comment found somewhere in Joseph Heller's *Catch-22*, "he knew everything about literature except how to enjoy it," I agree with Kivy that, to go in the other direction eventually leads to accepting that "ignorance is bliss." If understanding is not the only game in town, then what is—not understanding? Of course, the anti-cognitivist is not going to agree to this characterization, and instead will say something to the effect that "understanding has its place, but ultimately the appreciation of music comes down to feeling."

The discussion might be transposed onto the arguments about ethics made by Immanuel Kant and John Stuart Mill, stand-ins for the cognitivist and emotivist, respectively. The latter takes enjoyment (or happiness or pleasure or the avoidance of pain) to be the motivating category; there is not first of all something to "know," and, indeed, the sort of thing that makes one person exceedingly happy (attending a performance by the Chicago Symphony, say, or perhaps one by the Miami Dolphins) might evince the equal and opposite reaction from another. Kant proposed, instead, that there was a way to know right from wrong, and this knowledge was attained by applying the "categorical imperative"—"act only according to that principle that can be understood, at the same time, as a universal moral law." Happiness may consist in different things for different people, but this is not the case for basic ethical principles, Kant argued (and therefore he wanted to sever the question of what is right from the pursuit of happiness; I hasten to add, since some wag will undoubtedly want to point this out, that Kant lived before Mill and therefore was not responding to Mill personally, but instead to applications of the principle of utility to ethics, these applications having a long history that predates modern utilitarianism). Fine and good, you might say—or perhaps not—but still, even if there are universal moral laws, why think there are universal aesthetic ones?

Incidentally, we might further align Kant with Kivy—in a very general way—in that the point about universal moral laws might be reconceptualized thus: if we want to talk about ethics, then the subject of our discussion should be the question, "What is right?" If we want to talk about what might make for the greatest happiness for the greatest number, then that is another subject, insomuch as "happiness" here can only be the aggregate of the essentially ineffable pleasures of individuals. In the utilitarian framework, pleasures do not need to be explained, and in fact cannot in the end be explained, only recommended. Perhaps if I understood something that you say that you hear and take pleasure in when you listen to Beethoven, then perhaps if I am able to hear that same thing I will take pleasure in it as well. But perhaps not—and, so the argument goes, there is a point where all explanations will fall short, and I will either take pleasure in the music or I will not. Here, though, we see how Kivy is more in line with a Kantian framework, but also how he perhaps gets into a bit of trouble where it comes to the relationship between appreciation and enjoyment. If we want to *talk about* (or otherwise discourse upon) a musical work, then what else is there to talk about than what is good (or perhaps bad) in it? Perhaps, *knowing you*, I may infer something about a piece of music that you have only expressed feelings rather than ideas about (recognizing, of course, that "feelings" and "ideas" are rarely separable in practice, though they serve well enough here as analytical categories), but then I am inferring something about the music from something else I know, something about you. Otherwise, it may be useful to know your feelings on a particular work (I mean feelings expressed in terms such as "I love it" or "I hate it"), but we can go only so far in a conversation about our feelings. The utilitarian will say that this means there is also only so far one can go in a conversation about enjoying this or that piece of music. The trouble comes in the fact that the person who is shown "something" in Beethoven, or in the Sex Pistols for that matter, might respond, "I appreciate what's being done there, but I cannot say that I enjoy it." Supposing that we can take it for granted that Beethoven created a great deal of music that is to be appreciated, can we make the further step and say that the person who appreciates what is there *ought* also to enjoy it? That seems quite a leap, and, indeed, Kant makes no such leap when it comes to ethical questions—people are obligated to do what is right, whether they derive any happiness from it or not. In fact, in Kant's scheme, people should be actively suspicious of any course of action regarding an ethically significant situation where happiness is a potentially motivating factor. All of this becomes quite relevant when it comes to avant-garde movements in twentieth century music, for two reasons that I will turn to in a moment. One of the reasons has to do with the "it" or "something" *in* music.

For the emotivist or utilitarian, there is ultimately no more to the "it" that is "in" music (in this or that particular work) than something that stimulates our sensory surfaces in such as way as to bring about either pleasure or pain. Ultimately, then, there is nothing to talk about beyond whether to bring this something closer or to push it away.

At the same time, it seems likely that what Kivy would mean by "enjoyment" is more akin to the concept that has come down to us from Plato and Aristotle: *Eudaimonia*, happiness as pertaining to human flourishing. For my part, I think it is because Kant saw that "happiness," in the emerging commercial age, was being reduced to mere pleasure-seeking, that he proposed a strict separation between the questions of what is right and what makes a person happy. Clearly, the kind of enjoyment that comes from an active and ever-more-engaged understanding and appreciation of music pertains to a "deep down happiness" that is not at all the same as feeling "pleasured" and in fact may be at odds with it. Deeper happiness, for instance, may be tinged with melancholy; when Kivy talks about profundity in music, he cannot help but bring in the question of mortality (see, for example, pp. 202–18). Surely the pleasure-seeker would want to push that subject far away, as it does tend to bring one down a bit. At the same time, questions of the possibility of human flourishing and their relation to the true, the good, and the beautiful (or even the sublime) are quite marginal to the real question of our culture: what sells? This is a fundamentally thoughtless question (indeed, it only brings itself forward as a question in any intellectual sense when someone has the temerity to raise some other question, such as "what is right and good?"—to which the "answer" will be given, "hey, money talks, bullshit walks"), even if some thought or even some creativity goes into answering it, and perhaps there is even a point where the politics of pleasure and desire must also resist this thoughtlessness, a point where the human organism is not infinitely pliable to the imperatives of profit-making (the point where one is starving, for instance). But it is at that point that both thinking and creativity have some work to do, and the cognitivist framework can be recast as urging that there is a fundamental connection between the two.

Sometimes the cognitivist and emotivist positions are characterized as "objectivist" and "subjectivist," respectively—in the former case, there is an "it" out there to be analyzed and understood, while in the latter case there is ultimately just me and my feelings. The question of the "objective" and the "subjective" is a great deal more complicated than one would know from, for instance, "anti-relativist" critiques of "fashionable postmodern ideologies" or whatnot. Be that as it may, in arguing that the sort of knowledge of music that leads to appreciation need not be technical knowledge, Kivy takes us one step closer to seeing what his sense of understanding music is about:

> the more knowledgeable listener is just the one who has music at the center of his or her life; who listens to it frequently; who talks about it incessantly to anyone within earshot; who "gushes" over music and musical performance long and loud. This simple and direct correlation between the behavioral criteria by which we judge that someone gets from music intense pleasure beyond that of the ordinary person and the person of knowledge, either technical or informal, beyond that of the ordinary person, strongly suggests the conclusion that, in general, if not in every case, increase in understanding of music brings increase in enjoyment. (p. 118)

Not wanting to go back into the question of enjoyment and pleasure, and also questioning some of the terms that Kivy employs here, I think that we can still take away two basic points from this passage. First, understanding and appreciation of music involves *engagement* with music; music has to be important in one's life, not incidental to it. (This bears, of course, on a culture where most music is meant to be mere background and perhaps, in the largest sense, a mere "advertisement" for a society where everything important is just a background that one never pays direct attention to. I raise this here simply to provoke the reader to see that the issues discussed in this "intellectual exercise" actually have a great deal to do with the larger subject of this book.) Second, in showing that his "simple and direct correlation" can be drawn, I think Kivy has also made a good case for the correlation. The question again comes around to the consequences that would follow from *not* drawing the correlation. At the same time, although Kivy's purpose here is not necessarily to worry about this point, in stressing the relationship between the understanding *of* music and involvement *in* music, it is clear that his arguments about musical "knowledge" do not require some clinical or scientistic notion of "objectivity." (In other parts of the essay Kivy refers to musical works as "intentional objects," which adds further sophistication to the picture.)

Still, let us turn to the "it" and "what" of Kivy's inquiry—"It's only music, so what's to understand?" As with every other point in Kivy where on the whole I agree with him, I am "agreeing" in a way that most likely expands his arguments beyond where he might want to go with them. So, the "it" of music that can be an intentional object of understanding is something about the *form* of a particular work, and what it is about the form is what Kivy calls the "syntax" or "grammar" of the music. This grammar is captured in the understanding by more or less formal descriptions of it, which in either case demonstrate more or less well that one knows what is going on in the music. The account of musical "grammar" that Kivy gives covers the Western classical tradition from J. S. Bach and perhaps some time before to Brahms and perhaps some time after; clearly, his account is not meant to cover a good deal of twentieth-century avant-garde music or music outside of the European classical canon. Within the tradition that Kivy focuses on, a very simple test of whether someone understands the grammar of the music is whether they would know if something akin to a "grammatical error" has been committed. Because Kivy's analysis of this matter sheds light upon both the contemporary avant-garde in general, and avant-rock in particular, I will follow his argument out at some length. In his comparison of music with language, Kivy offers the interesting formulation that music "present[s] itself to us . . . as a quasi-syntactical structure: a syntax without a semantics" (p. 101). (For the moment let us address the question of syntax exclusively, returning later to the problem of meaning.) However, it is not difficult to see an objection to the idea that understanding music means understanding the syntax of music: there are many people who seem to have an appreciation of and deep involvement in music who would not be able to "parse" the "grammatology" of it (p. 102). Kivy employs characters from E. M. Forster's novel, *Howards End*, to press this point:

> Whatever else Mrs. Munt may understand and enjoy in Beethoven's Fifth Symphony, if she cannot enjoy its syntactical structure, she is so far from the heart of the matter as to be hardly an enjoyer of the *music* at all. Like Helen, she might just as well be hearing heroes and shipwrecks. And that conclusion is intolerable. It makes music, in one of its most important aspects, understandable and (hence) enjoyable only to the musical grammarians. (p. 102)

We perhaps see now another way to frame the basic question: What counts as musical *literacy*? To say that it is intolerable to deny the musical literacy of someone who cannot parse the grammar of a musical work is similar, then, to recognizing that there are many competent speakers and writers of, say, the English language who also cannot give a technical account of the syntax of the language. But in that latter case we do not say that the person does not understand English.

Perhaps what we say about such a person, then, whether it is a question of music or language, is that they display an informal understanding of syntax when they clearly know that a musical work or a conversation or a piece of writing is "going right" and when it is "going wrong."

Let us take up just one thread of this argument and now set aside whatever difficulties there may be in Kivy's larger position. If I could extend Kivy's basic claim (though perhaps further than he wants to go with it), I would simply restate the point about syntax in these rather vague terms: to understand a musical work is to have a sense of its form. Is to say this mere "formalism"? What of musical "content"? This is a complex issue that cannot receive a full treatment here, but there are a few things about it that need to be said, for the issue bears on many of the experiments in music that are discussed in this book. So, to be very brief and telegraphic: there is no absolute line that can be drawn between form and content and, furthermore, form *has* content. There are no absolute musical "forms" that fall out of the sky, all of them exist in a matrix of traditions, counter-traditions, and social relations. If a new voice is heard in music, a new theme or idea, this is also in some sense a transformation of form. At the same time, the expansion or transformation of musical syntax or form in the narrow sense is clearly central to the question of what is creative in art—to ignore this, as Kivy argues, is to go very far from the heart of things, to the point where it is unclear why it matters that we are talking about *music*. (This point can be seen very clearly if one considers "agit-prop" or "message" music, or at least some of it—the particular message may be well and good, and the "music" may serve as a *useful* vehicle for the transmission of the message, but what is the music doing *qua* music? Theodor Adorno argued that the further effect of this music is that, even while it may be directed against capitalism, it reinforces the capitalist mission of making everything instrumental to the cash nexus.) That a work of art may be "about" a profound subject does not in itself make the work profound.

If to be involved in music is to be involved in its form, then, how do we know when things are or are not "going right"? This is the thread that I want to pursue. Kivy argues that, in the case of the canon that is his focus,

> in music, unlike in ordinary languages, the occurrence of a true grammatical error is rare. Numerous times a day one hears "ain't" for "isn't" and "don't" for "doesn't." But clearly, we do not listen to the music of *bunglers and beginners*. A syntactical error in any music of the standard repertoire or its peripheries is uncommon and almost always arguable into the bargain. That is to say, we make every effort to be critically charitable and to try to see the "error" as "non-normal" grammar rather than as ungrammatical.

> . . . [W]hereas in everyday discourse we have no compunction about identifying various usages as ungrammatical, in musical works we tend to apply a principle of charity, if you will, whereby apparent ungrammaticalities . . . are, *as much as is possible*, understood as "grammatical" in a different style system rather than "ungrammatical" in the one in which they might appear that way. (p. 110; my emphasis)

One hypothesis that occurs to me on the basis of this passage is that the avant-garde has fundamentally to do with the "as much as is possible," in the previous paragraph, and with the mixing of grammars. Indeed, in the musical avant-garde in general, and certainly in avant rock, there is often the effort to involve the "bunglers and beginners" in music-making as a way of stretching grammars (perhaps to the breaking point) and crossing style systems by bringing fresh ears and ideas to the process. In an earlier passage than the one just quoted, Kivy referred to a composer (William Billings) who was "untutored and self-taught," arguing that, as this figure

> becomes more and more a part of the canon . . ., his mistakes will come to be seen and enjoyed as peculiarities of style, "original" departures from orthodoxy, and appreciated for their novelty and crude but rugged strength rather than derided as grammatical errors. . . . (p. 110)

Well, though there are significant exceptions, many of the figures discussed in this book are "untutored and self-taught"—that is the norm in rock music. On the other hand, exactly what is it that can be "taught" in music, and what can be taught when it comes to the avant-garde?

These questions may be simply the larger correlates of worries about how far we can go with the analogy to grammar.

> What, then, are we really talking about when we talk about the perceiving and enjoying of musical grammar? It seems as if we cannot perceive grammar of any kind without the possibility of perceiving the ungrammatical as well as the grammatical. Yet what I have

just said [about incorporating the "mistakes" of canonical figures into different grammatical systems] seems to rule that out for music. Well, not exactly.

> The experience of grammaticality in music is phenomenological; that is to say, we perceive musical syntax as a phenomenal property of the music. Since music does not—except in the most unusual cases—contain true "grammatical" errors, what we perceive is not the correct or the incorrect, for everything is correct. We perceive, rather, the "correct" and the "incorrect" as aesthetic properties of the music. Thus music gives us feelings, impressions of "rightness" or of "wrongness" resolving into "rightness," but what it seldom gives us is a genuine "ain't." If it seems to, it is because we . . . have not caught on to the style; have not learned the "language"; have not internalized the "syntax." (p. 111)

If one has internalized the syntax of a piece of music, and if there truly are "mistakes" in the music, then, even without any technical language, one might make significant observations about the structure of the music: "that passage should have zigged when it zagged," "this doesn't go with that," and so forth. But there are two closely related problems with this syntactical approach. First, we take it as a property of many (and perhaps most and perhaps all) important works of art that they establish their own rules for when things should zig and when they should zag and what goes with what. That is what makes works of art *creative*; that is the element of *poiesis*. So, second, a creative work will "abuse," if you will, or at least stretch, the established ways of hearing syntax.

When we come to the avant-garde, these issues are pressed to extremes. Having some mode, however informal, for describing the grammatical properties of music, Kivy argues, is

> what makes music, even to the untutored . . ., something other than a kaleidoscope of sounds. For there is nothing of syntax in the kaleidoscope's patterns: nothing is "right" because nothing is "wrong." [Anyone] unable to participate in musical grammaticality . . . would indeed be so musically impoverished as to be scarcely describable as a musical listener. *There may be musics without syntax*, but Western music is not one of them. (p. 114; my emphasis)

Now, it is not a very far leap from these comments to central issues in the avant-garde. Where has musical syntax been strained to the point of incomprehensibility? Is there some permanent crossing-over place? Clearly, "tonality" in itself is not that place. Are some of the works of John Cage, Cecil Taylor, and Sonic Youth simply beyond the pale of what can be understood structurally and grammatically?

At the beginning of the discussion I referred to Donald Davidson's arguments about thought and language. One of the things that he argues is that it doesn't make sense to say that nonhuman animals have language, we just don't know how to understand it. His argument is that one cannot tell the difference between a language that is "untranslatable" (even given sufficient effort and goodwill) and something that only sounds at first like a language. (In addition to the essays mentioned earlier, also see "On the Very Idea of a Conceptual Scheme," the title of which inspired the title of this section.) Another way to say this is that Davidson argues that we cannot make sense of the claim that there are "languages" that do not work at all in the way that the human languages we know work (and which therefore can be translated, on the whole, one into the other) and yet that are languages all the same—and can be recognized as such. For, what is it that one can "recognize"? There are languages where the basic syntax is different, or at least on the surface appears to be different, from whatever happens to be our "home" language. But the translation of one language into another shows that, at the very least, anything that would be recognizable as a language has to have grammatical structure.

Given the limitations (but holding, I hope, to the strengths as well) of the analogies of language and grammar to music that we have discussed here, we might wonder whether there truly can be a "music without syntax" that would be recognizable as music, as opposed to "not-music" (or perhaps, as was said by a famous jazz critic of John Coltrane's work, "anti-music"), the more common name for which is "noise." The paradox is that creativity in poetry occurs when language and grammar are pressed to the limit (which, to return to the earlier remarks about form and content, may also mean the expression of heretofore marginalized human experiences even within more "conventional" language), and perhaps somewhere beyond the limit. Davidson, in an essay that many analytic philosophers have not fully assimilated to their readings of his work, "A Nice Derangement of Epitaphs," argues that language is not a finished thing. He even goes so far as to claim there is "no such thing as a language," if by this one means some static entity consisting in syntax and words. In this respect, "the limit" that the creative poet (an expression that ought to be seen as redundant) places pressure upon is not some eternally designated line in the sand. Here I think the analogy with music holds plenty well—neither is there some immovable point where we can absolutely know the difference between syntax and the kaleidoscope of sounds. At least, this is the case where the experience of music—whether from the standpoint of the listener or the composer or the performer—is conceived as an experiment.

Earlier, I promised two reasons why Kivy's arguments bear on the avant-garde. I have just rehearsed the first of these reasons: the "it" of avant-garde music, the "what" that is there to understand, seems to be of a less "syntactical" character. But we might say, in the spirit of Kivy's argument that we cannot understand the "rightness" of the syntax without also having a sense of what "wrongness" might be, that avant-garde music is music that challenges us to consider that distinction at every or almost every moment in its unfolding. And it also makes us consider the distinction in it's very *idea*. John

Cage's work for piano, *Etudes Australes* challenges us to ask the following: Suppose we were to lay a transparency with staff lines embossed upon it over a chart of the stars as seen from Australia, and then to transpose the positions of those stars into notes on the staff—is there music to be found there? Is that a cockamamie way to conceive of musical syntax—when really all we have is a kaleidoscope of sounds (and silences) where nothing is "wrong" because we have no procedure, logic, or structure, to determine what would be "right"? Is *Etudes Australes* more a work of philosophy, in that it mainly causes us to raise questions about what music is, rather than a musical work itself? But, if so, why doesn't that property in itself make these *Etudes* an interesting musical work? These are the sorts of questions that avant-garde works force upon us.

The second reason has to do with the relationship that Kivy sees among understanding, appreciation, and enjoyment—and what one famous commentator on Western classical music called "the *agony* of modern music." Is avant-garde art meant to be "enjoyed"? Certainly, to begin with anyway, there were many people who did not enjoy the innovations of Beethoven or Stravinsky or Schoenberg or Coltrane or Taylor—and some of these, at least, still resist assimilation to enjoyment. Kivy does not discuss the avant-garde or rock music or, certainly, the avant-garde in rock music, but this is the place where I would take a stand for its importance and relevance. I am thinking of those terms that Kivy used to describe the sort of person who has music at the "center" of his or her life—they "gush" over it, they talk about it incessantly to whomever happens to be around, and so on. This reminds me, I'm afraid, of the typical sort of dilettante that one finds in the Western classical scene, a scene built around what I would generally call a "museum culture" of "the standard works." In some sense, I have to wonder how "important" music is for the person for whom it is so "important" that it is at the "center" of his or her life—because it has been my experience that the sort of person one finds in the "gushing about music" scene is one for whom music is not very much part of a more general human striving, but instead is someone who has found some precious niche to occupy. (I can't help but think of the Niles Crane character from the TV show, *Frasier*.) There are of course people involved in classical music for whom this is not a fair characterization, from Pablo Casals and Leonard Bernstein to Yo Yo Ma, but it is precisely because one sees in them this connection between music and the possibility of human flourishing. Clearly, they have wanted to take the great works of the standard repertoire out of the museum and reinfuse them with vitality. I would not argue that this vitality is at an end—*but,* when it comes to the audiences, I mainly see preciousness and posing. Naturally, they want to "enjoy" music as something "pretty" and soothing. In some sense, why would this not be the case? The main audiences for classical music—and I am not saying that many of these listeners are not musically sophisticated, that is not the point—demand that the standard repertoire be performed in the standard fashion again and again. Being in the museum is what is at the center of their lives. But one might quite plausibly make the argument that real "involvement" in music means not only appreciation for past achievements but also participation in (as a listener or as a musician or both) the kind of creativity that is not already packaged for the museum. And here I think we see a good deal of vitality in the experiments that are taking place within the context and on the basis of rock music—and its "untutored" aspects often help it to remain unassimilated to existing grammars.

While I agree with Kivy that there is not a "semantics of music," per se, we might still consider the hypothesis that a focus on the music of the museum culture places music in a context where the fact of music-making itself has diminished significance. We do not have to propose any theory of music as representation—such theories having been adequately critiqued by Kivy and others (see especially Kivy's *Sound and Semblance*)—in order to say that, still, the significance of Beethoven's Third Symphony having been inspired by the French Revolution is seriously diminished when the work is mainly presented to audiences who either know or care nothing for the Revolution or who find the whole affair a rather dreadful prospect. Music "matters" to these people in a way and in a context that itself does not matter.

However, it is undoubtedly the case that creativity in rock music has its own battles to fight when it comes to forces that diminish significance. We know very well the force that has assimilated much rock music from its beginnings (and that generates a good deal of rock music as "pre-assimilated")—simple commercialism will do well enough as the description of that. But rock music also came out of experiences of struggle and striving—in particular of the civil rights movement, Black liberation, and even class struggle understood broadly, and out of the whole political matrix of "the sixties." When it comes to avant-rock, it would be hard to convince me that any album blew the whole field open more than *Sgt. Pepper's Lonely Hearts Club Band*, even with all of the flaws that one might find in it in retrospect. *Up to a point*, the dynamic opened up by that album is still unfolding. It may also be that *this* energy of social and cultural rebellion, and its artifacts in music, has largely been assimilated to recognized grammars, and that the new forms of experimental rock music are taking their cue from elsewhere. That is a question for the rest of this book.

A final thought in the context of Peter Kivy's arguments. If music is significantly similar to language, this might help us with the question of whether avant rock is expanding the boundaries of music in general, or mainly of rock music. For instance, one might say of a certain literary stylist that he or she has expanded the boundaries of linguistic expression in English. Does it mean anything to say that such a stylist has expanded the boundaries of expression in language "in general"? Well, there does not appear to be such a thing as "language in general." Philosophers of language, following an impulse from Frege, toyed with the idea of a "metalanguage" that is the repository of *something*—meaning and reference are the usual candidates—that grounds what we say, but, after Wittgenstein, Quine, Davidson, and Derrida (among others), it is very difficult to sustain this notion. Still, there is translation, and it could be that a literary stylist in one language creates new possibilities for meaning that have implications for other languages or even for all other languages—given Davidson's argument that we cannot make sense of the idea of an untranslatable language. Is there at least this kind of sense to be made of the idea of "music in general"? I would say yes, but only in a time when the historical context of music allows for a great deal of cross-fertilization. In other words, we can now compare contributions to music across genres to a certain extent because there is now a culture that is larger than the particular genres. But this is also a good reason to not get stuck in the museum culture.

Having read this "manifesto" and perhaps taken a glance at some of the discographies for this book the reader can now see, I hope, the larger motivations behind the writing of this book. I want to try to understand where rock music has been and where it is going. I want to understand what creativity and innovation has been, is, and might be in this music. In the end, the idea of avant-garde rock music may not be fully sustainable, in part because it is not clear what the avant-garde in anything means anymore. The drive toward artistic creativity, however, leads some to seek out music not yet heard, and experimental rock is playing its role in this endeavor.

2. Rock music in postmodern times

Chevette had never been that much into music, not any particular kind, although in her messenger days she'd gotten to like dancing in clubs, in San Francisco. Carson, though, he'd been very particular about what music he liked, and had tried to teach Chevette to appreciate it like he did, but she just hadn't gotten with it at all. He was into this twentieth-century stuff, a lot of it French, particularly this Serge Something, really creepy-ass, sounded like the guy was being slowly jerked off while he sang, but like it really wasn't even doing that much for him. She'd bought this new Chrome Koran . . .

He had been taught, of course, that history, along with geography, was dead. That history in the older sense was an historical concept. History in the older sense was narrative, stories we told ourselves about where we'd come from and what it had been like, and those narratives were revised by each new generation, and indeed always had been. History was plastic, was a matter of interpretation. The digital had not so much changed that as made it too obvious to ignore. History was stored data, subject to manipulation and interpretation. . . .

"There is an ongoing initiative to bring the bridge community back into the fold, as it were. But the issue is sensitive. A matter of image, really, and that of course is where we come in." Harwood smiles. "A number of major cities have these autonomous zones, and how a given city chooses to deal with the situation can impact drastically on that city's image. Copenhagen, for instance, was one of the first, and has done very well. Atlanta, I suppose, would be the classic example of what not to do." Harwood blinks. "It's what we do now instead of bohemias, " he says.

"Instead of what?

"Bohemias. Alternative subcultures. They were a crucial aspect of industrial civilization in the two previous centuries. They were where industrial civilization went to dream. A sort of unconscious R&D, exploring alternative social strategies. Each one would have a dress code, characteristic forms of artistic expression, a substance or substances of choice, and a set of sexual values at odds with those of the cultures at large. And they did, frequently, have locales with which they became associated. But they became extinct."

"Extinct?"

"We started picking them before they could ripen. A certain crucial growing period was lost, as marketing evolved and the mechanisms of recommodification became quicker, more rapacious. Authentic subcultures required backwaters, and time, and there are no more backwaters. They went the way of geography in general."

—William Gibson, *All Tomorrow's Parties*

The status of rock music in these times is not any different from that of any other cultural form, except that, seemingly, rock music is one of the forms that has been especially chosen for liquidation. A recent *People* magazine (summer 2001) devoted to something it was calling "music" had photographs of about fifteen people on its cover. The fact that these were fifteen "individuals" says something already, about the way that the marketing of rock music is mostly slanted away from rock groups and toward "solo artists." Such "artists" have to be photogenic, of course. What of the essential rock idea that "the group's the thing"? Well, that doesn't fit very well with the way contracts work—no, the singer is the thing. Of the fifteen or so people on the cover of the magazine, I would count perhaps one or two of them as actual musicians.

Well, the particular musician's name that appears in the title of this book is Björk. But I wouldn't talk about her if I didn't think she was a real musician—yes, whatever *that* means. Björk is a singer, she has a pretty face, and is even a celebrity—though, lately, she is parodied here and there (*Mad TV*, for instance) as some sort of paradigm of a weird-crazy person. But she didn't make the cover of *People*, not the "music" issue in any case.

No, the centerpiece of the cover was reserved for Marshall Mathers, a.k.a. Eminem.

All right, fine, perhaps I am just preaching to the choir here, given the likely readership for a book of this sort. I do apologize for opening this final part of the book with a rant—except that I want to go a little further with it. When, in the 1950s, Theodor Adorno talked about the culture industry and the fully-administered society, and

Hannah Arendt talked about the banality of evil, both might have been exaggerating a bit for effect. But it is all coming true now, and perhaps their theses have already come true, and this affects the possibilities of culture. Rock music may have been affected more than any other form of culture, for two reasons. One of these has to do with the way that rock music became a kind of universal language of youth culture in the 1960s and 1970s. Although rock music began with closer ties to commerce than any other form of music before it, there was always an element of "breakout" (which is why I maintain that the progenitors, Little Richard, Chuck Berry, Jerry Lee Lewis, Bo Diddley, and the rest, were avant-garde in their way—they gave us new sounds, and opened doors to new musical possibilities). In the later 1960s, owing to the many ways that Western society was in upheaval (connected at every point to ways in which the Third World was in rebellion), this breakout led to greater autonomy for the creativity of rock music, and many musicians felt encouraged—I would even say by "forces of history," however vaguely defined and understood—to let their musical visions roam at least as far as the ear can hear (to mix metaphors). Unfortunately, because of the efficacy of this universal language, which was even able to involve people in their millions in experimental art (I keep repeating it: show me anything like this elsewhere in history), the powers-that-be have worked overtime ever since the middle-1970s to put that cat back in the bag. The fact that there are mass-circulation magazines devoting themselves to "music" without ever saying a thing about actual music (what I mean here is not just the "good stuff" versus the crap that *People* is covering, rather that, even with the disposable pabulum that is being covered, there aren't any words in the magazine that have anything to do with the actual music, but instead with celebrity biography) is one indicator that the culture industry has done a good job in this endeavor. Rock music may not be able to save the world, or even to change it very much, but it has played its part in the past, and not only as music but as emblem of a general cultural shift ("before and after rock" is a legitimate cultural, generational, and biographical indicator, I think), and therefore it must be neutralized, normalized, recuperated. So that is one reason.

The other reason is closely related to the first. A trivial example will serve here, unfortunately one that could be repeated *ad nauseum*. In November 1999 I happened to see the Foo Fighters on *Saturday Night Live*. Now, this is a band that I have nothing against, and, in fact, I am predisposed to like them, since their leader was the drummer for Nirvana (Dave Grohl). The song they played was fine, "it wasn't hurting anybody," as I like to say. But I felt a sense of "date inversion," from 1999 to 1966, in the sense that it was unclear to me what the Foo Fighters were doing in 1999 that hadn't already been done, and done better, by the Kinks in 1966. Now, I realize that this is the sort of thing that we old fogies of rock music say, that everything was better in 1969. Surely, if that is all that anyone of a certain age or older could say, we would have to be dealing with folks who just have their heads too much in the past. Radio is now fully attuned to this phenomenon, at least in the United States, so that there are stations in most *major markets* oriented toward each decade from the 1950s onward, in order to cover that decade when the listener of whatever age spent her or his formative years. Even within this narrow periodization, the "oldies," "classic rock," and, more recently, "eighties" and "nineties" stations tend to pick the silliest or most insipid records and play them over and over again, day in and day out. (But then, we aren't really dealing with discreet "stations" anymore, in the United States, because FCC "reform" has allowed a few media companies to buy up most stations, and they are programmed centrally.) Even people who think that rock music "hasn't been any good" since—name your date: 1967, 1969, 1972, 1977—but who at least followed the music closely up until that point, could easily think of program lists that would blow ninety-five percent of "oldies" or "classic rock" fare out of the water. Why is it that, on "classic rock" stations, we always hear insipid garbage such as Journey or Foghat or Ted Nugent (and not the sometimes great—or at least really cool—Amboy Dukes), and we rarely if ever hear the Beatles or Jimi Hendrix or Joni Mitchell, to say nothing of the Velvet Underground or Funkadelic?

Actually, this goes back to reason number one, or at least it does in the theory-snippet that I have started to develop regarding such music. Perhaps this is a perspective that only applies in the United States, but feminist writers and, from the other side of things, reactionaries, have looked at events such as the loss of the war in Vietnam in terms of an emasculation of the American male. Films such as *Rambo* and their ilk, among other reactionary political aims, play the role of pumping up the deflated male (and never by exposing the fact that, while American soldiers bear some responsibility for their role in an imperialist invasion, they were at the same time cannon fodder for a ruling class whose members—for example, Dan Quayle or George W. Bush—would, of course, never do any of the actual fighting). There is a kind of rock music, often called, and appropriately so, "cock rock," that I would even go so far as to call angry male jack-off music. Part of the effort—which does not begin as some sort of organized conspiracy, but instead simply follows the imperatives of commodification and empire (which, however, starts to look a little more conspiratorial at the point where a handful of corporations control almost all media)—toward the neutralization and recuperation of the creative and rebellious energies of rock music has been to bolster patriarchy and the general domination of women.

However, if it is the case that some, perhaps most, protestations that the Kinks or Cream or The Who did it better thirty or forty years ago are simply evidence of creeping (or raging) fogie-ism among "sixties people," surely it is not always out of order to make such claims? Part of what we are up against here is that, to talk about lengths of time such as "thirty or forty years" is something that even the most creative rock music may be ill-prepared to deal with. And yet, for rock music to be creative, and for it to remain creative, the timeframe and generational questions *must* be dealt with—I don't mean "theoretically," first of all, but by musicians.

In the preceding section,"Avant rock: the very idea," I argued that one way that the mainstreams and avant-gardes of rock music differed from those in jazz and European classical music is that there did not seem to be the kind or level of antagonism in rock music, an antagonism found elsewhere. The appreciator or creator of experimental rock music can also have a soft spot for Black Sabbath or the Allman Brothers or Madonna or that French guy named Serge Something, and not have to feel bad about it. Probably many of my fellow followers of experimental rock would agree with this assertion, but perhaps for a different reason than the one that motivates me. Lately there is a lot of talk concerning rock to the effect that it is all "pop" music—but that is a term that I am very ambivalent about. Indeed, the "pop" category seems to be just another way of moving everything over into Hollywood/celebrity territory. The problem with all those people on the cover of *People* magazine is not that they are singers. Good singers are musicians too, and singers such as Björk or Jon Anderson are musicians first, who happen to use their voices as their main instrument. No, the problem with the *People* magazine "singers" (including Lenny Kravitz, since they couldn't care less that he is a guitar player, too) is that the main quality for which they have been selected is that they are "frontpersons," and they are frontpersons because they are photogenic. Bully for them, but what does it have to do with music?

So now it has to be ventured, fifty years into the rock music enterprise, that perhaps something like an antagonism is opening up after all. The Foo Fighters are perhaps not 100 percent mainstream, and it is unclear what the term means in a time when the idea of a "counterculture" is increasingly hard to define, too. But then, the antagonism is perhaps not with the "mainstream" artists per se, but with the market and commodification—the groups and artists that are just repeating what was done better thirty-five years before are just playing their part for niche marketing. This is why the "entry level," pre-teen and teenage sectors of the market niches have come increasingly to resemble the "teen idol" system that has been in place in Japan for many years. Disposable pop stars are created for entertainment consumption by young consumers at this or that six-month or one- or two-year stage in their aesthetic development.

(For a period of months or perhaps a year or two, Korn or some such is the only band that matters; the world revolves around them. Then it is someone else. Then, after adulthood is reached, it's back to Korn or whomever was the big thing in that crucial moment.)

The dynamic is changing. In the last few years of the 1960s, a person could easily go from Jefferson Airplane and the Beatles and the Velvet Underground to King Crimson, because it was a generally hip idea to always look for music that was further out and that was aiming to be experimental. Part of what made that spirit possible was the fact that even the more mainstream groups were branching out and exploring. Of course, there continued to be pre-teen and teenage puff rock, which the "oldies" stations have now done a fine job of dredging up and displaying as if this is really what people were listening to in 1969. Well, it is true that the best-selling 45-rpm single in 1968 (at least in the United States) was "Ballad of the Green Berets" ("Fighting soldiers, from the sky …"). In a time of brilliant *albums*, reactionaries had their one song, so they pretty much had to go out and buy a copy. Despite the best efforts of the media corporations, the energy of that time was able to sustain the experimental spirit for at least a couple of decades. But now it is becoming increasingly clear that rock music, and experimental rock music, have entered a truly post-1968 era.

Not that there is any less experimentation now. Whether this experimentation has continued to come to real breakthroughs in creativity is another question, which we will turn to in a moment; the digital revolution in technology, however, affecting both production and distribution of music, has certainly opened a period in which more people than ever can attempt to realize their musical ideas. No, the question now is whether avant rock will start to be more like other avant-garde musics, produced, played, and listened to in arenas of its own, mostly small arenas, set aside from those forms of music (of whatever genre—jazz, classical, rock, JuJu, Indian classical, and so on) that are in some way or another more "popular" or "mainstream" or perhaps "acceptable" is the term. If so, perhaps we are on the verge of a new, "general avant-garde," one where differences in genre do not matter very much. That would be a double-edged sword. On the one hand, I think that it is good when genres do not matter as much as some more general orientation toward musical creativity. On the other, if a new "general avant-garde" emerges, it may not be out of the same universalistic spirit that motivated the cross-fertilizations of the 1960s. Without that spirit, it will be hard for experimental musicians to break free of their particular social niches, especially those who are shut up in the academy and hung up on pedigree. Broad-minded musicians such as John Zorn, Jim O'Rourke, Björk, and Fred Frith are making a very important contribution by cutting through that sort of thing.

Still, it seems likely that we are entering a period where "mass culture"—to use the old Marxist term that denotes the "culture" that the media corporations serve up through its myriad outlets, and that can be contrasted with something more like "popular" cultures that are actual expressions of the people—will become ever more stupid, and experimentalists will just keep trying to go off in new directions, "on their own," so to speak. But this can be a very vibrant "margin," and perhaps not as obscure as one might at first expect—the person sitting next to you on the subway or across from you in a restaurant may be into it, too, and perhaps only social anonymity keeps you from knowing this.

The musical career of Mike Patton is useful to reflect upon in this connection. In the late 1980s/early 1990s, Patton was the "hypnotic" singer and frontman with "pin-up looks" for the alternative rock band, Faith No More. (The sobriquets come from the *Rough Guide to Rock.*) Their reputation was built upon playing intense, no fooling around, rock. Given that I am the "wrong generation" for what they were doing, I did not find them especially adventurous, but at least they were lacking in pretension and they had more to them than just more "punk" attitude coming ten or fifteen years too late. (They also did a neat version of Black Sabbath's "War Pigs.") Then Patton also formed a side project, Mr. Bungle, that was a good bit more far out, with whimsical Beefheart-like elements. Their 1999 album, *California,* is especially good. But Patton must have wanted an outlet for music that is completely experimental, so, in 1996 and 1997 he did two albums for John Zorn's Tzadik label. The first of these, *Adult Themes for Voice* is quite radical, and yet it also looks backward. That is, it is an album of pieces entirely for solo voice (Patton's, that is) and microphone. Certainly this is "out" music for any "ordinary" rock listener, and for most of the more adventurous listeners besides. And yet it is also quite reminiscent of Yoko Ono's vocal experiments, especially "Fly," and we might also make a nod here to Cathy Berberian and Joan La Barbara. The latter's *Singing Through* album consists in vocal compositions by John Cage, and among the other musicians on the album is the percussionist William Winant. Winant's credits, as has been mentioned, run from Stockhausen to Sonic Youth, and he is also featured on Patton's 1997 Tzadik album, *Pranzo Oltranzista.* Obviously, what looms large as a question is whether those gestures that are quite "out" and experimental for rock musicians amount to more than a recapitulation of the main currents of twentieth-century avant-garde music, especially those from jazz and European classical music. Or, is something coming together, on the basis of rock music—or of musicians associated with rock, as the case may be—that will allow music once again to take the next step, or even to find the "different logic"?

Kudos and praise to Mike Patton for his experimentalism, but we might also learn something by asking about the demographics of his different musics. How many people who were into Faith No More are willing to go along with Mr. Bungle, and how many of those would go along with the Tzadik projects? Yes, of course, on one level, *who cares?*—what we care about here is musical experimentation and the spaces where it can occur. It has been very rare for this experimentation to be a broadly popular thing, the major exception being the utopian window that opened in the late 1960s and per-haps stayed open for a few years after the decade was over. The dynamic now is differ-ent from what happened with, for instance, John Coltrane in the last two or three years of his life. Coltrane had a big following, and then that following dwindled somewhat as he (and Rashied Ali, Alice Coltrane, and Pharaoh Sanders) moved into the territory of ever-increasing fragmentation. My sense is not that someone like Mike Patton, when he

is doing his own solo projects or Mr. Bungle, experiences a "dwindling" of the following that he had with Faith No More. I would venture that, instead, we are just talking
about two different worlds. Now, it is true, most Beatles fans (and, broadly speaking,
there are not many people who are not Beatles fans on some level) are not going to follow George Harrison into *Wonderwall* music, or John Lennon and Yoko Ono into
Unfinished Music #1. And yet, Beatles fans then and most likely now know that some
of the Beatles did some weird stuff on the side, some of it occasionally finding its way
on to an actual Beatles album (Yoko! Oh no!). By contrast, most Faith No More fans do
not know about Mike Patton's Tzadik albums, because, from their perspective, they
don't need to know about them, any more than they need to know about Cecil Taylor or
Karlheinz Stockhausen albums. So that is where I find the Mike Patton example instructive—after all, Brice Glace or Gastr del Sol were never on *Saturday Night Live*
(undoubtedly they should have been!), whereas Patton is a bona fide rock star.

Or, he was. The good music stores will have a selection of Tzadik CDs, sometimes
in a section called "avant-garde" or "experimental." Apparently Tzadik even put out a
guide for record store managers, on displaying and marketing avant-garde albums, with
the idea that a Tzadik display would be pretty much equal to this task. Well, you can't
blame them for trying, I suppose. But in any case, a great deal of what people know
about these things nowadays comes from word of mouth. Looking at it from the other
side, not of the "ordinary" rock listener, who might have been a fan of Faith No More
but would have a hard time wrapping his or her head around *Adult Themes for Voice*,
when I was first told about the Tzadik albums and that they were by Mike Patton, my
first reaction was, "who?" "You know, he was the singer from Faith No More." Well, I
recognized the reference, and I even had a Faith No More album ("War Pigs" sucked
me in), but what mattered to me much more was that John Zorn was putting this music
out, that it was for interesting instrumentation (or no instrumentation), and that musicians from the avant-garde scene such as William Winant and Marc Ribot (guitar) were
a part of it. So, my "avant-garde world" was disconnected, as well, from its own side,
from the rock world, even though I have nothing against "ordinary" rock music and
indeed listen to a fair share of it. When, in 1960, John Coltrane made *The Avant-Garde*
with Don Cherry and other musicians associated with Ornette Coleman, it was not necessarily regarded as something much further out than the trajectory he was already laying out with *Giant Steps* (1959). Now we are seeing a fragmentation of spheres, and I
would argue that only larger shifts in society, beyond the realm of music or "culture"
proper, will open the doors for "popular experimentalism" once again.

These shifts, however, may come in forms hitherto unseen. It isn't that Mike Patton
is "putting his reputation as a rock star on the line" with his experimental music. The
old forms of word-of-mouth still exist, actual conversations that people have in face-to-
face settings. For my part, I hope these forms will continue to exist, and I fear for what

sort of line will be crossed if the occurrence of these forms diminishes even more. But the same technology that allows more and more people (the temptation is to say "anyone" and "everyone," but, as yet, that remains a first-world prejudice) to make albums and engage in musical experiments, could also lead, finally, to the end of the star system. Cyberanarchists are fond of saying that "information wants to be free." Systems for downloading music online such as Napster and other forms of what essentially amounts to bootlegging may not yet spell the end of the bourgeoisie, not only because the media corporations will fight desperately to enforce their ownership "rights," but also because there is something not yet sufficiently transformational about young people who have the disposable income for their iMacs or whatever (mine is lime) supposedly not having the scratch for the latest Matchbox 20 album. All the same, the new information technologies have clearly opened a Pandora's Box wherein the very idea of private property starts to seem absurd, ludicrous, or just silly. Everyone knew all along that the "ownership" of music (and art generally) seemed a strange notion, which is why even many big rock stars have been swindled out of their own work over the years—this is just an extension of the fact that the super-rich individual who could purchase a Van Gogh for forty million dollars would never have gone anywhere near that wretched fellow in real life. So, we aren't there yet, but it would be hard to imagine that anyone doubts that major changes are coming. Many of these changes will be fought out in the institutions of bourgeois property relations (not only courts, but police crackdowns on hackers and others who come to possess "stolen" information), but there already are and will be more, at an increasing rate, subterranean movements that will transform the meaning of property, and perhaps first of all the meaning of "musical property." As these changes take place, one could imagine an even greater divide opening up between a "culture" of pap, pabulum, and pure hype, where the thing that makes a person a "star" (and not a "rock star," since there is very little "rock" in the sort of stuff that is valued primarily for its photogenic element) is that a large number of people may want to pay to see the performer at a concert or on cable TV, and a somewhat underground, word-of-mouth culture where there is experimentation and where we don't much care what the person looks like (even if mainstream journalists do not know how to write about much of anything else).

Perhaps, too, there has been a shift in the more experimental circles away from particular people or figures, and toward certain "scenes." In 1969 or 1972, say, if you were a person who was really into rock music, you almost certainly would have known about all or most of the significant groups or artists of the period. Now such encyclopedic knowledge is about to become impossible, unless you are independently wealthy or employed full-time to keep track of the sprawling confusion that is contemporary music. (On second thought, "independently wealthy" is a term that ought to be interrogated; is it not simply part of the apparatus of commodity fetishism to think that a person can be wealthy—or poor, for that matter, that's the point—apart from the fabric of social relations? So let's just say a "rich person with lots of time on his or her hands.") This is where good reviewers come in, people who can do some of the sorting that is necessary for figuring out what deserves at least an initial listen. Even some of these, I'm afraid, have been affected by the ever-present culture of hype—how could they not be? What I mean by a transition to the "scene" is that one travels in circles (some of them in cyberspace) where experimentation in music is valued, and someone mentions something that you haven't heard or heard of yet, and you respond by saying, "that sounds interesting, I'll have to check that out." Of course, this has always happened, but now it happens to a qualitatively greater degree.

Perhaps it is this more recent division of music into two worlds that has led some rock critics and listeners to look to Radiohead as the veritable messiahs of rock. It has been interesting to watch the amount of publicity, at least in the United States, that has attended the release of the two most recent Radiohead albums, *Kid A* and *Amnesiac*. Clearly, the bleak landscape painted by the group has captured the imagination of a nice cross-section of rock listeners, "young and old alike." Some people are saying that the appeal of Radiohead for folks who came of age in the late sixties and early seventies is that the music is reminiscent of some of the early Genesis albums. Being a member of that demographic myself, and having returned to the Genesis *Trespass* album (1971) for a few listens with the Radiohead question in mind, I would venture that there is something to this idea. But surely something else is animating the group's legions of younger listeners—though in both cases (and in the case of early Genesis, for that matter) this very likely has to do with that elusive "something about England." We in the States eat that "something" up, of course, and yet it is not easy to define what makes Radiohead appealing—or, at least it is hard to say what makes their appeal extend beyond that accorded to any other left-of-center and offbeat rock band.

I will have more to say on *Kid A* and *Amnesiac* at the end of this discussion, where I will also take up some other albums that appeared during the final stages of writing this book. But we wonder why it is that so many rock critics and listeners are pinning so much hope on this one band. Perhaps we have gone beyond the notion—a ridiculous one, in my view—of "the only band that matters," to something like the idea that "at least this is one band that matters." "Mattering," *in terms of music*, has become awfully difficult in this time when all of the "controversies" around rock music are extra-musical. Radiohead comes along and, bless their hearts, you have to pay attention to the music, because the lives of the band members do not seem that interesting otherwise. Sure, there is an existential vibe to the music that makes journalists look for some overwhelming dread on the biographical front, and one can find this angst in Thom Yorke and some of the others. But journalists cannot really write about angst the way they can write about what outfit Mariah Carey wore to the Grammies, and, even so, there is a legitimate connection to be made between existential moods and the group's music, and so we have to come back to that, the music. Being forced to focus, for once in a great while, on the actual music—having the music assert itself for a change, breaking through the "culture" of hyped-up junk—is something that serious rock listeners, musicians, and critics appreciate. Instead of following up their hit album, *OK Computer*, with "son of OK Computer," Radiohead changed direction, even while maintaining some continuity with the language they had begun to develop. (For one thing, for a band with three guitar players, there is very little that sounds like guitar on the two more recent albums.) So, even though I am not entirely convinced of the more messianic claims—nor has the group made these claims for itself—I say more power to Radiohead, and I hope that they keep making music the way they want to make it.

Where is experimental rock music heading?

In the end, perhaps the main contribution of avant rock to music more generally is simply a more extreme version of what rock is good at at its best in any case, the generous synthesis, or, put with a slightly different twist, "broad transmutation." The avant-rock musicians are the ones who have listened more broadly and more far afield from rock, and perhaps they have given greater and deeper consideration to the *ideas* in the music they are transmuting. However, are they generating many new ideas themselves, or are they mainly doing something "rock" with the ideas that come from elsewhere, especially other avant-gardes?

In fairness, there are general trends in avant-garde music, toward "noise" and "non-musical" sounds, toward fragmentation, toward the fracturing of narrative structure and the resistance of linearity, toward the inclusion of hitherto excluded voices, and others, that legitimately belong to rock music just as much or more than they belong to any other kind of music. Add to this the argument, heard at least since the 1950s, that ever since these and other trends were pushed to extremes—which is another way of saying, ever since John Cage—the idea of the musical avant-garde has either exhausted itself or, at the very least, been very much up for grabs. An article by classical-music critic Alex Ross, on the composer Gyorgy Ligeti, develops the trajectory in which avant rock arose very nicely.

> By the nineteen-seventies, the avant-garde had run its course, and the clearest signal of its obsolescence was the Beatles' "Revolution 9," which replicated the way-out textures of Stockhausen without the benefit of conservatory training. Composers, trumped by pop, began to search for a way back toward classical tonality. Some, like John Adams, plunged into the thick of Romanticism, but Ligeti was more cautious; his method of deconstructing and reassembling tonality on his own terms—"non-atonality," he called it—meant that Boulezian scolds could never accuse him of nostalgia. ("Ligeti Split," *The New Yorker*, May 28, 2001, p. 135)

It is interesting that Ross sees the 1970s as the point where, to give my own spin to it, at least certain parts of the music world were looking to see what could be done that would be both "beyond"—or, at least, *after*—Cage, and other than Cage. Ligeti's term, "non-atonality" is brilliant, though it must now enter into conversation with a musical universe where defining the difference between "tonality" and "atonality" is more or less impossible, as is hearing the difference. (Incidentally, as Ross mentions, Ligeti's great composition, *Atmospheres*, was used during the psychedelic sequences in Stanley Kubrick's *2001*. In 1962, Ligeti created a work called "Poeme Symphonique" for one hundred metronomes: "the piece had the look of a prank—a rotten egg tossed at the classical tradition. In performance, however, it cast a curious spell, one that the composer may not have fully anticipated," p. 134.) By the 1970s, rock music had become open to the whole world of music, and it had become an international musical language, with something of a "tradition" of its own. Arguably, a great deal of rock music since the 1970s, whether experimental or not, continues to come out of the dynamics and conflicts of that period. A good deal of recent experimental rock music seems to be looking for a way beyond the seventies dynamic. If Yes was listening to Beethoven, Sibelius, and Stravinsky (and Wes Montgomery, Chet Atkins, and the Beatles), some of the post-1968 generation seems to be saying it will instead listen to Cage, Stockhausen, Varèse, Ornette Coleman, Cecil Taylor (and the Sex Pistols and Robert Fripp). But now, we might say, *all of that* has been listened to and transmuted, so what's next?

Fifty years of rock—it is difficult to wrap one's head around that idea. In *Listening to the future* I say that it boggles my mind that Chuck Berry is now over seventy years old. There is more to this than simply, "gee, mister, you're really old!" There came a point about fifteen years ago (somewhere in the mid-1980s) where the question was raised as to whether certain aging rock stars should still be out on stage shaking their hips and whatnots. Again, this would seem to have little or nothing to do with avant rock, which is not generally associated with hip-shaking (except in the case of Björk, Iggy Pop—well, now I wonder if the list could actually be quite long). But the point is not only that rock is arguably a young person's game. The deeper question is whether there is something about rock music that is inherently anti-memory, a function of its having always been a thorn in the side of tradition—and even moreso in the case of broadly social traditions than in terms of music more narrowly understood. Surely there is a relationship between this anti-traditionalism and the way that even experimental rock musicians often seem to do no more than reinvent the wheel of other avant-gardes. The alternative would seem to be to embrace the "tradition" of rock—these fifty years—and to make a self-conscious effort to play a role in and extend this tradition. And this requires memory—and memory is not deeply valued in societies that have too many things that they would prefer to not remember. On the contrary, especially in the home of rock and roll, social and cultural amnesia is a big part of what allows this society to function. Rock music can either be a part of this problem—and since the beginning of post-1960s renormalization (which can be identified especially with the time of Reagan and Thatcher, and, for that matter, what might be called Mitterand's anti-1968 "socialism") this is mainly what it has been, mere "entertainment" with little or no critical function, and often the opposite. Or, rock music can serve as one means of the return of the repressed, which means not anti-memory, but, to borrow a term from Michel Foucault, *counter-memory*.

When I proposed the term, "generous synthesis," especially to describe what I saw as the musical dynamic of progressive rock, one of the things I had in mind was the following: in the 1960s, if a person was into the avant-garde, usually he or she would be into either the classical or jazz avant-gardes, and, if the two came together, it was often in the context of rock music. (I had lots of things in mind concerning this term, including the way that questions of class, race, gender, and sexuality play a role in music; see *Listening to the future*, pp. 21–54.) More recently, in experimental-rock circles, and inspired by certain philosophical currents that are often associated with the terms "postmodernism" and "poststructuralism," and perhaps with Gilles Deleuze as the figure most often invoked, we have entered a period of what might be called "transmutations that resist synthesis." Indeed, such a formula might describe the essence of postmodern music, or music that is deemed fit as a reaction to these postmodern times. One might associate this resistance to totality not only with Deleuze, but also with Theodor Adorno's famous statement that "the whole is the false," and with Jacques Derrida's arguments concerning the appearance of the new and unexpected.

I began this section by asking where experimental rock music is heading. It is in the nature of an experiment that no definitive answer to such a question can be given *a priori*, and, as abstract and theoretical as I tend to be in my discussions of music, I all the same think that the proof is in the pudding, and that it is best to listen to what is out there and try to understand it. So, after a few final observations I will turn to some recent albums.

We might consider the idea of "models" for the arts, and even "model arts." For instance, two model forms for the nineteenth century were the novel and the opera. What these two forms have in common is that they represent large-scale narratives in a time of not only History writ large, but also of the Hero, the historical agent. Personally, I have a great fondness for the novel, and, if push came to shove, I would probably say that the novel is my "model artform." But then, I have great fondness for Jean-Paul Sartre. In my book about him, *The Radical Project*, I discuss the fact that Michel Foucault had somewhat sneeringly said of Sartre that the latter was "the last great philosopher of the nineteenth century." Sartre not only lived in the twentieth century (1905–1980), he was sometimes referred to as "the philosopher of the twentieth century." The title of the relevant section in *The Radical Project* was "A philosopher of his time after his time." After all, if Sartre really was an anachronism in the twentieth century, then there would appear to be little to learn from him in the twenty-first. As improbable as it may seem for a book on Sartre, I compared what Foucault said with what Brian Eno had said about progressive rock, that rather than starting something new, it was really the extension (he might have said completion, even) of something old, namely late nineteenth-century Romantic classical music. Like Foucault, Eno argued that the time for such things had passed—not just Sartre or progressive rock, but even History, agency, and related notions.

Now, while it is the case that I read novels from many different genres, I have to admit a special fondness for science fiction, and, on any given day the likelihood is that I am reading a novel from this genre. As the reader undoubtedly knows, science fiction is somewhat suspect from the standpoint of "legitimate" fiction. That is a bizarre and ridiculous (and unsupportable) point of view, but there it is. Actually, I think that rock music and science fiction have this in common, and I will state the point rather bluntly: whoever thinks that creativity is not possible in either—and this is quite often the case with academics—is an ignoramus or a moron or both. There is plenty of actual creativity available in either rock music or science fiction, and that is all the further one needs to go on the "legitimacy" question. Science fiction has had its fans in rock music, Jimi Hendrix being a famous example; perhaps one sees a kind of "science fiction" perspective especially in progressive rock, even if this perspective might be considered quite "old school" by more recent standards. Actually, I like that idea—if some progressive rock is more in the mold of, say, Isaac Asimov, Arthur C. Clarke, or even Robert Heinlein (the reactionary dirty old man who, paradoxically, had an undercurrent of communalism, at least in novels such as *Stranger in a Strange Land*), then some more recent experimental rock, especially that in the techno and electronica genres, might be more associated with Philip K. Dick and William Gibson and other "cyberpunk" writers.

One thing that might be said of Gibson, one of my favorite writers, is that he is trying to tell stories in a time of fragmented narratives. Indeed, that is another reason, in addition to not having any more of a crystal ball to consult than any other informed reader, why the question "where is experimental rock heading" is a difficult one. Where is *anything* heading? The idea of the "heading" in this fragmented, one might say "cul de sac" time, is, to say the least, difficult, undecideable, and slippery. With the transmutations that resist synthesis it sometimes seems there is little more logic to them than simply "filling out the grid," just trying to see what can be set next to what. "Tres gut," "sehr bien," as I sometimes like to say—what Fredric Jameson famously called the "postmodern pastiche." There is a way in which John Cage's procedures are inverted by the more recent combinations. Cage tended to start with an idea, some way that sounds and silences could assert themselves such that human intentionality would not get in the way. Thanks to sampling technology, some of our more recent mixmasters are starting at the other end, and perhaps they do not get to something like an "idea" when they are done. Can we put *this* with *that?*—is the question; and, if *this* does not at first sound so good with *that*, then we have even more incentive to try it. Doing it this way is itself an idea, of course, and the mixmasters know this—and to invert Cage this way is no less "legitimate" (to use that ugly word once again) than to do it the other way. But we might worry that the consequence of such a procedure will be to simply fill out the grid of all possible sounds and silences—which would then also seem to be part of what motivates the orientation toward timbre that many experimental musicians have lately. And yet, what else is music to do? The narrative fragments do not quite form a chorus, much less a story, but perhaps they do say something about all of the voices and possible voices that are struggling to be heard.

Part of what I like about science fiction is the element of "listening to the future" (to coin a phrase!). In progressive rock one often finds this paradoxical (or even contradictory) combination of anti-urban and anti-technological attitudes with science-fiction visions of a future utopia. The term I came up with for this is "sci-fi medievalism." Whatever the merits of this strange combination (which I would associate somewhat with what might be called the "Romantic Marxism" of Raymond Williams and E. P. Thompson, which is also to say that there is something very "English" about it), we might again make a comparison with more recent trends, where attitudes toward technology, the city and the countryside, romanticism, the future, and utopianism are significantly altered.

It may be that the novel could never serve as a "model art" in our time not only because of postmodern fragmentation, but even more simply because ours is not a highly literate period. Film culture, whatever one thinks of it (I tend to take a rather dim view on the whole, though I recognize brilliance in film here and there), has had a tremendous effect on music, going back at least to the Velvet Underground and Andy Warhol, and perhaps taking a major leap with Brian Eno. The idea of the "imaginary soundtrack," often consisting in what Fredric Jameson called "image shards," is a major influence in experimental rock (and even some less experimental rock, as with U2's "Passengers" project, which Eno produced). But, to complete the thought, part of what I like about "listening to the future" is the idea that there might actually be a future that has humanity in it, even given all of the counter-possibilities that work to the contrary. That is, I take many science fiction novels, even some with what I might otherwise think of as a reactionary point of view, as expressions of faith in possible human futures. What I wonder about experimental rock today is whether there still has to be a connection between creative expression and something like this faith, so that even musical works that seem to celebrate fragmentation are reactions to a larger sense of narrative structure.

Even so, there comes a moment when such structures are essentially (or "practically speaking" might be the better way to put it) irretrievable, and another dynamic (or anti-dynamic) is in play, and there is no longer any connection with the "all that" of the nineteenth century, whether we are speaking of History, or even histories, agency, Sartre, or teenage symphonies to God. Has that moment arrived? Would it be a good thing for such a moment to arrive? Experimental rock music, along with the rest of cultural production, takes place around such questions, even if the artists are not always able to thematize them in these abstract terms.

Just to be provocative, I would say that the majority view on these questions, among those writing about avant rock, is what led many to criticize the epic work of techno music by Goldie, *saturnzreturn*. But then, I do not agree with the majority view—and yet I also do not think that one can take a novel such as William Gibson's *Neuromancer* seriously, as I do, and not realize that we are entering a world that will be very different, perhaps qualitatively different, than the world in which we read Sartre and listened to those symphonies. And so music has to be different also, even if in primarily taking a position of resistance to this emerging world.

▲ simple question: what is going on with groups? I have already referred to the saying in rock music, "the group's the thing." Even with groups that have strong leaders, or even what might be called "principal composers," there is a group dynamic that contributes to the uniqueness of rock as a musical form. Many pages ago I mentioned that many people think of Paul McCartney as a great singer and songwriter for the Beatles, without even realizing the Beatles also had a great bass player, and that walrus was also Paul. Another useful example is The Who, where almost all of the music was written by Pete Townshend, but the Who sound requires the distinctive musical voices of Roger Daltrey, John Entwistle, and Keith Moon. Take those stunning bass runs out of "The Real Me" (*Quadrophenia*) and you have a different song. Keith Moon's style of drumming is both unique and divisive—many musicians would put him in their top five (I would), while others wouldn't put him in the top one hundred. And Daltrey is one of the best "straightahead" rock singers. Ironically, simply as a guitar player, Townshend is the least distinctive of the lot. Personality-wise, the sometimes difficult relations among the band members also played a role in the musical output of the group. Another example that is possibly among the strangest is the case of Robert Fripp and King Crimson. Given that King Crimson has had little continuity of personnel over its more than thirty years of existence, including blocks of several years where there was no group at all, and given that the group exists when Robert Fripp convenes it, questions have been raised as to whether King Crimson is a "rock group" at all, at least in some more conventional sense. All the same, when King Crimson music incarnates itself in the form of the group, there is a dynamic that is entirely different from a project involving Robert Fripp and some sidepeople. The point is that even the examples that deviate somewhat from a more fully egalitarian situation, where every band member contributes equally to such things as composition, strength of musical voice, and say-so in the direction of the band, still confirm the basic ideal of rock music as a group production.

There are still plenty of rock groups, of course, both experimental and otherwise, but the group dynamics that were characteristic of bands in the period from about 1960 to 1980 or so seem to be in a state of transition. Taking experimental rock separately (though the same issues arise in rock more generally), there is a tendency either for individuals to work on their own, or for groups to be transitory and not last very long. Orienting the final section of part two of this book toward Björk and Jim O'Rourke is meant to be emblematic of this shift. I see four main reasons for the new and emerging situation, the first three of them simply aspects of the kind of social and personal relations that prevail in our go-go postmodern capitalist society.

Rock groups, at least in the classic period, involve friendship and other forms of personal bonding, in ways that are somewhat akin to being in marriages and families. Perhaps a qualified empirical researcher could examine whether the fate of the rock group dynamic has run parallel to the fate of marriages and families. It is simply harder these days to keep relationships together (whether these are relations of intimacy—and being in a band can be a very intimate experience—friendship, collegiality, or family membership). This will come as no surprise to anyone. The ability to hold a band together is affected by the same winds that whip other relationships around.

There are new logistical problems at the point where members of bands are living in different cities or even different countries or continents. Initially this sort of thing happened with major British bands, such as the Rolling Stones, for the purpose of avoiding taxes. Now it happens for all sorts of reasons, and quite often just because of personal taste in where a person would like to live. But what that says is that, if "the group's the thing," it isn't the main thing.

The newer forms of technology, and especially the digital revolution, have facilitated the scattering of band members, so that people can work together to some extent even if they are separated by hundreds or thousands of miles. We probably have not had enough years to see fully what is gained and what is lost in such arrangements. A parallel that might be useful here is with "distance learning" experiments in education, which some colleges and universities are seeing as a potential cash cow and possibly as a way of phasing out the costs and hassles of dealing with too many flesh-and-blood faculty members who are usually griping about something. Basically, the idea is that the instructor is in front of a digital video camera, and the student is watching a computer screen in the privacy of her or his home. "Discussion" takes the form of a chatroom or perhaps conference call. Rock groups that function similarly simply phone in their parts, so to speak, and then someone has to assemble them. One thing that is common to both examples is that the aim of the technology is to simulate to whatever extent possible the experience of being in the same room, but without the logistical issues involved in making that actually happen. Although I have not taken part in distance education experiments in my university, it is not unusual these days to find students having more and more of a "screen mentality"—a tendency toward the visual, an inability to take notes because anything important can be looked up on the World Wide Web later, a tendency to think of everything in terms of quantities of information, a tendency to tune in and out of class just as one would with one's computer screen at home. The technology that allows musicians to assemble works without being physically together may not have these sorts of problems to the same extent, but there is still a kind of disembodied sensibility involved in not being able to hash things out face to face. I could imagine that this technology will develop to a much greater extent, perhaps ultimately using holograms and multiple cameras and whatnot to simulate much better the experience of playing together. Even so, and without being overly judgmental about it, this technology is changing the way rock musicians work in qualitative and radical ways. One of those ways is that it is a very small step from not working with your band mates in a physical situation to just dispensing with the band altogether, and simulating what used to be the different roles of different musicians using technology. Some very good albums have been made this way, for sure, but the tendency now is for more and more musicians to go this way—because, after all, then one does not have to deal with logistics and personalities—and then the group becomes less and less "the thing."

Lastly, and again some sociology and demography would be useful here, but there seems to be a marked increase lately in the tendency to make a fetish of photogenic singers. The "group" is just a bunch of guys in the background, it doesn't particularly matter who they are or what kind of musical voices they have developed. Björk is a difficult case here, because, although she is plenty photogenic (much more than she is homogenic!), to the extent that her music features her voice (and often it doesn't), the music is not simply the servant of nice physical features or catchy melodies. Furthermore, as much as I like the Sugarcubes, Björk's post-group music is more interesting, and she brings together some very interesting musicians to play it. Björk, however, is the exception that proves the rule. Although the fetish for photogenic singers may not have much of an effect on experimental rock, certainly it is playing a role in decreasing the space and orientation toward groups. If experimental rock is not pulled in this direction by the general trend, this will still be further indication that we are now in a time when experimental rock and the rest of rock (and "pop" music) find themselves in two different worlds.

For my part, I will be happy if experimental rock does not go in the direction of almost exclusive focus on the singer, because I think that orientation toward the group is one of the great things about rock music.

Two of the dichotomies that have been set out in this book have to do with the questions of technique and composition versus improvisation. These dichotomies are somewhat operative in rock music generally, but they become especially acute in avant rock, or, we might say, what is simply happenstance in the rest of rock music becomes the source of controversy and principle in avant rock. It is one thing to not have so much in the way of technique; it is another thing to actively avoid or refuse technique, as a matter of principle. There are two ways, or perhaps stages, where this sort of thing becomes interesting and potentially innovative. The refusal of what might be called "conventional technique" (one attempts to become a very skilled guitarist on the order of, say, John McLaughlin or Steve Howe—I mention these two because they are very skilled with chords and time, and are not anywhere remotely near the legions of "lead guitar" wankers out there) might be interesting in some sort of "initial stage," such as we see with the Velvet Underground, where the refusal leads to the discovery of new sounds. I would associate this form of refusal especially with untapped possibilities of the electric guitar (and amplifiers). Sonic Youth would be among those who took this sort of thing further, and in a direction that was still interesting.

However, there comes a point where this form of the refusal of technique becomes no longer interesting, and where it cannot be musically justified on the basis that John Cage opened some door to it (Cage's motto was "make it new," and after awhile there is not much new in just letting an electric guitar play itself) or that Cecil Taylor is just "randomly bashing away" on his instrument (he isn't). So then it is time for a second stage of refusal, and this is where the refusal of conventional technique becomes a new language or nonconventional technique. To take a major example from jazz, it isn't the case that Pharaoh Sanders lacks technique. What is the case is that he has taken numerous "effects" of playing the tenor saxophone, especially overblowing and biting on the reed, and made his own language out of them. Surely, if this were the refusal of technique pure and simple, then any Tom, Dick, or Mary could pick up the tenor and do what Mr. Sanders does—and, of course, they cannot. When it comes to the way that such an approach has been taken within rock music, however, it is sometimes harder to discriminate between the merely lazy and the truly interesting. But this is where, again, I would hold up Sonic Youth as the exemplars—they have forged their own kind of technique that is largely outside of conventional playing.

To be good at creating and, shall we say, *spelling out* compositions is also a matter of technique, and I do worry that much avant rock is avoiding this technique in the name of improvisation or perhaps spontaneity. Unfortunately, the refusal of composition interacts a little too easily with a refusal to improve one's instrumental (or vocal) skills. What do I mean by "composition"? The reason I used the words "spelling out" is that I certainly do *not* mean that composition is only the ability to write out musical scores in the conventional way. Really all I mean is some form of communication whereby band members can decide to play (or not play) certain notes, beats, sounds, or silences at a certain time, a certain loudness, a certain force or lack of force, and so on. There seems to be a decline in either the ability to do that with any level of complexity, or in the desire to be able to play this way, or both. This kind of refusal of technique is not a healthy thing, it seems to me. I am thinking of the sorts of musicians or listeners from the sixties generation and younger, but especially younger, who are "not impressed" with groups that could play a work of the complexity of, say, "Close to the Edge" (Yes) or, just to rub it in, "Tarkus" (Emerson, Lake and Palmer). The goal of attaining virtuoso or near-virtuoso instrumental skills (which I define as mastery of the instrument to the point where complexity is not an issue) can be a double-edged sword, as everyone knows by now. And, it is a good thing that rock is a genre where everyone feels invited to participate, at whatever skill level. However: (1) we ought to be very suspicious of a false populism that has room for the refusal of technique (which is not the same thing as valuing simplicity over complexity), but not for the perfection of technique; (2) we ought to be very suspicious of the use of rock music's participatory ideal as cover for simply not practicing. In the United States, there has been a decline in school music programs and other venues for young people to learn to play an instrument. Technology plays a role, too, at the point where a young person comes along having never played any other instrument than a sampler or beat box. It isn't that there is anything wrong with this in some absolute sense, and perhaps musical instrument instruction will simply go the way of instruction in typewriter repair (the last schools for this craft closed in the 1990s). As with all paradigm shifts in culture, something will be gained and something will be lost. Some sort of dialectical evenhandedness would require that the commentator accept that what is lost is made up by what is gained. For my part, however, I cannot accept this—although I am fully willing to admit that this could mean that my present age renders me resistant to some of the changes that will undoubtedly come. Be that as it may, there is a danger of one-sidedness in the new music at the point where refusal of technique informs attempts at "improvisation."

Sermons about how we all need to keep working on our chops aside, however, the creative musician avoids being trapped by dichotomies, whether of technique or its refusal, or of composition and improvisation (which can never be strictly separated in any case), or what-have-you. If vocabularies have been exhausted, then some forms of instrumental virtuosity can become mere anachronisms, perhaps not unlike whatever particular skills associated with using a manual electric typewriter that are not transferable to using a personal computer. While it is not a pleasant thought, for me at any rate, that the violin or saxophone or bass guitar or drum set might at least retroactively be understood as simply forms of technology that can be surpassed and thereby rendered obsolete, this has happened before. But perhaps this time is not yet upon us, and, at the very least, it seems to me that there are new forms of electro-acoustic music still to be discovered in rock. One irony of some of the new music that is made entirely in the cybernetic domain is that, even while a significant part of it is meant as "body" music, it is far away from being tactile in its creation. Rather than shutting down creativity, then, the new elements that have emerged from electronica may very well be at the start of showing their possibilities. It is early days yet, and one hopes that there will be many years and stages of new interfaces to come.

Some final thoughts on music and chess . . .

> The enigmatic model of the *line* is thus the very thing that philosophy could not see when it had its eyes open on the interior of its own history. This night begins to lighten a little at the moment when linearity—which is not loss or absence but the repression of pluri-dimensional symbolic thought—relaxes its oppression because it begins to sterilize the technical and scientific economy that it has long favored. In fact for a long time its possibility has been structurally bound up with that of economy, of technics, and of ideology. This solidarity [solidity?] appears in the process of thesaurization, capitalization, sedentarization, hierarchization, of the formation of ideology by the class that writes or rather commands the scribes. Not that the massive reappearance of nonlinear writing interrupts this structural solidarity [again, "solidity" might be a better translation, although the French is indeed *solidarité*]; quite the contrary. But it transforms its nature profoundly.
>
> —Jacques Derrida, *of Grammatology*

> The wisdom of the plants: even when they have roots, there is always an outside where they form a rhizome with something else—with the wind, an animal, human beings (and there is also an aspect under which animals themselves form rhizomes, as do people, etc.). "Drunkenness as a triumphant eruption of the plant in us." Always follow the rhizome by rupture; lengthen, prolong, and relay the line of flight; make it vary, until you have produced the most abstract and tortuous of lines of *n* dimensions and broken directions. Conjugate deterritorialized flows. Follow the plants . . .

> Music has always sent out lines of flight, like so many "transformational multiplicities," even overturning the very codes that structure or arborify it [make it tree-like]; that is why musical form, right down to its ruptures and proliferations, is comparable to a weed, a rhizome.

> [U]nlike trees or their roots, the rhizome . . . brings into play very different regimes of signs, and even nonsign states. . . . Unlike a structure, which is defined by a set of points and positions, with binary relations between the points and biunivocal relationships between the positions, the rhizome is made only of lines: lines of segmentarity and stratification as its dimensions, and the line of flight or deterritorialization as the maximum dimension after which the multiplicity undergoes metamorphosis. . . . The rhizome is anti-genealogy. It is a short-term memory, an anti-memory. The rhizome operates by vari-

ation, expansion, conquest, capture, offshoots, ... What is at question in the rhizome is a relation to sexuality ..., the animal, the vegetal, the world, politics, the book, things natural and artificial . . . that is totally different from the arborescent relation: all manner of becomings.

Let us take a limited example and compare the war machine and the State apparatus in the context of the theory of games. Let us take chess and Go, from the standpoint of the game pieces, the relations between the pieces and the space involved. Chess is a game of State, or of the court: the emperor of China played it. Chess pieces are coded; they have an internal nature and intrinsic properties from which their movements, situations, and confrontations derive. They have qualities: a knight remains a knight, a pawn a pawn, a bishop a bishop. Each is like a subject of the statement endowed with a relative power, and these relative powers combine in a subject of enunciation, that is, the chess player or the game's form of interiority. Go pieces, in contrast, are pellets, disks, simple arithmetic units, and have only an anonymous, collective, or third-person function: "It" makes a move. "It" could be a man, a woman, a louse, an elephant. Go pieces are elements of a nonsubjectified machine assemblage with no intrinsic properties, only situational ones. Thus the relations are very different in the two cases. Within their milieu of interiority, chess pieces entertain biunivocal relations with one another, and with the adversary's pieces: their functioning is structural. On the other hand, a Go piece has only a milieu of exteriority, or extrinsic relations with nebulas or constellations, according to which it fulfills functions of insertion or situation, such as bordering, encircling, shattering. All by itself, a Go piece can destroy an entire constellation synchronically; a chess piece cannot (or can do so diachronically only). Chess is indeed a war, but an institutionalized, regulated, coded war, with a front, a rear, battles. But what is proper to Go is war without battle lines, with neither confrontation nor retreat, without battles even: pure strategy, whereas chess is a semiology. Finally, the space is not at all the same: in chess, it is a question of arranging a closed space for oneself, thus of going from one point to another, of occupying the maximum number of squares with the minimum number of pieces. In Go, it is a question of arraying oneself in an open space, of holding space, of maintaining the possibility of springing up at any point: the movement is not from one point to another, but becomes perpetual, without aim or destination, without departure or arrival. The "smooth" space of Go, as against the "striated" space of chess. The *nomos* of Go against the State of chess, *nomos* against *polis*. The difference is that chess codes and decodes space, whereas Go proceeds altogether differently, territorializing or deterritorializing it (make the outside a territory of space; consolidate that territory by the construction of a second, adjacent territory; deterritorialize the enemy by shattering his territory from within; deterritorialize oneself by renouncing, by going elsewhere . . .). Another justice, another movement, another space-time.

—Gilles Deleuze and Felix Guattari, *A Thousand Plateaus*

Well, we aren't going to unpack *all* of this. I'm not sure what it means to say that chess was played by "the Chinese emperor"—which one? Chess originated in India around 500 to 600 CE, taking a more modern form in Persia only a few decades later. Chess seems to have been spread around Asia by Buddhist monks, and perhaps even originated as a means for teaching religious and philosophical ideas. There was a "Golden Age of Islamic Chess" in the eighth to tenth centuries CE, and by about 1000 chess was widely known throughout Europe. There are a few who argue that chess actually originated in China; at the least the game was taken into China by Buddhist monks early in its history. (Some argue that chess is even much older than fourteen or fifteen hundred years. But neither this nor the Chinese origins hypothesis has been substantiated.) There are also Asian forms of chess, such as *Xiangqi* ("Chinese chess") and *Shogi* ("Japanese chess"), and it is most likely the former that was played by the aforementioned "Chinese emperor."

It is not quite true that all chess pieces remain "what they are," at least not since about 1475 CE. At that time "took place the most significant of all changes during the recorded history of the game," namely the convention whereby a pawn that makes it to the furthest rank can be exchanged for any other piece, and most often for a queen. (See *The Oxford Companion to Chess*, 2nd ed., p. 173.) Indeed, it was also at this time that the queen was instituted as a piece—previously the king was accompanied by a "first minister" (known variously as the Firzan, Firz, or Fers in the Persian world). Thus, in carnivalesque fashion—and, notably, this change occurred in Europe, not in India or Persia—the putative "least" of the chessmen can change both class and gender, and thereby become the most powerful piece on the board.

Go is considerably older than chess. Indeed, in one of the most famous Western manuals for the game, *The Theory & Practice of Go*, Oscar Korschelt writes (originally in German) that "Go is the oldest of known games." Korschelt cites sources that place the origin of Go at last as far back as 1000 bce, and possibly another thousand years before that. I would like to quote Korschelt's comparison of chess and Go at a little length, because—strange as it may seem—it sheds light on some issues in contemporary experimental music. Korschelt wrote his book in order to attract Europeans to Go; so, while it is interesting on all kinds of levels to compare chess and Go, Korschelt was also interested in showing players of the former the appeal of the latter.

> Our chess circles would recognize that the ingenuity and depth of skill in Go are fully a match for chess, and it would soon be cherished as highly as chess.
>
> Chess and Go are both antagonistic or warlike games, that is, they are both governed primarily by skill in tactics and strategy. But the form of conflict typical of chess is like the warfare of olden times in which the king was the center of the struggle and the battle was lost with his downfall. In this sort of knightly struggle victory or defeat was decided more through the exceptional virtue of a single noble or group of nobles than through the mass action of the commoners as parts of an overall strategy.

Rather than being the image of a single struggle as in chess, Go is much more like
the panorama of an entire campaign or complex theater of war. And so it is more like
modern warfare where strategic mass movements are the ultimate determinants of vic-
tory. . . . As in modern warfare, direct combat, without supporting tactics, rarely occurs.
In fact, to engage too soon in direct combat frequently spells defeat. . . .

Whether chess or Go offers more entertainment is a difficult question. Unlike chess
the combinations in Go are afflicted with some monotony because there are no pieces
with different styles of movement and because once placed in the field the stones are
fixed. But that defect is compensated for by the greater ration of combinations and by the
greater number of places on the board where the battle may rage. In general, two average players of fairly even skill will find more enjoyment in Go than in chess. In chess it is
fairly certain that the first of two evenly matched players to lose a piece will suffer defeat
unless he can exchange it for one of like value. Without such an exchange after a loss the
rest of the game is mostly an ineffective struggle against predictable defeat. (pp. 6–7)

Korschelt wrote *The Theory and Practice of Go* in the latter part of the nineteenth century, and this is a salient point. Much as Albert Einstein's teachers were recommending
that he pursue some field other than physics, because all of the basic problems had
already been solved (the rest was just mop-up, not needing a mind the caliber of
Einstein's), it was widely argued at the end of the nineteenth century that chess was
exhausted—it had run out of steam. It turned out, of course, that *steam* had run out of
steam, and what came in its place was special and general relativity and, in the case of
chess, the hypermodern movement.

Complex positional play came to the fore with the hypermoderns, such that what
Korschelt says about losing material in an exchange does not strictly apply. Ordinary
mortals playing through the games of Garry Kasparov or Viswanathan Anand or Judit
Polgar will certainly see no end of strategic complexity. But what does this say about linearity or what Deleuze and Guattari call "striated space," the sorts of things that many
contemporary avant-garde musicians, sometimes citing the aforementioned, are
attempting to escape?

Hypermodern chess, which was initially formulated by Aron Nimzovich and
Richard Reti, has much in common with "postmodern" trends in philosophy, architecture, and other forms of cultural and intellectual production, especially the displacement of the center. Nimzovich and Reti formulated their ideas in a Central- and
Eastern-European milieu that was exceedingly rich in intellectual and cultural ferment:
it was the time of Wittgenstein, Freud, the Vienna Circle, Schoenberg, Einstein, Kurt
Godel, the Prague Linguistic Circle, the "Blue Rider" painters, and so on. Displacement
from the center was the order of the day. I wonder if "chess," as conceived by Deleuze
and Guattari in their analysis, has more in common with Korschelt's late-nineteenth-
century conception than it does with the extraordinary complexity of chess since the

time of the hypermoderns. In other words, in what they say there are assumptions about what has been "played out," exhausted, or about what is in the end part of an authoritarian social structure that ought to be resisted—chess as the carrier of "state philosophy." This terminology is part of a recently emerged trend that calls itself "postmodern anarchism" or "poststructuralist anarchism," and which takes inspiration from Guy Debord and the situationists, and philosophers such as Michel Foucault, Deleuze and Guattari, and Jean-Francois Lyotard. (Notably, Jacques Derrida is cited less often, and Jean-Paul Sartre is often used as a whipping boy. See Todd May, *The Political Theory of Poststructuralist Anarchism*, and Lewis Call, *Postmodern Anarchism*.) Being a mediocre but enthusiastic chess player myself, and not knowing how to play Go (people ask me if I am going to take it up, but I tell them that I am too busy losing at chess at the moment), still, I think that chess still has some creativity to demonstrate—*its* historic moment has not yet passed. But then, I am one of those who still believes that the transition to a communist society must still pass through a period in which the working class and oppressed people constitute their rule in the form of a state (though not only this, of course).

Well, that is a larger question for social theory, and undoubtedly the thesis that chess still has something to give is not dependent on the idea that the dictatorship of the bourgeoisie has to be overthrown and supplanted by the rule of the proletariat (or is it?!). The reader may find it interesting, by the way, that Marx and Lenin were both avid chess players, and reportedly quite good ("for amateurs," as they say), while Mao would play Go at the drop of a hat, and recommended it to the soldiers in the Peoples Liberation Army as a school for strategy. This is far afield from music, but we need to learn from all three of these game strategists if we are going to change society. But then, I am sufficiently Hegelian to believe that there is some sense in which chess, Go, music, and social formations are all imbedded in a human history that is in some sense "common."

However, what comes a little closer to musical questions is the way that the chess/Go comparison resembles what I set up in the first part of this book as the Schoenberg/ Stravinsky comparison, which had less to do with their music per se than with the dynamic of "next step in the logic"/"some other logic." What has changed in the time since Schoenberg and Stravinsky were composing is that, while the search for other logics on the part of the latter, as well as Bartok, Gershwin, and others, was still fundamentally a gesture toward the "outside" of Europe from (to use Derrida's expression) "a certain inside," now it is undeniable that the Third World has begun to "stand up" (as Mao said of the Chinese people in 1949).

One might also, however, set the dichotomy not in terms of "another logic," but instead we might consider the idea of "escaping logic," or at least escaping certain entrenched logics, or trying to stay outside of them. Three little bits of information might prove useful here. First, while there are now computer programs that can beat grand-masters at chess, there are no such programs in the case of Go. We can safely assume that this has nothing to do with lack of computing skill in Asia. Instead, the existence of high-powered chess programs means that, at least up to a point, there are algorithms for playing the game. In other words, the mathematical complexity of chess, at least (if not the psychological and other forms of complexity), can be captured in formulas. Of course, every chess player beyond the most basic level applies some sort of formulas in playing—build strength in the center, protect your king, develop your pieces, advance your pawns, develop knights before bishops, don't trade pieces when you are behind in material, and so forth. There are exceptions for each of these rules, in actual chess practice, but the exceptions can be formalized to a point as well. Whatever the limita-tions of computer chess, the fact that it has been developed to a fairly high degree, while there is no such development in the case of Go, seems to speak to Deleuze and Guattari's claim that chess is characterized by "striated" thinking—it is much more "arborial" than "rhizomatic." The musical lesson would seem to be that, to escape lin-earity, one should look to a model such as Go rather than chess. Or, quite apart from whether one cares about these games and the kind of comparison I am taking up here, the point is that musicians might rightly wonder if a certain "Western" linearity is exhausted.

Second, if chess is a game of the "state-form," an interesting inquiry might be made into how both chess and Western musical forms have fared in parts of the world where the state is a relatively recent phenomenon. In a paper presented at a conference on Africana philosophy (at DePaul University, February 2001), Bruce Janz applied the Deleuze/Gauttari arguments about chess and Go to the question of state formation in Africa. Of course, the "state," in the modern, Western sense, has been imposed upon African territories by colonialist and imperialist powers, and it has been an almost unmitigated disaster. One might infer that chess would also not "work" well in Sub-Saharan Africa, and in fact this seems to be the case. When I raised this question with Professor Janz, he answered that there is a game that is played widely throughout Sub-Saharan Africa, called by various names, the simplest of which is "Mbao," and this game is much more like Go than chess. By the same token, it seems that the forms of "Western" music that fare the best in Africa are those that have at least partial African origins to begin with, namely jazz and rock.

I would like to add to this an anecdote that might shed further light on what was just said. Some years ago, when I was in graduate school, I shared an office with an African woman from Sierra Leone. Her training as an undergraduate in her home coun-try was in analytic philosophy, and she had come to the United States to do graduate work in this field, and in the philosophies of David Hume and Bertrand Russell. If you know anything about these figures and analytic philosophy in general, you know that the tendency is toward a kind of philosophical austerity. (I have done some work in this field and I find this tendency both a blessing and a curse.) One predominant trend within analytic philosophy is to apply Occam's Razor, as it were, to any subject (or object) that is not capable of formulation in logical terms or verifiable in public, empirical terms. My African officemate was an enthusiast of this trend. But one day, as we were chatting amiably in the office, she asked me if I believed in spirits, demons, ghosts, and the like. I said that I probably did not, at least in the way that she meant (now I'm not so sure), and I asked her if she did believe in such things. She said that, heaven help her, despite her whole philosophical training and orientation, there was an "African" side to her that could not help but believe in such things. Unfortunately, these two sides of her life were tearing her apart, and about a month later she had a nervous breakdown. This seems to me to be an exemplary case of "capitalism and schizophrenia" (to take the larger title of Deleuze's and Guattari's project, of which *A Thousand Plateaus* is the second part) of a sort that is not often discussed by postmodern anarchists.

Perhaps a political lesson could be drawn here that also applies to music. In the contemporary world, we have to look at the "next step"/"other logic" dichotomy in global terms, and this includes having an awareness of the way the world is constituted by a new, but violent "unity" ("one world, ready or not"), and by deep divisions. I think that I would say to Deleuze and Guattari that chess still has something to give, despite its limitations. I wonder if, in the appreciation they show for the music of Pierre Boulez in *A Thousand Plateaus*, they are not agreeing with this claim to some extent.

Third, it would be interesting to compare artifacts of what might be called "chess culture" to those of "Go culture." Here I must admit to both ignorance and frustration. There is a culture surrounding chess that yields something like a "chess aesthetic," in the form of novels, films, painting, and perhaps most of all, music. The valuable website maintained by New York composer John Greschak, "Connections between Music and Chess," traces "chess music" in classical music, jazz, and rock. Among the composers included are John Cage, John Lewis (pianist in the Modern Jazz Quartet, whose *The Chess Game* is based on Bach's *Goldberg Variations*), and Jon Anderson (from Yes), as well as others who are not named Jo(h)n. (To find Greschak's site, just put "chess and music" in your search engine.) My ignorance and frustration has to do with not knowing if there is a similar "Go aesthetic." My experiences thus far are limited to the novel *The Master of Go* by Nobel-Prize winner Yasunari Kawabata, and the anime film, *Ranma* $^1/_2$. Thus far my search for "Go music" has been fruitless, other than recalling that the group that the great Japanese percussionist, Stomu Yamash'ta, formed with the great Santana drummer, Michael Shrieve, back in the late 1970s was called "Go." I do not know why there would not be a culture of Go comparable to that of chess, so I am assuming that I simply have not found it yet. Perhaps the culture of Go is more oblique, less apparent; perhaps one would find such a culture in the composition of Toru Takemitsu, for example. But my larger point is that comparison of the artifacts of each culture might tell us something about what is supposedly a univalent or at most dialectical "Western" or "modern" approach to thinking and music, as opposed to a culture and thought of difference. And my even larger point is that I tend to think that, as experimental music begins to take the rhizome rather than the tree as its model, it will have to grow in that direction on the basis of the tree, the tree will have to evolve in that way. Otherwise, the tendency is to fall into mere exoticism and Orientalism.

On the other hand, there is a dimension of the "after Cage, what?" question that is mere Eurocentrism. This is the case even if—indeed, *especially*—the question is raised in purely "analytical" terms, because then the assumption is that the limits of Western reason are the limits of all possible reason. But when we go "beyond the West" (or "beyond rock"—and the lovely thing about rock is that it always wants to go beyond, it doesn't have any hang-ups about going beyond itself), to look for new sounds, we have to be aware that all vibrant musics are always looking for new sounds and new ideas. The Western propensity has been to approach the musics of diverse non-Western cultures as though they are static artifacts. The irony is that this gesture also reinstates linearity. The challenge is to transcend linearity from within linearity itself, not to simply jump from Western reason to some supposedly timeless non-Western cycle. To put it provocatively—as well as in a way that, I hope, leaves it clear that the "next step" must be an experiment, and therefore not susceptible to calculation alone—the challenge is to play "guerilla chess."

Sonic Youth, *nyc ghosts & flowers* (Geffen CD, 2000).
Yoko Ono, *A Blueprint for the Sunrise* (Japan Society/Harry N. Abrams CD, 2000).
R. L. Burnside, *Wish I Was In Heaven Sitting Down* (Fat Possum Records CD, 2000).
Tortoise, *Standards* (Thrill Jockey CD, 2001).
Stereolab, *The First of the Microbe Hunters* (Elektra CD, 2000).
Radiohead, *Kid A* (EMI CD, 2000).
——, *Amnesiac* (EMI CD, 2001).
King Crimson, *the construKction of light* (Virgin CD, 2000).
——, *Heavy ConstruKction* (Discipline CD, 2000).
White Out, with Jim O'Rourke, *drunken little mass* (ecstatic peace CD, 2000).
Björk, *Selmasongs* (Elektra CD, 2000).
——, *Vespertine* (Elektra CD, 2001).
William Hooker, *The Distance Between Us* (Knitting Factory CD, 1998).
William Hooker, Christian Marclay, Lee Renaldo, *Bouquet* (Knitting Factory CD, 2000).
Sonic Youth and guests, *Goodbye 20th Century* (SYR CD, November 16, 1999).

Once more into the breach. Looking at this list of albums, we might ask of the twenty-first century, Are we there yet? The rub is that, all of those who thought that Jean-

Paul Sartre was stuck in the nineteenth century will find that it is not so easy to get out of the twentieth, either. The avant-garde sensibility is not only one of "going forward," but also of momentous changes that come in the blink of an eye. Teleology *and* eschatology, line *and* unexpected—even monstrous—new things that appear seemingly without antecedents. Or perhaps I simply chose certain albums to consider at the end of this story—what's the *plot?* A predominant feeling in these albums, in any case, is a certain wistfulness, even if intermixed with a cyberpunk edge. On *Kid A,* Radiohead follows "Optimistic" with "In Limbo." Haunting line from the former: "I'd really like to help you man, I'd really like to help you man." If the world is at an impasse, then we explore that impasse—as Walt Whitman put it, "Society waits unformed and is for a while between things ended and things begun." Or W. H. Auden: "Nothing can save us that is possible." What looks like mere cynicism is sometimes instead a peculiar and vertigo-inducing version of the now barely-breathing wish for redemption and exhaustion from the mindless complexities of life.

My own wistful feelings are evidenced by the fact that there are no techno albums here at the end, and most of the music is played on instruments long associated with rock music. There are plenty of post-rock instruments here, however, with Jim O'Rourke on laptop computer, Radiohead's Jonny Greenwood on Ondes Martenot and Thom Yorke's voice running through vocoder, autotuner, and whatnot, Christian Marclay's turntable artistry, and Robert Fripp's and Adrian Belew's six-stringers rarely sounding like guitars. Indeed, for anyone who listened to King Crimson circa *Lizard or Larks' Tongues,* it is hard to imagine them as a "guitar band" in 2000, with the same instrumentation as the Kinks. *The construKction of light* doesn't sound anything like *Something Else* (ahem). But there they are: two guitars, bass, drums. Sonic Youth, too; Radiohead: three guitars, at least in principle.

There are a million labels now, many of them coming out of electronica. We have hip-hop, trip-hop, and I think trip-bop went across the radar screen somewhere along the way; soon enough we could have hip-trop, a beat-heavy and sampledelic version of Brazilian Tropicalia. Oh wait, Tom Ze and Arto Lindsay are already there. It is the time of the mixmaster (or mixmatrix), to be sure. Two other labels that might prove useful are "chamber rock" and "deconstruction." Both are familiar. Although some of the artists discussed here perform in larger venues (mainly Radiohead), most are found in more intimate settings. The basic idea is that even those artists who are capable of filling larger halls approach the gig with a non- or even anti-"arena rock" attitude. This is very hard in these days when rock fans have gotten very comfortable with the idea that a concert is a time for partying and incessant talking (on a cell phone, even), as if the music is background and sometimes annoyance. The sort of folks who would go to hear Stereolab or Björk or King Crimson are generally a bit better than this, but still. (The last time I saw King Crimson, which was late October 2000, as of this writing, there was a fellow sitting in front of me who would shout "Bruford!" after every piece. This was a version of the group that did not contain Bill Bruford—perhaps the reason for the shouting, but who knows?) As the worlds of mainstream and experimental rock get further apart, however, perhaps the chamber-rock sensibility will sink in further with the listeners as well. I think this would be a good thing, even if avant rock does not quite need to be played in conditions of concert-hall bourgeois respectability, because then the idea that an experimental-rock concert is a laboratory for sonic exploration is foregrounded. In addition, the connection between the performers and the audience is actually strengthened, because the common element is *listening*, not showing off.

R. L. Burnside might be called a "traditional" blues musician, but now he has fallen in with the hip-hop crowd. Avant rock is music that breaks with blues orthodoxy, so the question arises as to where that leaves the blues, proper. There are many great blues musicians playing today, of course, from Koko Taylor to Jimmy D. Lane, but can the blues be innovative even while staying within its own bounds? That's a hard one; it seems as if, as with country music, the parameters are fairly narrow, or else we aren't really talking about the blues (or country music) anymore. The alternative is to mix the blues with something else, as, say, the Jimi Hendrix Experience or Cream did with psychedelia. On Burnside's *Wish I Was* In *Heaven Sitting Down*, as well as his earlier *Come On In* (Fat Possum CD, 1998), the "blues parts" are plenty raw, and the "hip-hop" parts are, in a sense, mere scaffolding. The music is not so much a true synthesis or even hybrid, as a demonstration of what happens when you put two different forms side by side. It works. And yet the most powerful track is pure blues, plus a little bit of scratching, the album closer, "R. L.'s Story." Burnside's narrative of family members who have been murdered in small-town Mississippi, Memphis, and Chicago is sad beyond words.

Some might challenge the presence of Radiohead in a discussion such as this. Indeed, the excellent cover article on the group by Simon Reynolds (the title, "Walking on Thin Ice" has a nice Yoko Ono connection) in *The Wire* (July 2001) opens with three paragraphs of worrying about how some will say that, "a group with this kind of commercial heft and such a degree of mainstream consensus of praise behind them simply has no place on the front cover of a magazine known for championing mavericks and margin dwellers" (p. 26). Reynolds praises *Kid A* for playing a major role in "rejuvenating the moribund concept of 'post-rock'" (p. 26). The fact that the June issue of *Mojo* also featured a cover story on the group doesn't mean that *The Wire* is going commercial, but instead that Radiohead is doing something that people who care about the quality and future of rock music can appreciate. I wonder if the term might be "deconstruction." It's not only that the group zigs when you expect them to zag, or that they deal in fragmented narratives as well as anyone, but they have a very clever way of taking rock expectations and turning them inside out. Indeed, these last two points interconnect, because the whole synergy—the music, the singing, the lyrics—makes you think, "there's a story there, I wish that I could get to it." Someone is hurt—what happened to them? You know that you will never know, and yet you cannot turn away from wanting to be let in on the secret.

The specter of deconstruction is introduced here, too, because it seems to me that we have not really heard enough "Derrida music" to go with all of the "Deleuze music" that has been created in recent years.

There is some other hurt in these albums. Sonic Youth's *A Thousand Leaves* (1998) was already part psychedelic dirge in memory of Allen Ginsberg (especially the long track, "Hits of Sunshine"), and I wonder if the passing of the great bard still hovers over *ncy ghosts & flowers*—or perhaps the subject has broadened to mortality in general. The title piece is especially eerie, the lyrics and sense of dramatic build-up much more careful than what one usually finds with this group. The noise freak-out can be great, and no one does it better than Sonic Youth, but (the album's title song) "nyc ghosts & flowers" shows what attention to composition can reveal. Elsewhere on the album, Kim Gordon once again shows what it means to make a certain nonchalance into an artform, with "nevermind (what was it anyway)." Leaving the question mark off from the parenthetical question just reinforces the point. "Boys go to jupiter to get more stupider/girls go to mars, become rock stars"—not the greatest line, but funny. Of course, many boys do well enough at getting stupider right here on planet Earth. Sonic Youth is assisted by Jim O'Rourke on three tracks, and he also co-produced the album. As always, I wish for more bass in the music, not only to fill out the sonic spectrum— it's all very trebly, as usual—but also to get some contrapuntal action going with drummer Steve Shelley.

Much more sad is Björk's music for the film, *Dancer in the Dark*. Titled *Selmasongs*, after the main character in the film, there are moments of levity and even silliness, for sure, but even these contribute to a very dark sensibility in the context of the film as a whole. People seem quite divided on *Dancer in the Dark*, and on Björk's performance as Selma. My only ambivalence concerns the very fact of Björk appearing as an actress, because I would hate to see her taken away from music by the seductions of the film world. Reportedly she has said that this is the only film she will ever do. I wish her every success in this resolve, the problem being that she was pretty much amazing in the role. The film is not easy to watch; to me it was almost unremittingly tragic. Björk is not cute here, and rarely even coy. She is an awkward woman in a terrible situation, or a series of such situations, and her perseverance and optimism only make things worse. The ending is painful and heartbreaking. The whole film, and especially the ending, is an indictment of American "justice." The closing recapitulation of the opening "Overture," with its weighty, low brass, affected me physically.

So, Björk continues to do new things. "I've Seen It All," from the soundtrack, features Thom Yorke. (Apparently Björk and Yorke were supposed to perform a vocal duet at the 2001 Grammy Awards, but Yorke pulled out, and Björk was left singing with a tape, from whence derives some of the recent parodies of her as weird and crazy.) I had hoped to have a new, complete (*Selmasongs* is only thirty-two minutes long) Björk album to discuss here, and such an album was supposed to be released in June 2001, but it was delayed. And now, at the last moment—August 28, 2001—here it is, finally! *Vespertine* is Björk's first "album" since 1997's *Homogenic*. Expectations, accordingly, are running high—therefore, it would perhaps not be fair to make more than a few preliminary comments here. The instrumental elements of the album are somewhat similar to those found on *Homomgenic*, strings and electronic beats. The addition here is the use of choir and harp, the latter played by avant-garde composer and instrumentalist Zeena Parkins. Björk also uses musical boxes on several of the songs. As before, Björk has co-composers and co-arrangers on some of the songs, but she did most of the work herself. In that respect, I appreciated this statement from the *Urb* magazine cover story that accompanied the release of *Vespertine*: "While everyone thinks they know what she's about, few see Björk's true nature as a devoted music nerd and electro-acoustic composer who spends countless hours talking about snare sounds and editing noises on her laptop" (Tamara Palmer, "A different sort of bird," *Urb*, Sept. 2001, p. 125). Don't hate her because she's beautiful—instead, disrespect her because she's intelligent: that's what the photogenic crowd has figured out recently, and their instincts are true.

The term "electro-acoustic" comes up again in Palmer's article, and it is an interesting way to think about Björk's more recent music. Here is her own description of what she is doing, from an interview with Palmer:

> I'm really interested in blending together electronic music with our everyday life to prove that's actually how we're living . . . . I guess my attempt is to take just the life we're leading every day and make magic out of that. Just to be honest, those are the sounds [of life]; it's what we hear all the time . . . I like extremes, I guess: very raw acoustic things and then very pure electronic beats. To me, electricity comes from nature. Like acupuncture—something several thousand years old triggers the electricity that's inside us within our nervous system. (p. 125)

Even though there are a few new sounds and textures on this album, and even though in general approach it follows in the footsteps of *Homogenic*, it is actually a more austere group of songs, and very private. Even though they have their splashy and loud moments, all of Björk's albums are *quieter* than people tend to think—or perhaps it is hard to hear how quiet they are. *Vespertine* is the quietist of them all, and, with the possible exception of the first song on the album, "Hidden Place," there is a great deal of flow but very few "hooks." After the success of *Dancer in the Dark*, Björk might have been expected to go for even bigger pop success. Instead she is continuing to develop her conception. There is no guitar here, and the "standout" instruments are all of the "subdued" sort, primarily harp and celeste. One of the songs—"Sun in my Mouth"— quotes from poet e.e. cummings, and the final song features a sample from the electronica group Oval. To say that something is "vespertine," means that it comes forth at night, like the introspective evening prayers of cloistered nuns. Björk as a nun is a hard image to wrap one's mind around—the *cyborg* seems more appropriate—but there is an element to her persona, no matter how much she flamboyantly puts herself out in the world, that is fundamentally inward. Hence her evensong. But all of this is upon the first couple of listenings, and it will be interesting to see how the experience of this album fills out. Regardless of where *Vespertine* will eventually sit on the scale from good to very good to excellent, however, what is most gratifying is that Björk's commitment to creativity in music seems unshakable.

A *Blueprint for the Sunrise* is even shorter than *Selmasongs*, at about twenty-four minutes. It is also a "soundtrack," though this time for the *YES Yoko Ono* book that is the companion to the retrospective exhibit of the same name. I saw the exhibit in Minneapolis, and was thrilled that the "White Chess Set" was set up in a public area where people could play on it. We didn't get very far! Unfortunately, the *Blueprint* CD does not come with any information about who is playing on it. The music does not break new ground, really, but it does place Ono's vocal instrument in some new settings, including a grunge meets techno scenario that is provocative.

Wistfulness returns with Tortoise and especially Stereolab. The former has kind of "creeped out" its sound a bit, with metallic and alien noises intruding and drifting through the more friendly, vibraphone-led parts. I must say that I despise the album cover—indeed, it is a demon to be cast out. I'm not referring to the outer cover, necessarily, though here is another example of what looks like a studied, annoying nonchalance. Instead what I am referring to is the back page of the booklet, which is purportedly presenting the information on who plays what on the album. Please send contributions toward purchase of a good microscope! Am I the only one who is peeved by this sort of thing, album information presented in a way that can only be meant to frustrate the listener, to say nothing of wrecking his or her eyesight? There is an aspiration toward anonymity on the part of Tortoise, and indeed of many of those in the Chicago avant scene, and aspects of that are laudable, I suppose. Maybe the credits on the *Standards* cover are meant to reinforce that. The anonymous feel extends to the music, as well, but here I appreciate more the collectivity the group achieves. Is it so wrong of me to want to know, in the midst of this, who played that synthesizer riff? Perhaps. In any case, one of Tortoise's prime virtues is their ability to preserve space, and to avoid fighting greedily over who is going to fill it up. Percussionist John McEntire even describes this virtue in terms of passivity, but also in terms of democracy (Jim DeRogatis, "Tortoise's John McEntire: Post-Rock's Sonic Genius," *Modern Drummer*, July 2001, p. 90). I would say instead that there is a good deal of *active* democracy at work in Tortoise's music, a conscious collectivity that seeks and values the contribution of the other.

Significantly, in the interview cited above, the group that McEntire mentions in connection with Tortoise is Stereolab. (In addition to his superb, understated skills as a percussionist, McEntire is a talented sound engineer; he did some of the work on *Microbe Hunters* as well as *Sound-Dust*.) Both groups specialize in repetitive, groovy grooves, rendered sweet by instruments such as vibraphone or Farfisa combo organ, with minute changes over extended periods. This is not Philip Glass minimalism, or even *Discipline*-era King Crimson incrementalism, but it is not unrelated, either. It's the Serge Gainsbourg element, that avant-lounge thing. The previous album, *Cobra and phases*, had electric-Miles leanings; the new one is scaled back by comparison, and might be considered simply a further elaboration of the Stereolab sound. That being said, *Microbe Hunters* is a fine example of the Lab language. Of course, what they have over anything remotely similar is Laetitia Sadier's voice, which is also where the wistful element comes in. It would be easy to hear a merely nostalgic quality to not only the voice but also the combo organ, but I think the nostalgia is for what might have been after May 1968. One of my favorite things about Stereolab, therefore, is that they are very much a part of the "it's a different world now" form of post-sixties rock, and yet they still have that connection.

Always an episodic affair, King Crimson seems more so than ever. In the middle 1990s the group reconvened, with the *Discipline* formation of Robert Fripp, Adrian Belew, Tony Levin, and Bill Bruford, augmented by touch-guitar player Trey Gunn, and drummer/percussionist Pat Mastelotto. That was a lot of drums and wires (to recall the XTC album title), and the attempted "double-trio" never really jelled, at least in terms of compositions that made use of the possible contrasts. (Concerts were another story, especially in the case of improvisations, as 1996's *THRaKaTTak* demonstrated effectively.) On the other side of the expanded Crimson, Bruford and Levin went off to pursue other projects (including their joint effort, BLUE—Bruford Levin Upper Extremities, as well as Bruford's Earthworks; Levin also toured as the bass player for Seal). Apparently, four is the inevitable number for King Crimson: the Beatles have always been among the hovering spirits with Crimson music. Indeed, the Beatles spirit seems to be asserting itself even more in recent KC history. In the six-member group, the percussionists' division of labor was supposedly along the lines of Bill Bruford as Buddy Rich and Pat Mastelotto as Ringo Starr—sort of "lead" and "rhythm" drums. Trey Gunn has had to step into the bass role in the *ConstruKction* group, and, like Paul

McCartney (who took up the bass to replace Stu Sutcliffe and because John and George weren't having any of it), he has emerged as a contrapuntal and timbral innovator. (More on what the "bass role" means in Gunn's case in a moment.) Meanwhile, something of a "John and Paul" dynamic has developed between Robert Fripp and Adrian Belew. (Is there a shortage of a George Harrison in the group?) Maestro Fripp brings the edge, while Belew adds not only humor and melodicism (though many mistakenly assume that all of the "edgy" guitar solos are Fripp's, and this is far from the case), but also the occasional silly love song. As with Macca, this latter tendency does sometimes go too far.

However, having seen two performances by the most recent King Crimson in the fall of 2000, it is my view that the *ConstruKction* formation is the best version of the group since the *Larks' Tongues/Starless/Red* period from 1973 to 1974. Furthermore, this group promises to sustain itself and develop over a longer period than most of the other formations. Then again, the King could have withdrawn into another hibernation by the time this book sees the light of day. I hope not. I hope that the present KC keeps going for at least several more years this time. With the *Discipline*-era band, half of King Crimson's population was American. *Thrak* took the proportion to two-thirds, and now the *ConstruKction* band is at three-quarters—a long, strange trip for a fellow from Bournemouth (Robert Fripp), the remaining English member. I suppose there might be something to be said about the "American leanings" of the recent constitution of the group; there is the connection, through Adrian Belew, to Frank Zappa, someone else on the edge of progressive rock and who would not have accepted the label as regards his own music. Certainly Bill Bruford always looked to America in terms of the jazz that has influenced him so much. But most of all these sorts of logistics are typical in our increasingly globalized world (three of the four core members of Yes live in the United States now, for instance—though I probably wasn't supposed to mention them in this connection!). Still, it is strange to think of King Crimson convening, as it has for the past several tour preparations, for practices in Nashville, Tennessee.

Speaking of Music City, however, some avant-rock aficionados may be shaking their heads at a discussion of King Crimson at the end of this book. The fact that this group has been convened off and on since 1968, always to push the envelope of rock music, ought to count for something. King Crimson has maintained (with perhaps only a couple of minor lapses that appear all the more insignificant in the larger context) the highest standards of *musicianship* throughout these decades—and musicianship is not something that is always appreciated in the rock avant-garde. To return to the earlier categories and discussions, King Crimson has dealt with the question of technique through its transcendence—when you have sufficient technique, then it no longer appears as a musical question—and, though the music often leans toward improvisation, there is no shortage on the side of composition. In other words, Crimson has consisted in musicians who can have interesting musical conversations.

Sometime in 2000, Robert Fripp made the observation in his online diary (at the Discipline Global Mobile website) that the latest incarnation of the group is the first one that he would call "King Crimson as rock band." This after working through various other labels—progressive, art, fusion, heavy metal (actually, no one else called King Crimson this, to my knowledge, but Fripp said something along these lines in the *Larks' Tongues* era), and new wave. Well, there was never anything wrong with playing rock— you can be as creative there as anywhere, that's what groups such as King Crimson show. Still, now we do have King Crimson with two guitars, bass, and drums: no more mellotrons, reeds, violins, piano, double-bass, and so on, and the guitars are always electric ones. Now, it is true that the guitars are running through digital effects that allow them to sound like almost anything, and the fact is that they rarely sound like guitars. My one complaint here is that, except for a clever piano sample that Belew sometimes employs (at the *Thrak* concert I attended I assumed that Bruford was somehow doing it), there are not only no longer any sounds that have either the bite or the delicacy of acoustic instruments, there is also not that great acoustic/electric contrast that King Crimson (and other progressive rock groups such as Yes, Genesis, and Jethro Tull) used so effectively in the days of yore. (Edward Macan contributed a very interesting discussion of the acoustic/electric contrast, in terms of gender, in his book on English progressive rock, *Rocking the Classics*.) I think there is more that can be done with this contrast, and it would be nice to see the present KC configuration work with this. For now, they are pursuing a synthesis of sometimes unremitting heaviness, the interwoven fabric of great complexity á la the *Discipline* era, and then the occasional *song*, if you can imagine that.

Pat Mastelotto has come forward as what I would call the "Alan White" of King Crimson, and I mean that as the highest compliment. People who know me and my work on Yes know that I hold White in the highest regard. Like Alan White, Mastelotto has no shortage of technique, he comes from a more mainstream rock background, he is following Bill Bruford, and he has risen to the challenge and demonstrated that he has his own creative contribution to make. Pat Mastelotto was previously the drummer for The Rembrandts, famous mainly for providing the theme song for the TV series, *Friends*. (In the video for the song, Courtney Cox pushes Mastelotto out of the way and takes his place on the drum stool; I suppose that she had the first shot at the Crimson position, but she would have had to have taken a large pay cut.) His drumming is a bit heavier than Bruford's, as befitting the current direction of the group. Without compromising technique in any way, there is an element of Ringo Starr in what he is doing—and that is also the highest praise in my book.

Trey Gunn came along as a player of the Chapman Stick, a ten-stringed "touch" instrument that had also been played by Tony Levin in the previous two incarnations of the band. As I understand it, Gunn had also been a student in Robert Fripp's Guitar Craft school, so he may have been something of a protégé. But no more (not that there is anything wrong with being Robert Fripp's protégé, many of us would give our right arms for that); Gunn's solo albums show that he has his own musical conceptions, and what he is doing on bass has to be seen to be appreciated. The reason I say that is, in the present KC incarnation, Gunn is playing an instrument that was built specially for him, called the Warr Touch Bass. As with the Chapman Stick, both hands are involved in pressing down on notes, and only rarely is the right hand (in the case of a right-hander, such as Gunn) used for plucking or picking. Gunn's instrument, like the Stick, has ten strings. I don't know that the sound of this instrument comes across adequately on the studio recording (or perhaps it is the inadequacy of my stereo); in concert the sound is unreal, and, though obviously this is the bass player in me responding, it is very instructive to see how Gunn actually plays the thing. He is not only very good at playing countermelodies with the rest of the group, his two-handed technique allows him to play at least two independent lines on his own instrument. At the expense of being a little reductive, it is something like having some very deep and heavy pipe-organ pedals as a foundation, with Jaco Pastorius gliding and surging at will on top.

As for the studio album, some of the songs work better than others. For what I think is the first time, King Crimson has included a blues song on one of its albums. It is a thoroughly warped and very Captain Beefheartish blues, devoted to the notion of solving all of life's worries with Prozac, but still. "Prozac Blues" opens the album. It's a funny song, but it doesn't wear that well. (Oh well, a nod to Don and Frank.) I also found the closer, "Coda: I Have a Dream," to be weak, at least lyrically. (The album also contains an improvisation that follows the last song, attributed to "ProjeKct X.") In between these two bookends (which are not bad, just not sterling), *the construKction of light* is a very strong album. The title track represents a further development of the language of interweaving lines that was initiated with *Discipline*. "FraKctured" and "Larks' Tongues in Aspic-Part IV" hark back to the *Larks' Tongues* period, but bring that music forward through the subsequent Crimson music. "Part IV" is the most successful "Larks' Tongues" since the first one. "The World's My Oyster Soup Kitchen Floor Wax Museum" is a more interesting attempt at Zappaesque whimsy. Which leaves "Into the Frying Pan," the most Beatles-like piece on the album and, in my view, the most successful. The swerving, pitch-modulated vocals, and the insistent, "I Am the Walrus"-like instrumental track, are vertigo-inducing. Indeed, when I played the song for my wife, she insisted that I take it off as she thought it was going to make her physically ill. Of course, I complied but I had to tip my hat to the achievement.

When King Crimson is great, they are often even "more great" in the live context. *Heavy ConstruKction* is a valuable document in this brief. As a live singer, Adrian Belew has become much stronger in recent years. Highlights of the three-CD live set include the beautiful and melancholy "One Time," Belew's amazing acoustic solo performance of "Three of a Perfect Pair," and numerous improvisations featuring the trio of Fripp, Gunn, and Mastelotto.

Long live the Crimson King. I can only hope that there will be more King Crimson music to be played in this new century, and that there will be a King Crimson to play it.

William Hooker is quietly becoming a major force in the New York avant scene, especially in the company of either the Sonic Youth guitarists Lee Ranaldo and Thurston Moore, or musicians associated with John Zorn. *The Distance Between Us* is a little bit of a departure, strangely, in that it is a more straightforward jazz record, which all the same includes plenty of free playing, as well as two different arrangements of a Sonic Youth piece. Here Hooker leads a big group, including two saxophones, trumpet, and piano, as well as four different guitar players. Hooker represents the next phase in the progression of drumming in the school of Billy Cobham—jazz chops with a rock sensibility. More often Hooker is recorded in the duo or trio format, the latter being the case on *Bouquet*. The combination of Hooker with Lee Renaldo on guitar and Christian Marclay on turntables is the most effective of these small-group albums, I think. Personally, I am always interested in seeing new possibilities found for the trio format—perhaps it is the Buckminster Fuller or Hegel influence in me that takes three as the most perfect number (Pythagoras thought it was four), but the trio has the appeal that it is the most minimal form of the "group." The *Bouquet* band brings the noise, for sure, but they are most effective when they quiet down a bit. Hooker will remain an important force.

You know that there is an avant-rock *scene*, with its own scensters, when a new group appears with the words, "with Jim O'Rourke" added to its name. White Out also includes Lin Culbertson on synthesizer, flute, autoharp, and voice, and Tom Surgal on percussion. About half of *drunken little mass* (there are a lot of Catholics in Chicago!) was recorded live at two different clubs. My main interest in the album was to hear Jim O'Rourke jamming in a group context on what has become his main instrument in recent years, the laptop computer—Powerbook powertrio! O'Rourke also plays that outmoded box, the guitar, on the album. To be honest, I was expecting a good deal of "click-clack" music, but instead there is a nice sense of flow, especially thanks to Surgal's jazz chops. He is also good with the gongs. Sometimes I am not sure what is coming from the synthesizer and what from the laptop, but I do think O'Rourke and the group are taking electronic music into a new domain of improvisation. In some sense O'Rourke's use of the laptop is the latest realization of Brian Eno's notion of mixing board as musical instrument, except that the library of available sounds is increased practically to infinity, as is the ability to modulate waveforms. As with a good deal of cyberculture, especially of the *Wired*-magazine variety, there is both a forward-looking, *Neuromancer*-ish quality to the music, and a 1950s, space-age "zowie!" feel. Meanwhile, the album and song titles are more akin to fifties beat culture. As wide-open as the possibilities are with synthesizer and laptop, it is the presence of the drums and here and there the acoustic guitar that ultimately make the album interesting—not the mere presence, as if these acoustic sounds are some sort of relief, but instead the contrast. This is good avant-chamber rock, and the album shows that there are still many contributions to be made by electro-acoustic music.

But we aren't done with Jim O'Rourke yet, as he was one of the co-producers and musicians participating in an album that seems almost tailor-made for ending this discussion, *Goodbye 20th Century*, by Sonic Youth and numerous guests. A two-LP/CD affair, the album features works by major avant-garde composers from the twentieth-century, European avant-garde tradition, including John Cage, Christian Wolff, Yoko Ono, Pauline Oliveros, Steve Reich, and Cornelius Cardew.) One wishes for an additional "goodbye" album that would reprise Sidney Bechet, Louis Armstrong, Charlie Parker, Thelonius Monk—you get the idea.) For this effort, Sonic Youth is joined by Jim O'Rourke, William Winant, Takehisa Kosugi (who also contributes a composition), Christian Wolff, Coco Hayley Gordon Moore (daughter of Kim Gordon and Thurston Moore), Christian Marclay, and Wharton Tiers. As seems to be the order of the day around rock music these days, avant or otherwise, there is not any information provided regarding who is playing what particular instruments on any given piece. (Experience shows that it is not a good idea to make assumptions here, either. On SYR 3, one might have assumed that Jim O'Rourke was playing guitar or bass, when, in fact, he played drums on much of the album, and Steve Shelley played trumpet.) What we do learn here is that not all of the ensemble plays on every piece. Indeed, Yoko Ono's "Voice Piece for Soprano," only twelve seconds long, is performed by Coco Hayley Gordon Moore alone.

All four Sonic Youths, plus Winant and O'Rourke, performed on the three John Cage pieces presented here: two different versions of 1991's "Six," as well as a thirty-minute long rendition of "Four6," from 1992 (the year Cage passed away, just shy of his eightieth birthday). Julian Cowley's review of the album opens by paying tribute to the composer's philosophy of possibility:

> Arguably, the most important aspect of John Cage's legacy was not his body of work but the gift of permission he passed down to subsequent generations. Testing his anti-authoritarian stance to the point of paradox Cage assumed cultural authority that permitted musicians who followed him to expand their working definition of music, and enabled non-musicians to reconceive themselves as musicians. Composition as proscription has

in his wake been challenged by a sense of music as a basis for community, as an antidote to cynicism, a programme for exploration, or as therapy for mind and body. There have, of course, been challenges from elsewhere, but these have often promoted a particular musical style. Cage and his diverse sympathisers have tended to withhold definition, preferring to open up space which has enables others to act.

Sonic Youth's farewell to the century effectively says thank you to some of the enablers. (*The Wire*, New Year 2000, p. 78)

Yes to all of this, but who would have figured that the most fitting tribute to the enablers would come from a rock group? And yet, on the other hand, and despite everything (by which I mainly mean the culture of pap and pabulum), what could be more appropriate? Rock at its best is a music of open-ended possibility. Its avant-garde edge is simply where rock's ears are most open.

Although it is very hard to choose, probably my favorite pieces on the album are "Six for New Time" by Pauline Oliveros and "Burdocks" by Christian Wolff. The former was actually written for Sonic Youth by the composer, who is best known these days as the leader of the Deep Listening Band. Like Yoko Ono, Oliveros has had to find ways to function in male-dominated scenes; in 1961 she was the co-founder, along with Terry Riley, Morton Subotnik, and Ramon Sender, of the San Francisco Tape Music Center. Like Riley, Oliveros is sometimes associated with the beats, and her instrument in the Deep Listening Band, accordion plus the Expanded Instrument System, is exemplary of her Ginsberg-like preoccupation with breath. "Six for New Time" is also spacious and breathy, though here also with the eighth-note chiming guitars that is a Sonic Youth trademark. Part of the interest in the performance of "Burdocks" is not only the participation of the composer, as well as the whole rest of the assembled cast (excepting Coco), but also the fact that Wolff's concert premier of the piece almost thirty years before (1971) featured David Behrman, David Tudor, Frederic Rzewski, and Gordon Mumma. Sonic Youth and company give a quite different reading, of course, which is what makes life interesting.

On June 16, 2001, Sonic Youth performed pieces from *Goodbye 20th Century* at a one-off concert at London's Royal Festival Hall. They were joined by not only William Winant and Jim O'Rourke, but also John Zorn and Anthony Braxton. Glenn Branca and his trio opened. Sometimes things just come together.

And yet there is an unavoidable fragility to this music of our time, a music and a time when contingency asserts itself as never before—hence the feeling that not only the spirit of Cage is being reprised, but so is existentialism in its numerous dimensions. What's next? We don't know, and music now is becoming more about asking rather than presuming to have a definitive answer. Spread out, look, listen.

In the spirit of Cage's and Tudor's *Indeterminacy,* one last story from David Revill's biography of John Cage:

> Cage was also thinking of an opera, the instrumentation of which would include the pre-pared piano, based on the story of Mila Repa, a "Tibetan saint" who took the form of a thistle and floated over the landscape. He planned to employ the prepared piano, but the book which included the story had been borrowed from the library. By the time it was returned the idea of operatic narrative no longer interested Cage. (p. 103–4)

Surely this particular moment from Cage's larger aesthetic of freedom is a bit too close to the aesthetic of flippancy that is all too common in our postmodern times. Therefore, let us close instead with a different comment from Cage, as well as one from Brian Eno, cited in a lovely essay by David Toop on the idea of "generative music" (*The Wire,* May 2001, pp. 39–45). Cage, in his conversations with Joan Retallack (in the book *Musicage*), refers to the moment in his development "where the process of composing was changed from making choices to asking questions." Eno refers to a new approach to music that "is like trying to create a seed, as opposed to classical composition, which is like trying to engineer a tree." Rock music still has the capacity to ask more questions; it will have a future as long as it further develops this capacity.

Bibliography and further reading

General reference works

Buckley, Jonathan, and Mark Ellingham, eds. *Rock: The Rough Guide*. London: Rough Guides, 1996.

Carr, Ian, Digby Fairweather, and Brian Priestley, eds. *Jazz: The Rough Guide*. London: Rough Guides, 1995.

Buckley, Jonathan. *Classical Music on CD: The Rough Guide*. London: Rough Guides, 1994.

Yoko Ono/Beatles

Doggett, Peter. *Abbey Road/Let It Be: The Beatles*. New York: Schirmer Books, 1998.

Haskell, Barbara, and John G. Hanhardt. *Yoko Ono: Arias and Objects*. Salt Lake City: Peregrine Smith Books, 1991.

Kemp, Mark. "She Who Laughs Last: Yoko Ono Reconsidered." *Option*, no. 45 (July/August 1992).

Kozinn, Allan. *The Beatles*. London: Phaidon Press, 1995.

Munroe, Alexandra, with Jon Hendricks. *Y E S Yoko Ono*. New York: Japan Society/Abrams, 2000.

Ono, Yoko. *Grapefruit: A book of instructions and drawings*. Tokyo: Wunternaum Press, 1964.

John Cage

Cage, John, in conversation with Joan Retallack. *Musicage: John Cage Muses on Words, Art, Music*. Hanover, N.H.: Wesleyan University Press, 1996.

Greenaway, Peter, director. *John Cage* (from *4merican Composers*). New York: Transatlantic Films, 1985.

Hamilton, Andy. "Age of Chance." *The Wire*, no. 183 (May 1999).

Kostelanetz, Richard. *Conversing with Cage*. New York: Limelight Editions, 1988.

———. *John Cage (ex)plain(ed)*. New York: Schirmer Books, 1996.

Perloff, Marjorie, and Charles Junkerman, eds. *John Cage: Composed in America*. Chicago: University of Chicago Press, 1994.

Pritchett, James. *The Music of John Cage*. Cambridge: Cambridge University Press, 1993.

Revill, David. *The Roaring Silence: John Cage: A Life*. New York: Arcade Publishing, 1992.

251

Glenn Gould

Gould, Glenn and friends. *Variations*. Ed. John McGreevy. New York: Quill, 1983.

Gould, Glenn. *Selected Letters*. Ed. John P. L. Roberts and Ghyslaine Guertin. Toronto: Oxford University Press, 1992.

Ostwald, Peter F. *Glenn Gould: The Ecstasy and Tragedy of Genius*. New York: Norton, 1997.

Page, Tim, ed. *The Glenn Gould Reader*. New York: Vintage, 1990.

Payzant, Geoffrey. *Glenn Gould: Music and Mind*. Rev. ed. Toronto: Key Porter Books, 1984.

Tovell, Vincent, and Eric Till, directors. *Glenn Gould: A Portrait*. Toronto: Canadian Broadcasting Corporation, 1985.

John Coltrane, Cecil Taylor, and Miles Davis

Case, Brian, and Stan Britt. *The Illustrated Encyclopedia of Jazz*. New York: Harmony Books, 1978.

Corbett, John. *Extended Play: Sounding Off from John Cage to Dr. Funkenstein*. Durham, N.C.: Duke University Press, 1994.

Carr, Ian. *Miles Davis*. New York: Quill, 1984.

Jost, Ekkehard. *Free Jazz*. New York: Da Capo Press, 1975.

Litweiler, John. *The Freedom Principle: Jazz After 1958*. New York: Da Capo Press, 1984.

Nisenson, Eric. *Ascension: John Coltrane and His Quest*. New York: St. Martin's Press, 1993.

Rosenthal, David B. *Hard Bop: Jazz and black music, 1955–1965*. New York: Oxford University Press, 1992.

Spellman, A. B. *Black Music: four lives*. New York: Schocken Books, 1970.

Thomas, J. C. *Chasin' the Trane: The Music and Mystique of John Coltrane*. New York Da Capo Press, 1975.

Tingen, Paul. *Miles Beyond: The Electric Explorations of Miles Davis, 1967–1991*. New York: Billboard Books, 2001.

Wilmer, Valerie. *As serious as your life: John Coltrane and beyond*. London: Serpent's Tail, 1992.

Velvet Underground

Bockris, Victor, and Gerald Malanga. *Up-Tight: The Story of the Velvet Underground*. London: Omnibus Press, 1996.

Penman, Ian. "European son: John Cale." *The Wire*, no. 125 (July 1994).

Jimi Hendrix

DeRogatis, Jim. *Kaleidoscope Eyes: Psychedelic Rock from the '60s to the '90s*. Secaucus, N.J.: Citadel Press, 1996.

Progressive rock

Covach, John, and Graeme M. Boone. *Understanding Rock: Essays in Musical Analysis*. Oxford: Oxford University Press, 1997.

Cutler, Chris. *File Under Popular: Theoretical and Critical Writings on Music*. Brooklyn, N.Y.: Autonomedia, 1993.

Gimblett, John. "Larks' Tongues and Slapstick." *Stride*, no. 35 (1993).

Loydell, Rupert. "The Great Deception: King Crimson box sets, Art-rock, and popular music." *Stride*, no. 35 (1993).

———. "An Interview with Chris Cutler." *Stride*, no. 35 (1993).

Macan, Edward. *Rocking the Classics: English Progressive Rock and the Counterculture*. Oxford: Oxford University Press, 1997.

Martin, Bill. *Music of Yes: Structure and vision in progressive rock*. Chicago: Open Court Publishing, 1996.

———. *Listening to the future: The time of progressive rock, 1968–1978*. Chicago: Open Court Publishing, 1997.

Smith, Bradley. *The Billboard Guide to Progressive Music*. New York: Billboard Books, 1997.

Stump, Paul. *The Music's All That Matters*. London: Quartet Books, 1997.

Can

Bussy, Pascal, and Andy Hall. *The Can Book*. Harrow, Middlesex: SAF Publishing, 1989.

Gill, Andy. "We Can Be Heroes: Kraftwerk, Can, and the Return of the Krautrockers." *Mojo*, no. 41 (April 1997).

Jope, Norman. "So Far So Soon: An appreciation of German Progressive Music, 1969–1975." *Stride*, no. 35 (1993).

Young, Rob. "Inner space is the place: Can." *The Wire*, no. 158 (April 1997).

Steely Dan

Sweet, Brian. *Steely Dan: Reelin' in the Years*. London: Omnibus Press, 1994.

Punk

Azerrad, Michael. *Come As You Are: The Story of Nirvana*. New York: Doubleday, 1993.

Frith, Simon, and Howard Home. *Art Into Pop*. London: Methuen, 1987.

Gracyk, Theodore. *Rhythm and Noise: An Aesthetics of Rock*. Durham, N.C.: Duke University Press, 1996.

Heylin, Clinton. *From the Velvets to the Voidoids: A Pre-Punk History for a Post-Punk World*. New York: Penguin Books, 1993.

Lydon, John, with Keith and Kent Zimmerman. *Rotten: No Irish—No Blacks—No dogs*. New York: St. Martin's Press, 1994.

Marcus, Greil. *Lipstick Traces: A Secret History of the 20ᵗʰ Century*. Cambridge, Mass.: Harvard University Press, 1989.

———. *Ranters and Crowd Pleasers: Punk in Pop Music, 1977–92*. New York: Anchor Books, 1993.

Savage, Jon. *England's Dreaming: Anarchy, Sex Pistols, Punk Rock, and Beyond*. New York: St. Martin's Press, 1992.

George Clinton and P-Funk

Corbett, John. *Extended Play: Sounding Off from John Cage to Dr. Funkenstein*. Durham, N.S.: Duke University Press, 1994.

Brian Eno

Bracewell, Michael. "Eno's no bounds." *The Guardian Friday Review*, May 8, 1998.

Doerschuk, Robert L. "Brian Eno: On Simplicity, Context, and the Necessity of Urgency." *Keyboard* 15, no. 6 (June 1989).

Eno, Brian. Talk presented at the "Original Vision" symposium in Irvine, California, November 1987. *Stride*, no. 34 (1992).

———. *A Year with Swollen Appendices*. London: Faber and Faber, 1996.

Kelly, Kevin. "Gossip is Philosophy: Brian Eno." *Wired* 3, no. 5 (May 1995).

Rorty, Richard. *Contingency, irony, and solidarity*. Cambridge: Cambridge University Press, 1989.

Sinker, Mark. "Taking modern culture by strategy: Brian Eno." *The Wire*, no. 104 (October 1992).

Stump, Paul. *Unknown Pleasures: A Cultural Biography of Roxy Music*. London: Quartet Books, 1998.

Tamm, Eric. *Brian Eno: His Music and the Vertical Color of Sound*. London: Faber and Faber, 1989.

Toop, David. *Ocean of Sound: Aether Talk, Ambient Sound, and Imaginary Worlds*. London: Serpent's Tail, 1995.

Glenn Branca

Newquist, H. P., et. al. "The Outsiders: King Crimson, Frank Zappa, and the Noise School." *Guitar* 13, no. 5 (March 1996).

Sonic Youth

Appleford, Steve. "Come on, feel the noise: Sonic Youth gets back to basics." *Option*, no. 79 (March/April 1998).

Foege, Alec. *Confusion Is Next: The Sonic Youth Story*. New York: St. Martin's Press, 1994.

Kopf, Biba. "Notes from underground: Sonic Youth." *The Wire*, no. 171 (May 1998).

Valania, Jonathan. "Sound of Confusion: Sonic Youth." *Magnet*, no. 34 (May/June 1998).

Bill Laswell

Toop, David. "Telematic nomad: Bill Laswell." *The Wire*, no. 130 (December 1994).

Mills, Fred. "The Road Less Traveled: Bill Laswell." *Magnet*, no. 35 (July/August 1998).

Stereolab

Ali, Lorraine. "Mistakes were made: Stereolab's accidental pop." *Option*, no. 77 November/ December 1997).

Shapiro, Peter. "Laboratory secrets: Stereolab." *The Wire*, no. 149 (July 1996).

Valania, Jonathan. "The Now Sound: Stereolab." *Magnet*, no. 31 (November/December 1997).

Turntables, samplers, and the new electronic music

Barr, Tim. *Techno: The Rough Guide*. London: Rough Guides, 2000.

Bussy, Pascal. *Kraftwerk: Man, Machine, and Music.* Wembley, Middlesex: SAF Publishing, 1993.

Kopf, Biba. "White Line Fever." *The Wire*, no. 184 (June 1999).

Osbaum, Stacy, ed. *Urb* special issue on "The Future." Issue no.70 (December 1999).

Reighley, Kurt B. *Looking for the Perfect Beat: The Art and Culture of the DJ.* New York: Pocket Books, 2000.

Reynolds, Simon. *Generation Ecstasy: Into the world of techno and rave culture.* New York: Routledge, 1999.

Shapiro, Peter. "Turntablism." *The Wire*, no. 179 (January 1999).

——. *Drum 'n' bass: The Rough Guide.* London: Rough Guides, 1999.

Sharp, Chris. "Nature boy: DJ Vadim." *The Wire*, no. 158 (April 1997).

——. "Lone swordsman: Photek." *The Wire*, no. 159 (May 1997).

Sicko, Dan. *Techno Rebels: The Renegades of Electronic Funk.* New York: Billboard Books, 1999.

Tate, Greg. *Flyboy in the Buttermilk: Essays on Contemporary America.* New York: Simon and Schuster, 1992.

Toop, David. *The Rap Attack: African Jive to New York Hip-Hop.* Boston: South End Press, 1984.

Young, Rob. "Tools you can trust: To Rococo Rot." *The Wire*, no. 164 (October 1997).

King Crimson

Barnes, Mike. "Mobile intelligent unit: Robert Fripp." *The Wire*, no. 159 (May 1997).

Bungey, John. "King Crimson." *Mojo*, no. 73 (December 1999).

Fripp, Robert. "The Road to Graceland." *Stride*, no. 36 (1994).

——. *Discipline Global Mobile Newsletter One.* Salisbury: DGM, January 1997.

Tamm, Eric. *Robert Fripp: From King Crimson to Guitar Craft.* London: Faber and Faber, 1990.

Land of the rising noise

Keenan, David. "Signal to noise: Merzbow." *The Wire*, no. 159 (May 1997).

Lee, A. C. "Cyborg manifesto: Ikue Mori." *The Wire*, no. 172 (June 1998).

Roman, Annette, ed. *Japan Edge: The Insider's Guide to Japanese Pop Subculture.* San Francisco: Cadence Books, 1999.

Björk

Gray, Louise. "The idea of north: Björk." *The Wire*, no. 177 (November 1998).

Jim O'Rourke

Cox, Christoph. "Studies in frustration: Jim O'Rourke." *The Wire*, no. 165 (November 1997).

Young, Rob. "Invisible Jukebox: Jim O'Rourke." *The Wire*, no. 179 (January 1999).

Other artists discussed in Part 2

Barnes, Michael. "Guitars and monsters: Gary Lucas." *The Wire*, no. 172 (June 1998).

Cost, Jud. "Music from the Outer Limits: the Olivia Tremor Control." *Magnet*, no. 39 (April/May 1999).

Henderson, Richard. "Coming up for air: Pauline Oliveros." *The Wire*, no. 164 (October 1997).

Holtje, Steve. "Odd man out: James Blood Ulmer." *The Wire*, no. 171 (May 1998).

Keenan, David. "I was a teenage Jesus: Lydia Lunch." *The Wire*, no. 173 (July 1998).

Meyer, Bill. "Drawing of Sound: Red Krayola." *Magnet*, no. 27 (February/March 1997).

Mills, Fred. "The Unusual Suspects: Tortoise." *Magnet*, no. 33 (March/April 1998).

Penman, Ian. "Matters of Life and Death: Diamanda Galas." *The Wire*, no. 190/191 (January 2000).

Watson, Ben. "Lightning rod: Butch Morris." *The Wire*, no. 165 (November 1997).

Young, Rob. "Tangled up in blue: Portishead." *The Wire*, no. 178 (December 1998).

Synthesis and new vocabularies/Rock out (theoretical works)

Bertland, Michael T. *Race, Rock, and Elvis*. Urbana: University of Illinois Press, 2000.

Call, Lewis. *Postmodern Anarchism*. Albany, N.Y.: SUNY Press, 2002.

Constanten, Tom. *Between Rock and Hard Places: A Musical Autobiodyssey*. Eugene, O r e . : Hulogosi, 1992.

Davidson, Donald. "Thought and Talk." In Davidson, *Inquiries into Truth and Interpretation*. Oxford: Oxford University Press, 1985.

———. "On the Very Idea of a Conceptual Scheme." In Davidson, *Inquiries into Truth and Interpretation*.

———. "Rational Animals." In Ernest LePore, ed., *Truth and Interpretation: Perspectives on the Philosophy of Donald Davidson*. Oxford: Basil Blackwell, 1986.

Derrida, Jacques. *of Grammatology*. Trans. Gayatri Chakravorty Spivak. Baltimore: Johns Hopkins University Press, 1974.

———. *Glas*. Trans. John P. Leavey, Jr., Richard Rand. Lincoln: University of Nebraska Press, 1986.

———. "The Law of Genre." In Derrida, *Acts of Literature*. Ed. Derek Attridge. New York:: Routledge, 1992.

Eshun, Kodwo. *More Brilliant Than The Sun: Adventures in Sonic Fiction*. London: Quartet, 1998.

Gill, John. *Queer Noises*. Minneapolis: University of Minnesota, 1995.

Goehr, Lydia. *The Imaginary Museum of Musical Works: An Essay in the Philosophy of Music*. Oxford: Oxford University Press, 1992.

Gracyk, Theodore. *Rhythm and Noise: An Aesthetics of Rock*. Durham, N.C.: Duke University Press, 1996.

Griffiths, Paul. *Modern Music and After: Directions Since 1945*. Oxford: Oxford University Press, 1995.

Guitar World magazine. "1969: The Greatest Year in Rock." Series of articles, vol. 19, no. 6 (June 1999).

Harraway, Donna. *Simians, Cyborgs, and Women: The Reinvention of Nature*. New York: Routledge, 1991.

Hooper, David, and Kenneth Whyld, eds. *The Oxford Companion to Chess*. Oxford: Oxford University Press, 1996

Jameson, Fredric. *Postmodernism, or, The Cultural Logic of Late Capitalism*. Durham, N.C.: Duke University Press, 1991.

Kahn, Douglas. *Noise, Water, Meat: A History of Sound in the Arts*. Cambridge, Mass.: MIT Press, 1999.

Kivy, Peter. *Music Alone: Philosophical Reflections on the Purely Musical Experience*. Ithaca, N.Y.: Cornell University Press, 1990.

Korschelt, Oscar. *The Theory and Practice of Go*. Ed. Samuel P. King, George G. Leckie. Boston: Tuttle Publishing, 1965.

Krell, David. *Daimon Life: Heidegger and Life-Philosophy*. Bloomington: Indiana University Press, 1992.

May, Todd. *The Political Theory of Poststructuralist Anarchism*. University Park, Penn.: Penn State Press, 1994.

Nattiez, Jean-Jacques. *Music and Discourse: Toward a Semiology of Music*. Carolyn Abbate, trans. Princeton: Princeton University Press, 1990.

Perl, Jed. "Contemporary seriousness and the end of the century blues." *New Republic*, Nov. 8, 1999: 66–74.

Ree, Hans. *The Human Comedy of Chess: A Grandmaster's Chronicle*. Milford, Conn.: Russell Enterprises, 1999.

Reynolds, Simon. *blissed OUT: The Raptures of Rock*. London: Serpent's Tail, 1990.

Reynolds, Simon, and Joy Press. *The Sex Revolts: Gender, Rebellion, and Rock'n'Roll*. Cambridge, Mass.: Harvard University Press, 1995.

Rich, Alan. *American Pioneers: Ives to Cage and Beyond*. London: Phaidon Press, 1995.

Richards, Sam. *Sonic Harvest: Towards Musical Democracy*. Oxford: Amber Lane Press, 1992.

Rockwell, John. *All American Music: Composition in the Late Twentieth Century*. New York: Da Capo Press, 1983; new preface by author, 1997.

Sarig, Roni. *The Secret History of Rock: The Most Influential Bands You've Never Heard*. New York: Billboard Books, 1998.

Schiff, David. "Re-hearing Bernstein." *The Atlantic Monthly* 271, no. 6 (June 1993).

Schwartz, David, Anahid Kassabian, and Lawrence Siegal, eds. *Keeping Score: Music, Disciplinarity, Culture*. Charlottesville: University Press of Virginia, 1997.

Shepherd, John. *Music as Social Text*. Cambridge: Polity Press, 1991.

Silverstein, Robert. "Class of '69: Then and Now." *20th Century Guitar* (November 1999).

Subotnik, Rose Rosengard. *Deconstructive Variations: Music and Reason in Western Society*. Minneapolis: University of Minnesota Press, 1996.

Whiteley, Sheila. *The Space Between the Notes: Rock and the counter-culture*. London: Routledge, 1992.

Zorn, John, ed. *Arcana: Musicians on Music*. New York: Granary Books, 2000.

Index